ALSO BY BARRY WERTH

The Billion-Dollar Molecule:
One Company's Quest for the Perfect Drug

Damages

DAMAGES

ONE FAMILY'S

LEGAL STRUGGLES

IN THE WORLD

OF MEDICINE

BARRY WERTH

SIMON & SCHUSTER

SIMON & SCHUSTER
Rockefeller Center
1230 Avenue of the Americas
New York, NY 10020

SIMON & SCHUSTER and colophon are registered trademarks
of Simon & Schuster, Inc.

Designed by Liney Li

Manufactured in the United States of America

1   3   5   7   9   10   8   6   4   2

Library of Congress Cataloging-in-Publication Data
Werth, Barry.
Damages : one family's legal struggles in the world of medicine / Barry Werth
p.   cm.
Includes index.
1. Sabia, Tony, 1984—Trials, litigation, etc. 2. Obstetricians—
Malpractice—Connecticut—Cases. 3. Attorney and client—
Connecticut—Cases. 4. Developmentally disabled children
—Legal status, laws, etc.—Connecticut—Cases. I. Title.
KF228.S22W47   1998
344.73'0411—dc21   97-36949 CIP
ISBN 0-684-80769-6

For my parents,
Hilda and Herbert Werth

ONE

DONNA MARIA FITZGERALD GUNNED THE MOTOR OF HER 1970 DODGE DART, slipped through two lanes of traffic, and coasted to a stop just past the Woodrow Wilson Memorial Bridge on I-95, near Washington, D.C. Minutes earlier she'd invited a trucker she'd heard on her CB radio to pull over at a rest stop for coffee. He was trying to duck rush hour, said he didn't have much time, and offered to share his thermos instead. They said they'd meet after the bridge. With her daughter Shannon, five, prating with her dolls on the back seat, Donna smoked a cigarette and waited. At five feet one and 102 pounds, she had crow-black shoulder-length hair, a tough-pretty face, hard stance, and wary eyes.

Tony Sabia was a sinewy twenty-seven-year-old former Marine barreling south in an empty car carrier from his home in Norwalk, Connecticut. Possessed of what he calls a "raw attitude," he was jocular and blunt, and Donna liked the way he sounded. She wasn't disappointed when he climbed out of his truck. Medium height, he wore faded boot-cut jeans, a T-shirt with a beer logo, military-issue black-frame glasses, and a shaggy copper-brown perm. His combat boots were meticulously shined and he smoked Kools. They talked and drank Tony's coffee for about fifteen minutes. Donna was hard of hearing in one ear, so the hurtling traffic made it hard for her to hear even though she and Tony almost shouted. She told him she could drive a semi, and Tony said maybe he'd call some time and they'd drive together.

Watching him yank himself into his cab and roar off, Donna doubted the invitation was sincere. At twenty-four, she'd been on her own "a long time" and was skeptical of men. Her real father "wasn't around much," so her mother had divorced him, putting Donna and her two sisters up for adoption when Donna was three. After growing up in spare comfort in the Maryland suburb of Riverdale, outside Washington, she'd fled home soon after her eighteenth birthday, and her adoptive father had called the police to stop her. Within a year she'd had Shannon, whose father, a keyboard player with a bar band, was a nonpresence before and since. Two days before she met Tony, a guy she was seeing had asked her to marry him. "He just wanted someone to take care of the kids," she says drolly. "I was, like, 'I don't think so.'"

When Tony called a week later, Donna was surprised, then elated. They talked for hours that day and the next. Two weeks later he picked her up and they drove together to Houston, where they climbed on top of the truck, threw down a blanket, and tanned themselves. Donna hadn't felt so free in years. Tony gives a first impression of wiry belligerence. He smolders. He also chain-smokes and has a bopping insouciance, a bouncy working-class verve and integrity. Donna was taken with his smile—he had perfect teeth—and his bluntness. When he called the next time about a run to West Palm Beach, she packed up Shannon, drove to Norwalk, and left her for three days with Tony's parents and sister while she and Tony teamed south. Tony said it would be okay.

That—plus eight hundred dollars in long-distance telephone calls—was their romance. On the phone a week later, Tony proposed. "I don't know if that's exactly how he wanted to do it," Donna remembers. "But I didn't let him get away." So on the morning of May 4, Tony and Donna drove to the Arco station in Norwalk where Tony's father hung out after work, borrowed a hundred dollars, and took I-95 to Virginia. The next morning they went for blood tests in Arlington, bought two rings at an antique store, and picked a justice of the peace from the Yellow Pages. After the ceremony they picked up Shannon at kindergarten and Donna introduced Tony as her new father.

They merged their belongings and moved in with Tony's parents in Norwalk. The house was a vinyl-sided three-bedroom raised ranch in a luckless subdivision called Bound Brook Estates, locally known as Sunken Homes. One hundred and five lots on a reclaimed swamp, the neighborhood was in slow-motion collapse. In dozens of the lowest-lying houses, windows, walls, floors, and joists buckled and cracked. Pipes sheared and posts poked helter-skelter through wavy rooflines as houses sagged into the water table. The whole place, at the heart of Fairfield County, one of the wealthiest counties in America, was settling into the weak earth. With Tony's sister and her husband already in one bedroom and Shannon in another, Tony and Donna commandeered a twin bed in a basement playroom, the smallest room in the house. Tony bought a water bed, but his mother, fearing it would sink the house further, made him drain it.

His friends know Tony can be maddening; he has a chip on his shoulder, doesn't like bosses, seethes when he feels slighted and tends to get into fist-fights. Getting through to him when he's made up his mind, says one, is "like telling a stone wall to move." But he never doubted his duties as a husband or father. The night after he and Donna arrived in Connecticut, he foreswore long hauls and went to work with his father, driving for Standard News, a newspaper delivery company in Stamford. The work was backbreaking and mindless—heaving 20,000 papers, 40 to 50 in a bundle, onto a truck, then driving all night to drop-off points throughout southeastern Connecticut. The route, he says, took him places "the cops won't even go," so he bought a black 9-mm pistol, which he kept tucked under the seat of his cab. But the pay and benefits were good, it was a union shop, and Tony liked the solitude of the graveyard shift. Also, he could spend his days with Donna while Shannon was in school. For all its rashness it was not a bad start: they were in love, Tony was making money, they had a future. Shannon "resented the fact that I left her with people I didn't really know" when she and Tony first ran off, Donna says, but the girl was beginning to like Tony's father.

Then, too soon, they had trouble. After less than a month on the job, Tony hurt his back swinging a bundle of papers off the back of his truck. He slumped home, "lightning bolts," he says, shooting down his right leg. Donna had to lift him into bed. "I couldn't do shit," he says. Out of work and married just two months, he was operated on a few weeks later to remove a herniated disc. "They were wheeling him out of his room," Donna recalls, "and they handed me his watch. Nobody told me what to do. I was just standing there. That's when I found out he had a plate. I walked over and found these dentures in a glass by the bed and said, 'Where the hell did these come from?'" Two days later, friends brought Tony beer in the hospital, and, refusing painkillers, he shuffled down the street with them to a Fourth of July party, telling the nurses he'd be back in a couple of hours. He shrugs wryly: "I had my cane, I had my slippers, so I went."

Tony's health insurance paid for the operation and a private hospital room, but he hadn't been on the job a full twenty-six weeks, and when he was discharged, he lost his coverage. He got a lawyer to fight his insurer. Then the motor went on his van. "Two weeks after I got out of the hospital, I was pulling the engine," he says. "Donna went ballistic."

Donna had always worked. Before she met Tony, she'd waitressed at a Lum's, biking fourteen miles each way on an interstate when she couldn't afford a car. Now she started hostessing at the Silver Star Diner on the Post Road in Norwalk. Tony qualified for workmen's compensation, but money was still tight, and Tony's mother resented having to support them. The flash point was the phone—"my tombstone," Donna says, gripping a receiver. Missing her mother and sister, she called them every day. When she wasn't on the phone, Tony's sister was. Tony and his father avoided the issue, but as the bills piled up, Tony's mother bridled. There were other tensions: about cleanliness, about noise, about who was doing what around the house, about Shannon, about Donna's sleeping late. But with the phone, things spilled over. Finally, Tony's mother refused to pay the bill, and the service was cut. "That," Donna says, "was hard. The worst situation you could be in is to live with a man in his mother's house and also have his sister there. Tony's mother I tolerated because she was his mother. His father I had a lot of respect for. If he told me to shut up, I shut up."

In September, Donna awoke feeling nauseous. She bought a home-pregnancy test, took it home, and confirmed what she already knew, that she was several weeks pregnant. She and Tony quit sharing the twin bed, and though his back still hurt, he started sleeping on a sofa. He tried to go back to work, but the company wanted him in a desk job and he refused. To make ends meet he started selling marijuana, the only time in his life he did so, he says. Donna tried to stop him, but Tony says he couldn't see how else to provide for his family. He pledged to quit as soon as the company let him drive again.

Without private health insurance, Donna started going to the maternity clinic at Norwalk Hospital. The clinic charged $1,200 in advance, and Tony paid it in installments. Donna had gone to a similar clinic in Maryland when she was pregnant with Shannon and knew what to expect: crowded waiting rooms, grinding waits, harried nurses, now-you-see-them-now-you-don't doctors. Though she dreaded the waiting, she wasn't disappointed. Each time she saw the hospital, a maze of brick towers squatting fortresslike on a hill overlooking downtown Norwalk, she felt a vague comfort. She trusted hospitals; people in hospitals knew what they were doing.

Norwalk's clinic was staffed mainly by nurse-midwives, an arrangement just coming into vogue that served the interests of both the hospital and its obstetricians. Uninsured pregnant women like Donna had long been a problem for them both. Norwalk, a dour, fading nineteenth-century port city, was surrounded by some of the richest suburbs in America but was itself poor. The hospital was midsized, urban, and aging, yet because its local patient base was increasingly low-income, it had been forced to compete aggressively for insured patients, not only against richer community hospitals in Greenwich and Stamford but against world-famous university medical centers in New York and New Haven, both less than an hour away. Making matters worse, it had no house staff—low-paid doctors and residents—who at those other hospitals treated indigent patients at reduced cost.

Hence the three-year-old clinic. One in five babies at Norwalk was now a clinic birth, making the clinic one of the hospital's busiest services. Yet its

twelve or so affiliated ob-gyns were required to attend clinic patients on average only about five days a year, plus four weeks on-call for deliveries. Otherwise they were left to their private practices. There was a Wednesday clinic for
straightforward, low-risk pregnancies, and a Friday clinic for more complicated cases. To maintain staff privileges doctors saw clinic patients on Fridays
only, rotating monthly without pay. The plan had an undeniable appeal: the
hospital received the doctors' services for free, enabling it to cut costs, while
the doctors distributed the financial burden of serving Norwalk's growing
number of uninsured new mothers, who gained access to physicians they
normally couldn't afford to see.

Because Donna had had an uneventful pregnancy with Shannon and was
generally healthy, she was assigned to the Wednesday clinic. It was first-come,
first-served, and she spent the mornings squirming and reading dog-eared
magazines until she was seen. She stopped smoking. In November, Tony went
back to work and Donna got a job as a cashier at Kmart, which had begun hiring for the holidays. They were bringing in real money now, but the phone
was still shut off. After her clinic visits Donna called her mother from pay
phones.

Donna's belly grew quickly and Tony joked about it, crudely but in a way
that also made her laugh. He told her, "If it's twins, I'm gonna kill you and eat
the babies." His malevolence was feigned, but Donna was worried and knew
Tony must have been worried, too. What if there *were* twins? Where would
they put them? Their room was "wall-to-wall furniture" as it was. Besides the
water-bed frame, which now held a queen-sized mattress, there also was a
couch, a TV table, and, because they had no closet, a metal clothes rack. There
was a hanging bedsheet for one wall. Christmas was approaching and Donna
already felt faint after standing for eight hours at work. Her back was killing
her. She was so big already, she couldn't imagine carrying one baby, much less
two, another four months.

Because she was growing so quickly, the clinic sent her for an ultrasound
exam, on December 5. Donna hoped the test would show she was having just
one big healthy baby, and when she couldn't distinguish the grainy images on
the little black-and-white monitor in the examining room, she felt reassured.
Then the radiologist performing the exam told her he could see two hearts,
bladders, and stomachs. Donna laid her head on the table and cried.

She would remember him saying little else, but in a written report to the
clinic, the radiologist raised two concerns. The baby on the left, Twin A, appeared larger than Twin B, though how much was unclear. And, he noted,
there seemed to be a "moderate" excess of amniotic fluid, possibly indicating
other problems. These could include birth defects, congenital viruses, maternal diabetes, fetal heart failure, and the risk that one of the twins was thriving

at the other's expense, an imbalance which, if severe enough, could result in the death of the deprived twin. In his note the radiologist suggested that Donna be monitored with subsequent ultrasounds.

Donna was afraid to tell Tony the news about the twins. When she did, he lit a cigarette, clenched his jaw, and laughed: about his morbid threat, about the apparent conception date a week after he came home from the hospital with his bad back, especially about the twin bed. Whatever happened, he told her, they would handle it. Donna wasn't sure, but she believed him. She quit her job at Kmart, and started eating better and resting more.

With the discovery that she was carrying twins, Donna was switched to the higher risk Friday clinic, which cost another $400. Four weeks later, on January 5, she went for a second ultrasound. The smaller twin now had turned and was head down, allowing the radiologist to compare head sizes, which seemed slightly different. Overall, he estimated that Twin A weighed about 18 percent more than Twin B. Consistent development in twins is desirable, but as a tool for measuring fetuses ultrasound is notoriously inexact. In his report, the radiologist noted that the disparity might simply be within the statistical margin of error.

Whatever concerns were raised by Donna's sonograms were not reflected in her visits to the clinic. There she and the babies were thought to be thriving. They seemed to be doing so well, in fact, that two weeks after her second ultrasound the staff proposed that she see a doctor not every visit, as planned, but every other visit. Hospital guidelines for the Friday clinic called for "medical management," meaning that although the doctor on rotation was in charge of monitoring a patient's progress and directing care, he didn't have to examine the patient directly. The nurse-midwives were capable of that. The alternating-week arrangement was approved by the physician on staff for January.

Though Donna felt fine, her next ultrasound was on January 27. This time, the radiologist wrote, everything appeared normal: heart rates, amniotic fluid, even the relative sizes of the twins, which he estimated to be about equal. With the babies approximately the same size, and no further evidence of excess fetal fluid, he advised the clinic that a follow-up ultrasound might still be done, but only if "clinically indicated"—if either Donna or the fetuses seemed to have a problem.

Beginning her third trimester, Donna felt huge but in no way ill. Out of work and with little to do, she spent long hours again on the phone. She was often lonely and restless, and on an afternoon in February she took Shannon sledding on a local hill. She fell in the snow, hard, on her butt, she says. Scrabbling awkwardly to her feet, she laughed it off. Her body was becoming ridiculous. She looked forward to getting it back after the twins came.

Tony's health insurance was reinstated on March 1, but by then Donna had no thought of switching to a private doctor even though she could now afford one. She was at thirty-four weeks—almost at term. Moreover, she liked and trusted the nurse-midwives. She now knew all of them by name, and they knew her. Six years earlier, when she'd had Shannon, she'd understood little about giving birth. First she hadn't known she was in labor. Then she'd had no one to take her to the hospital. She'd ended up calling an ambulance and laboring alone for eighteen and a half hours: "Here I am not knowing any of the doctors," she recalls. "I'm spread-eagle for all these people, and they take an X-ray because they don't think I'm big enough to deliver her. After the X-ray I collapse." This time, Donna thought, she'd be prepared. With her mother and sister in Maryland and Tony's family offering little in the way of comfort, the midwives would be her allies during the delivery.

March in Norwalk was typically muddy and grim. At Sunken Homes new fissures appeared with the thaw. Sewer lines buckled under the shifting weight of some of the houses, spreading sewage underneath and unleashing a malignant stench. Tony's family was luckier: floors sagged, but held. Donna cleaned as much as she could, but the tensions with Tony's mother and sister, the latter also now several months pregnant, only increased. She fought with them—then, more and more, with Tony. They started looking for their own place, but everything was too expensive or too small. Donna seemed sullen and anxious, Tony coiled.

On Friday, March 30, Donna was examined during her regular clinic visit by Barbara McManamy, a nurse-midwife whom she'd seen on at least one other occasion, the day of her first ultrasound. McManamy had recently taken on added responsibility for running the clinic, and Donna thought her especially capable and caring. Slender, pert, intelligent—she had a masters degree from Columbia University—McManamy, thirtyish, was a young mother herself. She wore her sandy hair in a neat pageboy and her pale eyes were warm and blue. Donna trusted her.

McManamy examined her belly, measuring the position of the babies and hearing two heartbeats. It had been the midwives' suggestion to alternate Donna's clinic visits between a physician and a midwife, a decision McManamy felt strongly had benefited both Donna and the hospital. Because twins are generally smaller than singletons, the greatest risk to them is premature delivery. But Donna, at thirty-eight weeks, was now a week past the acceptable delivery date for twins, who because they develop quicker can also survive earlier outside the womb, and so the burden of care had shifted from preventing her from giving birth too soon to ensuring that she didn't deliver too late. McManamy told Donna she was doing great; the babies were of ample size and by every indication doing well, and so was she. To herself McManamy was even more emphatic; twin pregnancies, she thought, "don't go any better." At Norwalk as elsewhere, midwives struggle for professional respect. Donna's successful pregnancy was evidence to McManamy that they could collaborate with doctors even in difficult cases.

That night Tony wanted to go out with friends and he and Donna argued. Donna wanted to go with him; he didn't want her to go. When he got ready to leave, Donna tried to stop him, and Tony pushed her up against the wall, not hard but enough to startle her. "I was in front of the door," she says. "He moved me." Later, when Tony went to work, she shook the incident off.

Tony slept late the next morning while Donna straightened up the kitchen and mopped the floor. Taking this burst of energy as a sure sign she was about to go into labor, Donna swung between excitement and nervousness. She found it impossible, she says, to think logically about her situation. She and Tony, after a year of scraping by, were about to have twins, but they had no place to put them. Her mother had sent two big boxes filled with thrift-shop gatherings—receiving blankets, burp pads, bottles, clothes—but they had no bassinets and no place for them where they were living, a tiny room below grade in a swamp filled with fly ash. Her mother had crocheted matching blue baby buntings (at the second ultrasound, they'd found out that one baby was a boy but were unsure about the sex of the other), but otherwise they had no idea what to expect.

When Tony woke up that afternoon, Donna apologized. "Even though we had a fight the night before, and I didn't get my way, it always blew over," she says. Tony, too, was no longer angry, though he didn't show it. Whatever his anxieties, he preferred, now that he was back at work and earning good money, to concentrate on planning, and getting, ahead. Saturday was a big night for overtime. Because of the fat Sunday papers, Tony could go in early for "shape-time," work ten to thirteen hours, and "pick up six hundred, seven hundred bucks" for a night's work. He dressed, ate, and left the house early.

With Tony still at work, Donna awoke the next day, Sunday, April 1, 1984, alone. She was spotting and had light contractions. About eight o'clock she dragged herself up, went to the bathroom, and got dressed. Not wanting to disturb—or owe anything more to—Tony's family, she decided to drive herself to the hospital. Tony's sister, also a clinic patient, heard her opening the front door and grabbed the car keys. They arrived at the reception area at about eight-thirty.

Tony, stopping shortly afterward at the Arco station before heading home, was met by his father.

"You better go up to the hospital," his father told him. "Your wife's up there."

Tony, still in work clothes, shrugged. "No, I better go to the diner and eat. It's gonna be a long day."

~ ~ ~

Dr. Maryellen Humes was asleep when the phone rang at about 10 A.M. She was a handsome woman, forty-four years old, with tousled apricot-colored hair, trim features, and strong, tapered legs and hands. Even when she was exhausted, which was often, she moved with athleticism and authority, as if charging up a fairway after a strong drive. Humes slept the same way she ate, irregularly, the result of a busy and unpredictable life. Though she had a warm, gentle manner that patients appreciated, she made decisions in intense, pressurized bursts. Rousing herself, she anticipated the reason for the call. Two hours earlier she'd begun her first clinic rotation of the new year at Norwalk Hospital; for the next two weeks, besides attending her own patients, she was in charge of all clinic deliveries. Humes listened attentively. A patient named Donna Sabia was at the hospital in active labor with twins. She was at term—there were no red flags—but the second baby was in a breech position.

Humes dressed quickly as she weighed the situation. She was reassured by three things: that the caller was Barbara McManamy, that McManamy was at the hospital, and that McManamy knew the patient. As the only woman ob-gyn in the department and the most junior, Humes knew she might well have been contacted by someone less helpful, less simpatico, than McManamy. She also knew McManamy had trained at one of the most notorious public hospitals in New York City, North Central Bronx, a crucible for nurse-midwives equivalent to combat for thoracic surgeons. As she left the house, Humes thought that whatever the complications of delivering twins for a woman she'd never seen before, having to second-guess her next-in-command wouldn't be one of them.

Humes plotted Donna's delivery as she sped down I-95 in her Saab from Westport, the next town up the coast from Norwalk. She focused on the breech twin. She would need an ultrasound machine and someone from radiology to use it to determine the baby's position; someone with surgical skills to assist with a possible C-section, an anesthesiologist; a second pediatrician.

She arrived at the maternity suite by ten-thirty and was met at the nurse's station by McManamy. Breech births, so named because the buttocks are presented first, increase the risk of complications, including cord accidents and oxygen loss to the newborn which, if sustained, can cause brain damage. Humes told McManamy she thus was preparing for a C-section for Twin B if she couldn't turn the baby by hand. McManamy informed her that Donna's labor had progressed rapidly and that she'd been admitted by a veteran nurse, Mollie Fortuna. Hospital procedure called for checking fetal heart rates with an electronic monitor upon admission, but McManamy didn't mention fetal monitoring strips, and Humes, trusting those further down the hierarchy to tell her what she needed to know, didn't ask.

Down the hall Donna labored in a small, spare room. She writhed and screamed with each contraction as Tony's sister stood by anxiously, unable to help her. When Humes arrived, she introduced herself, then quickly examined Donna. She noted that her cervix was soft and slightly less than halfway dilated. Her waters hadn't broken, and Humes could feel the downward pressure of the first twin's head on her finger. The babies were coming fast; there was little time. Humes offered Donna her encouragement, then left to begin marshaling a medical team while McManamy stayed with Donna. Humes, who'd borne three daughters with "nary a drop" of painkiller, thought as she left the room that she'd rarely seen a patient more agitated.

From the nurse's station Humes made several quick phone calls—to Radiology; to Dr. Stuart Danoff, a pediatrician specializing in newborns; to Dr. Shubhinder Puri, an anesthesiologist—and asked them to stand by. She disliked leaving Donna, but made the calls herself because doctors in hospitals prefer to be enlisted for help by other doctors, not support staff. Humes then went across the hall to look for a resident to help with the cesarean. Discovering no other ob-gyns "in the house," she paged a physician's assistant in Surgery. Humes had done cesareans when the person scrubbing beside her was a staff nurse. She preferred a more skilled pair of hands. She kept trying.

The pace of Donna's labor picked up. Dr. Avelino Maitem, a Philippine-born radiologist fresh from a game of racquetball, arrived with a resident. Crowding with Humes into the labor room, they found Donna thrashing wildly. "Everybody was hysterical," recalls Maitem. Donna was grunting and begging McManamy for painkillers. She was on her back, sweating, crying, breathless. Maitem, who was skilled but not an expert at ultrasound techniques, had time only to sweep the transducer across the upper right portion of her belly. He, Humes, and the resident then retreated to discuss the position of the second twin as McManamy, exasperated, thought but didn't say, "Come on! This woman can't hold still like this!"

Humes and the radiologists left the room just before Tony arrived at about eleven. He was testy and taciturn, as alien here as at a convent. McManamy sensed in him a hostility that worried her enough to mention it to Humes. He hadn't slept and may have been reacting to Donna's overwrought condition and the chaos swirling around her. People were racing in and out of the room. Donna, heaving and grunting, barked that she hated him and wanted to kill him. Not one to say much when it's not called for, he absorbed it all watchfully, eyes like rivets.

Humes struggled to stay ahead by planning the logistics of the delivery. She ordered a room set up for a twin birth: two baby stations, both sides of the table; two bassinets; two ID tags; "double everything," says Tony. With Donna so far along, the first birth would be vaginal. Most likely it would go fast, leaving only minutes to assess the condition of the second twin before deciding whether to do a cesarean. Humes ordered Mollie Fortuna to ask the radiologists to don outer jumpsuits and shoe covers and stay nearby. Danoff, the pediatrician, was already there. A second pediatrician was paged. Humes went to change into surgical scrubs. Another patient laboring nearby was almost completely dilated and shrieking terribly—parallel havoc on the floor.

Hurrying, Humes took a call from a postpartum nurse, Shirley Brown. It was checkout time on the ward, and Brown said she needed Humes at once. "She said, 'Can you get over here? We've got patients to be discharged, we want to clear out these beds,'" Humes recalls. Humes told her she had a patient in tumultuous labor and was too busy to review charts and give home-care instructions to patients she didn't know. Brown persisted; Humes was the only one available. Humes consulted McManamy. They agreed McManamy would call her as soon as Donna was taken into delivery. Irritated, Humes left the delivery suite, fast-walking some fifty feet to the postpartum area.

Donna's labor had become "booming . . . violent . . . like she'd been shot out of a cannon," Humes acknowledges. Earlier, Donna had told McManamy she was happy finally to be having the babies—now she was too wracked with pain to speak coherently. Again, she pleaded for painkillers, but McManamy told her it could hurt the babies. Clutching Donna's face so close to hers that she could feel her breath, she exhorted her to hang on.

By eleven-thirty, Donna felt about to burst. With Humes still off the ward, McManamy and a nurse yanked the rails up on Donna's bed, shouldered it into the hall, and scrambled thirty feet to the delivery suite. Humes returned just as Donna, panting, her face almost the color of blood, climbed exhaustedly onto the delivery table, threw up her legs, and kicked the right stirrup so hard it clanged to the floor. McManamy positioned herself on the catcher's stool. "Push!" she yelled, and Donna obeyed. The baby's head appeared—a dark, hairy spot drenched in a torrent of fetal water. With a scissors McManamy slit an inch of Donna's perineum, which spurted blood. Donna didn't feel it. She bore down and screamed. With several pushes the baby's head was out. After another, McManamy held the slippery newborn in her hands.

She would not forget the feeling. The baby was limp, flaccid, like a sack of water. A boy, his limbs dangled and he was ashen, almost yellow. He made no effort to breathe. McManamy rushed to hand the baby to Danoff, who began to suction fluid from his nose and mouth. His Apgar score, which rates newborn vitality on a scale of 1 to 10, was 1. Zero is death.

Seeing what was happening, Humes scrambled to rescue the second twin. She requested the ultrasound transducer from Maitem, who stood by, and began scouring Donna's belly, thinking it might not be too late to take the baby by cesarean. It was. The baby came almost immediately, feet first, in a flurry of spasmodic pushes from Donna.

He was dead. Smaller than the other twin, his color was russet and his fetal water was lightly stained with meconium—feces—indicating prior distress. He was fully formed, and Humes noted that the skin on his buttocks and testicles was soft and beginning to slough off, as if it had been scalded. Having trained for four years as a pathologist before becoming an obstetrician, she knew at once he had been dead for some time. He was starting to decompose.

Watching, Tony and Donna were staggered. They didn't know what to think or feel, and their confusion was mirrored in the desolate faces around them. Danoff, steely-eyed, continued to work on the newborn, trying to resuscitate him. And Humes received the afterbirth, which Donna expelled in one final gasping paroxysm. Otherwise no one spoke.

With death, medicine becomes perfunctory. The hospital's procedures for dealing with stillbirths were to notify the admitting office; fill out a death slip noting sex, time of birth, weight and length; ascertain whether the family wishes to see the baby; clamp cord with plastic disposable clamp; cleanse baby; pad wrists and tie together; and remove body from delivery room as soon as possible. Tony saw the procedures differently: "They just threw him on the table like a piece of meat," he says.

As Danoff removed the surviving twin to the nursery, Humes cleared the room, leaving just herself, McManamy, Tony, and Donna. Humes says she was "crushed . . . distraught," but she also felt she needed to try to make sense of what had occurred and to comfort the Sabias. She examined the dead child and then, at greater length, the placenta. Fortuna came in inquiring about a yellowish discharge she said she'd seen earlier; Humes cut her off, thinking the timing of this inquiry inappropriate and insensitive. Then, cradling the dead infant, she showed Tony and Donna their son. She thought that to grieve properly they needed to see that he "wasn't deformed in any way." She knew parents often blame themselves for stillbirths and worry about having more children. "The purpose was to show them that this was a cord accident," she says. "I didn't want them to have nightmares."

She also showed them the afterbirth. It was blood-rich and glimmering. Humes noted that the three vessels in the second baby's umbilical cord lacked the usual protective coating and were rooted tenuously in the delicate membrane on the surface of the placenta, where they were exposed and vulnerable. One artery appeared to have torn some time earlier as evidenced by a blood clot near the site of the tear. Humes knew a more thorough investigation was needed to establish the precise cause of death; having done as many as four or five such investigations a week as a pathology resident, and knowing that they often required up to two weeks of rigorous examination and study, she was careful not to offer speculative conclusions. Yet as the Sabias recall it, she told them that the smaller baby had somehow slashed one of its cord vessels, shutting off its blood and oxygen supply, and that the other twin, sensing the danger, "gave his blood" to his dying brother through the vessels of the placenta. Ob-gyns call this exchange of fetal blood through the placenta "twin-to-twin transfusion," a phrase Donna remembered as "twin-to-twin gestation." Humes insists the phrase did not—could not have—come from her.

For Tony and Donna, the next twenty-four hours were a jumble. They had one dead son and one whose condition was grave and about whom they were getting scant information. Donna was moved to a recovery area, then to a room with a woman who'd just had a normal birth. When the sight of the woman's nursing was too much for her, the hospital gave her a private room and posted a DO NOT DISTURB sign. Tony's sister came up, and Tony left to tell his parents. Finally, Donna was alone. She cried inconsolably. "I was in a state of shock," she says.

A priest came in. He told her the surviving twin wasn't expected to make it through the night, and asked if Donna wanted him to deliver last rites. She said she didn't know and wanted to talk to Tony about it. The next morning Tony arrived early and the situation was different. The first baby was still alive, hooked up to a bank of machines in a critical care unit. He was having seizures but was breathing on his own. He wore an oxygen mask. Under five and a half pounds, he seemed to Tony no bigger than a cat.

Donna and Tony talked about names. Family was important to them both: it was all they had to bestow. Tony was Anthony Sabia Jr. They'd planned to name their firstborn son Anthony Sabia III and the second for Donna's adoptive father, William Thomas. Now they agonized, "How the hell could we say which name should live on, so to speak?" Tony says. They decided to hedge. They named the live baby Tony John. The dead twin they called Michael James. They liked the way it sounded.

All through the morning people came and went, including Humes and McManamy. Everyone was solicitous, caring; questions were broached gently. A nurse asked if they would allow an autopsy on Michael, to determine what had killed him. Tony said, "You're gonna cut him open, I'm gonna be there." The hospital refused. Tony says, "In Okinawa, I pulled a guy out of a jeep that got his legs blown off. I pulled people out of wrecks on the damn interstate." He had no doubt he could watch the dissection of his son and thought his job as a father demanded as much. Staring down the hospital, he felt vindicated. "I guess they were afraid I didn't have the stomach for it." When Michael was finally brought to them, Donna couldn't bear to hold him. He was wrapped in a cloth and still streaked from the birth. "How could they offer for us to say goodbye to our child and not bathe him?" Donna says, "I said to Tony, 'If you want, take a picture. I don't ever want to see him like that.'" It was the first time they realized that the boys were identical.

"I was lost," Donna recalls. "I didn't understand it. I didn't understand why Michael was gone and Little Tony was very sick. I even called the priest that baptized Little Tony. My brother Dennis and I had a conversation about

Michael, whether he would go to heaven or hell. The priest basically told me that Michael was in limbo, more or less. Because he was never really born."

As for Little Tony, they relied, as Donna had, on the hospital. "We accepted what was said," Tony says.

~ ~ ~

Humes strode into Linda Nemeth's office the next morning agitated and upset. Nemeth was the assistant chair of nursing, a veteran supervisor well respected within the hospital. Doctors in their professional relationships, especially with nurses, value competence and composure, and Nemeth displayed both. Equally to the point, Humes was her gynecologist and her mother's: they were friendly, and Humes needed a friend. Nemeth knew without being told why Humes was there. Doctors and hospitals call unfavorable results "bad outcomes." For insurance if not always for medical reasons, such mishaps are usually reported quickly. The news of the previous day's events in obstetrics had officially made the rounds that morning, amplified by the twitchings of the hospital's rumor mill.

Humes wasted no time: she wanted Nemeth to investigate Mollie Fortuna's actions during Donna's delivery. From the instant she'd held Michael Sabia she'd been gripped by bewilderment and anger. She was sure he'd died well before birth, certainly a day, maybe more. Yet Donna had been in the hospital for more than three hours before delivering and nobody had known she was carrying a dead child. Reviewing Donna's chart after the delivery, Humes had seen a notation made at 9:20 A.M. when Donna was admitted to the labor area. Under "FH," for fetal heart rates, it said, "A-170; unable to find Twin B?" The entry, made some forty minutes before McManamy called her at home, was in Fortuna's handwriting.

Humes's distress was palpable, and Nemeth could see where she was heading. Either Fortuna, the on-duty nurse, had reported the failure to locate a second heartbeat, presumably to McManamy, or she hadn't. Judging by McManamy's shock in the delivery room, Humes suspected it was the latter. (Fortuna says that she did report it.) In either case, Humes was allowed to proceed with the delivery without being told there was a problem.

Nemeth weighed the implications of Humes's complaint. The hospital had what she calls a "horrendous" outcome on its hands. Humes wasn't a hospital employee, but Fortuna and McManamy were. If either of them had failed to report vital information, and that failure resulted in injury, the hospital could be held liable in a lawsuit. Already, its "risk managers" were involved; senior administrators had been alerted. If the lawyers hadn't been called, they would be that day.

Nemeth was supportive but noncommittal. She told Humes to file a written account of the delivery. That afternoon she called Fortuna to her office. A labor nurse at Norwalk for more than twenty years, Fortuna was plainly distressed. Nemeth told her she was suspended for five days pending an investigation. That Friday, Nemeth called her in again and, with a union representative present, fired her. "I told her," Nemeth says, "that this was an inexcusable incident, so severe that we could no longer keep her on staff, and that she was terminated immediately." Later, under pressure from the nurses' union, Nemeth would write Fortuna a "very broad, bland recommendation" for a job at a nursing home.

Tony wanted to bury Michael on top of his grandfather. As he saw it, it was either open the grave of a family member for the sock-drawer-sized coffin, or a potter's field, and Tony resented even the thought of a pauper's burial. Shaken, his father gave his blessing, but his aunt, who maintained the gravesite, told Tony she'd have him arrested if he tried it. Piqued, she said, "Why don't you bury him with your sisters and brother?" As far as he knew, Tony was the oldest of three children—besides his sister, also named Donna, he has a brother, John. He knew nothing about any dead siblings. He asked his father about it but got no answer and so let the matter drop. He was too preoccupied to pursue the remark further. Resentfully, he thought, Here you got enough to deal with and you got an aunt that's throwing some bullshit in your face.

Burial was that Wednesday at St. John's Cemetery in Darien, in a plot for indigent children. The Metro-North commuter link to New Canaan bisects the graveyard, which is bordered on the south by the Noroton River, a narrow muddy stream still swollen that day from a month of spring rains. On the other side of the river sits a rock-crushing plant, today hidden behind a twenty-foot fence but at that time visible. The children's field consisted of two slivers of shaded bottomland at the river's edge. The gravestones were small and close together. Some of the children had lived a day, others a year. More than a few had died nameless, their stones reading only OUR BELOVED BABY or CORNELIO TWINS or BABY MALDONADO. In a gesture of respect, the gravel plant shut down its deafening machinery for ten or fifteen minutes when the Sabias' procession pulled up and halted.

Fewer than a dozen people huddled in the sunlight—Donna, Tony, their siblings, two or three friends. Tony's mother came, but his father, engulfed in a private grief, stayed home. Each mourner held a red rose. As two of the men removed the casket from the hearse, Donna stumbled behind them. She had come straight from the hospital and was wearing heels for the first time since the birth. She was so shaky Tony had to clutch her to keep her from collapsing. A priest who'd been conducting another funeral came over and said a few words, but Tony and Donna found no solace in prayer. "There really was nothing to be said," Tony recalls.

Afterward, Tony wandered off for a cigarette and made a discovery—a single flat headstone with the names of three other Sabia children: Karen, Elizabeth Ann, and his own name, Anthony Jr. They had died, at ages four, one, and eight months, respectively, in 1951, five years before he was born. He still didn't know what to think, but he associated the headstone, and his aunt's blurted comment, with a half-remembered taunt. He'd been in a fight as a teenager, and the other kid said something about his family and a fire. Walking back to the car, he assumed his parents had lost three children in an unmentionable tragedy, and had dealt with it by burying it and starting over. Figuring he'd probably have done the same, he decided not to bring it up.

Michael's death had consumed him and Donna, but they also felt thankful for Little Tony. He, at least, was alive. After three days in the pediatric special care unit—wired, intubated, and receiving around-the-clock attention—his seizures had diminished. Heavy doses of two anticonvulsives, phenobarbital and Dilantin, kept him sluggish, and he occasionally was short of breath and required oxygen. But his heart and lungs appeared generally strong. He had what the doctors called "positive suck reflex," and Donna was able to feed him. He opened his eyes and seemed more or less alert, although his pupils remained fixed and dilated—"nonreactive." He was moving all his limbs and responding to pain. Severely anemic at birth, he'd "pinked up"; the volume of red cells in his blood had increased.

Tony and Donna were hopeful. As an antidote to Michael's death, Little Tony's survival gave them what is most often urged on parents of stillborns—another child. True, he was a "twinless twin" (Liberace, Thornton Wilder, and Ed Sullivan were others), born live after a twin had died in utero and said to share a legacy of survivor guilt, pain, and loss. Still, Tony and Donna were encouraged. Elvis Presley's twin brother, Jesse Garon Presley, emerged stillborn moments before Elvis's birth, and his mother later said Elvis seemed born with the strength of both boys. Tony and Donna felt similarly about Little Tony. He had "given his blood" to save his dying brother. A more gallant act was hard to imagine.

They started thinking ahead. Donna blamed the tensions of the past several months, especially with Tony, on their living arrangement. "We wouldn't be living at his mother's house if he hadn't hurt his back," she says. "He swore to me he wouldn't bring Little Tony back there." That Thursday, the day Donna was released from the hospital, they took Shannon to see Little Tony, and she treated him sweetly. He still was dependent on around-the-clock care and far from ready to go home, but Donna for the first time glimpsed that he, much more than the death of his brother, would change their lives.

She and Tony knew Little Tony had suffered brain damage: that much the doctors had made clear. But how much and what kind they didn't know, nor did they ask. Their hopefulness worked like a baffle. They knew Little Tony's situation was perilous, but either didn't hear or didn't understand when the doctors brought up the future. Whether this was simply their walling out more pain or the cautious pessimism of doctors who knew it was too early to predict what would happen the next day, much less years from now—or, just as likely, the evasiveness of medical people conditioned to expect lawsuits when things go wrong and who may have feared Tony and Donna's reaction to more bad news—the result was the same: a disconnection. On April 13, for instance, Tony and Donna visited Little Tony after a night during which his heart rate had slowed dangerously. A CAT scan had shown some deadening of brain tissue that doctors thought was consistent with the cutoff of oxygen near the time of birth. Now they feared damage to that portion of the brain that regulated the heart. "Situation grave," a physician's assistant wrote in Little Tony's record, "family told of likelihood of impairment of intellectual function, etc." Yet the next day, the same physician's assistant observed: "Prognosis remains poor. Parents in to see patient—seem optimistic."

Tony went back to work. He found them a walk-up apartment on Flax Hill Road in south Norwalk. It was in a green, wood-frame double-decker, and though it was thirty-one steps up from the street, it was roomy and had a big kitchen, something Tony and Donna had always wanted. Across the street was the Miracle Temple Church of Christ; a few blocks away, a convenience store and a laundromat. Steel garbage cans lined the curb.

Donna pumped her breasts several times a day, delivering the milk to the hospital and sitting with Little Tony while he tried to take it from a bottle. On Easter, she says, "We all got dressed and went up to see him." They were pleased when the nurses took Polaroid pictures of all the babies and displayed them over their Isolettes. Tony cleaned the apartment, and managed to move in the last of their things on April 24. The next day, with Little Tony's prognosis now elevated to "fair," he was circumcised. Two days later, after a month in the special-care unit, he was released from Norwalk Hospital.

Tony and Donna stopped at the cashier's office before leaving the building. Though their health insurance covered 100 percent of Little Tony's hospital stay, Tony recalls, he was told he owed a balance of several thousand dollars. "I ain't giving you a dime," he snorted angrily. He and Donna left without paying. Then, after stopping at a drugstore for phenobarbital, Dilantin, Enfamil, and Pampers and at Tony's parents' house, they drove Little Tony and Shannon to the apartment on Flax Hill. Despite Little Tony's difficulties and the concerns of the hospital staff, they believed the worst was over. "We were excited," Donna says, "that after a month he was finally coming home and we were going to be in our own place."

TWO

HUMES DWELLED ON THE BIRTH LONG ENOUGH TO DETERMINE WHAT HAD GONE wrong and to assure herself and the Sabias that she had done all she could. She prided herself on her ability not to let her emotions undermine her competence, to be fully involved in everything she did, to stay focused and in control "no matter what." Yet her heart was also deep in her work; the horror of the twins' delivery didn't go away. Resuming her busy schedule, Humes delivered another 11 babies in the three and a half weeks that Little Tony remained in the hospital, sometimes two a day, while adding dozens of new patients to her practice roster. She attended an all-day workshop at Yale Medical School on the treatment of sexual problems. She tore out trees on her property, prepared a guest cottage to rent, signed up for a seven-month karate course, built a pen for a Bernese mountain dog she'd bought for her daughter, scrambled to hire an associate; "taking on too much, always," she says. She grieved for the Sabias, but as someone who stops to help at the scene of a disaster, then regrets the futility of her good intentions.

A woman of that vigorous yet often frustrated generation that came of age in the fifties, she is, in her own word, a "goop," after a children's book character who takes on many endeavors at once. "I've always got to have a major project," she says, "and it's got to be just out of reach." She was born and raised comfortably in Rochester, New York, the middle child of formally uneducated parents who encouraged their children to excel in school. Humes, a determined student, exceeded their hopes. Meticulous, diligent, and brimming with initiative, she graduated from Stanford University, then enrolled in the University of Chicago Medical School in the fall of 1961, one of just a dozen women in her class. The following year she married a Harvard Law School graduate, Roland Peracca, who worked for the Chase Manhattan Bank in New York.

Humes's medical training followed the arc of Peracca's career. She transferred to Downstate Medical School in Brooklyn and had two daughters, Martha and Sara, before graduating in 1966. Then Peracca was transferred to Puerto Rico, and Humes, learning Spanish, was a house physician for a year before interning at University Hospital in San Juan. After another daughter, Anne, was born in 1968, they returned to the Northeast, moving into a gambrel Colonial in Darien, Connecticut. Humes was thirty-one, living in an unfamiliar suburb with three preschool-age children, no independent livelihood, and a marriage that had foundered amid what she calls the "traumatic" dislocations of corporate life.

She trained in clinical pathology because it was a nine-to-five job and because she could do a residency at Norwalk Hospital, near to home. "Did I want to be a pathologist? No," she says. What compelled her were "things that are taxing, overwhelming, all-encompassing; things that suit *my* pathology."

What she wanted from her marriage was out. "Roland always said I couldn't make up my mind about what I wanted to do," she says, "Finally, I went to him and said, 'Okay. I've decided. I'm going to do a residency in obstetrics and gynecology. Then I'm going to divorce you.'"

Humes excelled in ob-gyn training at Stamford Hospital, becoming chief resident in her third year, although she was controversial within her department. In medicine, patients are the coin of the realm. Ob-gyn in Stamford, a city polarized between rich and poor, was at the time split between two groups—the "Waspy Old Boys," says Dr. Daniel Clement, another former resident, and the "Jewish Old Boys." Humes, neither, was also neither a typically subservient resident—she was almost forty—nor easygoing around male prerogative. She was popular with patients, strong, feisty, honest, and had plans to stay in the area. She also had ideas of her own, especially around the bread-and-butter issue of childbirth; a calm, accommodating manner; and a natural affinity with women. She clashed with the old order. "You could almost look at any of the doctors," says Clement, "and say, 'Rich patients . . . poor ones . . . rich ones . . . poor ones . . . middle class'—just by their behavior, background, and attitude. Maryellen had the appearance, demeanor, education, talent, background, and attitude to garner everybody. I think they all found her very threatening. They watched her like a hawk."

Humes gained her independence on schedule in the fall of 1979. Finishing her residency, she joined a pioneering woman ob-gyn back in Norwalk, Dr. Grace Gorham, who soon retired, leaving her with a busy solo practice. And, making good on the second part of her pledge to Peracca, she decamped with the girls, moving into a stone cottage on a wooded promontory in Westport.

It was in Westport, and in this house, that Humes aimed to complete the makeover of her world. The town is fashionable, picturesque, dropping down from the Yankee hills along the axis of a tidal river, the Saugatuck, then lying out amid the rocky headlands, broad salt marshes, and smooth beaches of Long Island Sound. It had long been famous as a haven for the creative and self-styled. Writers, artists, actors, and others from New York first colonized Westport by train, in the twenties and thirties, and soon were followed by a legion of cultural icons: F. Scott Fitzgerald, Elizabeth Taylor, Marilyn Monroe, James Thurber, J. D. Salinger, Edna Ferber, George Balanchine, George Gershwin, Oscar Levant, Bette Davis. Later most of the big names moved on as the Sound became polluted and more exotic enclaves beckoned.

Humes, as a woman alone, prized Westport for its beauty and its aura. Her stone house and studio on Old Hill sat on a sloping acre at the bottom of a winding lane, two doors from Neil Sedaka's. In the forties and fifties the property had belonged to an artist of the American West, John Ford Clymer, who painted more than eighty covers for the *Saturday Evening Post.* Before that the couple who lived there threw parties that a neighbor remembers lasting two to three weeks. Now the property was overgrown, a maze of low-slung boxes, mortared walls fourteen inches thick, a gnome's hut deep in a shadowy forest. Humes loved it the minute she saw it.

To call the place her refuge understated her need of it. The house was a wreck. The bathroom was rotting, causing damage to the neighboring rooms. A full-scale restoration, Humes thought, would be a "huge project . . . building a boat in a bottle." But Humes thought the house and grounds "a magical place" and thrilled to the challenge. She took down one hundred trees and replaced them with ornamentals—weeping hemlock, paper bark maple, copper beech. She blasted ledge, bulldozed a hillside, dug roots, laid drainage, sculpted from the slanting terrain a rock garden, perennial beds, a miniature orchard, fieldstone paths. She had the two-car garage remodeled to open onto a courtyard. She made grand decisions, then changed her mind. She would move an arch a foot to make everything fit in the kitchen, then tear out the kitchen. She reversed her mistakes, but relished making them—and paying for them—herself.

With three teenagers, the chaos and expense of reclaiming the house multiplied. As a single mother, Humes poured herself into her daughters and was, she says, "too generous with opportunity." She sent Martha to Pomfret and Colgate; Sara to Carlton and Barnard, with a junior year in Copenhagen; Anne to Loomis-Chafee and Cornell. She paid for their education largely herself, although Peracca helped with child support. "He decided I was a rich doctor and I could handle it," Humes says. Yet if she was a rich doctor, a rich *Westport* doctor, that wasn't how it felt. Humes built a big practice to support an active life, then worked so slavishly she had little time to enjoy either.

Everything she earned went out. She couldn't save. The pace only increased when, six months before Donna Sabia's delivery, Anne, her youngest, left for boarding school. Alone for the first time in almost twenty years, with little besides her house and career to occupy her, she hurled herself into both.

On occasion Humes sought escape but never, it seems, rest. She liked to take demanding vacations—cross-country skiing in Norway, bird-watching in South America—and when it happened that in January, around the time Donna was switched to the Friday clinic, she had a week with no deliveries and no surgery scheduled, she went rock-climbing in the California desert. Otherwise she worked, and plotted ways to meet her expenses. She had an architect redesign Clymer's studio so she could rent it. And she looked for an associate, finding one finally in December. When the woman showed up six months later, in June 1985, six months pregnant, Humes tried to accommodate her, but she needed someone who could work a full schedule and cover for her. Disappointed, she gave the woman until the end of the year to leave.

Alone once again, Humes bore down, worked harder, prodded the workmen at her house to perfection, grew impatient with the slightest lapse in her schedule. Those scarce times the waiting room was empty, she prowled the narrow hallway among the examining rooms in her office, phone jerked to her neck, good-naturedly bird-dogging her staff as if trying to will the world to keep up.

During his first year Donna took Little Tony to the pediatric clinic at Norwalk Hospital for his checkups. After these visits she sometimes took him to the labor and delivery floor to show him off. More than once she saw Barbara McManamy, the nurse-midwife who had delivered him. McManamy, like others at Norwalk during this period, was surprised by her behavior. She expected Donna to be bitter about the birth and angry and upset about the damage to Little Tony, and she worried that Donna might blame her and Humes. More to the point, she dreaded being "held in"—named—in a lawsuit, which she, like Humes and Linda Nemeth, thought had become all but inevitable the instant he was born. Anyone who worked in obstetrics braced now for being sued whenever a newborn was less than perfect; with lawyers renting billboards to solicit parents of children with learning disabilities, it was difficult not to. Not that McManamy thought Donna had cause, but something terrible had happened between her last clinic visit on Friday and Sunday morning, when the twins were born. Whatever it was, McManamy had been there on both occasions and hadn't known about it.

McManamy, who'd never been sued before, was haunted equally by her failure to anticipate what had occurred and the prospect of being swept up in a lawsuit that targeted that failure. She'd had trouble sleeping and eating. From the moment she'd held Little Tony, she knew from his lifeless condition that his injuries could only be catastrophic, and assumed Donna knew, too. Yet Donna, on her visits, seemed not the least aware of any of this, neither of his problems nor of the possibility of blame. She was proud of her son and friendly and gracious to everyone on the staff. McManamy's relief was palpable, overwhelming. "God gave you the right parents, Tony," she thought. "They think you're great."

He was a thin, stiff baby—"tight," Tony says—anemic and constipated and unable to roll over or sit up. Tony and Donna figured he was developing slowly. At home Tony sat with him on his knees, cycling his arms and legs, trying to loosen him, but on his own he didn't reach or grasp. He was sweet, never crying or fussing, and he slept through the night. Donna worried about him, especially about his seizures, but didn't consider him any trouble. He slept on a pillow in a laundry basket.

Donna took him out in a musical car seat. At the laundromat she set him on the big table while she folded. He disliked the fluorescent lights, got irritable, scrunched his eyes. Pain shadowed his face, now the image of Tony—gaunt, Mediterranean, with deep-set eyes and a thick shock of brown hair. Afterward, she sometimes took him to Tony's parents' house to see Tony's father, who, feet up on the cocktail table, cooed to him while rubbing his back and legs. Like Tony, his father treated Little Tony more tenderly than he did anyone else. He was sure the boy would come around. "My father had a bottle of Jack [Daniels] that me and Donna gave him for Christmas before Little Tony was born," Tony recalls. "He said he would open it the day Tony walked and talked."

Tony started working two jobs. During the day he drove a dump truck between Warren, a hill town an hour north of Norwalk, and construction sites in New York State. He got home around 6 P.M., showered, ate, and slept for an hour or two before Donna woke him at nine to go back to work. In the mornings he repeated the cycle. He worked nights Friday to Tuesday and days Monday to Friday. After about eight months he got into an argument with his day boss. "Guy started wanting me to work Saturdays," he says. "I told him, 'Forget it.'" Tony was earning more than $1,500 a week, most of it going out as quickly as it came in. He thought the boss resented his industriousness: "He didn't like the idea I was making more than him."

Besides his clinic visits, Little Tony went for physical therapy twice a week at Norwalk Hospital. Donna watched the therapist stretch him over a beach ball and work his arms and legs—range and motion exercises. The exercises were a lot like what Tony and his father did instinctively, and Donna felt encouraged. When the therapist left the hospital in March 1985, Little Tony was eleven months old and still making no physical effort on his own. The woman urged Donna to continue the therapy and referred her to an infant- and child-development program on Wolfit Avenue called STAR.

Entering STAR changed Donna's life more than it did Little Tony's. She had never thought of him as being handicapped, not like other children she'd seen, twisted in wheelchairs or with Down's syndrome. Yet now here they were, in a world of such children. Donna watched them uneasily, wondering if Little Tony would be like them, hoping—believing—he wouldn't. Once, in the hospital, she and Tony had seen a social worker, but Tony resented the idea. He thought it was like taking charity. Now, during Little Tony's therapy, Donna began meeting with other parents and a social worker named Rosalind Koffstein. It opened her eyes, she says: "We talked about anything we wanted to talk about—the kids, our problems, how we felt about it."

That month, March 1985, she and Tony moved back to Sunken Homes, renting a house directly across the street from Tony's parents. "It was puke green," Tony says. "There was no yard, no tree in the front, nothing: a real piece of shit." Inside was a shambles, but it was bigger than the apartment on Flax Hill, more convenient, had fewer stairs. They moved in the week before Little Tony's first birthday. With the house still a mess, Tony's parents gave the party at their house.

Eight days later, on a Sunday morning, Tony's mother phoned him in a panic. Tony's father had collapsed outside their bedroom. Tony dropped the phone. "I took off out of there, never touched the stairs," he says. "I took my father, put him on the chair. He was saying he was cold, but perspiring. He had a towel, kept wiping off his face, his forehead. It seemed like he didn't know what he was doing, like he was there and he wasn't. An ambulance came and they took him to the hospital. An hour later he was dead."

Tony tried to punch out the window of the limousine on the way to the funeral. Afterward, back at the house, he opened the bottle of Jack Daniels his father had been saving for the day Little Tony took his first steps. For a few days after that, he couldn't move the fingers of his right hand.

If Tony was wound tight, skirting violence, Donna was now lost. At STAR she was beginning to realize, in ways that Tony couldn't, how diminished Little Tony's abilities were. Sometimes it seemed, if they laid him on his stomach, he would try to push himself up, but there was no real progress. He seemed held back. Donna was gaining perspective—and losing hope. "We didn't know what Little Tony's needs were. I didn't understand why God would let a child live who couldn't do anything for himself. My faith in God was crushed," she says. Koffstein urged her to get more information about Little Tony's prognosis from the hospital.

Just feeding him was an ordeal. Donna had pumped her breasts for six months after he came home from the hospital, but Little Tony wasn't gaining weight and so she had switched entirely to formula. His sucking was labored;

it took him an hour or more to finish a bottle. Donna fed him three bottles a day. He also started eating cereal from a spoon, but he was losing weight. Donna worried about him. He was tiny. His seizures had stopped, but the hospital had taken him off phenobarbital and Donna feared that they would start again.

She found it increasingly hard to talk with Tony about Little Tony, or anything else. He was either at work, asleep, trying to sleep, or surly because he had just got up and had to leave. Each of them was overwhelmed, but the sources of their preoccupation were invisible to the other. Tony was always pissed at somebody at work, or about a bill Donna hadn't paid, or about how the house was a wreck, while Donna was beset trying to cope with Little Tony while managing seven-year-old Shannon's balkiness, getting meals on the table, and dealing with Tony's peevishness and rage. With Little Tony, Donna focused on all the things he couldn't do, Tony on the few that he could.

In July 1985, when Little Tony was fifteen months old, he was admitted to Norwalk Hospital after a routine clinic visit. He was pale and wasted. He weighed less than twelve pounds and his head circumference was below the fifth percentile. The first night, after being fed, his skin turned slatelike, almost purple, indicating a lack of oxygen in the blood. He was rushed to the special care unit, where it was noted he had "breath-holding spells," although no seizures. A week later he was sent home with instructions for a high-calorie diet consisting of whole milk, supplements, and Flintstone multivitamins. Tony and Donna mashed the vitamins into his cereal.

They say they still received no diagnosis, though hospital records indicate that one had been made. It was thorough and extensive: failure to thrive, microcephaly (abnormal smallness of the head often seen in mental retardation), severe developmental delay, spastic quadriplegia (spasms and paralysis throughout his body; cerebral palsy), status posthypoxic encephalopathy (brain dysfunction resulting from oxygen deficiency), and status postseizure disorder (seizures). Again the hospital, in its records, indicated "concern regarding the mother's conceptions of her child's illness and the bleak long-term outlook" and had a social worker investigate. A clinic pediatrician apparently told Donna of Little Tony's neurological status and prognosis, although Donna recalls only that "we knew that Tony had seizures. We knew he had some brain damage. We didn't know to what extent." Adds Tony, "Nothing was defined."

Donna pressed tentatively for answers. Encouraged by Koffstein and STAR, she started asking more questions during her clinic visits: Why wasn't Little Tony growing? Why wasn't he moving? What was wrong with him? At one visit, in early fall, a nurse left the room and Donna looked at Little Tony's records. She came across the words "mental retardation." When the nurse returned, Donna demanded, "Why didn't anybody tell us?" and the nurse said,

"We thought you knew." At her next visit with the clinic's neurologist, in December, he confirmed that the damage to Little Tony's brain was severe. He said the boy's mental and physical disabilities were profound and unalterable.

Donna blamed herself: "I ran through my head, 'Was it something I did? It must have been because I carried him.'" She thought the damage might have occurred when she fell while sledding with Shannon during her pregnancy, or when Tony shoved her out of the way the Friday night before the births. Bereft, she poured her heart out to Koffstein.

The clinic diagnosis only made Tony more protective. That Little Tony had problems was understandable to him; that his son's mind might be permanently diminished and his body incurably crippled was not. The void that lay behind Little Tony's eyes was obscured by his smile, which, as he approached his second birthday, was frequent and carefree. Back on anticonvulsives, he began laughing and cooing more, even babbling, and Tony and Donna began to hear through his inchoate mutterings the distinct beginnings of words—da, ba. He was eating three bowls of cereal a day, wearing a tuxedo bib that, with his thick hair, made him seem older, even distinguished—a young dandy. Tony would feed him from a spoon, saying, "Toe-knee!" then higher, "Toe-knee!" This singsong often elicited a slight turn of the boy's head and a gaping grin. This convinced Tony that his son could hear him, and that he knew who he was.

Donna's frustration with the clinic grew with each visit. Throughout the winter, as Little Tony ate more solid food, his constipation worsened. "He was hard as a rock," Tony recalls. Finally, one of the pediatricians told Donna to use an ice-cream stick to try to loosen his bowels. Donna stormed out. "On my way out the door he said, 'Make an appointment for your next visit,' and I said, 'I won't be back!'" she recalls. The following week she had a private session with Koffstein—her first. "She told me I had to go back," Donna says. "She said, 'If you want, I'll go with you.'" With Koffstein at her side for "moral support," Donna presented the doctor who examined Little Tony with a written list of questions. He answered them, she says, but hesitantly. It was the first visit with this doctor when she didn't feel uncomfortable.

The next month, April 1986, Donna found Little Tony a private pediatrician in Westport. Abruptly terminating a relationship that had begun almost three years earlier, the Sabias were no longer clinic patients at Norwalk Hospital.

~ ~ ~

For two years Humes had waited for the Sabias to find a lawyer and, though it had been clear to her from the outset that she'd done nothing wrong, sue her for malpractice. She was fatalistic about "bad babies," the doctor's term for brain-damaged infants. Some newborns, she believed, are bound to be defective. Things simply go wrong biologically or genetically or during pregnancy and childbirth. "You plant a packet of seeds," she says. "Do you expect them all to come up?"

But parents won't—can't—accept that, she thought. Bad babies are abhorrent to a society that believes itself entitled to perfect children. With Apgar scores interpreted anxiously as precursors to the SATs, and negligence lawyers trolling for victims on TV, most ob-gyns, Humes included, had by the early eighties come to expect that they would be sued whenever a child they delivered was at all neurologically impaired.

When no subpoena came, Humes counted herself lucky. She hadn't heard of a complaint against the hospital and so considered the matter closed. She lost track of the Sabias. What consumed her was her deteriorating relationship with her department. She had never got on with the "boys' club," as she called her all-male colleagues. No medical specialty has been so historically paternalistic, or so roiled by sexual politics, as ob-gyn, and Humes, intentionally or not, was a pot-stirrer. She was a feminist, at odds especially with the hospital's older practitioners, most of whom had gotten their training decades earlier when the fashion in childbirth was to treat it as a disease and when women in delivery were routinely laid out, sedated, cut, and had their babies yanked from them as if they were yielding a bladder stone. Her younger colleagues respected her, but as the only woman ob-gyn in the department, she drew away many of their patients, especially young educated women. As a solo physician she tended to be a loner, with no spouse to smooth her way socially.

The other ob-gyns in Norwalk, and many of the nurses, simply thought her opinionated and inexperienced. But because of her status and politics they seemed less tolerant of her than if she'd been a man. "She was basically a beginning practitioner in a system that offered her no support," recalls McManamy. "Nobody was willing to take her aside and say, 'Come on. I've been doing this twenty years. Let me mentor you a bit.'"

In her early years at Norwalk, Humes had been criticized for using a vacuum extractor, a suction device then beginning to challenge forceps in impacted births. Humes was the only one in the department using it, and sometimes there were problems. Babies' scalps suffered contusions, causing superficial bleeding. Their heads were temporarily elongated as the suction drew tissue fluid into their scalps. The device was safer than forceps—in extreme cases, the suction broke and the vacuum cup pulled off before causing serious harm—but it was a new technology, and some of her colleagues distrusted it. A departmental meeting was held, from which Humes says she was excluded, to review her cases, and she was ordered to call the senior attending physician whenever she employed the device. The chairman at the time, Dr.

Daniel Adler, liked Humes and defended her, but he'd recently been succeeded by a Canadian, Dr. John Whetham, with whom she clashed. Humes thought Whetham sexist and had complained about him. "If I started feeling paranoid about my work there, I had reason to."

In early May, shortly after Donna withdrew from the clinic, Humes received a letter from Dr. Clifford Feller, chairman of the ob-gyn department's peer review committee. Such committees are the front line for evaluating evidence of physician misconduct. Feller wrote that it was the "consensus" of the department that Humes should review Donna Sabia's delivery, particularly with regard to the "lack of fetal monitoring of Twin A (Little Tony), with the eventual outcome of an Apgar 1 infant." Reading the letter, Humes bristled. Why, suddenly, was she being asked to review events that had happened more than two years ago, concerning a child she hadn't technically delivered? And what consensus was Feller talking about? At the moment, she was more concerned with finding someone to cover for her so she could attend her daughter Martha's graduation from Colgate at the end of the month. That no one was willing to fill in for her only stoked her paranoia, while raising the (for her) unacceptable possibility that she might not be able to make the trip.

As often when her frustrations ran together, Humes reacted rashly. On May 12 she answered Feller's letter, calling it "abrasive" and "inaccurate." "You state 'consensus' of the Department of Obstetrics and Gynecology," she wrote. "As a member of the department I was not aware that a census had been taken at all in this case." Still, Humes pledged to cooperate "in any case where my interpretation is required." The next day Feller wrote back, correcting himself and asking Humes for a written account of Donna's delivery by June 1.

Humes fretted over what had sparked the committee's interest in the matter now. It made no sense. Peer reviews of bad outcomes generally take place soon after they occur. Memories are fresh then, and remedies, if necessary, timelier. (Besides, she thought, hadn't Fortuna's firing been enough?) By the same token, if, as Humes feared, Whetham was trying to discredit her, why had he waited? She concluded the Sabias must have hired a lawyer after all, and that inquiries for hospital records had invited the review, although, as hospital officials knew, that wasn't it, either. All they knew was that the Sabias had stopped bringing Little Tony to the pediatric clinic.

Humes hadn't lost touch with her former colleagues at Stamford Hospital, seven miles away. When the chairman there, Dr. Morton Schiffer, learned about her trouble finding coverage and the hostility she felt in Norwalk, he invited her to join his department. Humes leapt at the invitation. Why grovel? she thought. If they didn't want her at Norwalk Hospital, she'd leave. She'd taken on another new associate, an aggressive young doctor from Colorado named Cela Doppelt, and together they could see patients in both locations, funneling them to Stamford for their hospital needs. Hospitals are to doctors what arenas are to professional athletes. Though in most cases they don't work for them directly, they require their facilities. Likewise, hospitals need doctors to supply them with patients—business. For Schiffer the logic of recruiting Humes may have been clinched by the fact that she would be bringing with her a patient list of 5,000 women, all previously spoken for by Norwalk Hospital.

"I often leap first and figure it out afterward," Humes says. Now, in July and August, as she began sorting out the ramifications of the move, problems emerged that were more than logistical. Schiffer needed a recommendation from her current chairman, Whetham, to place her on staff. But Humes's life had become overwhelming even by her standards, and, seldom politic, she had neglected an important bit of protocol. In the frenzy of attending Martha's graduation, negotiating with Schiffer, expanding her practice to include Doppelt and a third associate, Dr. Irene Komarynsky, finding and setting up new office space in Stamford, maintaining her normal flat-out schedule, and wedging in a rafting trip to the Southwest, she had failed to answer Feller's initial request for an accounting of Donna's delivery and at least two subsequent requests. Intentionally or not, it appeared that she was avoiding an investigation of a grievous outcome with which she'd been involved. Whetham, even if he'd been so inclined, could hardly recommend her as long as she remained under such a cloud.

Little was clear about her failure to answer except that Humes was leaving the hospital—fast. And though *she* knew why she was going, indeed regarded the move as a step up, others seemed to interpret the confluence of events differently. Talk began, first among other ob-gyns, then among nurses and receptionists, finally among other doctors and people on the fringes of the department, that Humes was either fired or was forced to resign for avoiding Feller's peer review. From there rumors flew that Humes had botched a twin delivery two years earlier, leaving one child dead and the other profoundly brain-damaged, and now refused to face the consequences. Humes's leaving, the peer review, and Donna's delivery all became intertwined, imparting a stain that wouldn't easily wash off. In Stamford, Schiffer took to endorsing Humes publicly, standing by her at meetings, to calm concerns about why Norwalk Hospital hadn't recommended her.

Humes wrote officially to Whetham on August 14, long after he apparently knew, to tell him of her plans and to explain the reasons for her departure. "We have found the academic environment at Stamford Hospital truly exciting," she wrote, "and the warm, supportive demeanor of colleagues and administrators there most welcome." She ended with a personal note:

> I leave Norwalk understandably with some feelings of sadness as I have
> many fond memories of my long association with the hospital, dating back

to my residency in the department of pathology. Perhaps it was my vacation, rafting down the Colorado River through the magnificent Grand Canyon, or maybe it is the fact that my best childhood friend is terminal with ovarian cancer, or maybe it was my recent eldest child's college graduation that reminded me that our time on this earth is short and precious and the best move may be to move on. Thank you in advance for understanding.

Sincerely,
Maryellen Humes

≈ ≈ ≈

Donna sagged in the late-August heat. She was pregnant again, not due until March but already uncomfortable. She hoped she wasn't having twins. She and Little Tony, slumped in his car seat, sat alone under a shade tree at a picnic. Through STAR, she'd found him a spot in a summer camp at a state facility for the handicapped in Norwalk. A small wooded campus of low buildings, it was unmarked from the street. Still ambivalent about such settings, Donna kept to herself.

Mary Gay thought she understood Donna's wariness. "I was watching my kids and I recognized this woman," Gay recalls. "Not who she was, but she had a confused, bewildered look on her face, one that parents of handicapped children recognize. She just looked like me." A large-boned, forceful woman in her early thirties, Gay approached Donna. An effusive former artist, now a realtor, she held little back and tended to envelop strangers with her warm, insistent manner. Gay's six-year-old son Michael jounced around her. She was sweet with him but also rough, like a lioness cuffing a boisterous cub.

The women talked. Gay, who lives in Westport, had immersed herself in Michael's problems ever since learning four years earlier that he had cerebral palsy and was severely autistic. She was a survivor of a world that Donna was just discovering. She felt its insults deeply, was voraciously intent on redressing them, described her life in apocalyptic terms, and loved her son. Watching Little Tony, she thought she knew instantly the reasons for Donna's "stupor." It was clear to her that he was extraordinarily disabled; in May, after withdrawing from the pediatric clinic, Donna had taken him to Yale–New Haven Hospital, where doctors confirmed that on top of everything else, he was effectively blind. But Donna seemed unable, or unwilling, to accept these limitations. She pointed out another boy shambling with the stilted, outturned gait typical of brain-injured children, then asked Gay with a mixture of curiosity and hope, "Is my boy going to look like that?"

"I knew right then she was totally clueless," Gay recalls. "A feeling went through me like, 'You poor sweetheart.' It was obvious this child was profoundly brain-damaged, but she didn't know how bad he was, and I wasn't going to be the one to tell her. I almost couldn't deal with it," she says. "I wanted to connect her oblivion with a lack of intelligence. I wanted her to be stupid—for her own good, almost."

Gay recognized Donna's vulnerability and wanted to help as other mothers had helped her, but not by upsetting her. She steered the conversation toward more neutral ground.

"How's your husband dealing with it?" she asked.

"He doesn't really deal with it," Donna said.

Gay nodded. "Listen, I know what you're going through," she said. "I thought I was going to die until I went to a support group. You should go to one, and bring your husband."

Donna laughed hoarsely at the thought of Tony sitting around with strangers for the purpose of self-help. "No," she said. "He'd never do that."

Gay was emphatic. "Look, Donna, my husband's the same way," she said. "His attitude is, 'They're all geeks. I don't want to have anything to do with those people.' Men think there's something wrong with the whole family when there's a handicapped kid. You're going to have to trick him. He won't go to meetings at other people's houses, but if you have one at your house . . . This is something you have to do for yourself."

Gay then asked Donna about Little Tony's birth. She believed, as many people do, that most cerebral palsy resulted from oxygen loss before and during delivery, that it wasn't the babies who were bad but the doctors and hospitals who brought them into the world. Donna told her about the twins and about going to the clinic at Norwalk Hospital. Michael Gay had also been born at Norwalk, and Gay's interest, keen before, now spiked. When Donna told her about the dead twin and about Tony giving his blood to save his brother, she choked back tears.

Now Donna did the consoling. Seeing Gay's sadness, wanting to cheer her up, she took Little Tony's hand and said, "But look what we've got here. At least he's still alive." Gay was dumbstruck by Donna's equanimity, thinking to herself, At what cost?

She peppered Donna with more questions about her prenatal care: Which doctors had she seen? What kind of monitoring had she received? Donna had never been grilled quite this way, and had to force herself to remember. She told Gay about the midwives and the rotating doctors and her visit with Barbara McManamy on Friday when McManamy told her everything was fine.

"And then I got delivered by this other lady, who was the doctor . . ." Donna said.

Gay burst out sobbing. She reached for breath, "literally spun around," she recalls. "Maryellen Humes?" she asked.

Donna nodded.

Gay had been trying to contain herself but now came undone. Seven years earlier, when she first learned she was pregnant with Michael and Humes was new in practice, Humes had become her obstetrician. She'd liked Humes, admired her, and was sympathetic, though not militantly so, to her "natural" approach to childbirth. Though she'd gained sixty pounds, Gay's pregnancy was uneventful. After a long labor, however, her progress slowed. Humes and the labor nurse listened intermittently to Michael's heartbeat, but, not wanting to strap Gay down, didn't use electronic fetal monitoring, which correlates the child's heart rate with maternal contractions. When Michael was born, he wasn't breathing. His eyes, Gay remembers, rolled back in his head and he was limp. Humes revived him by inserting a tube in his trachea.

A few days later Gay had thanked Humes in a note, saying, "It's very evident that you care very much. You'll always be very special to us." But when she began to realize years later that Michael was brain-damaged, she seized on the birth as the cause, and sued Humes for malpractice. As the suit ground on, Gay came to believe unshakably that if Humes had monitored her electronically, she'd have recognized Michael's distress and delivered him by emergency C-section. She blamed Humes for the devastation of her world, with a ferocity even her husband had come to fear, and saw in the legal system her one hope for redress.

Gay asked Donna whether Humes had monitored her electronically. When Donna said no, Gay first felt outrage "that this woman had screwed somebody else up"; then "exhilaration, that I'm gonna get her again, and complete fury, that the system would let this happen."

Gay blurted, "I'm going to call my lawyer. I think you have a case."

Donna didn't know how to respond. She and Tony had never considered what had happened to them anything more than fate. They'd spent two and a half years just coping. She didn't think that Humes, whom she'd barely seen and could hardly remember, had somehow destroyed Little Tony the way Gay seemed certain she had devastated her own boy. But she had developed enough animosity toward the clinic doctors to think them capable of negligence and of covering for their mistakes. She listened hard as Gay went on. "I really don't know whose fault it is," Gay said. "But it's your responsibility to do this, because if your child needs help when he grows up, this may be the only opportunity you'll have to provide for him."

By now Gay was reeling. Seeing in Donna a reflection of herself, she felt an almost obsessive compulsion to usher her, if not toward a lawsuit, at least toward a lawyer, *her* lawyer, so that "he, as a professional, could tell her what to do." Donna looked at her quizzically, but Gay pressed her, saying, "It's very emotional, Donna. It's the most heart-wrenching thing you'll ever go through."

She didn't tell Donna the worst of it, how enraged and obsessed she'd become. Gay's lawsuit had been brought almost five years earlier and still hadn't been resolved. During that time Michael's prognosis had worsened. Meanwhile, doctors had told her he might improve with immediate and extensive therapy, but she couldn't afford the $40,000-a-year cost, and had come to feel, with increasing desperation, that even if she won her case against Humes it would be too late to help him.

This frustration had sundered Gay, making her feel "cracked down the middle." She cried and cried, often inconsolably, and behaved in ways she herself thought extreme. Twice she had driven her car into Humes's small parking lot and sat there, trembling and sobbing, unable to remember afterward how she'd gotten there or why she'd gone. Years before the Internet boom she increasingly escaped at night into the anonymity of chat rooms, holing up in a playroom over the garage and staying until morning. "If it wasn't for the computer, I'd have been dead," she says. "I was able to go on-line and be the saddest person, or else be somebody completely different, without a handicapped kid. I could be whoever I wanted." She came to resent the real people in her life, her family and friends, because she felt no matter how much they supported her it was never enough.

"Just let them review the case," she told Donna sadly. "See what they've got. You have a responsibility to do this for your son."

THREE

GAY WANTED DONNA TO MEET WITH MICHAEL KOSKOFF OF KOSKOFF, KOSKOFF & Bieder in Bridgeport, the state's largest and poorest city, thirty miles up the coast from Norwalk. The firm specialized in large personal injury cases, particularly medical malpractice claims, and its frequent multimillion-dollar verdicts made headlines statewide. Mike Koskoff was the only son of its celebrated founder, Theodore "Ted" Koskoff, from whose sizable shadow he still was emerging at age forty-six. As a teenager, the younger Koskoff had had two missions: to be an actor and to "redistribute the wealth." Now, with his polished courtroom performances, his national reputation for winning major product liability and personal injury suits, and his status as perhaps the best "medmal" lawyer in Connecticut, he liked to say he'd found a way to do both.

More than client and attorney, Gay and Koskoff had become, in the course of suing Humes, public allies. Realizing that her son was retarded and that Humes might be to blame had shattered Gay, but discovering that she might lose her only chance to help him because of a backlogged legal system had moved her to speak out. Driven by a combination of guilt and fury, she resolved to let others know just how such an injustice could occur and how it nearly had destroyed her family.

Koskoff and his partner Richard Bieder, always looking for clients compelling enough to advance the firm's political agenda, provided Gay with a platform by recruiting her to head the Victims' Rights Association. The group, existing largely on paper, was created by the Connecticut Trial Lawyers Association, with which Koskoff had long been involved and which was perennially at war with the state's preeminent business interests—the Hartford-based insurance giants—over the issue of civil liability. While the insurers crusaded for fewer lawsuits with smaller verdicts, the lawyers promoted the opposite agenda. Gay was a "figurehead," she says, Koskoff having assured her there was no real work or responsibility involved. All she had to do was stand up, be an example, publicize her plight.

Connecticut's civil courts, like those of many states, had long been clogged, a situation the Koskoffs considered a threat both to the Constitution and to lawyers like themselves who worked on contingency. When Gay's suit was filed in 1981, it joined more than 60,000 others waiting for a court date in a state with just 125 full-time superior court judges. The average wait for trial was about five years, twice that of, say, Pennsylvania. The delays hurt plaintiffs and, potentially, the public, as Gay's inability to pay for timely treatment for her son showed. But it was the trial lawyers—who financed their cases up front, didn't get paid until those cases were resolved, and generally took a third of most awards—who led the outcry. As a victims' advocate, Gay inveighed against the state's judicial delays, serving both her own agenda and that of the lawyers, who proposed making it easier to get cases to trial by doubling the number of judges and courtrooms. She appeared on TV, lobbied legislators, and addressed the 99th Congress. She "became a butterfly," she says, "going around to other people saying, 'I have a handicapped kid. Do you have a handicapped kid?'" Often during interviews she broke down sobbing while her son Michael climbed on her lap and licked her face. In Connecticut, Michael Gay—thick black hair, sweet discombobulated smile, wandering eyes never quite focusing—became a poster boy for delayed civil justice.

A few weeks after Donna met Gay, she and Tony left Little Tony with a sitter, then sped up I-95 in Donna's brown and white '79 Chevy Blazer to the Koskoffs' office in Bridgeport. They didn't know what to expect. "We didn't know if we had a case because the doctors never elaborated," Tony says. Donna, anxious, thought they were going "for answers . . . to find out if we had a case." "I still didn't believe that anyone had done something wrong," she recalls thinking, "but if they did, I wanted something done about it." Tony thought the visit "would be a waste of time basically" but decided they had nothing to lose since "it was a no-money thing going in"—they'd have to pay the lawyers only if they brought suit and won. Tony had come straight from work, hadn't slept, and wore what Donna calls his "accept me as I am" uniform; boots, jeans, and T-shirt. Donna "tried to make myself presentable," she says, in a loose-fitting outfit but not a maternity dress.

Tony pulled off the highway onto Golden Hill Street near downtown. It was an odd location for a thriving, nationally known firm, an area so notorious and crime-ridden that the Koskoffs had been forced in recent years to offer private car service to suburban clients too fearful to make the trip alone. The city had been for a hundred years, until the mid-sixties, a busy industrial center. Manufacturing plants and munitions factories thundered alongside a rumbling seaport. Now, Main Street was a grim gauntlet—pawnshops, unisex hair salons, squalid bars, boarded-up storefronts—as Bridgeport slouched toward bankruptcy, the first major American city to go Chapter 11.

Tony parked the car in an alley between the city's old county courthouse and the former Stratfield Hotel, a rambling brick building recently converted to subsidized housing. He and Donna entered through a rear door under a faded window sign advertising bail bonds, and were directed to the Koskoffs' offices. During Bridgeport's salad days, the suite had been the hotel's grand ballroom. Now it held two tiers of cubicles stacked around a painfully bright, two-story, seventies-style reception area—white quarry-tile floor, royal blue carpet, modern spiral staircase, a burbling fountain lit up from within by colored floodlights. The color scheme was orange and blue, a homage to the New York Mets. Counting cousins and spouses, seven of the firm's thirteen lawyers were family members. The clannishness, like the decor, flowed from patriarch Ted Koskoff's bold tastes and rich enthusiasms.

A short, bearded, middle-aged lawyer named Joel Lichtenstein came out of one of the downstairs offices to greet them. They had expected to meet with Mike Koskoff, but Lichtenstein explained that he screened the cases Koskoff argued in court. Unlike most of the firm's other lawyers, he never tried cases. Instead, he culled from the parade of sorrow that trudged through his office those tragedies that appeared at the outset winnable, and valuable enough, for the Koskoffs to take on. Donna had assumed she was the one who was shopping, but in truth it was the other way around. The firm turned down 95 percent of those who came in with possible malpractice claims. It never advertised. Largely because of Lichtenstein, it didn't have to.

Lichtenstein ushered them to his office and invited them to sit. As Donna spoke, he was stunned by the enormity of her loss. "My God," he recalls thinking. "What could be worse than for a mother to lose one baby so close to term and have the other baby so deeply damaged? I just couldn't believe that a woman could be so close, and suffer this kind of tragedy. Not in the modern world."

Hearing so much sorrow, interviewing so many broken-hearted people he knew he would turn away, Lichtenstein had developed a deft sincerity. His office manner combined several professional attitudes—an undertaker's solemnity, a psychiatrist's empathy, a banker's perspicacity, a doctor's concern. He claimed to feel deeply the suffering of those shattered by illness and injury, and at age forty-two, an Orthodox Jew up from the Bronx, responded with pained weariness to their "horror"—a word he pronounced, with a conspicuous heaviness of spirit, "hawroar."

He also understood the other side. Before joining the Koskoffs in the early seventies, he'd been vice president of a small New York insurance company, defending doctors against malpractice claims: he knew how doctors thought and how to value cases. Lichtenstein liked doctors and believed, perhaps too generously, that they liked him. But he also distrusted them when it came to their own fallibility, and he was a one man antidefamation league when it came to their slanders against lawyers. He was a frequent radio caller and scorching editorial page letter writer, often moved to lash back whenever he felt his profession was under attack.

Lichtenstein says he was horrified by Donna's story, but disbelief and indignation were baseline emotions for him. To ascend to outrage, the threshold for taking a case, he needed evidence that Donna's medical treatment was both incompetent and contributed to Michael's death and/or Little Tony's problems. He asked her to recall in detail her visits to Norwalk Hospital, whom she saw and when, scribbling her answers on a clean white legal pad. He stopped, raising his pen, as she began naming those who treated her during delivery. "Knowing it was Dr. Humes," he recalls, "who I didn't have a high regard for from the Gay case, made me immediately suspect."

Lichtenstein was always careful, no matter how tragic their stories, not to inflame potential clients. "I work very hard to make sure that they never leave the office with a great hatred of the medical process," he says. "If they carry over a hatred for doctors, nurses, hospitals, they're going to have an awfully tough time in the future." But his own presumption that Humes was implicated was already leading him to suspect that Donna had a case.

Finally, after an hour, Donna asked him what he thought. He was noncommittal. He told them only that he would look into it, and asked her to sign a release so that he could obtain her and Little Tony's medical records from Norwalk Hospital. In fact, Lichtenstein knew he had a more urgent problem: Connecticut's two-year statute of limitations. Plaintiffs in medical malpractice cases had that long from the time an injury was "sustained or discovered or . . . should have been discovered" to bring suit. But Michael Sabia's death and Little Tony's injuries had occurred in April 1984, two and a half years earlier.

Lichtenstein believed Tony and Donna when they said they didn't suspect until after Donna's conversation with Mary Gay that Little Tony's injuries might have been caused by "something someone did." He also knew there was ample case law to support them, and that what mattered was when the misconduct believed to cause the injury was first suspected, not when it took place. But he worried that by not coming to him sooner, Tony and Donna might have waited too long for him to be of help. He was careful not to inflate their hopes.

As they were leaving, he explained the firm's fees. Tony and Donna would pay nothing if the Koskoffs looked into the matter but decided not to represent them. If they brought suit, they would pay only if the Koskoffs won, in which case the firm took a third of the damage award, plus expenses. The arrangement was standard among personal injury lawyers, although some had lately begun to charge forty percent in more difficult cases, particularly medical malpractice claims.

Heading back to Norwalk, Tony recalls feeling perplexed—"like a fish out of water," he says. The concept of medical negligence was still foreign to him. Donna, who accepted it as a possibility, felt she knew no more than before and tried not to think about it. She was more worried now about Tony. Gay was right about him; not that he thought having a handicapped kid made him a "geek," but that she couldn't tell what he thought, he kept everything wrapped so tight. He was like a machine. He almost never slept. He ate ravenously and lost weight. He seemed to be burning himself up inside, and Donna couldn't help read into his oblique stare a molten rage—toward the world but also toward her. He seemed happy about her pregnancy, and she hoped for his sake that she would have a normal, healthy boy, and that maybe that would blunt some of his anger.

In October, Tony had a week off. He told Donna he needed to get away and that he was going to visit an old friend in New York. He gave her a phone number where she could reach him. While he was gone, one of Little Tony's classmates at STAR died, and Donna came unraveled. "This little girl, Jessica, was absolutely gorgeous," she says. "Beautiful long brown curls." Donna called the number in New York, but Tony's friend said he hadn't seen him and didn't know where he was. Donna says she was a wreck. She called Tony's brother John. She knew Tony had had other girlfriends before they met. Now she suspected he'd gone to visit one of them in Arizona and that he'd lied about it because he wasn't coming back. Trembling, she told John if he talked with Tony; "Tell him somebody passed away, but not somebody in the family." Afterward, she tore into old phone bills to see who he'd been calling.

Donna sent flowers to Little Jessica's family and signed the note both from her and Tony. She went alone to the funeral and the wake, sobbing over the open coffin as she imagined, for the first time, that Little Tony might also die, and that Tony would leave, and that there would be nothing left for her. For the rest of the week Tony never called, although one day she saw his truck parked behind a limousine business belonging to a friend of his. She suspected he'd stashed it there and had John drive him to the airport.

The night before Tony was supposed to return to work, Donna prepared a candlelight dinner. She asked a friend to take Shannon and Little Tony for the night. "I waited and waited and waited," she says. "He didn't show up." Finally, hours late, he opened the door.

"What'd ya think I wasn't coming back?" he asked.

Afterward, they talked. Tony said he'd never thought of leaving for good. But it was years before Donna would find out where he'd been. Whenever she asked, he told her it was none of her business. Eventually, she found out that he'd been in Arizona, just as she'd suspected, but Tony refused to apologize or confirm whom he had visited.

≈ ≈ ≈

Once Humes resolved to do something, she lost her tolerance for encumbering details; having decided to leave Norwalk, all she wanted was a clean break. But the hospital, for reasons of its own, refused to allow it. During the first week in October, she received a registered letter from Dr. Albert Burke, Norwalk's chief of staff. Burke said it had become "absolutely necessary" that Feller's peer review committee receive a written summary of Donna's delivery. "Should you fail to comply within seven days," Burke wrote, "I shall be required to act on your pending request for Courtesy privileges and bring this matter to the attention of my counterpart at Stamford Hospital."

Humes sat down and wrote Feller a hasty, one-page reply, but, typically, failed to save herself extra recrimination by delivering it right away. She held onto it for at least three days after Burke's deadline, inviting a second ultimatum from John Whetham, the department head with whom she clashed. "I am presently sitting with the request from Philip D. Cusano, president and chief executive officer of Stamford Hospital with regards to your application," Whetham wrote. "Until I am convinced that you have fulfilled your commitment in a satisfactory manner, I cannot respond to this request."

Humes still resented having to comply with Feller's peer review but realized now she had little choice in the matter. Reluctantly, she mailed him her account, in which she addressed the question of fetal monitoring raised repeatedly by Feller over the past six months:

> Continuous fetal monitoring was considered in this twin gestation but was
> not possible given the patient's lack of cooperation. There was no occasion
> to consider an alternate mode of monitoring as Mrs. Sabia's competent,
> experienced attendants reported that repeated checks of fetal heart tones
> were normal.

Whose heart tones Humes didn't say, though presumably she meant Little Tony's. It scarcely mattered. Her response only added to the committee's confusion, and to the sense that Humes still wasn't cooperating despite her earlier pledge. In her first written account at Linda Nemeth's request, two days after the delivery, she'd said she hadn't been told of any trouble with Donna's labor. "I was allowed to plan the management of this delivery . . . trusting that Mrs. Fortuna had found all parameters of her evaluation of her patient in order," she wrote. Now she seemed to suggest that it was Donna's violent thrashing and "combative behavior" that prevented all those attending her, including Fortuna, from monitoring the twins. Either way, the committee wasn't reassured. They needed to know directly from her just what she'd done, and why.

The problem for Humes was that she wasn't leaving Norwalk, not entirely, nor could she leave without the hospital's blessing. She was keeping her office on East Avenue, along a busy stretch of formerly good houses converted to professional buildings about a mile from the hospital. She planned to see most of her patients there, and wanted to assure them that she could rush them to the nearest hospital in emergencies. Meanwhile, she'd received excellent references from the ob-gyn staff at Stamford Hospital, but its administration was withholding privileges pending a recommendation from Whetham and Burke.

The more the pressure on Humes escalated, the more impatient—and suspicious—she grew. Increasingly, she saw the investigation into Donna's delivery as a witch hunt, an attempt by the boys' club to get her just as she was about to be rid of them. The facts, she felt, spoke for themselves. She'd come to assist with the delivery of a high-risk "service" patient she'd never seen, the victim of a horrific maloccurrence that had started and ended before she got there. For two years there had been nothing, not a word. Then this. What did they want from her? Humes wondered. Couldn't they see she'd done all she could for the woman? The damage was already done. She was a good, dedicated doctor. All she wanted was to take care of her patients, work hard, have a life, garden, be left alone. She was too busy for this. Why were they persecuting her?

Humes had suffered in silence throughout the years of Gay's lawsuit, but now her feelings pushed to the surface. The smart thing to do would have been to cooperate. She could only lose by appearing not to. But being sued by Gay and the Koskoffs had been the most difficult experience of her life, causing her by turns to feel vexed, disgraced, vilified, self-pitying, distrustful and, above all, alone. It was like fighting a guerrilla war. Humes felt assaulted on all sides, plagued by the terrible uncertainty of not knowing who was a friend and who wasn't. For this reason, capitulating to even a routine examination of her professional conduct became neither easy nor simple. Even if she wanted to cooperate, her instinct for self-protection told her not to. Besides, by now, early fall, the hospital had received Lichtenstein's initial requests for Donna's medical records. And, as Humes well knew, the stakes had jumped.

New calculations were in play. Norwalk, like most hospitals, treated such requests as routine, not bothering even to inform its lawyers since most inquiries never amounted to a claim: why pay lawyers before you have to? Peer reviews like Feller's were themselves confidential—not "discoverable" in a lawsuit—meaning the Koskoffs couldn't find out what was said and what action the committee took. On the other hand, Connecticut had what was

known as "joint and several liability": any party found even partially responsible for causing an injury could be "held in" and forced to pay the entire
damages. In other words, if the Sabias eventually brought a lawsuit, the results
of Feller's investigation couldn't be used against the hospital or Humes; the
state had recognized that medical centers would never investigate their own
mistakes and try to correct them if such efforts, inherently acknowledging
blame, could be used against them in court. But the results of the peer review
could bear heavily on who eventually paid, and in what proportion, if either
Humes or the hospital tried to evade accountability by faulting the other.

Humes's hesitancy reflected these new tensions. She knew that she and
the hospital were unalterably opposed. Whatever had happened during the
last days and hours of Donna's pregnancy, the machinery was now in place to
find someone to blame, and how she and the members of the boys' club responded might well determine who it was. They, after all, had managed
Donna's care virtually up to the moment Humes was called in to deliver the
twins. And it was their investigation. It was her or them.

Humes had no appetite for finger-pointing. Ob-gyns were already the
most commonly harassed of all doctors, with three-quarters of them now being sued for malpractice during their careers, more than a third of them three
or more times. Yet to submit to being blamed oneself was professional suicide.
Humes, already traumatized by one lawsuit and fearing another, and long at
odds with her colleagues, at times became so riled that she lost sight of her
own interests. Now, with the hospital bearing down on her, was one of those
times.

∽ ∽ ∽

In November 1986, about a month after Humes responded to Feller's peer review, *Gay v. Humes* was settled quietly in Stamford Superior Court. During
the summer, Mary Gay had written to the judge assigned to the case, an
arthritic black jurist then nearing retirement named Robert Levister, pleading
with him to put it on his calendar. Surprisingly, he agreed. Gay recalls that
Mike Koskoff was shocked when he phoned her to tell her the news, although
he says he thought the case would soon be reached anyway. But Gay's determination—and the results it brought—never surprised him. He knew Gay to
be a formidable force. Indeed, he and Lichtenstein had initially tried to reject
her case against Humes, but changed their minds after she refused to hear it.
"What do you mean?" she'd told Lichtenstein on the phone. "Of course, you're
going to take it."

Gay readied herself for trial by stalking Humes's attorney, a small, mild-
mannered Bridgeport defense lawyer named Arnold Bai, in court. Bai was

then working on another obstetrical case involving a girl who was born with brain damage while the obstetrician in charge was performing an abortion elsewhere in the hospital. For two weeks Gay, a staunch pro-lifer, got dressed each day in her best clothes, drove to Norwalk, and stared Bai down like a would-be assassin from the back of the courtroom. "I was in total control of that situation," she recalls. "I had his number. I ruffled his feathers. I did it intentionally. It was my kid who was next. I wanted him to know that I knew what he was doing."

With the trial set to begin, Gay, her husband, and her son attended a pretrial conference with Levister in Stamford. Mounting the courthouse steps with Koskoff, she broke into sobs—"like a faucet," she says. Later, in chambers, Michael Gay acted out of control and, with Koskoff and an associate of Bai's watching apprehensively, Gay cuffed him. Levister admonished her not to be rough with him in front of a jury. "Be sweet with him. Just let him be himself," she recalls him saying. Levister, the first black judge in Connecticut history, then took Michael Gay on his lap and the boy, uncontrollably affectionate, "slimed the judge's face," Gay says. According to Gay, Levister then dismissed the family, turned to Bai's associate, and said, "This woman needs some money." Humes had $1.25 million in malpractice coverage. The judge thought Gay deserved something more than $1 million. After a brief discussion Koskoff and Humes's lawyer agreed to settle the case for $1 million.

Gay says she was stunned when Koskoff came out to tell her the news. "Here I was," she recalls, "and these people are putting a freaking price on my son's head. What could be more barbaric than putting a price on your child's life. It was evil." Later she would have a different reaction, regretting that she settled for "too little" and wishing she had gotten more.

Humes learned about the negotiations later that day from Bai. She had always believed Michael Gay's problems were simply "a poor outcome." "Malpractice?" she'd ask. "What malpractice?" But Bai had long urged her to get out of the case as soon as possible, for her own good. "You don't want to be sued for more than your coverage" he'd counseled. Now Humes accepted his logic, though it pained her to do so. Already, Gay's media forays had left Humes feeling not only wounded but exposed. Most of the time Gay didn't refer to her by name, but a recent article in an alternative weekly had identified Humes as the defendant in Gay's lawsuit, and Humes had been upset by the publicity. A trial, she thought, could only be ruinous, especially now with her mounting dispute with Norwalk Hospital and Lichtenstein's enquiries about Donna's delivery. Bitterly, she told Bai to work up the settlement documents.

$\approx \approx \approx$

If Humes had been on bad terms with Feller's committee to this point, now they were at war. Litigation-sensitive, they both postured. Meeting with Whetham less than a month later, on December 5, Humes, on Bai's advice, refused to discuss Donna's complaints. "Accordingly, the meeting was terminated," Whetham wrote back in a strong letter meant to document—"paper," in legal jargon—their discussion. In mid-January, Burke, the chief of the hospital's medical staff, also again wrote Humes. Attempting to speed the matter to a close, he directed her to meet with Feller's committee within two weeks to answer its questions or risk "summary suspension." Humes wrote back to protest the meeting. She said she would attend only if Bai could be present "since the proceedings . . . might have future legal repercussions."

Lawyers begat lawyers, which begat a semblance of action. On February 5, 1987, nine months after Feller's initial inquiry and thirty-four months after Donna's delivery, Humes finally met with Feller's committee. Both sides came girded for confrontation, but despite the acrimonious buildup, it quickly became clear that there was little to discuss. Humes gave her account of the birth. There were several questions. Less than a half hour later the committee concluded that her conduct had been appropriate under the circumstances. With no disciplinary action taken, Burke and Whetham agreed to recommend Humes to Stamford Hospital, and Stamford accordingly granted Humes full privileges.

FOUR

LATER THE KOSKOFFS WOULD WANT TO KNOW WHAT KILLED MICHAEL SABIA AND ravaged Little Tony. But not now. Through the fall and into the winter of 1987, Lichtenstein tackled a simpler set of questions. What were the facts? Could he find other doctors to say there was malpractice? By whom? Was there sufficient insurance coverage on the other side? Had they "blown"—exceeded—the statute of limitations? Ballpark, what was the case worth? Lichtenstein didn't need to know the whole story, just that it was worth pursuing.

He started with a time line. Poring over Donna's hospital records, he noted several red flags. By early 1987, twin pregnancies were by definition "high-risk." Since more could, and often did, go wrong with multiple births, and since improved monitoring made it possible to intervene, doctors routinely watched women with twins more closely. Yet Lichtenstein couldn't see that Donna had received any special attention other than being switched to the higher-risk Friday clinic where, he noted, she'd been examined mostly by nurse-midwives who generally were barred from managing complicated pregnancies. Lichtenstein didn't know whether Norwalk Hospital had special procedures for monitoring twins, but Yale–New Haven, the state's premier medical center and the main teaching hospital for Yale Medical School, was famous for developing such protocols. And Norwalk was affiliated with Yale.

Of the dozens of pages of Donna's chart, Lichtenstein focused mainly on two, the labor and delivery summary, and not only because of Humes's involvement. Almost all obstetrical malpractice cases target the birth period, for decisive reasons. That's when it's easiest to show a link between the actions of doctors and nurses and, if there's brain damage, the loss of oxygen presumed to have caused it. To prove malpractice, a lawyer must show three things: that a doctor or hospital acted negligently by not adhering to a well-accepted standard of care, that there was harm done, and that the negligence caused the harm. Lichtenstein knew the Sabias' best case, especially in light of joint and several liability—the legal doctrine holding that with two (or more) defendants, in this case Humes and the hospital, each might have to pay for the other's misconduct—was to concentrate on Little Tony's brain damage and tie it to a botched delivery. Anytime before Donna went to the hospital that Sunday was a sea of grey, when things could go awry at any moment and proof of causation, hence blaming, might be unsustainable.

Lichtenstein thought the labor and delivery notes revealed considerable negligence, both by the hospital and Humes. The labor nurse, Mollie Fortuna, had indicated at about nine-thirty that she couldn't find a heartbeat for one of the twins, yet there apparently was no attempt at electronic fetal monitoring from then until both babies were delivered—vaginally, no less—more than two hours later. What the hell were they doing all that time? Lichtenstein wondered. That one twin was already dead and out of harm's way failed to diminish his outrage. To him Humes was a repeat offender. He'd seen this before, he thought, with Michael Gay; some conviction against using fetal monitors and doing C-sections had clouded Humes's judgement, with the result a terrible tragedy.

Suing doctors, Lichtenstein had come to hold himself equal to them in his ability to detect their mistakes, but he didn't rely on intuition and ego alone. He dug into medical texts to find out what was being taught about treating multiple pregnancies in 1983 and 1984, when Donna was attending the clinic, and the relevant period for determining what was then a reasonable standard of care in cases like hers. He combed the literature for articles on twin gestation and electronic fetal monitoring. He also sent Donna's records to a prominent academic physician for confidential review. Later he'd need to find medical experts who would testify publicly, but now Lichtenstein only wanted to know that he was on the right track. His source was the chairman of ob-gyn at a major teaching hospital, someone who never testified but was willing to review, discreetly, a few charts a year. "When he says to me I have a case, I know I not only have a case, I have a homicide," Lichtenstein says. He recalls the consultant telling him he could start thinking about buying a place in the Bahamas.

The Yellow Pages are awash with the full-page ads of lawyers who would have heard this, thought they'd struck gold, and phoned Donna. Lichtenstein disdains such people as the low, regrettable end of his trade. He says he especially resents how their fast-buck tactics twist the thinking of the sad, sick people who parade through his office and often take it out on him. Another lawyer has told them their case is worth $750,000, or $2 million, or $4.5 million, they say: How much can Lichtenstein promise them? Somebody else is screaming within the first five minutes about the outrageous injustice they've suffered; is Lichtenstein such a bad lawyer he can't see gross negligence when it jumps up at him?

But Lichtenstein hadn't become successful by selling himself, or cases, short. He had several tests for accepting a claim, and a pattern of negligence, no matter how compelling, was only the first. Far more important was how a case was likely to stand up in front of a jury. Mike Koskoff, who lectured other lawyers widely on the proper screening of cases, once wrote: "The preparation of a malpractice case prior to suit must be geared towards trial and not settlement. Insurance companies are not eager to settle malpractice claims and only do so for adequate reasons when confronted with well-informed counsel ready to go to trial." Koskoff's rationale was simple. Lawyers knew they had to be selective because they might have to live with a case for a decade or more. A claim like the Sabias' could easily cost $100,000 in time and expenses before it got to trial, where a firm could lose its entire investment. The Koskoffs' success meant they could afford to take risks that other lawyers couldn't, but it also enabled them to shrink those risks while maximizing their payouts, by taking only cases they thought they could win in court and nurturing them for the long haul.

Here was the Koskoffs' credo, and the key to their success. They were trial lawyers, trial *advocates.* They could imagine no higher calling than to try to sway a jury to their side and to this end worked every file in the office as if it were headed to court. They politicized every case, making it a battle of right and wrong, crusaded for their clients, and spurned easy settlements. Ted Koskoff, Mike's seventy-three-year-old father, was identified perhaps as closely as anyone in the country with the idea that a trial lawyer's job was to stand between the abuse of power and the individual, preferably in the "public arena" of a courtroom. A fervent champion of "victims' rights," Koskoff had been elected president of the nation's organized trial bar, the Association of Trial Lawyers of America (ATLA). Meanwhile, Michael had done as much as any lawyer in Connecticut to apply his father's brand of militant trial advocacy against doctors and hospitals.

Now that Lichtenstein had a sense of the merits of Donna's story, he began discussing it with the younger Koskoff, wandering into his office and curling up in a chair across from his desk. Mike Koskoff was four years older than Lichtenstein but looked younger. He was angular and reedy, taller than Lichtenstein by a few inches at about five feet nine. Twenty years earlier he'd first gained attention as a young radical lawyer defending alleged street criminals, and he still enjoyed his image as a firebrand, albeit one who was comfortably and respectably aging. He had a helmet of salt-and-pepper curls receding prematurely over a high-domed forehead, militantly arched eyebrows, a long slender nose, dark mustache, receding chin, and sinuous neck. He resembled Art Garfunkel, bristly and intense but in a mild, reassuring sort of way.

His office was cramped—all the offices but Ted's were—but in his lair Koskoff had about him an uncommon ease. Pushing back in his executive chair with his jacket off as Lichtenstein spoke, his legs extended and loafered feet propped on his desk, he exhibited a loose-limbed self-confidence. But Koskoff was no *vitellone*—"little veal," as Italians call the milk-fed sons of important men who don't measure up. During the past decade and a half he had tried dozens of cases that surpassed technically anything undertaken by his father. A gleaming power wall of plaques, many from grateful civil rights organizations, attested to his ongoing political commitment and ability to win demanding cases in the highest courts.

As he and Lichtenstein brainstormed, there really was only one question: Could they get the case to trial? Did it have the elements? If it did, and they liked it, and they thought it would bring in enough to satisfy them and the Sabias, they'd take it. Yet that raised another standard, one having to do only tangentially with medicine and law. Trials, as any courtroom lawyer knows, are only nominally about law and truth. More often, they're about the personalities and charisma of the lawyers themselves. Trials are a form of theater, and the ability to weave dramatic stories and portray them grippingly in court—as someone once wrote of Ted, to "give the jury a tune it can whistle after the show lets out"—was as much a Koskoff trademark as crusading for those they believed to be victims.

This was the other distinction that made the Koskoffs perhaps unique among the lawyers Donna might have gone to. Besides their politics, they were known equally for their flair for performing and love of the spotlight. Even in Bridgeport, where the city's patron saint and one-time mayor, P. T. Barnum, proclaimed himself the "Prince of Humbugs," and in a profession that values appearance over fact, the Koskoffs stood out, as Mike says, for the "family value" of unabashed theatricality.

"We're show people," he says.

≈ ≈ ≈

Negligence lawyers were bottom feeders when Ted Koskoff started practicing in Bridgeport in the years after World War II—hardly what the dramatic young Koskoff had in mind. He'd grown up in modest comfort in New Haven, in the shadow of Yale, the youngest of seven children and the family prize. His parents were grocers who had performed in Jewish theater in Russia, and Koskoff nearly dropped out of law school during the Depression to play the cello before his brother, Yale, a neurosurgeon, convinced him that he needed a profession. During the war, he'd made a fortune—and avoided the draft—by opening an ammunition factory. When the war ended, the factory turned to making collapsible metal rakes, but the implements were poorly designed and broke on the second or third use. Koskoff, thirty-three, lost every-thing.

Bankrupt and jobless, he decided to launch his legal career by approach-ing some of the city's successful lawyers. "Look," he told them, "just send me cases you don't want, and I'll try them. And whatever I get for them, I'll split with you."

"He would go into court," Mike recalls, "and try these junky personal in-jury cases—tough ones where there was very difficult liability: falldowns, small injuries, questionable injuries—and come out with wins. That was how he made his reputation, by trying civil cases that everybody thought were complete losers and getting plaintiffs' verdicts."

Ted Koskoff loved going to court. Perhaps more to the point, the court-room loved him, as the camera loves some movie stars. As theaters of dramatic conflict, of war writ small, courtrooms have their own production values, and in the fifties, before lawyers started to have to look good on TV, no personal characteristic was more rewarded in court than sheer forcefulness—the power to persuade. Koskoff, Churchillian, was almost perfectly fitted to his role.

Koskoff was and acted large, at six feet and 235 pounds a bald barrel of a man draped in elegant three-piece suits and wreathed in rich cigar smoke even when he couldn't afford such luxuries. Much later, when he owned a white Rolls-Royce and sent his driver every three weeks to the Owl Shop, a New Haven tobacconist, to buy a half-dozen boxes of $4 hand-rolled Do-minican Questarays, then gave them to everyone he met, he was famous for his grandiosity. But from the beginning what was most notable about him was that he could stride into a court of law and make it his own.

"No matter what the case," Mike recalls fondly. "No matter what his level of *knowledge* about the case, or the level of complexity of the case, or who the opponent was, or who the judge was, he would feel absolutely comfortable walking into the courtroom—being a lawyer, being an advocate; like an actor walking out on the stage where he felt in total control of every line and every prop because of years of training. That was the feeling you got, of an actor who could walk into any role at a moment's notice and play it as it should be played.

"He would always say, 'You try a case by impression, not by detail.' That was his basic approach: put on the witnesses, let them say whatever they want, try to waltz them around a little on cross-examination, and *then* give the final argument. Because as far as he was concerned, that was the whole case. He didn't have a whole lot of confidence in what a witness was going to say, but he knew that when he gave his final argument *he* would be able to say what the case was about, with such authority that a certain number of people were go-ing to believe it."

Lichtenstein recalls watching the elder Koskoff decades later, when he was in his seventies and ailing, ask a judge for permission to sit down to address the jury during a final argument. The judge agreed, and Koskoff proceeded to ambulate slowly around the courtroom dragging, with painful dignity, his heavy wooden chair. "Every eye was riveted on Ted," Lichtenstein says. "What happened before that I don't think anybody in the courtroom remembered."

"My father had a saying," Mike says. "'Never run when you can walk, never walk when you can sit, never sit when you can lie down'—the exact opposite of your aerobic personality. He also patented another famous line: 'You can't try a case on your knees.' You can't go into court constantly being a supplicant—applying for this, and may-Your-Honor-please this. He said, 'This has got to be your courtroom. You've got to tell the jury what the case is about.' And it was certainly true of him. When he went into a courtroom, the judge might preside and think he was in charge, or might want to be in charge. And the other lawyer would fight like crazy to maintain some presence. And so he would allow the judge to make rulings, and he would allow the other lawyers to speak. But it would always be out of a sense of largesse."

Koskoff's mastery of trial law and zest for self-promotion led him to champion not just the rights of plaintiffs but of lawyers. In speeches and articles he criticized the low repute of his trade. "Personal injury lawyers at that time were pretty much viewed as ambulance chasers," Mike recalls, "not very capable of doing big things and not very capable of having an impact on society." The elder Koskoff strove to change that. He began telling audiences of negligence lawyers that to gain respect and influence—while making, it went unsaid, better money—they had to become more competent, raise standards. Many of them, he knew, were at the bottom of the legal barrel because they belonged there. They dressed badly, spoke poorly, and came from marginal law schools. A lot of them never saw a courtroom, extorting quick settlements from insurers who found it easier to pay them something to make them go away.

In the fifties Koskoff was among the first personal injury lawyers to join the National Association of Compensation and Claimants' Attorneys, a trade group then comprised primarily of those representing victims of industrial accidents. NACCA's main purpose was to raise the image of negligence lawyers, something, Mike Koskoff notes wryly, "they were only partly successful in doing and for a limited period of time." Still, by the time it was replaced by a more broad-based organization of trial lawyers, ATLA, in 1972, Koskoff was known throughout the profession as one of its lions.

Increasingly, Koskoff had his choice of lucrative cases. He remained personable, without false modesty, but throughout the Connecticut bar there were people now who considered him peerless, and his standing sharply improved. He defended a state senator accused of murdering his wife and got the charge lowered to manslaughter. He was called in to defend Dare to Be Great entrepreneur Glenn Turner and Turner's lawyer, F. Lee Bailey, on mail fraud charges (which were later dismissed). His fame reached an apotheosis of sorts in 1976 when he represented Johnny Carson's first wife, Jody, in a custody fight. "The following week Johnny Carson was on *The Tonight Show* and said, "When I die, if I ever come back, I want to come back as my wife's lawyer,"" Mike Koskoff still recalls.

"I think that most people probably took the joke as being about my father having made lots of money," he says, "but I don't think that's the way [Carson] intended it. I think having spent several days in Litchfield, Connecticut, with my father, it was really the idea that here was a person who was so comfortable with himself, so self-satisfied and sure at every moment that what he was doing was the most important thing that you could be doing in life, and who was doing it at the level at which it should be done, he's just the person you wanted to be.

"Everybody who knew my father believed Carson saw that, and that's what he was talking about."

Mike Koskoff had no desire to become a lawyer or follow in his father's footsteps. All he wanted was to act. As a skinny teenager in Stratford, a Bridgeport suburb, he became an acolyte at the American Shakespeare Theater there. He "did nothing" in high school, went to Brandeis University, but returned within a year to Stratford, where he enrolled at the Shakespeare Academy and gravitated to the avant-garde circle of the late Will Geer. Later TV's curmudgeonly Grandpa Walton, Geer was then in professional exile, a compatriot of Woody Guthrie, who'd been blackballed for his refusal to name names during the McCarthyite purges in Hollywood. Koskoff was drawn to Geer's cult of radical politics, folk music, and theater, but soon doubted his own talent for the stage. "I came to feel that I was not the best actor in the class," he says, "and something about being a 'bad actor' deterred me from continuing."

The law beckoned, feebly at first, an alternative to the draft. The Vietnam War had begun, and after finishing college at the University of Bridgeport, Koskoff realized he didn't "have the luxury of doing nothing." He'd become active in student politics and was an early opponent of the war. Meanwhile, the civil rights movement had imbued him with "a heightened sense of justice, of people getting fucked." In 1964 he surveyed the menu of academic graduate careers and found them dismal—"ineffective." Only by becoming a lawyer, he felt, could he be a "potent force in society." Like Humes a decade later when she opted to become an ob-gyn, he decided to enroll in the University of Connecticut Law School as a political imperative.

Ted Koskoff had never pressured his son; now he had no need to. "The only thing I could see myself as was a trial lawyer," Mike says. "And I knew that the firm offered me the best opportunity I'd ever have. I hated every minute of law school. I didn't like my fellow students. The irony, of course, is that they all went into 'secure jobs' with big firms, and ended up losing their jobs and not getting rich. And I chose the scummy, low end of the profession."

Money was a distant afterthought. For a radical lawyer starting out in 1967, law was an instrument of social change, not a way to become rich, and Koskoff, newly married, was content to make $5,500 in his first year. His earliest cases, like his father's, were "other people's junk." "I didn't know how to charge very well," he concedes. What the younger Koskoff knew was that he had found a role in life that fit him as well as it had his father. By the time he entered practice, urban poverty and racial tension had polarized most cities. Black communities, including Bridgeport's, had erupted violently. There were daily skirmishes between blacks and police, and crime had become deeply politicized. For lawyers like Koskoff, a sharp-edged, outspoken twenty-seven-year-old with a passable Afro and bushy beard, the law had become the very flash point of the struggle. Crisscrossing the lines, he felt he had a major part to play and, as a lawyer, a kind of diplomatic immunity. He could agitate and be a rescuer at the same time. He was totally in character.

"What I would do in defending criminal cases was to find out what the person was charged with and read the statute very carefully," he says. "Then I'd try to think of every reason in the world why, even if my client did everything the prosecutor and police said he did, they still should throw out the case. I'd file motions, move to suppress the fruits of the arrest, move to throw out the searches, whatever might work."

He also learned to counter the larger injustices he saw by bringing lawsuits. He and other lawyers sued the Bridgeport police for brutality and won a settlement. They sued the city twice in federal court to hire more minority police and firefighters and won both times. Eventually, they sued the City of New Haven for illegal wiretaps, harassing phone calls, vandalism, infiltration into local organizations, and terrorism. By the end of the decade Mike Koskoff had discovered "the idea that whatever it was, you were in a position to do something about it simply by bringing a lawsuit."

On a May morning in 1969 a factory worker casting for trout on the Coginchaug River, about twenty-five miles north of New Haven, found the partly submerged body of a black man. The victim's wrists were tied, around his neck was a noose made from a wire coat hanger, and there were bruises, burns, rope marks, and ice pick wounds on his chest, arms, and buttocks. He'd been shot twice at close range, in the head and chest. Within months twelve members of the Black Panther Party, including chairman Bobby Seale, were charged in connection with the murder. Police said they had conspired to torture, then kill, the dead man, a member of the Panthers' New York chapter named Alex Rackley, because they thought he was a police informant.

The discovery of Rackley's body incited a wave of charged events in Connecticut. No organization at the time inflamed passions more than the Panthers, and perhaps no political figure was deemed more dangerous than Seale, who'd been gagged and shackled during that year's Chicago 8 trial. New Haven, tense and simmering throughout the decade, flashed over. Yale, forced to close by students striking over the Panther prosecutions, verged on rebellion as 4,000 marines and paratroopers were deployed to contain what one federal official called impending "racial violence, widespread destruction and even assassination in New Haven." A Panther leader named David Hilliard told students: "If anything happens to Bobby Seale, there will not be any lights for days in this country. Not only will we burn buildings, we will take lives. We will kill judges." Antiwar activist Tom Hayden called Seale's upcoming trial "the most important trial of a black man in American history." Yale President Kingman Brewster mused famously, "I am skeptical of the ability of black revolutionaries to achieve a fair trial anywhere in the U.S."

Both Ted and Michael were called to help with the Panthers' legal defense. Michael, who'd never tried a murder case, leapt at the opportunity. "I figured it was right up my alley," he says. "There was no money in it. It was a hopeless case." But Ted wanted assurances that the Panthers wouldn't turn the proceedings into a show trial in which the legitimacy of the charges, or the legal system itself, was challenged. Hayden had said in a speech in New Haven, "Facts are irrelevant in this case," but the older Koskoff was an immigrant's son with an immigrant's faith in the Constitution; he revered the legal process. Ultimately, the Panthers and their lawyers agreed, assigning the Koskoffs to defend a polite, soft-spoken twenty-four-year-old New Haven party leader named Lonnie McLucas, one of two men the state had charged with actually killing Rackley. Scheduled first, McLucas's trial attracted national interest as a "dress rehearsal" for the proceedings against Seale, who was charged with ordering Rackley's execution while in New Haven for a speaking date at Yale.

The trial lasted thirteen weeks, throughout the summer of 1970. A sideshow atmosphere prevailed outside the courthouse: at one point Mike Koskoff drove to Kennedy Airport to pick up Panther cofounder Huey P. Newton, who was also met there by Jane Fonda, Donald Sutherland, and numerous undercover agents, and was so assiduously trailed by two cars of agents that they practically followed him into his driveway. The trial itself, however, was almost scrupulously nonpolitical. The Koskoffs' defense was that McLucas—"that schnook," Ted Koskoff called him in his closing—had been victimized by the prosecution's star witness, a Panther enforcer named

George Sams, who had a history of mental derangement. They conceded that McLucas, terrified of what Sams might do to him if he didn't cooperate, shot Rackley in the chest, but argued that it wasn't murder because Rackley was already dead from a bullet fired by another defendant. The jury—ten whites, two blacks—deliberated thirty-three hours over six days, longer than any jury in Connecticut history, before convicting McLucas of conspiracy but acquitting him of the murder charge.

Ted Koskoff pronounced himself satisfied. "The judge was fair, the jury was fair, and in this case, a black revolutionary was given a fair trial," he was quoted as saying in *Time*. Some observers gave greatest credit to Koskoff himself: "McLucas was fortunately defended by a brilliant trial lawyer, Theodore Koskoff of Bridgeport," *The Nation* reported. "Mr. Koskoff did not seek to stage a political extravaganza . . . he carefully, and wisely, characterized his client in terms which the jury could readily understand and accept." By humanizing McLucas as a victim of an abusive and powerful Sams, the Koskoffs had won an improbable victory. And they had broken the state's case against Seale, which depended on Sam's testimony that he had heard Seale order Rackley's death. With Seale eventually acquitted on all charges, New Haven and the criminal justice system were spared.

The Panther trial divided the Koskoffs' history into before and after. "Suddenly, we were very high-visibility," Michael recalls. "People started coming to us with all kinds of cases. Anybody who viewed themselves as antiestablishment wanted us to represent them." Yet despite their newfound celebrity, they had little to show for it. The Panther Legal Defense Fund had promised $5,000 for expenses, but in the end paid much less. Father and son lost even more on their next famous case together, representing John Pardue, a Steve McQueen lookalike whose exploits had led to the largest bank robbery investigation in FBI history. They were starting to select a jury in Bridgeport when Pardue was shot five times by a U.S. marshal as he tried to escape from a holding cell downstairs from the courtroom. Rushing to the scene, Ted said, "I guess you didn't have much faith in us, John." Pardue died from his wounds, and the Koskoffs received no fee.

~ ~ ~

Since 1968, Mike had taken only a few medical malpractice cases. "Medmal," then a mostly uncharted field, was the opposite of criminal defense work, in which the prosecution had to organize, construct, and prove its case while defense lawyers only had to chip away at it. Bringing a malpractice suit, like any civil case, meant investigating, figuring out what happened. *You* were the prosecutor. *You* had the burden of proof. Although you didn't have to dispel all doubt, you had to show you were more right than the other side. After crusading against social injustice, Koskoff felt uncomfortable suing doctors, whose image as selfless healers he still accepted. "It took some doing at first," he says, "because I was a product of the middle class."

What motivated him was the challenge, and the money. Less than a decade old as a legal subspecialty, medical malpractice was pushing into esoteric areas of medicine and yielding huge verdicts. Only two other firms in the state, in Hartford and Stamford, were set up to handle big cases. A quick study, Koskoff saw a chance to get in early on a growing market. He liked mastering complex medical issues and the "magic" of making abstruse biological events real for lay juries. And once he got over his squeamishness, he found he liked going after doctors, whose refusal to stand against one another publicly amounted, he and many lawyers felt, to a conspiracy of silence. Doctors, hospitals, and insurers were rich and powerful; his clients weren't. Koskoff says he was able to justify suing medical people, and making good money at it, by deciding he was still working to share the wealth.

He hired Lichtenstein in 1972. "We made a decision to introduce Joel to the Connecticut Bar as a specialist in malpractice," Mike says. "He was not a trial lawyer. He was someone who could take a stack of records and tear it apart, not be intimidated by it, figure out what happened and what should have happened." Two years later Koskoff had his own defining moment as a young malpractice lawyer. On trial in the case of a man who'd walked into a hospital in Sharon, Connecticut, with a back injury and left several weeks later permanently paralyzed from the neck down, he had a traction order blown up to many times its original size. Discovering that it had been forged and postdated to cover for an earlier order so aggressive that his client's spine was "literally torn apart," Koskoff gave it to the judge, who immediately excused the jury and read the physical therapist who'd signed it his rights. With the case settling for $650,000, of which Koskoff and his cocounsel split a third, the episode removed any doubt for Koskoff that what he was doing might be just as potent politically, and vastly more lucrative, than defending black revolutionaries.

Koskoff's reputation as a malpractice lawyer quickly grew. Unlike Ted, he didn't try cases by impression as much as by mastering complex technical information and assembling it skillfully for juries. He'd acquired Ted's confidence in himself, but he also understood the value of a well-constructed case. Ted had become a top trial lawyer by mastering himself and the courtroom, but malpractice cases rested largely on the vagaries of medicine, which, as its practitioners liked to point out, was as much art as science. Michael, with his extraordinary acuity and recall, developed a courtroom style that owed more to method than personality. People who'd watched them both in court began saying that Michael was better.

After the Panther trial Ted also changed course, becoming a national spokesman for the trial bar. In twenty years plaintiffs' lawyers had gone from the fringes to the very heart of American business and politics—and had created a powerful backlash. Lawyers were still boisterous, emotional, and disdained, but by the seventies Americans were retaining them to sue one another at a rate never seen before. Their impact on society was profound. "The seventies were the setting for bringing down on the nation the old Mexican curse, 'May your life be filled with lawyers,'" one commentator observed miserably toward the end of the decade.

In 1979, on his second try, Ted Koskoff was elected president of ATLA, making him leader of the country's 55,000 personal injury lawyers, the group chiefly responsible for both the litigation explosion and the growing reaction against it. Wearing enormous tortoiseshell glasses and cutting an opulent figure, he traveled the country imploring ATLA's members, as always, to elevate their standards. Advocacy is the art of persuasion, he told them, so learn to be persuasive. Like a drama coach, he lectured on the virtues of courtroom technique, from voice ("Cadence and contrast . . . some words should be caressed and held back, not let go") to dress ("When you address a jury in a navy blue suit, white shirt, and dark tie, you are presenting a powerful, riveting appearance") to phrasing ("Simplicity is important. It has been said that eloquence is vehement simplicity").

He coached his colleagues on how to craft opening arguments, cross-examine witnesses, and make defendants squirm: "Ask a doctor in a malpractice case, 'Doctor, if you had to do it all over again, would you have done the same thing?' If he says yes, you say to the jury, as the conscience of the community, 'Are you going to put this monster out in society so he can do this thing again?' If he says no, say, 'Well, okay, he was honest, he made a mistake.'" And he exhorted his colleagues to use their growing status and wealth to donate politically and make themselves felt, something they did so concertedly that ATLA became, like the National Rifle Association in its heyday, a Washington rarity: an unbeatable lobby. As an industry, plaintiffs' lawyers have only had one legislative issue—the right to bring lawsuits against as many defendants, and for as much in damages, as the courts will allow. During Koskoff's term and for the next fifteen years, Congress never once voted to abridge those rights, despite the bitter and unanimous opposition of American business.

Whatever the Koskoffs' stylistic differences, success transcended them. By the mid-eighties, Koskoff, Koskoff & Bieder was a powerhouse nationally among small firms. The economics of plaintiffs' work had changed. In Ted's day a hardworking trial lawyer could make good money by churning through a large volume of small cases. Now, largely because of Michael, the firm had reduced its volume dramatically, taking only select cases with high liability. Brain-damaged babies were among the biggest; yielding fees in the millions, they became a specialty of the firm.

Together the Koskoffs prospered. Ted, of course, had acted rich even when he wasn't. Michael, who with his wife Rosalind, also now a lawyer with the firm, had four teenagers, embraced the material comforts his father loved much more slowly and ambivalently, but he caught up over time. He learned to dress as elegantly, installed a massive flagstone patio and pool off the living room of his outsized suburban Colonial, took tennis vacations in the Caribbean and theater jaunts to London, and drove a blood-red Jaguar with a plush leather interior and a car phone.

It was a good life, a charmed life, and father and son celebrated by living well. They ate at the best restaurants, always taking the check no matter how big the party. They listened to good music, enjoyed good plays, drank good wine, talked with studied appreciation about Mozart and Shakespeare and Schubert. They lived life as it should be lived, thoughtful and unrushed and unconflicted, and where, if one had the good fortune to live in southern Connecticut, it should be lived. In Westport.

"The biggest problem," Lichtenstein says, recalling his discussions with Mike Koskoff about the Sabias, "was we had one dead baby and one live one. We spent a lot of time talking about whether we should have actions on behalf of each. The deceased twin was gone; there was nothing we could do to bring that baby back. We decided that the most important thing was not the loss of one twin but the life of the other, because that's what had to be taken care of by the parents and society."

There were other, more pecuniary reasons for their thinking. Koskoff knew he'd be happy to argue the Sabias' case before a jury. It had, in his view, the essential dramatic elements: sympathetic plaintiffs, unsympathetic defendants, plenty of negligence—in Lichtenstein's taut phrase, "a double disaster." But even triability wasn't the final measure of a good case. That was damages: How much could the victims reasonably claim to have lost? Under Connecticut law, wrongful death claims in obstetrical cases were allowed substantial value, $1 million or more. But death damages were hard to evaluate and seldom brought that much at trial. Juries had mixed views of parents who seemed to be trying to profit from the deaths of their children, and awards were calculated on the basis of lost lifetime earnings. Tony Sabia, though he made good money, was a high school dropout; Donna was unskilled. No child of theirs was likely to become a brain surgeon, so lost income for the dead twin would probably come in low.

The big prize, they knew, was Little Tony. The cost of his medical care alone could run into the millions of dollars, and that didn't include his pain and suffering, which was incalculable. Koskoff wasn't callous: he knew that the financial and emotional strains of taking care of a totally disabled child frequently sink even the best-equipped families. Recovering enough money to ensure a lifetime of quality medical care could make a profound difference in all of the Sabias' lives. But he also knew that as a plaintiff, Little Tony was a gold mine—if he survived. "I'd have taken this case even if I knew Tony wasn't going to live," Lichtenstein says, but clearly, the incentives to do so would have been far fewer.

Koskoff didn't want to risk Little Tony's claim by focusing too broadly. Juries, he thought, liked things simple, and suing on behalf of a stillborn would muddle their case. For this reason he argued against including the distress from Michael Sabia's death in any complaint on behalf of Donna. In fact, Michael's death was a major problem for any lawsuit, and Koskoff and Lichtenstein knew it. If he died as a result of negligence, that let Humes off, since he appeared to have been dead many hours before she arrived on the scene. It was equivalent to the McLucas defense in the Panther trial, which, as the Koskoffs argued it, went, "Yes, he shot Rackley, but he didn't kill him, because Rackley was already dead." Alternatively, if what killed Michael also injured Little Tony, nothing Humes did or didn't do could have changed it.

After weeks of going back and forth Koskoff and Lichtenstein decided to sue on behalf of Little Tony and Donna but not Michael, even though his loss—his life—was greatest. Lichtenstein called Donna on a Sunday afternoon in February to tell her the news. Strategically, he knew this was the right decision, though he and Koskoff also were confirming a nineteenth-century complaint about a bias in civil suits: that it's "more profitable for the defendant to kill the plaintiff than to scratch him."

Donna and Tony were encouraged by Lichtenstein's call, but only slightly, and only in passing. Tony thought Lichtenstein was "a brain"; if he thought they had a case, maybe they did, maybe someone really had done something wrong. But bringing a lawsuit didn't solve anything, and Tony, especially, had no time for efforts that didn't help them cope with their immediate problems. A lawsuit wasn't going to put his sons back together, and he and Donna were too overwhelmed to dwell on what else it might do. "It wasn't a priority," he says.

Not that Lichtenstein made much of it either. After deciding to file suit, his first job with new clients was to dampen their hopes that a court case might change their lives. It might be five to ten years, if ever, before they went to trial. Little Tony could die during that time. They could lose in court. Lichtenstein didn't want clients so worked up that in the end a crushing disappointment led them to hate or worse yet, as was known to happen, sue him and the Koskoffs. With so many lawyers around, lawsuits alleging legal malpractice were also increasing, and personal injury lawyers had to watch what they promised. Lichtenstein soft-pedaled, and Donna thanked him politely but dully, without enthusiasm.

In February, the day before Humes's confrontation with Feller's peer review committee, Little Tony had hip surgery in Newington, a children's hospital upstate. One hip was improperly formed and the other pulled out of its socket. For five hours doctors remolded his joints, reinforcing them with steel plates. They cut and repaired the tendons and muscles leading to his feet, to relieve some of their splaying and tautness, and released his testicles, which had never descended. When he came to after his anesthesia, Donna says, he bawled hellishly. It was the first time she'd heard him cry.

Eight months pregnant, Donna slept in the hospital on a daybed throughout his week-long stay. She began keeping a journal and wrote affectlessly about the experience: "Tony and I went this morning for a screening conference in the apatheater," she wrote. "It was a little bit uncomfortable because they had Tony on a table, undressed, and the resident doctor basically discussed Tony's problems, then asked if anyone had any questions."

After returning home, she managed, but barely. Little Tony remained in a body cast for six weeks, and with Donna almost due, washing and feeding him became harder than ever. Tony "expresses himself a little bit more than he used to," she wrote in her journal a few days after bringing him home. But his expressiveness was slender comfort: his needs were overwhelming.

Donna had another problem. With Shannon, now nine, she was brusque and inattentive but felt she couldn't help it. She'd never planned to neglect her; it just seemed that ever since she met Tony, something or someone else always got in the way. For a fourth-grade writing assignment, Shannon wrote about Little Tony, "My brother is spatial because he is handicapped. He has seizures. A seizure is when you don't get enough oxygen to the brain. . . . Tony gets a lot of attention. He is so small because of being handicapped. He is two years old and can't crawl." When Shannon brought the assignment home, Donna told her how proud she was of it. Then Tony vomited and Donna had to scurry to keep him from choking.

It was all she could do to get by. The day Lichtenstein filed the lawsuit in Bridgeport Superior Court, March 2, found her wrestling with more pressing concerns: "Tony started back at STAR," she wrote in her journal. "Quality care aid never showed up."

The court complaint, eight pages, contained a long list of allegations. Lichtenstein still didn't know what had caused Little Tony's brain damage, so he covered every possibility. There were two counts each on behalf of Little Tony and Donna; the first against Norwalk Hospital and "its servants, agents and employees," the second against Humes. Lichtenstein prided himself on not taking a shotgun approach, suing every conceivable defendant, but Koskoff thought that because Humes was fulfilling an obligation to the clinic they might want to claim her as an "agent" of the hospital. Though they considered Humes largely at fault, suing the hospital for its role in the birth was, literally, extra insurance.

Of the eighteen allegations against the hospital, half involved Donna's visits to the clinic. These included failing to treat her pregnancy as high-risk; not having adequate procedures for handling twin pregnancies and not following the allegedly inadequate ones the hospital did have; not monitoring the twins regularly with ultrasound; and providing nurse-midwives, instead of doctors, to treat Donna. The remaining allegations concerned the birth itself, among them ignoring the fact that a fetal heartbeat couldn't be heard on admission, delaying an ultrasound, failing to do a timely C-section, and failing to have an obstetrician attend Donna as soon as she arrived at the hospital.

Altogether, the complaint alleged, Little Tony had been made to suffer "serious, permanent and painful injuries" which "have caused and will continue to cause [him] to suffer great mental and physical pain and anguish." Donna, the complaint said, had suffered "psychological, physiological and emotional distress" so "painful, serious and permanent" that it was difficult for her to carry on or enjoy a normal life.

The counts against Humes were equally grievous. By not examining Donna sooner and, after an ultrasound, delivering the twins immediately by C-section, Humes failed "to exercise that degree of care and skill ordinarily and customarily used by physicians specializing in the field of obstetrics and gynecology," Lichtenstein alleged. This "carelessness and negligence" had also caused Little Tony and Donna extreme suffering and economic loss.

Humes received the subpoena from a deputy sheriff in her office, about lunchtime. Having been through the experience before with Mary Gay made it no less difficult. All that she had feared from the beginning, and had left off fearing, was happening. She was again to be hunted down, blamed, scorned, less than a month after her former colleagues—doctors who not only knew but had sought to codify the very standard of care she was now being charged with violating—had absolved her.

Humes knew that she would carry on, but that she was now a target. And for what? She didn't fault the Sabias: they were only doing what they had to do. It was the lawyers she loathed. She was certain that they had twisted the truth to manipulate the Sabias into hating the very people who had tried to help them. How else could they possibly blame her? Who did the Koskoffs advocate for, really? No one but themselves, Humes thought. For their own greed, she believed, they would sacrifice anyone. She considered them vile.

Donna delivered her baby, Heather Rose, on March 28 in Norwalk Hospital. Though she and the hospital were now in litigation, it never occurred to her to go anywhere else: her doctor had privileges there; where else would she go? The hospital made no acknowledgment of the lawsuit, but Linda Nemeth, the nursing supervisor Humes had visited the day after she'd delivered the twins and who had fired labor nurse Mollie Fortuna, kept tabs on Donna and the baby as an unofficial ally. Loyal to the hospital, sympathetic to the Sabias, mindful of the Koskoffs, she felt strongly that it was in everyone's interest for the Sabias to have a good experience this time. Donna's delivery and aftercare were uneventful.

On March 31, her first day home, Donna placed Heather in the crib with Little Tony. It was the day before his third birthday, and Donna hoped the new baby would stimulate a reaction from him. "Neither one of them seemed to care much for it," she wrote in her journal, adding, "Over the weekend Tony ate really well. Now that I'm home, he doesn't seem to want as much."

Little Tony's appetite had been strong for over a year. As long as he was burped well, he kept his food down and put on weight. There weren't many parental rewards in caring for him, but this was one of them. Eating was one thing he could do, a solid achievement in a life otherwise devoid of progress. But now he didn't seem to want to eat. Several weeks later, on April 20, Donna wrote in her journal: "Tony has been vomiting all day over the past three weeks. His appetite has gotten very poor." Donna called the doctor, who advised her to give him clear liquids, but he continued to vomit. When she called again, her doctor told her to bring Little Tony to the emergency room at Norwalk Hospital. That night he was put on an IV and a heart monitor. He still couldn't eat. The next afternoon his IV slipped out, and Donna wrote: "His right hand and arm blew up like a balloon so now the IV is in his left arm. Nurse is putting warm compresses on to draw fluid out."

Dr. Murray Engel, the neurologist Donna had first confronted eighteen months earlier about Little Tony's diagnosis, and who still treated him at the hospital, ordered an electroencephalogram. It showed no changes; there was no apparent neurological reason why Little Tony couldn't take food. He still was vomiting, and was moved to the critical care unit, the same unit in which he'd spent the first four weeks of his life. "No TV, no radio, no sound stimulation which he needs," Donna wrote. "Tony is in room by himself. I try to visit every day but its real hard because of new baby."

On April 23, 1987, Little Tony stopped eating entirely. Whenever Tony or Donna or an aide who knew him from STAR tried to feed him, he shut his mouth determinedly or yanked his head away. For the next several days he continued to vomit despite being fed through a tube. An upper GI exam showed no obstructions. Eventually, nurses were able to sustain IV feedings of 1,000 calories a day, and Little Tony began to regain some of the weight he'd lost. "Dr. Woodward [Little Tony's pediatrician] is having a CAT scan ordered in the next day or so," Donna wrote. "She has spoken with Dr. Glassman, a gastrologist or something like that. . . . Could not go visit Tony on Monday. We had a broken sewer line."

Little Tony eventually was diagnosed with gastroesophageal reflux; he had more pressure in his stomach than in his esophagus, forcing the contents of his stomach to back up. This is a common ailment, the principal symptom of which is heartburn, and in most sufferers—pregnant women, runners, the obese—it is easily treated with antacids and a sleeping position in which the head is raised. But Little Tony's wasted condition, refusal to eat, and unresponsiveness made his situation dire. Woodward and Glassman explained that Little Tony needed more calories to grow; without them he would die of starvation. Tony and Donna could either learn to feed him at home through a tube inserted in his nose, in the hope that his appetite might someday return, or he could have surgery to have a permanent feeding tube sewn into his stomach. Tony and Donna didn't see that they had any choice. He was three years old and weighed eighteen pounds.

Little Tony was operated on at Yale–New Haven Hospital on May 15, his second major surgery in four months. Tony and Donna learned to manage his pump-feeding apparatus and to mash up and inject antiseizure medications into his feeding tube in order to keep him at home, but medically a major divide had been crossed. Even the slender independence that he had developed by taking food had now been cut away. He couldn't sit up, roll over, hold up his head, talk, or control his bodily functions. And now he couldn't eat. By any measure his long-term prognosis took an irremediable turn for the worse. His dependence was now total.

Tony, typically, saw the development differently. He saw Little Tony's refusal of food not as a measure of his helplessness or decline but as an extraordinary act of will, a triumph. Nobody believed he could do anything for himself, but he had made himself *not* do something; he had stopped eating the day Donna brought a new baby home from the hospital. And if he had the will to do that, then he must have it to do other things. Tony began to believe more than ever that imprisoned inside Little Tony's spastic, crippled, possibly agonized little body existed a whole person with feelings and awareness. A good boy. His son. "If he decides he wants to eat again, he will," he began to tell people. "If he decides he's going to walk, he's going to walk. If something kicks in upstairs, who's to say what he can't do?"

Donna disagreed, but she was so distraught she was willing to believe almost anything. Her youth had gone, and the decision to put Little Tony on a feeding tube had been almost too hard to bear. It was at about this time that she discontinued her journal on Lichtenstein's advice. In the lawsuit, he said, a journal might be discoverable. They might be called to provide it as evidence to the other side.

FIVE

As a profession, ob-gyn was born in blood. The learned physicians of the late eighteenth and early nineteenth centuries who delivered childbirth from the ancient realm of midwifery into the modern world of scientific medicine also slaughtered untold numbers of women with their own hands—inadvertently at first, then out of prideful ignorance, by refusing to accept that they were spreading deadly infections. For the next century and a half, no other medical specialty would have to confront such an agonizing truth about itself. When one finally did, with abortion and later birth injury, it was again obstetricians. No other group of doctors is so peculiarly encumbered by the possibility of causing pain and suffering while attempting to do good. The dangers of the birth process itself and the triagelike dilemma of caring at once for two patients, mother and baby, sharpens this ambiguity.

The field of obstetrics began in Europe around 1750 with the realization by male doctors that women in labor could be assisted through physical manipulation. Before that time the passage of the fetus from the uterus through the birth canal was scarcely understood. In difficult labors those trying to save a mother's life had no choice but to kill an impacted child and remove it by whatever barbarous means possible. Then academic physicians in England, France, and Germany determined through doing careful autopsies the precise reproductive anatomy of women. Viewing the uterus and birth channel mechanically, as a kind of pump, they began devising interventions to ease the passage. Their manipulations were often grisly. Wielding an armamentarium of hooks, knives, perforators, and grippers, early obstetricians frequently inflicted torturous violence on both mother and fetus. But in many complicated labors they were able to save the lives of women *and* their children, an extraordinary advance.

Once the province of midwives with no formal education, obstetrics surged. It was one of the few areas of general medicine where doctors had the knowledge to alter a likely fatal outcome. Doctors who saw obstetrics as a gateway to lucrative family practice were drawn to the field. Soon, however, calamity struck. At almost all early lying-in hospitals, outbreaks of a mysterious fever raged through the wards, in some years and some seasons deadlier than others, but with a terrifying consistency. Within hours of giving birth, previously healthy women came down with infections that rampaged through their bodies. Febrile and delirious, many of them died within days of blood poisoning, their abdomens bursting with pus. Though the symptoms of childbirth fever had been known for centuries, in some hospitals up to 70 percent of women now contracted the disease and up to a quarter of them died.

Hospitals, only recently elevated from warehouses for the destitute sick, became feared and reviled as charnel houses. Meanwhile, among women who delivered at home with midwives, and even among poor women who self-delivered in streets and alleys, childbirth fever was all but unknown. What caused the infections was beyond medical comprehension. It would be decades before French chemist Louis Pasteur would prove that germs, not vapors and humors, caused infectious disease; still longer before a young English surgeon named Joseph Lister would discover putrefying bacteria in septic wounds, thus pioneering the practice of antiseptic surgery. Obstetricians, helpless in the face of so much dying, ventured their own theories—from self-poisoning by vaginal fluids, to a specific disease entity like smallpox, to the poverty and perceived immorality of many hospital patients, to the foul stench emanating from the body cavities of victims.

Among the first to propose a connection between the epidemics and the new practice of obstetrics was a young American, Dr. Oliver Wendell Holmes. Holmes, a professor at Harvard Medical School, had studied in Europe and was celebrated for combining learnedness with common sense. Hearing accounts in Boston of women's deaths and of the deaths of doctors who had done autopsies, he theorized that some doctors were carrying the disease from patient to patient, and that they'd picked it up doing postmortem examinations on infected women. Doctors, he suggested, were carrying the lethal material on their examining fingers and instruments. Obstetricians, scandalized, attacked Holmes bitterly. A famous Philadelphia physician denounced his theory as a "vile, demoralizing superstition"; another blamed him for cruelly and heedlessly alarming patients. Doctors were gentlemen, they protested, and gentlemen have clean hands: What Holmes was suggesting was impossible. Despite his lack of proof, Holmes persisted. "The time has come," he wrote in 1855, "when the existence of a private pestilence in the sphere of a single physician should be looked upon, not as a misfortune, but a crime."

By then Holmes's contention was supported by the work of a zealous Hungarian obstetrician, Ignaz Semmelweis. Semmelweis had practiced in the 1840s at the Vienna General Hospital, where there were two obstetrical divisions, one run by doctors and medical students, the other by midwives. Autopsies were then the supreme instrument of medical education, and doctors and medical students each performed several a day, racing back and forth without washing between the morgue and the delivery area. Keeping careful records, Semmelweis noted that the incidence of childbirth fever was ten times higher in the doctor-run division than in the ward run by midwives, who did no autopsies. He further showed that by making doctors wash with a chlorinated solution between examinations, he could reduce the cases of childbed infection in the doctors' division to the level of the midwives' division.

Semmelweis was denounced if anything more vehemently than Holmes, perhaps because obstetricians in Europe had, literally, more blood on their hands than those in America, where most women still delivered at home. True, their metal hooks and knives often left women wounded and bloody, but the new obstetricians were saving lives with them. And, pre-Pasteur and pre-Lister, Semmelweis couldn't produce scientific evidence that doctors were somehow transporting unseen putrid material on their hands and introducing it into those open wounds.

Evangelical in his zeal, Semmelweis made himself a scourge, attacking the continent's leading obstetricians in the darkest terms. "I declare before God and the world that you are a murderer," he wrote to one; and to another, "Herr Professor has proven that in spite of a new lying-in hospital, furnished with the best equipment, a great deal of homicide can be committed, if only one possesses the necessary talents." "For many a conscience-stricken obstetrician," medical historian Dr. Sherwin Nuland writes, Semmelweis's conclusion that those who failed to follow his precautions were massacring their patients was "an appeal to self-condemnation . . . too heartbreaking to bear." And yet it was true.

At the same time that Semmelweis was conducting his research—the 1840s and 1850s—an English orthopedist investigating the causes of childhood deformities confronted obstetrics with a less direct but equally discomfiting challenge. Dr. William John Little, founder of the Royal Orthopedic Hospital in London, was himself clubfooted. He also was a visiting physician at the Asylum for Idiots, in Earlswood. There Little observed hundreds of children whose bodies were spastic and rigid, who today would be said to have cerebral palsy. Many of them also had convulsions and were mentally retarded. Tracing their medical histories, Little concluded that a substantial number of their disabilities had resulted from "abnormal parturition, difficult labors, premature birth and asphyxia neonatorum [oxygen deprivation during labor]."

Never before had a physician theorized that birth asphyxia could cause permanent brain damage. The discovery of oxygen by the radical English minister and chemist Joseph Priestley was less than a hundred years old. It had been less than seventy years since Antoine Lavoisier, a French chemist later beheaded during the Reign of Terror, demonstrated the essential role of oxygen in all biological activity. Little's observation that a lapse in respiration before or during birth could cause a "mischievous state of affairs" similar to drowning—"suspended animation," he called it, resulting in blood stagnation and ultimately "congestions of the capillary system of the brain"—was daring on all fronts.

Obstetricians didn't know how to respond. The implication that those attending difficult labors had any role to play in causing mental and physical deformities was so unusual—idiots and cripples were thought to be the work of God or a result of immorality—and compared to the carnage in the lying-in hospitals, so benign, that Little's claim, based on two hundred cases, was greeted less with opprobrium than curiosity. "The difficulty there appeared to be in discussing this excellent paper, arose, no doubt from the entire novelty and originality of the subject," a British doctor said in 1861 after Little defended his work before the Obstetrical Society of London, then three years old. "Dr. Little had brought before the obstetric world new matter for inquiry of the highest interest."

But Little's findings also put the obstetrical world on notice: Now that it had made intervention its cornerstone, what doctors did or did not do to ensure oxygen flow to the fetus during labor would have major consequences both for the children and, later, themselves.

What saved the new obstetricians from condemnation, if not ruin, was the law, and lawyers. In both Europe and the United States, doctors were protected from criminal prosecution by common law doctrine and statutes governing wrongful death. As long as they could show that they were honestly trying to help and had a reasonable expectation of doing so, it was almost impossible to convict them when patients died. On the other hand, since death was a public (criminal) wrong, civil negligence suits offered little remedy, no matter how clearly a doctor was at fault.

Doctors, and ob-gyns in particular, operated with virtual impunity. When, for instance, a doctor in America as late as the 1860s gave a patient ergot to induce contractions, which caused her uterus to rupture; then dissected and removed the fetus to save the mother, inadvertently removing some of the woman's intestines; then finally told the patient that "if she had anything to say she had better say it"—she died several hours later—he was able to avoid being sued by offering the dead woman's husband $300. The law was as primitive as the medicine it safeguarded. Whatever punishment doctors feared, it was not from lawyers.

Even with the first significant wave of malpractice suits in the Northeast from the mid-1830s to the mid-1860s, doctors and lawyers tended to remain on the same side. Like priests, members of the same privileged caste, they had specialized education and training that set them apart from society. Highly regarded by others, cosseted by their shared prestige, they perceived each other as gentlemen at a time when a man's honor often counted more than his deeds. As historian Kenneth Allen De Ville notes, "Physicians did not believe that lawyers were unredeemable villains but felt instead that they constituted a misguided, underinformed, but 'noble sister profession.'" Abraham Lincoln, a defense lawyer before he went into politics, once chastised a plaintiff who had sued his doctors after surgery. In the process of repairing his broken leg, they had made it several inches shorter than the other: "Well!" Lincoln remonstrated. "What I would advise you to do is get down on your knees and thank your heavenly Father and these two doctors that you have any legs to stand on at all."

Most Americans excused doctors for their failures because of the great good they did. But doctors did not as readily excuse lawyers. By the end of the Civil War their professional cordiality had become strained, as doctors began to see lawyers not merely as misguided but malicious. Holmes, who a few years earlier had challenged obstetricians to address their culpability for childbirth fever and had even called their recalcitrance a "crime," now saw on the horizon something even more unsettling and ominous: lawyers and lawsuits. "The [medical] profession," he wrote, "has just been startled by a verdict against a physician ruinous in its amount—enough to drive many a hardworking practitioner out of house and home—a verdict which leads to the fear that suits for malpractice may take the place of the panel game and child stealing as a means of extorting money."

Doctors were awakening to an unnerving reality: that they could be held accountable by the lay world for their mistakes. And though most early malpractice suits were unsuccessful and the legal system overwhelmingly favored well-meaning physicians, they had no trouble identifying the enemy. When Holmes's son, future Supreme Court Chief Justice Oliver Wendell Homes Jr., returned from fighting in the Civil War, he announced his career plans to his father. Replied the elder Holmes bitterly, "What's the use of going to Harvard Law School. A lawyer cannot be a great man."

~ ~ ~

Humes wanted as her lawyer Arnold Bai, who had represented her in the Gay case. She had no affection for lawyers as a group, but she respected and admired Bai. A small man, physically unimpressive, he spoke with a lisp, but he was meticulous and shrewd. For many years he had dominated the state's medical defense bar as Aetna Life & Casualty Company's lead outside counsel in malpractice cases.

Until the early eighties Aetna was the only malpractice insurer in Connecticut: if you were a doctor, and you were sued, Bai was your attorney. Soothing and supportive, he counseled doctors to go on with their good work while he took care of their problems. It was a powerful balm, as doctors historically won 90 percent of malpractice cases at trial and Bai excelled at persuading jurors to sympathize with physicians.

Humes trusted Bai to represent her interests. He was nearby in Bridgeport and knew the Koskoffs well enough to join them for lunch. They might try to intimidate her, but not him. Yet after being subpoenaed, she got a form letter from her insurer, St. Paul Fire & Marine Insurance Company, informing her that it had referred her case to another firm. The country's largest malpractice carrier, St. Paul had moved aggressively into Connecticut after Aetna had pulled out, and was now parceling out cases, exploiting the pent-up competitiveness within the state's insurance defense bar to keep down its legal costs.

St. Paul's local claims people considered Bai overpriced and refused to use him. Bai charged top dollar—$800 a day for depositions and court time—and had a reputation among insurers for padding. Plaintiffs' lawyers like the Koskoffs are widely scorned for taking contingency fees, but defense lawyers, billing by the hour, have the greater incentive to drag out questionable cases. St. Paul, a multibillion-dollar company, had ventured into professional liability because it was profitable, but profits shrank when carriers misjudged which cases to try and which to settle. St. Paul's district manager, a street-smart twenty-year veteran named Mike Kaufman, hated being told through years of pretrial wrangling that a case was a winner only to have a lawyer turn around at the last minute and say he needed $2 million. The lawyer ran up a fat fee while Kaufman had to explain himself to the central office. Kaufman believed this was Bai's style.

St. Paul referred Humes's case to Montstream & May, a small firm of a dozen lawyers located in a wooded office park in Glastonbury, a fast-growth Hartford suburb about an hour from Westport. The inconvenience alone dismayed her; how, Humes wondered, was she going to meet with these people? Yet it was the implied slight—St. Paul hadn't consulted her—that riled her. Humes wanted someone to represent *her*, not her insurer. But Bob Montstream, the firm's forty-nine-year-old founder and lead partner, seemed to her to be an eager captive not just of St. Paul, but of the entire insurance industry, of which Hartford was a kind of Vatican. His offices were located in a modernist brick box with a stark atrium and computer-generated art in the lobby. The building was owned by Connecticut General, a giant Hartford-based insurer, and its tenants were all insurance companies or firms that catered to them. In the social geography of upscale Connecticut, Montstream's office was about as far from Westport as one could get, and Humes worried about whose interests Montstream would be serving, hers or St. Paul's.

On the night of April 27, as doctors in Norwalk scrambled to determine why Little Tony had stopped eating, Humes called a claim representative at St. Paul to complain about the company's choice. She was strident, and the following day, the representative, Bill Suerkin, papered the conversation in a certified letter back to Humes. He told her to reread her policy, which stated that St. Paul reserved the right to choose a lawyer and that Humes was obligated to "fully cooperate" in its investigation of the case. "Should you fail to comply with these requirements," Suerkin wrote, "you will be seriously jeopardizing your own coverage and protection." Humes understood the code. She was being put on notice: if she continued to protest, she risked losing not only the right to a lawyer but $2 million in indemnification, her policy limit.

Humes was exasperated. She couldn't conceive of remaining uninvolved in her defense. She was not like some doctors, who could dissociate themselves from being sued, reducing the process to a cost of doing business, letting a lawyer do the dirty work while they soldiered. Bai had told her not to take it personally, but she had to. She was certain of her innocence, yet she was being attacked. And now she was being assigned a lawyer she didn't know and didn't want, while some functionary at her insurance company, which she paid $102,000 a year to indemnify herself and an associate, threatened her if she didn't do things their way.

She felt herself being drawn step by step into a dirty game, a game that everyone else seemed to sanction and enjoy. All these people, these *men*—the Koskoffs, the Norwalk Hospital boys' club, St. Paul maybe—needed a scapegoat, her. And the tragedy was, she thought, it had nothing to do with who she was, or what kind of doctor she was, or even what she may or may not have done during the two and a half hours she was in charge of Donna Sabia's care. All it had to do with, Humes felt was her being available—and vulnerable.

The real cost of being a defendant again assailed her. When you were on the defensive, you lost your ability to protest, your control, Humes thought. You were isolated, demonized, whispered about. Worst of all, people stopped seeing you as a doctor, as someone with vital, lifesaving skills who sat up night after night, cadging naps on gurneys, giving up your own life for your patients. How many difficult births had Humes managed? How many incompetent residents and nurses had she covered for? How often had she stood operating without sleep while some anesthesiologist yabbered about his sail-boat or asked to turn up the music in the operating room? How many times had she done an exquisite C-section, bringing out a pink baby, getting control over the bleeding and suturing the uterus so deftly that the woman could de-liver her next three children vaginally, then rushed off to sit encouragingly for twelve hours with a woman so desperate for a vaginal delivery that Humes had to question whether it would destroy her not to have one. How many male obs, she wondered, would just have done the second C-section in order to make a golf date and not have cared?

Humes tempered St. Paul's refusal by hiring Bai anyway, as her private counsel. For $10,000, he would bird-dog Montstream while looking out for her interests. And he would supply moral support, which Humes knew she would need. Montstream, meanwhile, only wanted to find out what kind of case he'd taken on. Contrary to Humes's suspicions, he believed a lawyer's first obligation in an insurance defense case was to the defendant. There were mal-practice carriers that ignored their policyholders' desires, but St. Paul didn't consider itself one of them. As the country's leading insurer of doctors, it cul-tivated a high-quality image promising both prestige and performance. Most physicians felt entitled to elite representation, so St. Paul knew it couldn't merely "dump" cases by settling early or refusing to pay the best expert wit-nesses or skimping on its investigations; plenty of other liability carriers were ready to move in if it did. Montstream knew the Koskoffs would spare no ex-pense to win the Sabia case. St. Paul, for its own reasons, expected him to do the same.

He also understood that the case was problematical. Though he sympa-thized with Humes and thought her a victim of circumstance, he was trou-bled by her inconsistency. To argue that she'd done no wrong, he'd have to develop a scenario to counter the one devised by Lichtenstein and Koskoff; namely, that Humes had failed to meet the standard of care by not staying with Donna, monitoring the fetal heart rates and delivering Little Tony sooner, by C-section. But the hospital records were a mess, and Humes's two subsequent written accounts were contradictory, the first blaming Fortuna, the second, Donna's wild thrashing. Nothing was more damaging to a defen-dant's credibility than a changed story—nothing except committing one's loose ends to writing.

It didn't help that Humes now believed that leaving the labor and deliv-ery area to discharge other patients may have caused her to lose "focus" on Donna's labor, or that she'd signed the labor and delivery summary without filling it out, leaving Fortuna and two other labor nurses to complete it later on. Jurors might normally be sympathetic to doctors, but they were unlikely to be impressed by a physician who seemed unwilling to assume responsibil-ity for her actions. None of this added up to malpractice, but that wasn't the point. The point was the relish with which Mike Koskoff would dissect Humes on cross-examination. Montstream wasn't encouraged.

Strategically, he knew he had two possible lines of defense: standard of care and causation. All he needed was to make a reasonable case for one of them, since it was up to Koskoff to demonstrate that Humes had both erred *and,* in so doing, injured Little Tony. At St. Paul's suggestion, Montstream now sent all of Donna's hospital records to a consultant, a Harvard-trained ob-gyn named Alan Pinshaw, to address the standard-of-care issue first. Easier to prove, it could obviate the matter of causation entirely, saving both time and money later on. A burly South African, Pinshaw was a staff ob-gyn at Harvard Community Health Plan, a well-regarded Boston HMO, and an instructor at Harvard Medical School. The son of a lawyer, he was a ruddy, vociferous man with strong opinions and a quick wit who'd become interested in law and medicine simultaneously. At age fourteen, a brick wall had collapsed on him in his native Pretoria and mangled his foot. While he was in the hospital recovering from surgery, his father sued the building's owner, winning 4,000 pounds. Pinshaw thought trial lawyers were "bullshitters," but after much introspection, he says, joined the "expert industry" to help inject some truth into the process of litigation. "Lawyers don't look for truth," Pinshaw says. "They look to put their opinion in as favorable a light as possible."

On July 27, four months after Montstream first received Humes's file, Pinshaw sent him his preliminary report. Most lawyers remind consultants not to write down their opinions and to purge their computers and shred their files; if the news is bad, they don't want the other side learning about it during discovery. Most such consultations therefore are conducted by phone and exist, in the end, only in lawyers' notes and in the often conflicting memories of the parties. But Pinshaw wrote a comprehensive review that went on, in final form, for some fourteen pages. For the first time, an outside physician evaluated Donna's treatment in toto, on the record, trying to piece together all that had gone wrong. Pinshaw pulled no punches. He thought Humes had twice violated the standard of care: by failing to order continuous fetal monitoring for Donna once she got to the hospital, then by leaving the labor area to discharge patients. Though he believed labor nurse Mollie Fortuna "quite inexplicably" had misled Humes and that McManamy had an "independent duty" to monitor both heart rates, he thought Humes would "find difficulty arguing that she rejoiced in the knowledge that 'all was well' with the twins." In hospital settings, the doctor is the "captain of the ship"—ultimately accountable. Humes would gain little trying to hide behind the lapses of her subordinates.

Montstream found considerably more cause for hope in Pinshaw's view of Donna's treatment during pregnancy, in which Humes had no part. It was here that Pinshaw was most critical and shed the most new light—despite erring about a key premise. Just as the Sabias would recall Humes telling them, he concluded that what caused Little Tony's brain damage was a loss of oxygen when he bled into his twin brother Michael. Taking this bleeding into account, and noting that at birth Little Tony weighed almost 20 percent more than Michael, he theorized that what caused Michael's death was the condition known as twin-to-twin transfusion syndrome. In twins who have this syndrome, the larger twin siphons nutrients from the smaller one, becoming plethoric—having too much blood—while the other becomes anemic. In fact, it was Little Tony who was anemic at birth, while Michael had so many red blood cells that he appeared flushed.

But if Pinshaw was wrong about this one detail, he was right that the twins were being nourished unequally, and that Norwalk Hospital hadn't detected it. This, he concluded, was the "primary and most far-reaching" lapse in Donna's treatment: the decision not to monitor the growth of the twins regularly during the last third of her pregnancy. Pinshaw believed that by sending Donna for repeat ultrasounds, the clinic doctors would have seen that Michael was doing, if not poorly, not as well as Little Tony. They would have done further tests to assess Michael's well-being and, seeing evidence of distress, would have taken both twins by C-section. "Premature delivery of this pregnancy," he wrote, "would have been accomplished with the delivery of two live twins." The boys would have survived. Humes would have remained in bed that Sunday morning.

Pinshaw on balance was no easier on Humes than he was on the hospital. He thought there remained a "salvageable situation" at least as late as nine-thirty on the morning of Donna's delivery, and that had Humes moved to take Little Tony even an hour sooner, he might have suffered "less long-term disability." Of the delivery itself Pinshaw wrote, "Numerous profound deviations from the standard of care worsened an already probably irretrievable situation."

But Pinshaw opened for Humes's defense a welcome second front. The more it appeared that the hospital had been negligent before Donna's delivery—that the damage had already been done—the less likely it was that a jury would find Humes culpable. The strategy was to push the time of Little Tony's injuries back to the period before Donna went into labor, before Humes even entered the picture.

Montstream and St. Paul now recognized that it was as much in Humes's interest to prove that the clinic was to blame as that she was not. In law as in politics, it helps to have good enemies. Norwalk Hospital's obstetrical clinic, the province of the boys' club, now became the best enemy Humes's defense team could find.

$\sim \sim \sim$

Once a case was filed, Joel Lichtenstein stood aside. He had become too valuable at winnowing cases to slog through the prolonged fact-finding that followed. He now limited himself to memo-writing and kibitzing at the firm-wide lunches that Ted had instituted and that were a cherished Koskoff tradition. In March, after Lichtenstein had brought Donna's suit but before St. Paul retained Montstream, he routed Donna's file to Karen Koskoff, Mike's younger cousin and one of several associates now working up medical cases for the firm. A former criminal defense lawyer, Karen specialized in psychiatric malpractice, which often took the form of sexual abuse. She also came from the family's medical side: her father Yale, whom she revered, was the neurosurgeon brother who had urged Ted to take up a profession.

Karen, a divorced single mother, had worked on only two brain-damaged-baby cases and found them distressing. But as she pored over Donna's chart, she felt compelled to find out more. "I was looking for two things," she recalls. "What procedures were in place to make sure that this didn't happen? And, who was in charge of this complicated pregnancy? What I found was the people involved had nothing to follow. It was a tragic game of telephone." Donna's care, she concluded, typified "how poor people are treated by the system."

Even among the Koskoffs, Karen was known as a true believer. She grew up in Pittsburgh, where her father, chief of neurosurgery at Montefiore Hospital, the city's top academic medical center, had gained national attention for doing radical brain operations and was one of the first department heads to hire a black resident. At free-form Goddard College in Vermont, she decided to become a lawyer after visiting Michael and Ted during the Panther trial, then cut her teeth as a $30-an-hour court-assigned lawyer in Washington, D.C. "I was making so little money," she says, "I would have been eligible for a court-appointed lawyer myself."

The Koskoff men still preached the firm's mission of fighting the powerful on behalf of the powerless, but they had become powerful themselves, and vulnerable to charges of taking only big cases while profiting from their clients' suffering. Not Karen. Tall and willowy at age thirty-five, with pale eyes, a drawn complexion, and sharp features framed by a torrent of frizzy brown hair, she generally looked as if she'd just come from organizing a rent strike. Dressed in pullovers and long print skirts, brimming with earnest outrage, she embodied the progressive reputation that had made the Koskoffs famous.

Karen's job was to amass all the relevant facts in *Sabia*, a grinding process known optimistically as "discovery." She knew what to expect—very little. The goal once a lawsuit has been filed is for both sides to come to a common understanding of events. Without this there can be little hope of a focused trial or fair result. But lawyers have far more interest in gaining information than in yielding it and are disinclined to make things easier for their opponents than they have to. Now that *Sabia* was in litigation, it was up to the lawyers to submit each other written questions, called interrogatories, which they were supposed to review with their clients and return. Ostensibly, they sought this information to flesh out their knowledge and prepare for the next state of discovery—depositions—in which they interviewed each other's witnesses under oath. But Karen knew that wasn't how it worked. With most written discovery, she notes, "everybody objects to everybody's else's questions." The case bogs down; then, after a period of meaningful delay the lawyers come back and horse-trade, saying, "We'll withdraw this question if you answer that one." The trick was to think strategically, to elicit the information you thought you needed without surrendering anything vital to the other side.

In April 1987, around the time Little Tony stopped eating, lawyers for all three sides in *Sabia* exchanged their first interrogatories. Karen, seeking to confirm that Donna's care had been as disorganized and haphazard as Lichtenstein's documents made it seem, submitted a seventeen-page questionnaire to the Stamford law firm of Ryan, Ryan, Clear & Deluca, which handled most of Norwalk Hospital's malpractice defense work. Karen knew Pat Ryan, the firm's senior partner, and liked him. So did Mike Koskoff, who disdained most defense lawyers on principle but who considered Ryan capable and charming. They both believed Ryan, a paradigm of the silver-haired, politically wired, small-city Irish defense lawyer, would respond in a businesslike manner. He did. He assigned an associate, Donna Zito, to the case, and she promptly stonewalled. Zito refused to answer twenty of Karen's twenty-nine interrogatories and twelve of her fifteen document requests based on two main objections. Either the information Karen wanted was privileged, she explained, as with her requests for incident reports and peer review minutes. Or, she said, Karen was fishing, as with her attempt to get the names, job titles, and addresses of everyone who treated Donna at the clinic.

Zito gave up next to nothing. Karen managed to learn, by asking if the hospital privileges of any attending physician, staff member, or employee "were terminated, modified or restricted" as a result of being involved in Donna's treatment, that Mollie Fortuna "left the hospital's employ in April 1984," but not whether Fortuna was fired or whether her role in the birth had been investigated. And she found out that Norwalk's main liability carrier was the Travelers Insurance Company. Beyond that, she discovered almost nothing new.

Not that she herself was more forthcoming. At the same time Zito was formulating her objections, Karen was reviewing forty-seven pages of interrogatories from Montstream, which she felt delved unfairly into the Sabias' personal lives. Montstream seemed to want to find out everything he could about them, and Karen, a staunch civil libertarian, recalls being offended.

Some of the questions she considered fair game: the precise nature of Little Tony's injuries and Donna's complaints, which doctors they'd gone to, when, what they'd been told. But most she believed were aimed at learning details about Tony and Donna that Montstream could use against them later on: where had they been born? lived? worked? Had they ever been married to anyone else? Had they ever been sick? Had Donna ever had a miscarriage?

Karen answered Montstream's motion on July 30 (three days after he had heard from Pinshaw), yielding less than Zito had to her. She provided all Donna's known addresses for the previous ten years and the names of Little Tony's doctors. But she balked at supplying the names of Tony's employers and other people he and Donna had talked with about the case. All personal questions, such as whether Donna had filed federal or state tax returns in the three years prior to Little Tony's birth or even her Social Security number, Karen considered "harassment" and refused to answer pending a court ruling. "Just because you've put a claim to suit doesn't mean you waive all your rights to privacy," she says. "Defense lawyers try to get information that the plaintiff is a bad woman, for credibility issues at trial. I wasn't about to do their work for them."

Karen's dealings with Montstream characteristically went from bad to worse. By midsummer she thought the most compelling negligence in Donna's case was that no one had been in charge, least of all Humes, who inexplicably seemed to have gone AWOL during the delivery. Montstream, she thought, only wanted the case to "go away." For the next sixteen months the two of them dodged each other's attacks while exploiting lax court deadlines. They pleaded, moved, objected, amended, stalled, and issued strong letters without—except on rare occasions—talking to each other.

There was little to talk about. Karen had concluded that Montstream's strategy, typical of defense lawyers, was to blame the victim, and that he probably thought he could bully the Sabias into dropping their complaint against Humes. At the same time, Montstream was being goaded by St. Paul's Mike Kaufman, who resented the fact that the company had been dragged into the matter in the first place and wanted it disposed of. "We really thought the hospital should have defended and indemnified [Humes]," Kaufman says. "She was blackmailed in a way, because she couldn't practice at the hospital unless she worked on-call at the clinic. We didn't think it was our problem."

Montstream had initiated the sparring on June 1 by asking the court to rein in Donna's claims. Lichtenstein in his complaint had sought to tar Humes with as much blame as he could, and Montstream had reason to fear that if the Koskoffs claimed her as an "agent" of Norwalk Hospital, making each liable for the other's mistakes, she could be held in for more than just her part in the delivery. He also may have assumed that Lichtenstein didn't know what effect Humes's actions had on the birth outcome and was being vague to cover himself. Montstream urged the court to curtail the issue, sharply. Humes, he argued, had entered the case only after Donna had been in labor for two and a half hours. Thus she shouldn't be liable for anything prior to that, including the failure to do an ultrasound as soon as Donna arrived on the labor floor, which would have shown that Michael Sabia was dead.

Karen, not surprisingly, objected, saying in effect that if Humes wanted to argue the limits of her accountability at trial that was fine, but that the case shouldn't be "litigated by way of a request to revise" the original lawsuit. The court overruled her. It ordered her to amend the original complaint against Humes to clarify that Humes had no role in Donna's treatment during pregnancy. Karen had filed her objections promptly, but now, after the court decision, she hesitated. She was busy with other cases in greater need of attention. Moreover, she had no relationship with Montstream, and was still more interested in his yielding to her requests than in meeting his. For a year she did no work on the amendments.

She and Montstream were now tangling over other issues that added to the slowdown. She thought Montstream was dragging his heels in response to her pleadings; he thought she was trying to prevent him from questioning the Sabias directly. Lawyers are entitled to depose each other's witnesses prior to trial, and both he and Ryan had questions for Tony and Donna that they didn't want them rehearsing with the Koskoffs. For this reason they hadn't included them in their interrogatories. Montstream especially was pushing for the Sabias' testimony, but Karen had failed to "produce" them. Four times between February and August 1988, Tony and Donna were scheduled for deposition but Karen had canceled each time. She was in no hurry to submit them to what she knew could be a painful replay of the birth. Meanwhile, it was now up to Karen to close her pleadings, to show the court that her interrogatories had yielded sufficient grounds to continue the case.

Finally, on September 30, 1988, sixteen months after Montstream first asked the court to narrow the case against Humes, Karen moved to force the issue. Little Tony was now four and a half, about the age at which the extent of birth-related brain damage becomes fully clear, and a time when parents frequently hit bottom. Confronted with mounting evidence that their son most likely would never develop beyond infancy, Tony and Donna were becoming more discouraged. Meanwhile, Mike Koskoff, familiar with this timetable, had begun to worry how long Little Tony might live and whether the Sabias could hold out.

Feeling that she needed to move the case along both for the Sabias' sake and for the firm's, Karen moved for a default judgment against Humes. "Default" means that a defendant offers no defense and thus concedes. Karen knew this wouldn't happen, but by enlisting the Court, she was trying to force Montstream to answer the last of her interrogatories. Montstream objected, then retaliated with a motion of his own. Noting that it had been more than a year since the Court had overruled Karen's objections to amending Lichtenstein's complaint and that she still hadn't produced a revised version, he moved to have the case against Humes dismissed.

Ten days later Karen filed the amended complaint, but Montstream persisted. Responding to the revised allegations, he again asked the Court to throw out the suit, this time for violating the two-year statute of limitations. He wasn't contesting the complaint: he was saying it was barred, since the Koskoffs had brought it too late. Montstream kept up his attack, pushing Karen on several fronts. Even as he tried to get the case thrown out, he kept prodding her to revise and narrow it. On December 8, after talking with Karen on the phone, he wrote her asking for still more amendments to the complaint. He especially wanted her to drop the wording in Lichtenstein's original suit that said that Donna observed Humes's "negligence . . . at the time or times at which the negligence was occurring" and that Humes "knew or should have known" that her conduct would be harmful to Donna and Little Tony.

"Each of these constitutes a Catch-22 along the lines of 'when did you stop beating your wife? . . . '" Montstream wrote. "In each case, an admission constitutes an admission of negligence, and in each case, a denial can be construed as an admission of negligence." Of course, if Donna actually suspected that Humes was negligent during the birth, two years and eleven months before she sued, that would support Montstream's claim that the Koskoffs had blown the statute of limitations.

The next day a Bridgeport Superior Court judge ruled in favor of one of Montstream's earlier motions, giving Karen four months to get the case moving or else face having it dismissed. Three days later, Montstream filed yet another motion for dismissal—his fourth in two months. Noting that the Sabias had now missed a total of seven scheduled appearances for deposition—two more in November, and one on December 12—and that the cancellations had led to "the frustration of the discovery process on the part of the defense counsel," he urged the Court to enter a "nonsuit" against Tony and Donna. The implication was, if the Sabias didn't consider it important enough to honor a subpoena, maybe their case against Humes wasn't serious, just a bad-faith act of harassment by their lawyers.

Karen was boxed in. Long afterward she would lament that the months of jockeying "didn't advance the case in any meaningful way," but she now knew what she had to do next. She would produce the Sabias for deposition.

SIX

PAT RYAN HADN'T BECOME ONE OF THE BEST MEDMAL DEFENSE LAWYERS IN Connecticut without being an actor himself, and as he urged Donna to make herself comfortable in the hard spindle-backed chair in his conference room, his role became clear. He would play the don.

At fifty-eight, Ryan fit the part. He was a former corporation counsel for the City of Stamford, where he'd been born and where more than a dozen *Fortune* 500 companies fleeing New York City had relocated, their glass and steel skyscrapers abutting some of the state's meanest slums. Stamford was a city riven between rich and poor, black and white. A broker by inclination and an insider by design, Ryan was at his best treading nimbly between camps.

He projected an easy eminence. He had the prominent white hair, ruddy complexion, and unperturbed smile of a bishop. His posture, slightly stooped, was professorial, suggesting a lifetime of reading aloud on his feet. In conversation his sharp blue eyes either swept restlessly above black-framed half-glasses or lingered with empathy for his listener. He had eight strapping children, all grown.

It was Ryan's personality that rival lawyers most admired and feared. Mike Koskoff, who anticipated meeting Ryan at trial in *Sabia*, would match his courtroom skills against anyone's. But he dreaded facing those with great charm, lawyers who could win over juries because they were impossible not to like or—he'd seen this with his father—were so charismatic that jurors wanted to please them. Koskoff put Ryan in that category. Going up against him in court, he thought, was like facing the actor Pat O'Brien in one of his worthy-priest roles.

Ryan's appeal as a lawyer was that he didn't act like one. Instead of aggression and partisanship, he practiced what he called the "rule of reason." At depositions he didn't bash or berate witnesses, he befriended them. Now, facing Donna, even though his purpose was clear—to protect Norwalk Hospital—this didn't prevent him from dispensing sympathy and kindness. Ryan was a businessman; he took the long view. "I don't try to antagonize people unless there's some reason to do it," he says. "And there's no reason to offend a party that you may have to come to agreement with some day."

The room, like Donna's chair, reproduced a sterner, earlier New England. Once the master bedroom of a somewhat grand brick Colonial a mile from downtown Stamford, it had an unused fireplace, a carved mantel, a gilded Federalist bull's-eye mirror, framed lithographs of bewigged English jurists, a small private bath, and floor-to-ceiling law books. Boxed overhead fluorescent lights gave the surfaces a stark glow.

Nine people clustered around the heavy glass-topped conference table as Ryan, eyes sweeping sagaciously to meet each gaze, slid in at the head. On his right, a few feet away, was Donna, then Karen Koskoff, then Tony. Along the opposite flank were two young associates of Ryan's, Beverly Hunt and Margaret Gaffney, then Humes and Montstream, then at the far end, an associate of Bai's, Madonna Sacco. A court reporter sat off to the side, a stenographer's machine mounted in front of her on a steel tripod.

Ryan sought to break the ice with a few consoling remarks; he'd seen too many bad baby cases to think them anything but tragic, for everyone. But his attempt was rebuffed by a permafrost of deep tensions. The Sabias and Humes, inadvertent adversaries, faced each other for the first time since the day after Donna's delivery. Humes and Karen, though they'd never met, shared a knee-jerk contempt. Donna emanated free-floating confusion, Tony sullen rage, and Humes resentment toward Montstream. Humes had come, as she would to almost all of the depositions, to hear what was being said against her, and she possessed the dour, militant aspect of a one-woman truth squad. Wherever Ryan looked, there was hostility, mistrust, uncertainty, recrimination.

Not that he himself wasn't involved. As Norwalk Hospital's main emissary, Ryan was pivotal to each concern, each knotted relationship. The hospital was as much a target of the Sabias' allegations as was Humes, and as codefendants, the hospital and Humes had a special antagonism. Liability was often a zero-sum game: how much Humes and the hospital would be held accountable, and might have to pay, depended in large part on how effectively each blamed the other. The more the case focused on Donna's labor and delivery, the truer this became. And so Ryan and Montstream, with Sacco monitoring, viewed each other as warily as they did Karen and the Sabias. Maybe more.

Regrettably for Humes, no one from Norwalk Hospital was present—Ryan would make his report later—and so he became for her, too, a proxy, suspect by association. Meanwhile, like Montstream, Ryan wasn't alone in representing his client's side of the case. The hospital was self-insured, but Travelers Insurance held its excess coverage, meaning the company would have to pay anything above the first $250,000 if the Sabias prevailed. Travelers had its own lawyer in the case, Ronald Williams of the Bridgeport firm of Williams, Cooney & Sheehy, peering over Ryan's shoulder just as Bai and Sacco peered over Montstream's. Ryan mentioned for the record Williams's involvement, and his absence that day.

Ryan noted these crosscurrents only to brush them aside; lawyers are valued for their ability to weave through emotional war zones. What riveted his attention now was Donna. Nearly five years after she'd entered Norwalk Hospital to have her babies, everyone involved in the outcome, or a proxy, was in this room solely because of her. Yet Ryan still didn't know, almost two years after she'd filed suit, what she thought, whom she blamed, what—other than money—she wanted. To defend the hospital properly, he needed to know who she was, her perceptions and feelings, how she would play in front of a jury. He needed to know her weaknesses.

Donna was nervous. Karen had coached her earlier in the week on what to expect. She knew she must think carefully before she answered, and that she should not answer questions she wasn't asked. But she was afraid and was sure everyone else in the room knew it. Depositions, she understood, were a test. The goal was to find out what you believed and get it on the record so it couldn't be changed. But lawyers also tried to trip you up. Karen had explained that both Ryan and Montstream, as lawyers for the other side, would ask the questions and that she, Karen, would object if she thought they were trying to lead Donna on. But Donna worried that she might be intimidated into saying the wrong thing.

As Ryan spoke, she turned sideways to face him, straining to hear with her good ear and twisting her small hands under the table. Unlike Tony, who'd come in his work clothes—jeans, boots, a T-shirt, and, because it was winter, a plaid flannel shirt, unbuttoned, with tails out—she was dressed formally, in a dark suit, and her shoulder-length black hair was freshly permed. Her voice was husky from smoking, and she wanted a cigarette. Despite Ryan's soothing, she found no comfort in her surroundings.

Ryan began by questioning her about Little Tony's birth. This was still, Alan Pinshaw's opinion aside, the most critical period as far as the Sabias' complaint was concerned, and Ryan wanted to hear Donna's story while sizing her up as a witness. Mindful of the statute-of-limitations issue, he also wanted to establish for the record when she had come to believe there may have been negligence on the part of the hospital and Humes. He questioned her gently, circularly, slipping from the birth to her meeting with Mary Gay, then back to the birth. Then, after about twenty minutes, he started to zero in. From Donna's initial account, he was uncertain whom she held responsible, and the potential liability of the hospital's employees concerned him.

"Okay," Ryan said. "So, as I understand it, when you were taken up to the labor room, the first person who came to see you was a nurse?"

"Yes," Donna replied.

"And she was the one with whom you had the conversation about the heartbeat that you told us about?"

"Yes. She made a statement about not being able to pick up a heartbeat from Baby B."

Ryan had earlier asked Donna if Mollie Fortuna, the labor nurse, had indicated to her that the twins were in trouble, and Donna had said no, "She didn't alarm me or anything like that." Now Ryan wanted to be sure no one else had aroused her concern.

"Then there was a midwife that came into the room at some point?" he said, stating more than asking.

"Yes."

"And was there any conversation with that person?"

"Yeah," Donna said.

"I mean other than chitchat. Did she say anything—"

"No. She asked how I was feeling. Once I got up into the labor room, I was having contractions."

"Okay."

Donna continued. "She helped me breathe through the contractions, get me focused on her or something, so I could breathe through the contractions."

"And she was helping you, being generally supportive?" Ryan suggested.

"Yes. I was yelling at her to give me something for the pain, and she said, no, no, it's better for the babies not to."

"Do you recall any other conversation that you had with her?"

"No."

"All right," Ryan said. "And then the ultrasound procedure was done. Do you recall any conversations you had with those people, the technicians that did that?"

"I don't even remember who did the ultrasound."

"You don't know what the person looked like?"

Donna shook her head no.

"Do you recall whether he was Oriental or a Chinese-looking person?" Ryan asked, apparently referring to Maitem, the Philippine-born radiologist.

Karen cut in sardonically: "She was in labor, Pat. She was busy."

"I'm not quarreling," Ryan said, turning back to Donna, "I'm just trying to find out what you recall. So you have no recollection?"

"No."

Ryan was so far reassured. Donna, it seemed, bore no hostility to Fortuna, McManamy, or Maitem, all of whom worked for the hospital. He went on.

"Now, afterwards, did somebody tell you that there had been a problem with the deliveries?"

"Yes."

"And who was that?"

Donna looked away, down the table, a courtroom-style identification. "It was Maryellen Humes," she said.

"And what was that conversation?" Ryan asked.

"She brought the placenta over to my husband and myself. The way she explained it to us was that Baby B mashed the cord and Tony—Baby A— sensed the problem and was sending blood and oxygen to the other baby."

Humes scowled. She didn't recall telling the Sabias what she thought had happened to the twins and resented that Donna was allowed to say she had. But Humes was there only as an observer. She stewed in silence.

"And that was the cause of the problem?" Ryan continued.

"Yes."

"Was there any discussion as to when that had occurred?"

"No."

"So that as I understand it," Ryan said, "the only conversation you ever had with anybody was the conversation you had with Dr. Humes following the delivery when she brought the placenta to you and your husband and said that there was some problem with the mashing of the cord."

"That's what we were told, yes."

"And there was no discussion as to when that occurred?"

"I don't remember who told us that whatever had happened, happened between Friday and Sunday. I believe it was one of the midwives that made that statement. But I honestly don't know . . ."

"But you're clear it wasn't Dr. Humes."

"Right."

Ryan didn't know what had happened to Donna's twins, nor was he immediately interested. He was more concerned with disarming her, turning the tables—finding an escape. Like Montstream, he thought he had one in the two-year statute of limitations. Little Tony's injuries were clear from Day One. If Donna suspected negligence around the time he was born or during the next nine months, the statute would be blown. Ryan could scarcely believe she hadn't suspected something, despite her earlier answers. Finding a deep pocket to go after was now the first thing most people thought of when a birth went bad. Ryan pressed her, subtly at first, then vigorously.

"So you're saying here that after Dr. Humes told you that on that date, it never crossed your mind until you talked with Mary Gay in August of '86 that maybe somebody should have done something sooner at Norwalk Hospital which could have prevented the injury to Tony?"

"No."

"You never thought of that?"

"No."

"You never thought that somebody should have had a C-section that morning, and maybe Tony—"

"Not at the time I didn't."

"It never entered your mind?" Ryan said skeptically.

"No," Donna said.

Ryan went on, a bit incredulous. "You were just chatting, and she questioned the absence of the use of fetal monitoring devices during your delivery?"

"Yes."

"And that you might have a lawsuit. All right. So I take it, then, up until that day you were never aware that what happened to either twin was the result of any wrongdoing or negligence of anybody. That was the first inkling you had?"

"Yes."

"Okay," Ryan said. "So you were never in any fear of injury to yourself because you were watching things that you thought were negligent, say, on behalf of Dr. Humes?"

Karen clarified: "You mean at that time." Like Montstream and Ryan, she understood the apparent inconsistency between Donna's court complaint, which said she observed Humes's and the hospital's negligence while they were occurring, and her claim that she had no idea that anyone had acted wrongly until almost two and a half years later when she met Mary Gay. Karen hoped to defuse the issue by sticking to the truth, which was that while Donna witnessed what she later suspected was negligence, she didn't recognize it as such until long after the birth.

"At that time, yes," Ryan said.

"No," Donna repeated.

"And you were never in any fear for any injury to yourself as a result of anybody's poor judgment or poor medical management?"

"No."

Trusting there was nothing more here, Ryan tacked. "Now prior to April, to Tony's birthday, during the course of your pregnancy you went to the clinic a number of times?"

"Yes."

"Did you ever have any perception or feeling that the treatment you were getting during the course of your pregnancy at the clinic was poor medical treatment?"

Not wanting Donna confused or to misspeak, Karen interjected again: "You mean at the time that she was treated?"

"At the time, yes."

"No," Donna said. "I never felt that anything was—anybody was doing anything wrong. I thought everybody was doing everything they were supposed to do."

Ryan asked the question directly. "Okay," he said. "Then is there anything else that you feel that any of these defendants did wrong, I mean were professionally wrong in doing or not doing?"

"As of this date?" Karen asked.

"As of the whole pregnancy, the date of the clinic and right on through the delivery," Ryan said.

"Thinking today, my feelings on it today?" Donna asked.

Ryan turned suddenly blunt. "Yeah. What are your claims of negligence against the defendants?"

"Well, I'm feeling now I probably should have had an emergency C-section or something done."

Ryan intuited correctly that "something done" meant fetal monitoring. As he'd suspected, the sum of Donna's complaint seemed to be what Mary Gay first suggested to her: a straightforward botched delivery. Relieved, he tried to steer her into foreclosing all other claims against the hospital.

"Okay," he said. "So these are the only two things that you have in mind personally today?"

"Yes."

"And that's what you think—I mean that's your understanding of the lawsuit?"

"It's just that if something had been done earlier, I'm thinking that maybe my other son might be here and maybe my son now wouldn't have the problems that he has."

Ryan went on: "Now this lawsuit deals only with Tony. There's no other lawsuit as a result of the stillborn twin. So I take it that there is no claim being asserted against the hospital or with anybody with regard to that twin?"

"Yeah."

"So we're just talking about Tony. With regard to Tony, is there anything specific that you feel, even today, that should have been done other than those two criticisms?"

Before Donna could answer, Karen objected. She thought the question called for a medical opinion beyond Donna's competence or ken. But she let Donna answer pending a ruling by the court.

"No," Donna said.

Ryan held no great hope that the explanation for Little Tony's injuries was anything other than a late-stage fetal injury: the fact pattern, and the presence of the dead twin, all but guaranteed that something disastrous had occurred near the time of delivery. But Ryan was obliged to explore all possibilities, among them, most notably, heredity. A sure defense in a bad baby case was the successful insinuation that the bloodlines were bad, not the doctors and the hospital. Ryan now pursued this.

"Do you have brothers and sisters?" he asked Donna.

"Yes, I do," she said.

"And how many brothers and sisters do you have?"

"One sister and two brothers."

"Are they natural brothers and sisters, or stepsisters or -brothers or what?

"My brothers are stepbrothers. My sister is my real sister."

"Your natural sister then," Ryan said. "Has she had children?"

"Yes."

"Has she ever had any problems with having children or giving birth or miscarriages?"

"No," Donna said.

"How about your parents, your family? Are you aware of any family history of your mother or your grandmother with children?"

"No. I don't know my family history."

"You don't know of your family history one way or the other?" Ryan asked, apparently surprised.

"I was adopted," Donna said.

"So you have no knowledge—"

"Well, my adoptive parents, you know, I have talked with them about Little Tony, and they have not ever mentioned to me that there was ever anything like that in my family's history."

"Okay," Ryan said. "So it's just silence."

Donna nodded.

Ryan, with his soft spot for suffering, couldn't help but be moved. Donna seemed tough and smart and apparently honest. She might not have a shred of a case, but she'd endured a great tragedy and survived; juries responded to that. He had to hand it to the Koskoffs. They had picked well.

"Tony lives at home?" he continued, shifting direction.

"Yes," Donna said.

"And who takes care of Tony during a typical day?"

"I do."

"You do?"

"He goes to a program. He had a program during the week; he goes four hours a day."

"And what is Tony's general—I mean very generally, what is his condition now?" Ryan asked. "What is it that he can do?"

Donna had been upset by Ryan's questions about her family. She didn't like to have to spell out that she was adopted. Now she just felt sad and empty. "Nothing," she said. "I don't know how else to explain it. He can't sit up or roll over or—"

"So he can't walk. He has to be carried from place to place?"

"Yes."

"And is there anything special that has to be done for him, I mean in the way of apparatus, when he's sleeping?"

"He's on an all-night feeding pump. We have to hook him up to the pump about eight at night. He's supposed to have two bolus feedings during the day, which is when we feed him through like a syringe into the button," she said, referring to Little Tony's feeding tube, which she and Tony inserted into a round plastic receptacle imbedded in his abdomen.

"Does he eat orally?" Ryan asked.

"No. Very, very little."

"He needs total care, then? He can't take care of himself to any degree?"

"No."

"And he can't walk, and he has to be carried wherever he's going?"

"He can't talk. He can't tell you if there's something wrong."

"Do the doctors say he's going to have any improvement, as best as you can say? Are they hopeful?"

Donna looked wearily at Ryan, answered in a low voice. "They don't feel that there ever will be," she said.

Ryan paused. He was finished for the time being. Thanking Donna for her answers, he yielded to Montstream. Shifting in her seat, Donna was struck immediately by the difference between the two lawyers. Montstream had none of Ryan's grace, nor, it seemed, any real curiosity about her medical treatment or allegations. He made no effort at rapport. What seemed to interest him most was her credibility, how she stood up to questioning. Bad cop to Ryan's good, he began to poke hard and deep into her personal life, starting with Shannon.

"Now, you have had a former birth of a child, your oldest daughter, age eleven?" Montstream said from the opposite end of the table.

"Yes," Donna said.

"Does that daughter live with you?" he asked.

"Yes."

"And what grade is she in?" Montstream asked.

"Sixth."

"And academically how does she do?"

"Average."

"What do you mean by 'average'?"

"She could do better. She's a bright child, but she could do better than she's doing."

Montstream prodded: "What do you mean by that answer?"

"She's having problems with a couple of her classes where she doesn't understand how to do the work, and I'll try to talk to her and get extra help from the teacher, and she doesn't want to do it."

"Have you talked with the guidance counselors at school regarding this?" Montstream persisted.

"Yes, I have."

"Over how long a period of time?"

"I spoke with the guidance counselors back in October. I haven't spoken with them since that time."

"Has this daughter received any counseling of any kind outside the school arena?"

"No," Donna said, feeling neglectful.

"Have you had this child tested in any way outside the school arena?"

"She was tested for hyperactivity back in—I think it was '79 or '80. 1980."

"And what was the problem at that time?"

"She was real antsy a lot of times. We thought maybe she might be hyper, but she tested negative. They said she was fine, she's just a very active child."

Ryan later would dismiss what he considered Montstream's third degree. He saw only negative value in trying to tie Tony's injuries, profound as they were, to something as slight as a sibling's jumpiness. The downside—that you might so offend the plaintiffs as to harden their hostility toward your client— outweighed the risk. But Montstream took seriously his obligation to Humes and St. Paul, which was to explore alternative theories. Any demonstration that Donna and Tony may have contributed, even slightly, to Little Tony's injuries would undercut their claims against Humes and the hospital. Montstream persisted.

"Do you smoke?" he asked.

"Yes, I do."

"For how long have you been smoking?"

"Fourteen years," Donna said.

"During the course of the pregnancy with Tony, did you continue to smoke?"

"No, I did not."

"Did somebody advise you not to smoke during the pregnancy?"

"I don't think so. I just quit automatically."

"Why did you do that?"

"I didn't feel it was safe for my child."

"Do you drink alcoholic beverages of any kind?"

"Once in a while."

"During your pregnancy with Tony, did you consume alcoholic beverages?"

"No," Donna said.

"At any time?"

"No, I did not."

"Why not?" Montstream asked.

"Because it's not safe for my child."

"Where did that knowledge come to you?" Montstream was nothing if not thorough.

"It's just common knowledge," Donna said, "that if you smoke or drink it's going to affect your baby."

"When did that knowledge come to you, what year?"

"I don't remember," said Donna.

"Were you being treated for any other reason during your pregnancy with Tony for a medical condition of your own?"

"No."

"Do you take any medications on a regular basis?"

"No, I do not."

"At the time you were pregnant with Tony or just prior to the pregnancy with Tony, did you take any medications?"

"No."

"Have you used any so-called recreational drugs?"

"No."

"Have you had any miscarriages?"

"No."

"You mentioned that you have a natural sister. Were you separated as children?"

"No, we were not," Donna said.

"You and your sister were adopted by the same family?" Montstream asked.

"Yes, we were."

"At what age were you adopted?"

"I was three."

"Do your adoptive parents know who your biological parents were?"

"Yes."

"Are your biological parents alive?"

"I have no idea."

"Do you know who your biological parents are?"

"I know their names. I don't know anything else about them."

"Have you ever tried to make contact with your biological parents."

"I've thought about it," Donna said, "but no, I have not."

Donna recoiled from Montstream's pressure. He "just didn't get it" about her family, she recalls, how being adopted had separated her from any sense of birthright, of being connected to the past. She didn't know what he was driving at. And he gave her no help. After abruptly finishing his questions about her family, he launched directly into Donna's recollections of the delivery, as if reading down a list.

"While you were in the labor room," he asked, "were you restless?"

"Very," Donna said.

"Were you moving about?"

"Yes."

"In what way were you moving about?"

"Trying to get comfortable in the bed. The midwife had to try to come over and get me calmed down to try to breathe through the contractions."

"Were you hysterical?" Montstream asked.

"No."

"If you needed to be calmed down, you were excited," Montstream said.

"I was in pain."

"Did you have to be restrained at all?"

"No."

"Did anybody hold you, a person, as opposed to a restraining device?"

"No."

"Were you making loud noises?"

"Yes."

"In what way?"

"Screaming from the pain."

"And between contractions, how were you?"

"Exhausted," Donna said.

"Were you noisy?"

"No."

"Were you thrashing around between contractions?"

"No."

Humes, who wasn't allowed to speak except to either of her attorneys, frowned deeply. It wasn't true. Donna had been wild, a tempest, she thought. McManamy saw it, too. How, Humes wondered, could this woman be allowed to lie this way?

Montstream, pointed before, now turned inquisitorial.

"When is the last time you spoke with Mary Gay?" he asked.

"Probably over the summer," Donna said. "It's been a while."

"Did you go to Mary Gay's house?"

"No. I've never been to her house."

"Has she been to yours?"

"No."

"Is Mary Gay married?"

"As far as I know, yes," Donna said.

"And her husband's first name?"

"I don't know."

"Did you ever meet him?"

"I believe I did once."

"Talked to him on the phone?"

"No."

"You have a deafness of a particular ear," Montstream said. "Is that a result of a disease or an accident?"

"Not as far as I know," Donna said.

"Your other ear is okay?"

"Yes."

"Your eyes are okay?" he asked.

"Yes."

"Have you ever had kidney problems?"

"No."

"At the time of your pregnancy with Tony, were you taking antibiotics for any illness?"

"No."

"Prior to the birth of Tony, had you taken any birth control pills?"

"Yes," Donna said.

"Diet pills?"

"No."

"Any female hormone medication of any kind?"

"No."

"Vitamins?"

"No."

"Tranquilizers?"

"No."

"Vitamin supplements?"

"No."

"Do you have any heart problems?" Montstream badgered.

"No."

"Have you ever had any seizures?"

"No."

"Do you have any pets at home?"

On he went—dogs, cats, traffic accidents, X-rays, recommendations for surgery—until he exhausted his checklist. What the grilling was worth seemed to elude even Montstream. A week later he gave it just a single line in his report to St. Paul, a rambling seven-page single-spaced letter to Kaufman at St. Paul's. Personal history aside, Montstream wrote, "The bottom line of claimant's feeling is that the lack of fetal monitoring is a major issue."

Nothing in Karen's coaching had prepared Donna for Montstream's interrogation. Yet just as he finished, Ryan said he had a few more questions, and Donna understood she wasn't through. The deposition had begun at 10 A.M. It was now 1:30. Dazed and hungry, Donna turned back to face Ryan another time.

He questioned her about Little Tony's seizures, their frequency and treatment, then asked whether she and Tony had any photos of Little Tony and Michael, the stillborn. He was trying to find out if she had any documentation that would add to her testimony. Donna explained that she had not wanted any pictures of Michael because the hospital hadn't cleaned him up. She also said she had very few pictures of Tony. Once, she said, when she took him to a professional photographer at Sears, the camera's flash drove him into a seizure. She hadn't been willing to try again after that.

Ryan pressed further. "You have no records with you today," he noted. "Have you kept any records or any notes or any diary or any writings about any of this entire experience of yours?"

Donna hesitated. "Not really. I haven't, no."

"So when you say not really—"

"Well, I think about it. I mean it's something I'll never forget."

"But as I understand it, there's no writings that you have at home, or given to your employers, a diary or letters or notes."

"No," Donna lied.

"Or memorandums, or recordings of any kind?"

Donna shook her head.

Montstream interjected: "Was the answer to that question 'no'?"

"No," Donna said flatly.

It was over. Donna had taken coaching well, Karen thought. As defense lawyers, Ryan and Montstream were trained to see plaintiffs as malingerers, but Donna had been calm and credible. She hadn't risen to their bait or become hysterical or angry. Except for a few small tactical deceptions, like her answer about the journal, she'd told the truth, bluntly and without fanfare. Mike Koskoff, paraphrasing Vladimir Horowitz, once counseled about the presentation of witnesses, "You want to play Bach like Chopin and Chopin like Bach"—don't overstate the obvious, but don't underplay subtlety, either. Karen thought Donna had been restrained, dignified, and powerful. Koskoff would no doubt be pleased.

∼ ∼ ∼

Tony, Karen feared, would be another matter. His deposition was scheduled for after lunch. Karen had thought he might be drunk that morning when he arrived, until he explained that he was bleary-eyed and unkempt from working all night. He'd been drinking coffee nonstop, his usual fill of seven or eight cups between the time he got off work at about 6 A.M. and noon, and all through Donna's deposition he'd sat seething, jittery as a sniper. As a criminal lawyer, Karen had dealt with tough men, but she'd rarely seen anyone so tightly coiled. "I was very worried," she recalls, "about how he was going to do."

By the time Ryan began to question Tony just after two o'clock, he had been up for almost twenty-four hours. Ryan led him through the events at the hospital, gaining little that was new, then returned, as with Donna, to their delay in filing suit.

"When was it," Ryan asked, "that first it ever entered your mind that this whole incident may have been the result of somebody's negligence or fault?"

Tony answered gruffly. "When my wife come home. I don't remember when it was. She said she had been talking to somebody and one thing led to another."

"So you heard your wife talking about a conversation she had with a woman by the name of Mary Gay in August of 1986?"

"Correct," said Tony.

"At some picnic at this special camp in Norwalk?"

"Correct."

"And you had never thought before that date as to why this event occurred, or whether it could have been avoided?"

Karen burst in: "Objection, it's a compound question."

"It is," Ryan said.

"If you can break it down," Karen asked.

"Do you understand the question?" Ryan asked Tony.

"Norwalk Hospital has professional people working there, correct?" Tony asked, retaliating with a question of his own.

Ryan seemed caught off guard. "Yes," he said, stopping and redirecting himself. "I'm asking the questions," he said. "It's just a procedure, but—"

"I'm just trying to answer it," Tony said.

"But I mean, are you through?"

Tony paused. "That's why we went," he said.

"Okay. So I take it that you would expect that Norwalk Hospital is professional, and you would expect them to take care of things?"

"That's it."

"And did you ever think when things didn't go right they didn't take care of things properly?"

"No," Tony said. "I figured I would be informed of it if something did occur."

Tony was a trucker and a veteran. He trusted those who knew things he ought to know to tell him. Watching Tony handle Ryan, Karen's confidence in him soared. She'd worried about Ryan's attempt to make the Koskoffs blow the statute of limitations; now she doubted it would work. Ryan needed for Tony to admit that he suspected negligence early on and then lied about it. What he got was a naive, almost religious faith in doctors and hospitals to tell their patients the truth, no matter how upsetting. As Karen would later put it, "It was suddenly very clear that light didn't go on until the day Donna met Mary Gay and told Tony about it." Witnessing Tony's dignified ignorance, her apprehension about him vanished into sympathy and affection.

Ryan asked a few more questions, then deferred to Montstream, who cross-examined Tony briefly about Little Tony's birth and his and Donna's conversations with Humes before turning to Tony's own health problems.

"Are you nearsighted in both eyes?" Montstream asked.

"Yes," Tony said.

"Have you ever had a cleft palate?"

"Excuse me?"

"Do you know what a cleft palate is?"

"No, I don't."

"An opening in the lip or a palate inside the mouth," Montstream explained.

"Oh, yes," Tony said, thinking he understood. "I have a plate."

"Is that a dental plate?"

"Yes."

"You had surgery due to the removal of some teeth?" Montstream concluded.

"That's it."

"Have you ever had epilepsy or seizures?"

"No," Tony said.

"Do you have any problem with hearing?"

"No."

"Do you have any kidney problems?"

"No."

"Do you smoke?"

"Yes, I do."

"How much do you smoke a day?"

"About a pack and a half."

"Do you smoke at home?"

"Yes, I do."

"At the time Donna became pregnant with Tony, you were a cigarette smoker at that time?" Montstream said.

"Yes, I was."

"Do you have diabetes?"

"No."

"At or about the time of the pregnancy, the beginning of Tony, had you used any recreational drugs?"

"No," Tony said.

"When you arrived at the labor room," Montstream said, segueing abruptly, "were you aware that only one heartbeat had been heard by a nurse putting a stethoscope or something on Donna's abdomen?"

"I was informed, yes."

"Did that mean anything to you?"

Tony was defiantly matter-of-fact. "No," he said, although in truth he had long regretted not asking whether it indicated a problem.

"Did you make any inquiry about it?" Montstream asked.

"No, I did not," Tony said.

"During the time Donna was in the hospital, did you make any inquiry concerning the missing heartbeat?"

"No, I did not."

"At any time subsequent have you made any inquiry of a medical person concerning that missing heartbeat?"

"No, I have not."

"Do you participate in the care of Tony?" Montstream asked.

"Yes, I do."

"What specifically do you do?"

"Just about everything," Tony said. "Feed him, bathe him, get him dressed, give him therapy, range in motion, try to get him to talk. That's it."

Try to get him to talk . . . Hearing the words, Karen says, she suddenly fought back tears. Glancing at Ryan, she believed he also seemed moved.

"Have you been given direction on what to do by a physician?" Montstream asked.

"That's a two-part question; yes and no," Tony said.

"Well, would you care to explain your answer?"

"You watch TV?" Tony began to ask, then squelched himself. "Excuse me, I'm sorry."

"It's been a long day, it's okay."

Tony reconsidered his answer. "It's just common sense," he said.

If Tony's rough simplicity was heartbreaking to Karen, all of the lawyers also knew it might work against him at trial. His "raw attitude," as he put it, would likely cause jurors, who had their own prejudices, to see him one of two ways: Either he was a rough but heroic working man so blindly devoted to his son that he couldn't see the boy's limitations and would do anything for him, including adapting home treatments from TV; or else he was a crude hothead, stubborn and brutish and undeserving of sympathy. Montstream, noticing Tony's edgy physicality, sought to bring it out.

"Do you walk with a limp of some kind?" he asked.

"No," Tony said.

"Do you have any bony problems of any kind?"

"Just my weight."

"Your weight," Montstream repeated. "Can you clarify that for me?"

"I eat like a horse, can't gain weight. I had disk surgery five years ago, lower lumbar. They fused a disk. And ever since then my weight's gone downhill, and I eat, eat, eat. Can't put no weight on."

"What was the reason for the back surgery?"

"It enlarged, wouldn't reduce itself."

"Was this the result of an accident of some kind?"

"At work, yes."

"Had you any back problems prior to that time?"

"No."

Tony felt like a yo-yo. First Ryan's smooth stroking, then Montstream's interrogation. All through the morning he had thought of how he would like to answer the questions they had asked Donna, but the lawyers refused to give him a chance. Testy, he found himself suddenly back again with Ryan, who under the trial-like rules was allowed to reopen his questioning based on new information uncovered during Montstream's cross-examination.

"The first question I have," Ryan apologized, "may sound silly to you, but it's really not silly. But in my questioning of your wife, I came to the conclusion that she's a very smart person. Do you agree with that?"

"Yes, I do."

Ryan perched. "Do you want to say something else?"

"Yeah. Sometimes she's too smart for her own damn good."

"That's true of all women," Ryan agreed.

Karen snickered inaudibly. So did Humes.

Ryan went on. "All right. I just have one other question, and that is what is your understanding of what was done wrong, if anything, with regard to this pregnancy and delivery of your wife?"

"I don't know if I can answer that correctly," Tony said.

"Okay. I take it that you have some—"

"Personal feelings."

"Yeah," Ryan said. "I mean you're a party to this suit. You have brought this suit on behalf of your son, Tony, and therefore I assume that you are of the opinion that there was something about the care and the treatment that your wife received during the pregnancy and during the delivery process that was below standard, so to speak; is that a fair statement?"

"I'd say yes."

"Okay. And what is it you think they did wrong? What should have been done that wasn't done?"

"Can I consult with my attorney first?"

"Well, I'd prefer if you didn't, if you can answer the question. If you can't answer it, that's okay, too."

"I think there were things wrong for the simple reason, you know, that the hospital, the doctors, being professional people, went to school for all these years to learn what they're doing. And I think that things that probably happened shouldn't have happened as far as care and everything else—"

"Okay. Anything else—"

"Because to me," Tony went on, "the only stupid question is the one not asked. I found out the hard way. And I get very upset and antsy about it. And that's it."

"Okay, let me ask you this," Ryan said, shifting his approach. "You told us about one conversation you heard at the clinic that you—As I understand it, you went once with your wife to her visit at the clinic, just once?"

"Um-hmm."

"And during that time you heard a conversation about the fact that your wife had twins, and it might be easy or it might be hard?"

"You twisted the question around," Tony said.

"I didn't mean to. Let me ask you this. I didn't mean to twist it. What was the conversation you heard?"

"It was about twins, like a high-risk pregnancy due to the fact that one could breech and they would probably go C-section after the other."

"So if there was some difficulty, they would proceed to a C-section?"

"True."

"Was that your understanding? At the day of the delivery, keeping that conversation in mind, you and your wife never made any inquiries as to why they weren't proceeding to a C-section?"

"No," Tony said.

"From your answer a couple of answers ago," Ryan said, circling back, "you said there was some question nobody's asked of you that's a question that should be asked?"

"Excuse me?"

"You said there's a question asked of you that nobody's asked a couple of answers ago; no? Did I misunderstand you?"

"It's possible," Tony said.

It was three o'clock when Montstream resumed his questioning, also for the second time. He asked about the discharge nurse, Shirley Brown, who'd brought the stillborn Michael to Donna's room when she was in recovery. The fact that no autopsy had been performed might make it hard, if not impossible, to determine later on what had caused Little Tony's injuries, and Montstream wanted to clarify why one hadn't been done.

"Did Mrs. Brown indicate any specific reason as to why an autopsy might be recommended?" Montstream asked.

"To find out why it happened, I guess. I don't recall offhand, because at the same time they came back in with the goddamn death certificate."

"At the same time that they were asking you about the autopsy?"

"Right," Tony said. He had all but had it with explaining himself. "And she told them to get out again."

"She is who?"

"Mrs. Brown."

"I'm sorry, I lost the train of thought there," Montstream said. "Mrs. Brown asked you to sign the death certificate?"

"No. Mrs. Brown told them to get out."

"Who was it that Mrs. Brown told to get out?"

"I don't know. I don't know. I was upset enough as it was."

"Are you upset right now?" Montstream asked.

"I'm upset, I'm tired, I'm hungry," Tony snarled.

"All right. I've noticed your hands are shaking a little bit."

"Yeah."

"Why is that?"

"How would you like to be up since yesterday afternoon?"

"Is that an answer to the question I'm asking?"

"No, I guess not. I'm tired. I'm getting upset."

"Do your hands normally shake?"

"No."

"Have you seen any physician concerning the shaking of hands?"

"No, I'm a hyper person," Tony said.

"Are you taking any medication for that?"

"No."

"Are you taking any medication on a regular basis?"

"I was taking it for a sinus infection, that's it, about a month ago."

"You're not in any long-term therapy of any kind?" Montstream asked.

"No."

"Or medication of any kind?"

"No."

"I have nothing further," Montstream said.

It is the purpose of depositions to establish for trial what witnesses will say and how they'll play to a jury. Lawyers read into these proceedings what they want. Tony's and Donna's credibility had been an issue for all sides. Now that they'd been deposed, some doubts had been erased.

Ryan now knew the hospital faced a serious complaint. A child had been devastated and his parents were sympathetic people—they loved their son. What's more, "explanations like the mother's a heavy smoker weren't really going to carry the day," he would later say, an apparent slap at Montstream. The case was going to be tried on medical grounds, not on the character of the plaintiffs. Damages might well be huge.

Ryan approached Tony as the Sabias were leaving, shook his hand, and said something like, "Don't worry. Things will work out." He meant only to be consoling, a voice of hope, but Tony interpreted it differently. He thought Ryan was telling him that the hospital saw the legitimacy of their claim and would find a way to settle it. Not understanding that Ryan had no authority to imply such a conciliatory posture, indeed that he risked destroying his relationship with Norwalk Hospital and a possible malpractice claim by intimating that he had, Tony seized on the remark. The hospital was going to do right by them, he was now sure.

Karen was wrung out, yet elated. When she got back to the office, Mike Koskoff asked her how it went. "Really good," she said. "I cried."

Only Montstream seemed to think that the Sabias might have made themselves vulnerable to counterattack. In his report to St. Paul's Kaufman the following week, he described Tony as "a tall, thin, nervous-looking gentleman, who appears easily excitable," adding that "he does not appear as bright as his wife, and would make a fair to good witness on his own behalf." Whether this is all he conveyed is unclear. Kaufman, who never set eyes on the Sabias and received his information through Montstream's firm, years later would recall believing that Tony was a "drug addict" with "an unsavory past"—by St. Paul's calculus, a decided plus.

SEVEN

WHEN KAREN WAS GROWING UP IN PITTSBURGH, HER FATHER KEPT THE BRAIN OF A habitual criminal named Millard Wright in a formaldehyde jar in the attic, and she liked to spook her friends by taking them up to see it. Wright was Yale Koskoff's most famous subject. In 1947, Koskoff performed a lobotomy on Wright, the first and perhaps only attempt to control criminal urges with radical surgery. Like many experiments, it failed. After leaving prison, Wright not only returned to a life of crime, but also became a more efficient criminal. The operation apparently severed only his anxiety about stealing, not the impulse to steal. "Never was he better, never more skillful, never more daring," Yale Koskoff later wrote. "Now there was no clumsiness, no mistakes. He never had to hurry."

The failure—Wright eventually killed himself, in prison—haunted Koskoff for the rest of his life. But it also led him to consider the physiological basis for anxiety and, ultimately, suffering. In the late forties and early fifties he did other lobotomies, on cancer patients. The operations involved severing the cablelike nerve bundles that connected the prefrontal "thinking" brain to the "feeling" brain of the midcortex, on the theory that "a certain internal conflict will come to an abrupt rest." The operations severed no known pain pathways but greatly reduced the *experience* of pain. Patients who needed morphine every two to four hours now required no narcotics. They felt the sensation of pain but no longer dreaded it; they didn't suffer. Koskoff, drawing on other studies, began to define suffering as a distinct entity—pain plus anxiety. Coupling his observation with new theories of depression, he concluded that the true basis of suffering was fear and despair, not physical pain.

On his annual visits to Connecticut he described his theory to Ted, who seized on its legal implications. Most of Ted's law practice at the time involved trying small personal injury cases—car accidents, slip-and-falls, workman's compensation claims. He noticed he had clients whose disabilities far exceeded their level of trauma; people, for instance, who complained of persistent and debilitating back pain after a low-impact fender-bender, or who became overwrought and dysfunctional after a concussion. Typically, doctors and insurers dismissed their distress as neurotic. Their bosses tended to treat them as malingerers and sought to deny them benefits. Worse, the courts refused to compensate plaintiffs for suffering unconnected to physical impairment. With no way to put a price on mental anguish, damage awards lagged. Negligence lawyers simply had no basis for arguing that defendants should be held liable for fear, anxiety, and stress the way they were for wounds, breaks, and fractures.

Ted immediately saw in Yale's theory just such a rationale. That suffering was a syndrome distinct from pain offered limited utility to doctors, who short of lobotomizing their patients had no remedies for it, but it electrified the thinking of trial lawyers, who realized that even if suffering couldn't be remedied, at least it could be compensated—in court, with payments for damages.

Over the next thirty years, together and separately, in articles and speeches, the Koskoffs championed the idea of legally compensable suffering with enormous effect, especially among plaintiffs' lawyers. As Ted would argue in his lectures, "You just can't make someone feel another person's pain." But fear, despair, anguish—these were the essence of good drama, and an effective lawyer could make them sing. "The real money," Ted once wrote, "is in your capacity to demonstrate and argue misery, suffering and disability." Over time, as court rulings expanded and favorable verdicts increased, suffering became the emotional centerpiece of many civil lawsuits, the subject that aroused juries' greatest sympathies and ratcheted damage awards to new heights. Suffering, largely because of the Koskoffs, became a staple of trial practice and a boon for personal injury lawyers.

Now, after the Sabias' deposition, Karen realized the extent of their torment. Whether Little Tony suffered was anyone's guess, but it was clear that as a family they had been shattered by the experience of his birth and that their anguish had become chronic. It could not be treated, nor would it go away. That the Sabias suffered, and that their suffering would increase the damages due them, was beyond dispute.

Typically, Tony and Donna had a more urgent concern: money. They could never get ahead. Starting about a year after Little Tony's birth, Donna had begun working on and off at Standard News with Tony. She filled in, stuffing and bundling papers. Shape-time on the night shift was midnight.

Donna would report, the only woman, and by 2 A.M. she'd know if they needed her for the rest of the shift. She hired a high school student to live in and paid the girl $3 an hour when she wasn't asleep to take care of the kids.

Even with Donna's income, and Tony's two jobs, Little Tony's medical expenses were a constant drain. Tony had Blue Cross, which covered hospitalization but reimbursed them only 80 percent for doctors' bills. When Little Tony was in Newington for his hip surgery and at Yale to receive his feeding tube, the bills had poured in for months afterward, piling up on the kitchen counter. "I used to rob Peter to pay Paul," Tony says. "I once told a doctor who called up wanting his money, 'I've got a stack of bills four inches high. Right now you're on top. If I put you on the bottom, you don't get anything.'" The Norwalk schools paid for his day program and the Sabias got some help from Services for the Blind, but Little Tony's needs were relentless. Every doctor he saw referred him to another.

The more Tony and Donna worked, the further behind they fell. Part of it was the house. After renting for three years, they had saved enough for a down payment and in mid-1988 bought the raised ranch on Southwind Drive, across the street from Tony's mother's. The house was one of a few in Sunken Homes to be built on steel piers; it was relatively well supported even though the pilings hadn't hit bottom. But it was shoddy from years of neglect, and the yard around it was sinking into the fly ash that covered the original swamp.

Tony, determined to build up equity, became compulsive about improving it. He scraped off the topsoil and brought in a hundred loads of fill—"every sidewalk in downtown Stamford," he says—to shore up the sagging property. Never skilled with tools, he taught himself to repair cracks and broken pipes. Working slavishly, he became a grim-faced do-it-yourselfer, pouring money and sweat into one project after another until the house stood out as one of the best kept in the neighborhood. The ground around it may be sinking, Tony told people, but the house itself was solid, a rock.

Pride in the face of doom. This had been Tony's answer to the world ever since Little Tony's birth. Kenzaburo Oe, the Japanese novelist, wrote of having a brain-damaged son that at first it left him so ashamed that he considered letting the boy die of neglect. In *A Personal Matter* he wrote, "I'm neither such a tough villain that I can wring the baby's neck nor a tough enough angel to mobilize all of the doctors to try to keep the baby alive somehow no matter how hopeless a baby he may be." Tony, finding himself to be just such a tough angel, never let it rest. When a coworker asked him why he and Donna didn't put Little Tony in an institution, he seethed, "He's my kid, and I ain't giving him up, and I don't give a fuck." He might live in Sunken Homes, but he wasn't going to surrender his house to the weakening earth. Whatever God dealt him and his, he would not quit trying to improve it. "Someday Little Tony's gonna walk," he'd say. "Make assholes of everybody."

≈ ≈ ≈

FEBRUARY 14, 1989

Humes was home alone when the phone rang. It was late, near midnight. The caller was her business manager, Karen Brooks. "Turn on *Nightline*," Brooks said. "You have to see this." With anyone else Humes might have resisted. She never watched TV, was too restless for it, preferring when she had snatches of time at night to play the piano or violin, or read. But Brooks was Humes's closest confidante and ally. More to the point, Brooks managed her finances, which always had been perilous and which now, with tuition bills and home projects, and the cloud cast by back-to-back lawsuits, had begun to preoccupy them both. Humes didn't know what she would do without Brooks's counsel on money matters. "I'd be dead without her," she says. "She's God's gift to me."

Humes switched on her set. Ted Koppel was intoning stiffly about the skyrocketing cost of medical malpractice insurance. It was a subject that lately had consumed Humes almost as much as being sued by the Sabias. The previous September her malpractice premium had soared to $155,825 for her and an associate. Since Humes owned the practice and paid the other woman a salary, she bore the full cost. It was more than she herself was earning working eighty to a hundred hours a week. Alarmed, Brooks had tried to switch to another carrier but was told that no other insurer would even consider an application from Humes as long as there was a pending claim against her.

Humes had sought relief by prodding Montstream. Twice in November while he was seeking a dismissal in *Sabia,* she wrote him letters pleading for an update. "I am eager to know if there has been any change in the status of the Sabia case," she enquired, adding, "Is there a chance that depositions will be given soon?" Whether her urging had any effect, Humes never knew; her own deposition was scheduled next, in three weeks. What she hadn't told Montstream, who she still considered an agent of St. Paul, was that her financial situation since the company's latest rate hike was now so precarious that she and Brooks both feared that she might go under.

They had reason to worry. Humes's malpractice coverage now consumed 19 percent of the annual revenue of Women's Medical Associates, her professional corporation—an eightfold increase in five years. Since the mid-seventies, other doctors, ob-gyns especially, had been forced to move, quit, or work for somebody else because they couldn't afford to insure themselves and stay in private practice. These defections generally were blamed on the second "malpractice crisis" in a decade, though the term was misleading. There had been two stretches, one each in the seventies and eighties, when liability insurance rates for doctors had shot up so quickly they made coverage impossible for some. But both times the crisis had been attributable to the cost and availability of insurance, not an outbreak of bad medicine.

The *Nightline* report aimed to clarify the issue. An investigation by the Minnesota Department of Commerce found that outsized profit margins, not increased costs, were driving up liability premiums, and that St. Paul especially had been guilty of price-gouging. The probe compared doctors' liability premiums, which had tripled between 1982 and 1987, with several indices usually cited by the insurance industry as proof of a genuine "crisis"—number of claims, payouts for settlements and verdicts, legal fees, even the bugaboo of frivolous lawsuits. While all those indicators had stayed flat throughout the period, St. Paul's net profit from its malpractice lines averaged 25 percent a year, spiking to over 45 percent in 1988. St. Paul rejected the Minnesota report as "not worth the paper it's printed on," but *Nightline* hired an independent insurance expert to review the findings and he found them valid. As Koppel asked rhetorically: "Is the skyrocketing cost of medical malpractice insurance really justified, or are doctors and their patients being taken for a ride?"

Humes's resentments flared as she watched the report in her cluttered living room. Worrying endlessly over money was the one thing she had in common with the Sabias. She, too, was dogged by financial pressure, had three kids to support, owned a house that was a sinkhole for her ambition and her hubris, worked without end, juggled bills, and felt that no matter how hard she slaved she had no real security. Like Tony and Donna, she was buffeted by out-of-control medical costs, and this added sharply to her sense that she, too, had suffered. Clearly, her suffering was preferable to theirs, but Humes considered their situations equally unfair.

And for what, she thought? So St. Paul could reap huge profits by taking more out of her business than she did? So that when unfortunate people like the Sabias, desperate for money, had only one recourse to pay for a lifetime of medical care—finding someone like her to blame—she got a company-assigned lawyer who, she felt, couldn't care less about her innocence? It was extortion, Humes believed. Doctors were fodder—for angry patients, predatory lawyers, their own craven insurers. Sometimes Humes thought she should go "bare"—uninsured. It couldn't be any worse than this.

As an ob-gyn and for the most part a solo practitioner, Humes in fact had been doubly squeezed. When she'd first started practicing in 1979, medicine was still a kind of a semipublic trust. Most doctors worked for themselves. They charged what they wanted, cossetted by a fee system that allowed them to pass costs on to third-party payers. The more patients they saw, the more they earned. Humes left her marriage and became an ob-gyn trusting that this golden age would continue, that she could do well simply by doing good.

But things soon changed. By the time she delivered Little Tony in early

1984, a whirlwind had swept through the world of medicine and transformed it into a business. Powerful new forces had driven doctors into the stiffest competition they'd ever known—medical costs rising twice as fast as inflation, too many doctors and hospitals chasing too few patients, insurers cutting back on reimbursements, soaring liability premiums. Ob-gyns, hit by more malpractice suits and larger awards than any other doctors, were especially caught in the shear between spiraling costs and falling revenues. Many joined or formed groups, which helped cushion the shocks. But for those who remained largely on their own, like Humes, there was only one answer: work harder, see more patients.

Starting out with little aptitude and less enthusiasm for business, Humes had at first decided, as with all else in her life, to manage her finances herself. Yet by the summer of 1985 she could no longer administer her burgeoning practice—she had taken on her first associate—and so she hired Brooks, a part-time restaurant manager from Westport and a patient of hers. An energetic, take-charge woman in her thirties, Brooks was appalled by Humes's fiscal disarray. Although she had been paying an accountant $480 a month, her corporate taxes remained unfiled. She had a stack of unpaid bills that Brooks believed vendors had inflated on the premise that doctors could afford to pay extra. Her payroll was a nightmare. Commandeering Humes's books, Brooks requested, and got, check-signing authority. She clamped down on what Humes took out of the business, refusing to give her raises even when she asked for them. Working all the time, Humes became her own hireling.

Brooks's greatest problem was how to manage Humes's output. Humes's associate soon left, and Brooks discovered the near-hopelessness of running a business whose sole producer was a solo ob-gyn. Brooks would schedule a day of appointments, then have to reschedule again and again as Humes, with no one to cover for her, kept being called away for deliveries. It was like trying to run a company with one machine that kept going down. Humes had other help in the office—nurses, secretaries—but she alone generated the revenue that kept it afloat.

Humes's liability premiums were initially among the least of Brooks's worries; her first year Humes paid $22,936, less than 6 percent of her annual gross, for $2 million in coverage. Then, in 1986, Humes's own malpractice crisis hit. Irrespective of her settlement with Mary Gay in November, her coverage jumped to $43,000, almost twice what it had been two years earlier, and 9 percent of her gross. The next year the cost for her and an associate soared to $102,000, or 19.5 percent of gross income. Suddenly, one in five dollars that came into Humes's practice was going for malpractice insurance. With her already aggrieved feelings about malpractice suits, Humes seized on the increases with mounting alarm. They symbolized her onerous financial strain, her sense of being indentured.

For Brooks the issue was simpler: how to get more income into the practice. Humes hoped to solve the problem by hiring still another associate: they could split the overhead and share coverage; Humes could work less and have a life. But Brooks knew that, because of St. Paul's premiums, that was impossible. The cost of additional insurance, plus salary and benefits, would more than offset what even the hardest-working ob-gyn could bring in. They were stuck, Brooks knew. There was only one solution for generating more revenue; Humes had to see more patients.

Now, watching *Nightline,* Humes was infuriated. While she'd suffered, it turned out, St. Paul had been profiting mightily. And yet she also felt galvanized, saying later that the report "got me going" and "really did change things in a major way." By the next day she had her plan. She resolved to fight the Sabias' complaint and St. Paul's depredations jointly, as two heads of the same beast. No matter what the sacrifice, she was determined to "put all that I have on the line" both to exonerate herself and to preserve her practice. "I thought," she says, "there's no amount of pain I won't endure to accomplish this."

She wrote away for the Minnesota study and put a copy in her waiting room for her patients to see. She also sent it to local HMOs with which she did business. Demanding "just compensation," she threatened to pull out if they didn't raise her reimbursements. "We are attempting," she wrote to one, "to pay these exorbitant [premiums] by drastic reorganization measures and salary cuts. Recent developments have given us hope that we will see the end of this extortion by the insurance industry. Meantime, we have to pay the bill."

Malpractice—both the allegation of it and its recasting as a business, legal, and moral issue—now became for Humes a crusade. She had always been political, had always seen obstetrics, with its history of control and exploitation of women, in political terms. But now, like more and more of her colleagues, she resolved to campaign for what would soon be called, inaccurately, "malpractice reform." What Humes strove to contain were not the abuses of bad medicine but soaring liability premiums.

In the next few weeks, as she prepared for her deposition, Humes came to see the issue of malpractice as a kind of Hydra. The more she fought it, the more new heads it grew. She was newly resolute but also newly anxious, fearing that it would destroy not only all she had worked for—her career, reputation, and independence—but her sense of who she was. In a way, it already had. Seeing the misery and confusion in the Sabias' faces in Ryan's office, hearing the horror of their lives, she understood that she long ago had ceased to be anything for them but a chance to redeem something for their loss. A last and only hope. "I'm a policy," she would say, her resignation neatly if unintentionally signaling the alienation of doctors in the new medical age.

EIGHT

HUMES STEELED HERSELF FOR HER DEPOSITION. NOW THAT SHE HAD RESOLVED TO fight back, she reviewed her conduct during Donna's delivery and concluded once again that it hadn't affected the outcome. "The real problem for me," she would say, "was having been there." She resented having to account to hostile lawyers for her actions. But Humes prided herself on her tenacity, and she came to see the deposition as a chance to vindicate herself and her profession by taking a stand simultaneously against the Koskoffs, the hospital, and St. Paul.

She reviled the Koskoffs, especially Michael, but it was Karen, not he, who would be deposing her, and the two women had too much in common to dismiss each other. Both were single mothers whose ex-husbands were lawyers. Both held political views that drove them to fight a medical system they believed abused women and to work with similar clients, many of them poor. A woman in mid–Fairfield County, say, who had cervical cancer and whose mother had taken the synthetic estrogen DES during pregnancy might turn to either of them, or both, for help. They were on the same short list.

They also were strong-minded women in hidebound male professions. Clarence Darrow once told women lawyers in Chicago, "You can't be shining lights at the bar. . . . You have not a high grade of intellect. You can never expect to get the fees men get. I doubt if you [can] ever make a living." A leading nineteenth-century obstetrician wrote similarly of women doctors, "They have not that power of action, or that active power of mind, which is essential to the practice of a surgeon. . . . [Their] feelings of sympathy are too powerful for the cool exercise of judgement." Both Karen and Humes had had to prove themselves to male colleagues who didn't believe they were smart enough, or unemotional enough, to do their jobs. Under other circumstances they might have been friends.

Where Karen diverged from the women's health orthodoxy—and Humes—was the issue of birth management. She'd seen enough families suffering with brain-damaged babies, and believed firmly enough in the potential of medical technology to prevent bad outcomes, to question the movement's glorification of the *experience* of childbirth. Her own son, Teddy, had been born by crash C-section, and though her relief at having a healthy child was powerful, she'd struggled afterward. "I felt like a failure," she recalls. "This is the one thing that you should be able to do. You're not supposed to do anything else, but you're supposed to have a child naturally." She came to see those who demonized the arsenal of modern obstetrics—ultrasounds and electronic fetal monitoring and epidurals and cesareans—as dangerously wrongheaded, "the dark side of feminism." And she cringed when she heard women complain of "doctors doing C-sections so that they can get to their golf games," though she knew such things happened. So what? What mattered more: a healthy baby or a satisfying delivery?

Coming into Humes's deposition, Karen knew Humes's birth politics made her vulnerable at trial. Not that she thought that Humes didn't monitor or do C-sections on principle, even at the risk of damaging an infant; self-interest alone sufficed to make even the most pro-woman obstetrician aggressive, and Humes's cesarean rate was indeed near average, about 22 percent. But Mike Koskoff liked to raise the issue in court of *why* there was malpractice, and he would surely try to steer a jury toward certain questions: Why hadn't Donna been monitored? Why hadn't it been discovered that she was carrying a dead baby and another that was profoundly distressed? Why hadn't Humes taken both boys sooner? Why, in his words, had she "futzed around"?

These were the central claims of the case, and they suggested, on the face of it, a reluctance by Humes to intervene, to act decisively. If Humes had hesitated to meet the standard of care out of some misguided obligation to help Donna deliver naturally, or some sisterly deference to the nurses and midwives, Karen wanted to establish it now. Her job was to find out exactly what had happened from the moment Humes was called at home until the delivery of Baby B.

Humes arrived at Koskoff, Koskoff & Bieder on March 7, 1989, in high dudgeon. She had worked flat-out since the *Nightline* show, honing her resentment, and she came in determined and focused. The firm had moved to new offices, the entire fifth floor of a new building in Bridgeport. Elsewhere, the beige stucco and glass tower would have seemed a typical suburban office block, but in Bridgeport it became an emblem of the city's distressed hopes. Across the street sat a weed-choked lot advertising a bold urban redevelop-

ment scheme, ambitiously titled the World Trade Center, that the city government would promote with great fanfare but never build. Explains Mike
Koskoff, "They figured Arab terrorists would only blow it up anyway, so they
decided, Why bother?"

Humes noted the sleek anonymity of her surroundings. There was a dark
granite water-wall fountain in the atriumed lobby and a security desk that led
to a bank of richly paneled elevators. The Koskoffs' reception area seemed furnished out of a showroom, with oversized white satin sectionals set off by
what looked like a pastel reproduction of a Renoir and Japanese-style table
lamps. The conference room resembled the board room of the small, successful corporation the firm had become. Sixteen high-backed leather chairs surrounded a burnished twenty-five-foot conference table. Outside, traffic
swooped along a six-lane highway. Minus the Sabias, the assemblage was the
same as at Ryan's office six weeks earlier: Humes, Montstream, Sacco, Karen
Koskoff, Ryan, and Beverly Hunt. A doctor and five lawyers. Humes grimaced
at the odds.

Karen led off the questioning, but unlike Ryan with the Sabias, she offered
no warmth. She marched Humes through a recitation of her credentials and
her understanding of Norwalk's protocols, then began establishing a time line
for Donna's delivery.

"Okay," Karen said, drawing from a list of questions scrawled on one of
several yellow legal pads in front of her. "Now how was it that you were called
to come to this delivery suite?"

Humes cleared her throat, responded forcefully: "I was called by Barbara
McManamy, the nurse-midwife."

"And what did she say to you?"

"She reported that there was a patient, Donna Sabia, who had been admitted in active labor, that she had a twin pregnancy, and that all parameters
were normal on admission, except that she was concerned that the first baby
was cephalic presentation, the second baby breech."

"When she said 'all parameters normal,'" Karen continued, "what was
your understanding of what she meant by that?"

"Well," Humes said, "she explained that the patient—that the patient was
at term, her due date I believe was in mid-April. Also, she was in active labor,
that the only thing that was of concern was the position of the babies, fetal
hearts had been checked and were normal."

"Fetal hearts plural?" Karen asked.

"Yes."

If Karen was surprised by Humes's assertion, she didn't betray it. Un-
recorded phone conversations are notoriously difficult to reconstruct. Karen
thought she'd never know what Humes and McManamy had said to one another that morning by phone, but the substance of their conversation was

critical, since it would explain their subsequent actions. She went on. "Okay. Did she indicate to you that an ultrasound had been performed?"

"No," Humes said as if stating the obvious.

"Did she indicate to you that there was difficulty in locating the heartbeat of one of the twins?"

"No."

"And so when you received this call, you came to the hospital, I take it?"

"Yes."

"And would you have come down regardless of whether or not there had been a breech presentation?"

"Absolutely," Humes said.

"When you arrived on the scene, can you tell us the first thing that you did?"

"I spoke with Barbara McManamy in person."

"Okay," Karen said, "and what did she tell you?"

"She, as I recall, pretty much reiterated what she had said over the phone. Telephone conversations are characteristically brief, because the point is, I have to come in. So I came in and then she told me that she was with the patient, the patient had been admitted in labor, and the findings we've discussed."

"Did you ask to see any fetal-monitoring strips?"

"I don't remember that I did," Humes said purposefully.

"Would it have been your custom to review fetal-monitoring strips?" Karen asked.

"Yes, it would have."

"So that even though you can't remember specifically in this case, would it have been your practice to ask for those strips for your review?"

"Yes."

"And why was that your practice?"

"It was the practice to do a monitor strip on a patient when she was admitted to the delivery room."

"For what purpose?"

Humes was pointed: "As a check of the fetal hearts, check of the well-being of the infant, or infants in this case."

Karen could easily hear Michael turning this last exchange back on Humes at trial: *And, Doctor, isn't it true that you violated not only the hospital's standard of care but your own standard of care in not asking to see fetal-monitoring strips for Mrs. Sabia?* But Humes's assertion that she knew nothing about there being any tapes also posed a problem. Karen had always found it inconceivable that in more than three hours at the hospital, Donna had never been continuously monitored, not even for a few minutes. Seven months earlier her disbelief had turned to suspicion when, in response to one of her interrogatories, an associate of Ryan's, John Mullin, confirmed that there were in fact fetal-monitor tracings for Donna, but then failed to produce them despite several requests. Karen had concluded that the strips had either been destroyed or else that the hospital was covering them up, neither of which would have surprised her. It would have helped if Humes had seen them. That she hadn't only added to the mystery.

"Do you recall," Karen continued, "whether or not you asked her any questions regarding the condition of Donna Sabia and the twins at that time?"

Humes hastened to reassert that she hadn't been remiss. "Oh, yes," she said, "I mean—"

"Tell me the conversation."

"As I recall, our concern focused on the—this malpresentation of the second twin. That was our primary focus, and I prepared for a cesarean section. . . . I introduced myself to the Sabias and explained the whole situation."

Karen noted to herself the inconsistency with the Sabias' testimony, who recalled never meeting Humes until the delivery. She continued.

"It was your understanding at the time that the stillborn baby was alive; is that correct?"

"Yes, there was no—"

"And you said you were preparing for the C-section primarily because of the breech presentation; is that correct?"

"Not *primarily*," Humes said. "That was the reason."

"Now, when you came in, did you examine Donna Sabia?"

"Yes, I did."

"Can you tell us what your findings were?"

"She was screaming and writhing in pain, thrashing to an extreme degree. There are not too many patients you see in labor more agitated than she was at that time."

"And did you make a determination as to why she was so agitated?"

"Some people are and some people aren't," Humes said, "but she was in very active labor by that time, so I'm sure she was in a lot of pain. Some people tolerate it better than others, but she was making very rapid progress."

"Did you make any assessment during your examination of fetal well-being?"

"No."

"Did you either put a fetal monitor on Donna Sabia or direct that one be put on her?"

"I did not put one on. I don't recall directing them. This patient, as I stated, was extremely agitated. I don't believe putting a monitor on her would have been at all possible."

"How about an internal monitor? Would that have been possible?"

"Possibly. Still—you can place a scalp clip, but you still have to have a toco"—a device for estimating contractions—"or an external strap on this patient. She was writhing in pain and kicking and screaming at the time."

Karen sneered inwardly. She'd noticed that there came a point in the testimony of most defendant doctors where they pleaded, in effect, extenuating circumstances: *The hospital was crazy that day. The support staff was AWOL. The patient was uncooperative.* She wasn't impressed. Doctors were *supposed* to remain cool and competent, no matter what the circumstances. Up to now she'd been willing to concede that Humes might have been misinformed and misled by the hospital staff, but this blaming the victim was, Karen would later say, "too calculated." She went on.

"From what you observed when you were in the room with her, did there come a time [when] she was able to be calmed down to some degree?"

"Not in any major way, no. She was intermittently more agitated than other times, but as a whole she was very agitated throughout."

"All right. But it was your belief that she wasn't so out of control that she would have required some kind of medication to calm her down; is that correct?"

"Well, it would have been—"

Montstream, quiet up to now, interrupted. "Objection as to form," he said. He didn't want Humes led into contradicting herself, saying Donna was too wild to monitor but not wild enough to sedate. It was a Catch-22: If Donna was really so out of control that Humes felt she had to calm her down with sedatives, Humes would have been able to monitor the twins and discover there was only one heartbeat; but because she let her go without medication, she hadn't known that Michael Sabia was dead. Montstream, by objecting to the way the question was put, was preserving his right, as lawyers say, to cure the problem later on at trial by getting Humes's answer thrown out. Humes heeded his cue. She took a minute, then answered safely in the abstract.

"It would have been my inclination," she said, "to encourage her not to take medication since the delivery was imminent. She was making rapid progress and anything she would take would be a depressant."

"Okay," Karen said, turning to the well-being of the twins. "So you were not personally monitoring Donna Sabia, but others were?"

"Yes."

"And did they put a fetal monitor on Donna Sabia?"

Humes was defiant. "You'd have to ask them."

"And do you recall whether or not *you* asked if there was any difficulty?"

"I don't recall whether I asked, no."

"Okay," Karen said. "So there came a time when the delivery took place. Describe the delivery. What happened?"

"The delivery was very uneventful in the sense that the first baby was delivered spontaneously by Barbara McManamy, as per our arrangement. She had been with the patient and was—that was our agreement."

"Okay. What was the condition of Baby A, Tony Sabia, at the time of his birth?"

"He was in poor condition."

"Okay. And what were his Apgars at one minute?"

"Apgar at one minute was 1."

"And there was no respiratory effort, from what you could assess?"

"Immediately after birth, yes," Humes said, "but let me add, you can have a baby that's totally flaccid with no respiratory effort, and certainly they would have a heart rate and tone. I mean, a lot of things could be present immediately that would be totally reversed by one minute."

"Was there anything that you observed at the time of Baby A's birth which would have indicated that he was anoxic"—without oxygen—"prior to birth?"

Humes saw at once the trap that Karen was laying for her. If she admitted knowing that Little Tony had suffered from a loss of oxygen, she might be forced to concede that she should have known about it earlier and taken some action. On the other hand, she was a doctor, and at the time Karen was referring to, there had yet to be a complete investigation into the cause of his condition. All that was clear was that Little Tony was born, as doctors say, depressed, not why. Humes answered safely, strenuously. "No," she declared.

Karen persisted: "And what was the condition of the stillborn infant at the time of the delivery?"

"The baby was macerated, slightly. His skin was sloughing."

"Did you make that physical examination or did someone else?"

"I made the examination of the infant, yes."

"And from your examination can you tell us what estimate of time you have in terms of the baby's death."

"The baby was macerated, a small area of the buttocks and testicles. That was the only place, as I recall. The fact that it was macerated would lead me to believe that it had been dead for some time. I can't tell you whether it was a week, or a day, or two days."

"Okay."

"But it was not instantly. It was not intrapartum. I was sure of that."

"Why were you sure of that?" Karen asked.

"Because there was maceration."

Karen, absorbing the implications, went on. "All right," she said. "Once Baby B was delivered, the placenta, I take it, was delivered?"

"Yes," Humes said.

"Would you describe the condition of the placenta?"

"Yes. I looked at the placenta very carefully in hopes that I could understand why the second baby was stillborn. The cord that corresponded with Baby B had a velamentous insertion"—the arteries were splayed at their roots and attached only to the membrane, instead of being wrapped in a tight coil, insulated by protective jelly, and anchored to the placental wall. "One artery was torn, and a corresponding place on the margin of the placenta had a thrombus (an obstructive blood clot) in it."

"Okay. And what was the significance of this torn artery and this thrombus?"

"I felt it was the cause of death of the second baby. The disruption in the circulation of that baby."

Karen so far had stayed safely within the period of Humes's involvement, but she now strayed into uncertain territory—the days before the birth—granting Humes an unexpected opportunity to state her case. Sensing her advantage, Humes grew resilient.

"Now, when you say that the artery was torn," Karen asked, "what would have caused the artery to tear?"

Humes said, "It's a very small vessel, maybe a few, three millimeters in diameter. You have a very active fetus. It's probably a wonder it doesn't tear more often, frankly. It's very fragile."

"How does the fetus tear it?"

"By moving, pulling on it. As I said, it's normally covered with Wharton's jelly, so normally would be impossible to tear. But in this case you have one three-millimeter artery by itself, that was the baby's lifeline."

"Were you able in examining the placenta to determine whether or not any of the arteries or veins were in communication with each other?" Karen had consulted by now with a doctor who'd guessed that the cause of Michael's death and Little Tony's injuries was twin-to-twin transfusion syndrome, the flow of blood from one twin to the other first suggested to Montstream by Harvard's Pinshaw. She also wanted to confirm the Sabias' story about being told that Little Tony was damaged by giving his blood and oxygen to his brother.

"That wasn't obvious to me," Humes said. "Often communications are deep within the placenta. I didn't take sections of it, so my examination was not as complete as it would have been in a pathology lab."

"Okay. And did you assess the placenta at all for the purpose of determining why Baby A, Tony Sabia, had problems at the time of his birth?"

"No, I mean, other than to notice that the portion of the placenta which connected to Tony looked all right, grossly."

"What did you tell the Sabias with regard to their children in the delivery room?"

"I remember showing them the placenta," Humes began, "and telling them that this was a cord accident and explaining that the cord likely tore sometime before the birth and that it likely was a considerable amount of time, not when she was in labor."

She went on. "I also remember showing them the stillborn baby. I showed them the maceration. I'm not sure how much they understood about that, but I did discuss it with them."

"Did you tell Donna Sabia that Tony Sabia, the Baby A, who lived, was attempting to give blood to the dead baby?"

"No, I did not," Humes said firmly. "I did not presume to speculate what was the problem with Tony."

"Let me ask you this: Did there come a time when you found out that Tony Sabia had some problems, some medical problems?"

"Oh, I was aware Tony Sabia had problems from the first moment of life."

"And what was your understanding on April 1, 1984, of the nature of his problems."

"He had—he did not have normal respiratory effort of a newborn; he did not have muscle tone; he did not have reflex irritability and he had poor color. Those are the factors in the Apgar rating, so that was apparent in the first minute of his life."

"Did there come a time when you found out that he had been at some point hypoxic"—partially oxygen-deprived—"or anoxic?"

"This baby had difficulty from the time of birth and I don't presume to explain why."

"Blood gases were taken of him, weren't they, do you know?"

"Again," Humes said, "this is all the pediatrician's bailiwick, so—"

"All right. Do you have any ideas as to what caused the problems?"

"I'm not—no, I don't know why the baby was depressed."

Karen had a second purpose in examining Humes—to implicate Norwalk Hospital. Strangely, if not unexpectedly, the two women now became tacit allies, dismaying, for different reasons, Montstream and Ryan.

"Have you ever," Karen asked, "spoken with Barbara McManamy about what happened to Tony Sabia during the delivery?"

"Yes, I would have certainly had conversations right after the fact; we both were in a state of shock."

"All right. And can you tell me what she said in that conversation?"

"We felt very badly, both of us, and we had shared this with Donna and her husband. I remember we talked about the fact that we did not continuously monitor this patient, and how impossible that would have been, given the patient's combativeness."

"Can you explain whether or not there would be any way that Tony Sabia would have been oxygen-deprived because of the velamentous cord of Baby B?"

Montstream objected to the form of the question since it called for speculation that might be self-incriminating for Humes. Still, he allowed her to answer.

"There was an abnormal placenta," Humes said, "and it was certainly my impression that the outcome of the pregnancy could be better understood by examining the placenta. As to specifically how the velamentous cord and the thrombus related to the condition of the first baby, it wasn't clear in my mind, no."

"Has it become clear since?"

"I have some thoughts about it, but—"

"Okay, what are your thoughts about it?"

"Well, I think the placenta needs close study. You mentioned the twin-to-twin transfusion syndrome. That's certainly a possibility."

Karen asked Humes to review a pathologist's report prepared by the hospital. Humes thumbed through it, having studied it earlier.

"Is there any finding in this report which indicates that there was a communication of the vessels between Baby A and B?

"Is there any finding in this report?" Humes repeated.

"Yes."

Again, Montstream interrupted, glowering. "Karen, the report speaks for itself. Are you asking for a state of mind? If so, I give her direction not to answer and I object to the form as well. I have given you direction not to answer, Doctor, on the state of this particular question."

Karen changed tack. "Do you know whether or not a peer review was held in this case?"

"A peer review. I did meet with one, with a committee of my peers on one occasion," Humes said.

"Involving this case?"

"Yes," Humes said.

"And can you tell me, as a result of that peer review, were any actions taken against you, for example, your privileges suspended or anything like that?"

"Objection," Montstream said, "and I would direct the doctor not to answer; there's a statutory issue here." He was referring to Connecticut's law protecting hospitals from having to disclose the results of internal probes.

"Same objection," Ryan said.

"Do you know whether or not a peer review was held involving any midwife?"

Before Humes could answer, both lawyers repeated their objections. Karen, thwarted, looked down her lists, then said she had no further questions and yielded to Ryan.

"You were present at the deposition of Donna Sabia, Mrs. Sabia?" Ryan said, peering above his half-glasses.

"Yes," Humes said.

"With regard to her conversation with you immediately following the delivery of the second twin, I recall that you informed her that there was a twin-to-twin transfusion involved in this pregnancy, between each fetus."

Humes corrected him. "I think she used the word 'twin-to-twin gestation.'"

Humes wasn't merely niggling. "Twin-to-twin gestation" was a malapropism, with no medical meaning. It wasn't a term that Humes, a trained pathologist, would have used, and Donna's recalling it, Humes felt, strengthened her claim that it hadn't come from her. She also meant to warn Ryan not to put words in her mouth.

"All right," Ryan said. "Did you communicate to her that there was vascular communication between these two fetuses?"

As Humes said no, Montstream jumped in. "Excuse me. Let him finish the question before you answer."

Ryan began again. "Am I correct that I understand your testimony that this stillborn fetus expired somewhere from a day to a week before the date of delivery?"

"Yes," said Humes, "plainly the extent of the maceration was such that this could not have happened intrapartum, yet it could have happened since the time of the previous clinic visit, so I think it's possible that the baby was dead for twenty-four—"

"Hours or so?"

"Or forty-eight hours before, yes. It certainly was not an intrapartum event."

Ryan juggled his concern over Humes's chronology, which implicated the hospital alone, with his desire to see that she be held accountable for the delivery. Unsuccessful at budging her on the first, he now pushed her on the second.

"Do I understand that you had a specific discussion with the Mc—what's her name—McManamy—"

"Barbara McManamy. Yes."

"—as to who would deliver the twins?"

"Yes."

"And I understand that there was a conversation in which it was determined that she would be the person who delivered the twins?"

"No," Humes said.

Ryan recast the question. "She would deliver the *first* twin?"

"She would deliver the first twin, yes."

"And what was it that she said and you said, do you recall?"

"I prefer to use 'understanding,' in that I can't remember the exact conversation. But it was not an accident that she delivered Tony Sabia, having done the episiotomy. It was understood that I would focus my attention on the safe delivery of the second baby."

Ryan went on. "You used the world 'consultant' on the day of the delivery. Did you consider—what did you mean by the use of that word? Is that a word of art in medicine?"

"I don't remember in what context."

"Well, let me ask you this: were you the attending physician at the delivery or were you a consultant?"

"Oh, all right. I was the attending physician, but I was called by the midwife, consulted by the midwife."

"You were the attending physician of this patient at the date of delivery; is that a fair statement?"

"Yes."

"And you were in charge of the treatment being provided; would that be a function of the attending physician?"

There was only one possible answer. "Yes," Humes said.

Afterward, Karen would say, "Humes was a good deposition for us. Number one, she communicated malpractice. She didn't handle the delivery when she was there, and she nailed the hospital. The problem for us was twin-to-twin transfusion. We still didn't know if they were asserting that as a defense. I didn't know if they were being cagey, that they were planning to spill it on us, or if they just didn't know."

Humes left the Koskoffs' offices after nearly five hours in much the same state she had arrived in—calmly militant and irate. Also newly self-critical. After years of resisting any suggestion that she'd erred, under Karen's interrogation she now saw that for her own protection she should have handled Donna's delivery differently. "If I'm culpable," she would say, "it's that I didn't take charge in a way that I should have. It was a matter of misplaced trust and misplaced confidence."

Those she'd trusted, of course, were Fortuna and McManamy. Such reliance on hospital staff was vital in obstetrics, where, as McManamy says, "One minute you're standing around having coffee and joking together and the next minute you're up to your knees in blood." But now there seemed no question that Humes should have asserted herself more, been more authoritative. She should have demanded to see monitoring strips even though there was no hint of fetal distress. She should have refused the charge nurse's request to discharge other patients. In short, she would say disgustedly, she should have acted more like a man, "drawing up lines, saying 'I will do this, I won't do this.'"

"It was stupid," she says. "I was doing a lot of secretarial-type stuff. I didn't delegate as I should have, and I didn't focus on what was essential. Had I acted more defensively, I wouldn't have had a problem."

Humes remained as convinced as ever that her lapses made no medical difference, since the damage to the twins was already done. She was as certain that she hadn't committed malpractice or harmed Little Tony as Karen was certain that she had. It only mattered, she thought, to her. "For my own well-being, to be above reproach, I should have stayed with Donna Sabia. Do I think it would have made any difference to the outcome? No. To myself? Yes, absolutely."

After returning to her office, she buried herself in her letter-writing campaign against St. Paul, which since the *Nightline* report had deluged the country's doctors with letters denying that it had overcharged them. She wrote her state senator and state representative. She sent a certified package to Connecticut's insurance commissioner, Peter Kelly, that included a videotape of the program, a written transcript, a copy of the Minnesota claims study, and an urgent appeal saying, "We have borrowed money to expand our practice in two communities hoping costs (malpractice being the largest) will plateau before we are forced out of business."

In the days and weeks ahead, she wrote to the Minnesota insurance commissioner featured in the broadcast, the American College of Obstetricians and Gynecologists, the Connecticut Society of American Board Obstetricians and Gynecologists, Inc., follow-up letters to Kelly and several state legislators, Ted Koppel, and the director of government relations of the Connecticut State Medical Society, telling this last person, "We have no hope of changing carriers until an outstanding malpractice case against Norwalk Hospital and me is settled."

The Sabia case and Humes's financial worries now merged so seamlessly that it was impossible for her to imagine gaining relief from one without the other. And indeed, when a month later she got a form letter from St. Paul informing her that as a "result of our regular countrywide rate review" the company was cutting malpractice premiums in Connecticut by nearly 10 percent, she was barely encouraged. Connecticut wasn't Minnesota. Insurance interests ruled the state. Frustrated at not hearing from Kelly, on May 8 she sent him still another certified letter, the third in two months, with a copy of the St. Paul notice and a plea for rate relief. Ten months later Kelly would reply, "For this line of business in the State of Connecticut, it does not appear that [malpractice] rates are excessive."

But by then Humes had all but surrendered any hope of government action, leaving everything to hinge on resolving the legal claims against her.

NINE

LITTLE TONY LAY AWAKE IN HIS BED, EYES FLUTTERING. HIS HEAD WAS SMALL AND ovoid, wide at the cheeks and tapered on top, like a water balloon. He had a helmet of coarse, dark hair, and there were reddened, crusty sores over much of his scalp. His face was to the wall, but Donna could hear him rasping. His mouth was open, and his tongue lolled aimlessly over his gums, which were inflamed and bled easily, and over the jagged spokes of his teeth. Except for his breathing, he was quiet. A scratchy clock radio near his head was tuned low to Norwalk's classic rock station, WEFX.

He was on his back, wearing only an extralarge Pamper and white socks, and stomach acid oozed from the base of his feeding tube, splotching his abdomen with an angry rash. Not that he could do anything about it. Other than the meaningless tremor of one foot, his body was inanimate. His limbs were thin, doughy, filigreed with body hair and tortuously splayed. His balled fists were twisted almost at right angles to his forearms, and his legs bowed out sharply. He looked like a marionette with clipped strings. He was five and a half years old.

It was about 7:30 A.M. when Donna came in to get him. She hurriedly disconnected his gastric tube and dabbed his rash with ointment. "Hiya, Tony," she said. "We're going to the doctor today." At the sound of her voice, his head lurched and rolled halfway over, slowly. His mouth widened ambiguously into the shape of a grin, and he emitted a hollow, open-throated groan. He sounded like Chewbacca, the doglike "wookie" in *Star Wars*.

Usually, Donna waited a half-hour after taking out his G-tube (gastronomy tube) to give Little Tony his antiseizure medicine, a mixture of Dilantin and phenobarbital capsules that she ground up into solution and injected into his stomach "button" with a baster-sized syringe. Because the drugs often made him retch, she liked to give his stomach a chance to settle, but now she was in a rush. The lawyers for Travelers Insurance, Williams, Cooney & Sheehy, had arranged for Little Tony to be examined by a pediatrician specializing in genetics, to see whether his condition wasn't hereditary. The appointment was at nine-thirty at the University of Connecticut Health Center in Farmington, an hour and twenty minutes away. Donna had asked for a later time, explaining Little Tony's digestive problems, but the firm couldn't reschedule. Scrambling, she injected Little Tony with his medications, then dressed him in a polo shirt, clean shorts, and unscuffed running shoes.

Donna grunted as she hoisted him into a molded hard-rubber seat that doubled as a car seat. Again, Little Tony groaned. Before he'd given up eating, he'd been undernourished and slight; his floppiness hadn't been a problem. But now he'd gained so much weight, so quickly, that his doctor had had to cut back on his nighttime feedings. Suddenly, he was heavyset, and all dead weight at forty pounds. Donna often wondered how much longer she'd be able to lift him. Unlike Tony, she no longer imagined that he might some day walk on his own.

Dr. Robert Greenstein was a senior figure at UConn, a full professor of pediatrics and codirector of the division of human genetics. As a consultant, he was paid by Travelers' lawyers both to evaluate Little Tony for possible genetic problems and to give an opinion about how long he might live, given his disabilities. Such consultations were routine. Travelers had a single primary interest with any malpractice claim: to determine, worst case, what it was worth, in order to put aside enough money in reserve. Insurance companies and the tens of thousands of people who work for them adjusting claims don't measure success and failure by whether those claims are won or lost, but on how well the *risk* of losing is anticipated and managed. That's how they make their money. They pool premiums and invest them, then count on a high enough return so that even after they compensate their losses there's a profit. Travelers, a sprawling financial empire with assets of $56.4 billion, might eventually want Greenstein to testify as an expert, at trial. At the moment, however, the company's needs were more basic. It wanted to know whether Norwalk Hospital had an alternate defense in claiming that Little Tony's problems were a freak of nature, and if it didn't, what it might cost to take care of him for the rest of his troubled life.

Greenstein had reviewed five volumes of Little Tony's medical records and was well aware of his condition, including his feeding problems. The boy hadn't thrown up in the car, and as Donna arrived at the medical center, she remained hopeful that he might hold down his meds. Waiting for the doctor, she sat with Little Tony in the small examining room, cooing his name. He was sweating, his eyes lurching frantically as if tracking a fast-moving train at close range. Donna shielded his gaze from the overhead fluorescent lights.

Greenstein entered. As he introduced himself, Little Tony began to cough. The rushed schedule and long car ride had been too much for him after all. He vomited, spattering Greenstein with a dark, viscous bile as Greenstein began his examination. Nothing in Little Tony's medical records indicated a history of birth defects, but Greenstein's job was to spot anomalies. He started at the top of the boy's head and worked methodically toward his feet, noting initially how hairy Little Tony was: the low hairline, coarsening of the eyebrows, hirsutism on his back, arms, and legs. These, he thought, were probably side effects from the Dilantin, although he couldn't be sure. Likewise, Little Tony's scalp outbreak and swollen gums. Inspecting his ears, Greenstein observed that they were folded laterally at the margins, also possibly indicating a genetic disorder.

He studied the size and shape of Little Tony's head at length, measuring its circumference, which was at the fiftieth percentile for a six-month-old. It was evident that the boy's brain had long ago stopped growing, and since there had been no stimulus for the vault to grow, his skull had fused in infancy. Entombed within, at best, was an infant's primitive brain, perhaps one-third the mass of what was normal for a child Tony's age. Hereditary causes for such severe microcephaly were relatively rare; what was more common were problems during pregnancy—maternal diabetes, German measles, and high exposure to X-rays during the first trimester—none of which, Greenstein knew, were indicated in Donna's hospital records. Still, he didn't rule out a genetic link. Completing his examination of Little Tony's head and face, he noted that his other features were normal. His neck was supple, lungs clear, and heart steady. There were no murmurs.

Inspecting Little Tony's abdomen, Greenstein observed that the scars from his operations were well healed and that he had no areas of tenderness or masses. He speculated that the broken skin around his G-tube might be due to a fungal infection. Little Tony's spine appeared straight. His hands were narrow, with long, tapering fingers. The flexing of his arms and legs was what would be expected with severe cerebral palsy. Other than pointing downward, his feet appeared normal.

Two weeks later Greenstein reported his findings to the lawyers. He confirmed that Little Tony suffered from "severe to profound" cerebral palsy, microcephaly, a chronic complex seizure disorder and near-total blindness, and that "his developmental prognosis is considered very limited since it is unlikely that he will progress much beyond his current level of functioning." Although he mentioned Donna's adoption and the deaths of Tony's three siblings before he was born, he stressed that there was "no history of mental retardation, microcephaly, seizure disorders or other genetic syndromes on either side of his family." Nevertheless, he suggested sending Little Tony's blood for chromosomal analysis "to rule out the possibility of an associated genetic cause," particularly with regard to his small head size, ears, fingers, and hirsutism. He offered no opinion as to the general cause of Little Tony's disabilities.

If Greenstein's report disappointed Travelers, his view on the child's life expectancy was explosive. "In my medical opinion," he wrote, "given the nature of Anthony Sabia's medical and health complications, it is likely that he would live only 40% to 50% of what would be expected for the average healthy male in the United States today. If the average male is expected to live 74.4 years, then Anthony would not be expected to live beyond 35 to 38 years of life."

Time is money in malpractice cases in the purest sense. The longer a plaintiff lives, the greater the damages. Future medical care, lost income, loss of life's enjoyment, pain and suffering—each claim increases in value with each new uptick in life expectancy. It had been enough that Greenstein thought the damage to Little Tony wasn't genetic, that his condition would never improve, and that he'd need around-the-clock care for the rest of his life. But that he might live another thirty years or more catapulted the value of the Sabias' claim, propelling it to the very high end of Travelers' caseload.

A little over a month later, toward the middle of October, Karen Koskoff received a letter from Beverly Hunt, an associate of Ryan's who'd now taken over the day-to-day handling of the case for the hospital. "We would like to pursue having a meeting among interested parties for the purposes of discussing settlement," Hunt wrote. The letter was copied to Ron Williams of Williams, Cooney & Sheehy, and to William O'Donnell, director of Travelers' strategic claims unit.

Karen couldn't understand what Ryan was up to. She didn't know Hunt and had no inkling of what would have precipitated such an offer, although she doubted it was serious. Probably, she thought, Ryan was just fishing for an asking figure to take back to Travelers. Even so, you didn't request a settlement meeting, especially this early on, if you thought you had a solid case. She talked the matter over with Mike Koskoff. Bypassing Hunt for Ryan, she wrote back cautiously on October 16, thanking Ryan but declining the invitation to talk. "I need to depose a rather large number of hospital employees so that the case can be properly evaluated," she wrote. McManamy and Fortuna had been scheduled for deposition in September, but had been canceled and were now rescheduled for early December. Karen was eager to hear what they would say. Having not yet received Greenstein's report, she wondered what Ryan knew that she didn't.

~ ~ ~

DECEMBER 6, 1989

Barbara McManamy stepped off the elevator, took one look at the overstuffed furniture in the Koskoffs' reception area, and froze. Oversized furnishings weren't alien to her; she lived comfortably with her husband and two children in a "five bedroom, suburbo-mom Colonial" in Wilton, one town over from Westport. But these were power couches, she thought. They served the express psychological purpose of making those who sat in them feel small.

McManamy had reason to feel intimidated. She'd been afraid, almost from the instant she'd delivered Little Tony's lifeless body, that she'd be named in a lawsuit. She'd been greatly relieved when she hadn't, and thought the Sabias had spared her because they "had good feelings about the nurse-midwife group." In fact, there was no loyalty involved: the nurse-midwives didn't have enough liability coverage and probably not enough assets to warrant a separate action, unless, of course, deeper pockets couldn't be found— but they were. Ultimately, McManamy had been called by the Koskoffs as a "fact" witness, a seemingly more neutral role but one that troubled her almost as much as if she'd been a defendant. As "the one person from the hospital's side who knew the story," she feared being forced to incriminate the hospital, Humes, or both. She was burdened miserably by the choice. "Driving up to Bridgeport that day," she recalls, "I was really on edge."

She was accompanied by Bev Hunt, who'd coached her in preparing her testimony. McManamy had quit her job at Norwalk Hospital during her second pregnancy, in September 1985, more than four years earlier. Because she wasn't a named defendant, the hospital had no legal obligation to represent her. Yet on the day she received her deposition notice, there was a message from Hunt on her answering machine at home. She didn't know who Hunt was and was ambivalent even about talking with her—she assumed Humes had also been sued and that Humes and the hospital would be at each other. But she called Hunt back and right away "felt safe with her."

Hunt came to her house, showed her a videotape on how to answer questions, explained what would happen at the deposition—"who would be there and how they would protect me," McManamy recalls. She prepared her for the "ferociousness of the Koskoffs," telling her they were the "number-one plaintiffs' attorneys in Connecticut." McManamy calmed down when she realized she was being called as a witness, not a defendant, but she also perceived that the hospital was desperate to enlist her testimony. "My sense was that they knew how bad this was from the beginning," she says. "Their attitude seemed to be, 'Talk to us because we're looking for a way out of this.'"

Hunt shared none of McManamy's unease. A compact woman with a firm bearing and a determined smile, she was a fierce hospital loyalist: she knew exactly which side she was on. At forty-four, her reddish-brown page-boy was greying slightly, and she had lively, penetrating eyes, mainly hazel but flecked with slate grey, blue, and gold. Before becoming a lawyer she'd been a nurse, then a nursing teacher, then a supervisor, for almost twenty years, and was a staunch defender of "hospital people . . . my people." She had a master's degree in education from Columbia, where McManamy had received her midwifery training, and had gotten her law degree at night, from UConn, while working full-time at Stamford Hospital. On her first day as a lawyer, in September 1988, Pat Ryan had come into her office, tossed the Sabia file on her desk, and told her she'd be working on it. She'd been thrilled. She'd gone into malpractice defense "mostly because of Pat" she says. Now they would be working on a major case together. Soldiering alongside Ryan for Norwalk Hospital, Hunt's ambitions had come ablaze.

With Hunt next to her in the waiting room, McManamy felt relieved to have taken the hospital's help. "She made it clear to me that in situations like this you have no friends," McManamy would recall. "You do what you have to do to protect yourself." The notion of dog-eat-dog wasn't new to McManamy, but it was foreign to the highly interdependent world of obstetrics, and she'd been uncomfortable with it at first. She knew that much of the questioning would be about why Donna wasn't monitored and why she, not Humes, had delivered Little Tony: she knew equally that because she had been a hospital employee, the way she characterized each of their responsibilities might be damning on the question of who was liable—the hospital or Humes. And yet when she had worried about what effect her testimony might have on Humes, Hunt had told her, in effect, "Maryellen's a big girl"—she'd been protecting herself just as aggressively.

Reluctantly, McManamy had come to see that Hunt was probably right. "Being a midwife, I knew I could hide behind the doctor managing the labor, which might protect me but didn't take away my moral obligation," she says. "Still, I made a clear decision that the Koskoffs would never hear that. I'd suffered plenty for this, and making myself a sacrificial lamb wasn't going to change it. I decided I was going to go in and speak the party line." Defendant or not, McManamy resolved to take the hospital's side.

It was seeing Humes, seated at the end of the oversized table in the Koskoffs' conference room, that undid all her resolve. She hadn't considered that Humes would be there—*could* be there. Suddenly, she was stung by guilt and fear. She and Humes had been friendly before Donna's delivery. As the only woman obstetrician in Norwalk, excluded by the boy's club, Humes had gravitated to the nurse-midwives, and the midwives had regarded her as supportive of their position. Then she and McManamy had shared the horror of Donna's delivery. Yet instead of bringing them together, it had driven them apart. Knowing that there would probably be a lawsuit, McManamy had pulled away, deliberately affecting a "psychic break." "I knew someday I was going to be deposed, and I didn't want them to ask me how many times Maryellen and I had dinner together," she says. "I wanted the answer to be none."

Now McManamy was haunted by the bleak finality of their estrangement, the inevitable betrayal. She says, "It wasn't as if I did a really good job for the hospital, I'd be screwing Maryellen. I just knew that by telling the truth it wasn't going to be good for her. I also worried about how what Maryellen would say might affect me."

Taking her seat next to Hunt, McManamy was weak with anticipation. She was shaking; her stomach was knotted. She tried to avoid Humes's wounded glare, focusing instead on Karen Koskoff, who again would lead off the questioning, although Karen was hardly a promising ally. Though she respected the work of midwives, Karen thought hospitals used them primarily because they were cheaper than doctors. It was like hiring a paralegal to do a lawyer's work, she thought; they could follow orders, but they didn't have the competence or judgment to make important decisions. Karen hoped to wring from McManamy an admission that she'd been in over her head, and that Norwalk Hospital had deliberately placed her there. Letting her off the hook at Humes's expense would release the hospital from a large part of its liability, something Karen was determined to avoid.

She thus began questioning McManamy about Donna's care during pregnancy; specifically, why the twins, known to be developing unequally, hadn't been monitored more closely in the last trimester. It was still an article of faith among the Koskoffs and Lichtenstein that by not doing repeat ultrasounds the hospital had failed to anticipate whatever caused Michael Sabia's death and Little Tony's injuries, though they didn't know how their injuries had occurred. If Karen could find enough negligence, it might not matter. A jury could become angry enough with the hospital not to care.

"Did you ever attend any meetings with any physicians about Donna Sabia's care and treatment while she was in the clinic?" Karen asked.

McManamy answered crisply: "No, I did not."

"Did any exist, to your knowledge?"

"Not to my knowledge."

"Do you know whether any of the physicians who saw her in the clinic sat down with the midwives to discuss her care and treatment at any meetings?"

"I don't know."

Hunt interrupted: "Can you elaborate on what you mean by meetings? Meetings meaning what kinds of people were involved?"

"Were there any discussions about planning Donna Sabia's pregnancy?"

"Not that I'm aware of," McManamy said.

"Did you ever hear anybody at Norwalk Hospital discuss whether or not serial ultrasounds should be performed on Donna Sabia?"

"I never heard that."

"Did you ever hear anybody talk about stress tests or nonstress tests being performed?"

"I did not."

"And you never suggested that stress tests or nonstress tests be performed, is that right?"

"That's correct."

"And you never suggested that serial ultrasounds be performed?"

"That's correct."

"Now," Karen continued, "can you tell us what the position of the twins was at the time of the last visit?"

"Yes. By abdominal palpation, I made a note that Twin A was a vertex with the head dipping into the pelvis and Twin B was a breech."

"Did you inform anybody of that?"

"No, I did not."

"You would assume that they would know that that was the situation because of what you had documented in the record, I take it?" Karen said.

"That's correct."

Until now Karen had intended to show that Donna's pregnancy had been managed by default, that McManamy, with nothing more than a hospital chart to guide her, had been abandoned by the clinic's doctors as surely as had Donna. She'd subtly encouraged McManamy to feel like a victim. Turning to the birth, however, she had a different purpose entirely. She wanted to show that McManamy had an independent responsibility to care for Donna, and that as the hospital's main agent at the labor and delivery she was, in effect, "vice president"—there to help Humes, but clearly in charge in Humes's absence. It was a distinction that wasn't lost on McManamy, who became more obtuse the more Karen turned inquisitorial.

"So you were able to determine at the time Donna Sabia was admitted to labor whether or not there was fetal well-being?" Karen said.

McManamy braced herself, recalled Hunt's admonition not to let Karen overstate her responsibilities. "I have the skills to determine that," she said. "That was not my role at the time."

"Whose role was it?"

"The nurse is usually the person who admits the patient, and makes a report to the person who will be managing the labor."

"Who is the person managing the labor?"

"That would be Dr. Humes."

"Where was Dr. Humes?"

McManamy hesitated. "Dr. Humes was—I called Dr. Humes from the hospital to tell her that Donna was there."

"So, until Dr. Humes arrived at the hospital, who was responsible for Donna Sabia?"

"Well," McManamy said, "it's common practice that a physician is not at the hospital when a patient arrives, but they're still responsible for the patient."

Humes felt the wind go out of her, as if she'd been kicked. They were laying it all on her, she thought. McManamy wasn't going to take any of it. She felt stupid for not having seen it before. They were sacrificing her, and McManamy was their Brutus. The whole tragic mess was going to be her fault.

Her eyes locked on McManamy, who seemed to squirm as Karen continued, "Weren't you responsible for making sure that she was properly monitored until Dr. Humes arrived?"

"I was not," McManamy said.

"Who at the hospital was responsible for making sure that she was properly monitored until Dr. Humes arrived?"

"In situations where the physician manages the labor, the nurse is the person who gathers the data and then reports it to the physician."

"Who was the nurse?"

"Mollie Fortuna."

"What was your role?"

"My role in a high-risk pregnancy that's managed by an obstetrician is to be a familiar face to the patient. Often the patient would not have met the obstetrician who would be there at delivery, but would probably have met the midwives. To be a familiar face and to act as a labor support person."

Here was McManamy's "party line." Technically, she was correct: according to hospital protocols, the doctor was in charge. But McManamy knew that wasn't how it worked in practice. The doctors depended on the nurse-midwives to be their eyes and ears and hands. They expected them to run things when they were out of the room. Indeed, the midwives wanted it that way, had fought hard for the privilege, and were proud of it. McManamy wasn't lying, but she wasn't telling the truth, either, and both she and Humes knew it. The pain of the moment rose up between them, a cold, repellent space. From then on, McManamy's answers had a Nuremberg-like distance.

"So you are testifying today that it was not your role to assess the fetal well-being of Donna Sabia?" Karen asserted.

"I am."

"Are you testifying that it was Nurse Fortuna's responsibility to assess the fetal well-being of Donna Sabia's pregnancy?"

"It was her role to listen to the fetal hearts, take the blood pressure, make note of the labor pattern."

"Was one of your responsibilities to direct the nursing staff with regard to the assessment of fetal well-being?"

"It was not."

"Well, was there anyone at Norwalk Hospital who was physically in the hospital responsible for assessing the fetal well-being while Dr. Humes was on her way to the hospital?" Karen pressed.

"Common practice is that the nurse would collect the data and report that to the obstetrician who is en route."

"So, for a period of an hour, is it correct that there was no physician at Norwalk Hospital in charge of Donna Sabia's delivery?"

"That's correct," McManamy said.

"And during that period, did you monitor or assess her in any way for fetal well-being?"

"I did not."

"Did you direct anyone to do that?"

"I did not."

"Do you recall whether or not there was a fetal monitor monitoring the infants?"

"There was a fetal monitor in the room," McManamy said. "I do not remember it being on Donna."

"Did you ever look at any fetal-monitoring strips?"

"I did not."

"Did you ever at all personally try to assess the fetal well- being?"

"I did."

This was a surprise to Karen, who sought to develop the point. "What I'd like you to do," she said, "is show me in the records the first time you did that."

"There's no note in the record indicating that," McManamy said.

"There's no note?"

"No."

"Why don't you tell me, since there's no note, the first time—why don't you tell me about the first time you assessed the fetal well-being?"

"Okay," McManamy said. "Donna had a lengthy ultrasound, during which I coached her through her contractions. After everyone left the room, I turned on the fetal monitor to try to listen to the twins."

"Was the ultrasound used to identify the fetal hearts?"

"I don't know."

"Did you ask anyone at Norwalk Hospital to use the ultrasound to determine the location of the fetal hearts and whether or not the fetal hearts were in fact functioning?"

"No, I did not."

"During the period of time before Dr. Humes arrived, did you assess the fetal well- being?"

"No."

"Did you order ultrasound?"

"No."

"Did you consider ordering ultrasound for any reason?"

"No. I anticipated that Dr. Humes might want to do that, and I mentioned that to Mollie Fortuna."

"Was there any difficulty at that time in finding both fetal hearts?"

"At the time of the ultrasound?"

"No, during this period before Dr. Humes arrived."

"Okay," McManamy said. "Mollie came to me and said, 'I'm having trouble hearing Twin B.'"

"And what did you do in response to that?"

"I reassured her that that's a common situation when you have twins in labor, and to try again."

"Did she try again?"

"She did not report back to me again after that."

"And you never followed up during that period to determine whether or not she heard the second fetal heart; isn't that right?"

"That's right, I didn't follow up."

"And you assumed, I suppose, that she had heard the second fetal heart because otherwise she would have told you?"

"That's correct."

"All right," Karen said. "And obviously we now know that she didn't hear the second fetal heart, couldn't have?"

"That's correct," McManamy said.

"All right. So that there was—aside from one time when a nurse heard one heartbeat, there was basically no assessment of fetal well-being; isn't that right?"

"I don't know, because for most of that time I was making rounds on the postpartum unit, discharging patients, so that I was not in the room the entire time."

"So all of the care and treatment of Donna Sabia was left up to this nurse?"

"That's correct."

"And if the nurse caring for Donna Sabia felt there was a problem, according to hospital protocol she would have known to inform someone?"

"That's correct."

"And who was the person she was supposed to inform?"

"She would have informed Dr. Humes."

"But how could she have informed Dr. Humes if Dr. Humes was en route to the hospital?"

McManamy paused. "I don't know," she said.

Karen turned to the subject of Little Tony's delivery, asking McManamy to recall the birth.

"It was rapid," McManamy said. "Donna felt the baby coming, we looked, the baby was coming, and then the baby was born. It was uneventful. He was obviously depressed and was immediately handed over to Dr. Danoff." By her syntax she was able to avoid mentioning that she had been the one to hand him over.

"What was said at the time Tony Sabia was born?" Karen asked

"I believe that I said to the Sabias that the baby appears distressed, and is not breathing well, and that the pediatricians are working on the baby and therefore they wouldn't be able to hold him right away."

"What did Dr. Humes say?"

"Dr. Humes was managing the delivery of the second twin."

"When you say that she was managing the delivery, can you tell us more specifically what she was doing?"

"She was at the patient's perineum and had asked the radiologist to scan the uterus so she could see what the position of that baby was and then make a plan for delivery."

"And can you tell us what happened then?"

"What happened then, to the best of my recollection, is that the second twin was born and appeared to be stillborn, and had some macerated skin, no muscle tone."

"Did Dr. Humes say anything about why Tony Sabia was born depressed?"

McManamy halted. She was obviously distressed, fighting back tears. "When she talked to the Sabias afterwards, she showed them the placenta, and showed them that, and told them that there was a possibility that Tony had given his blood to his brother."

Karen pulled back, though McManamy could sense where she was heading. "Let me ask you a little more specifically," she said. "How long was the conversation between Dr. Humes and the Sabias?"

"It was probably ten minutes. Dr. Humes, myself, and the two Sabias closed the delivery room door so they would have some privacy and Dr. Humes spent a long, gentle time with them, helping them to understand, as best we could at the time, what had happened."

"Okay. So, as best you can remember, would you tell us exactly what she said to the Sabias at that time?"

"As best as I can remember, she showed them the placenta, she told them that sometimes twins will send their blood to their other twin, they give their blood to their brother and that makes them very anemic and therefore very depressed, and she asked them if they wanted to hold Twin B and see the baby, that she would wrap up the baby in a blanket."

McManamy had been on a thin edge. Now she broke through, sobbing. It seemed to everyone, especially Hunt, that she was overwhelmed by recalling the birth, but that was only part of it. She also was crying for herself, for the unendurable burdens implied by Karen's inquiries, accusations summed up by the question "Was I responsible?"

It was something she'd only dared ask herself covertly. Like Humes, she believed that Little Tony's brain had been asphyxiated when he bled into his dead brother. But how had she not known about it? The possibilities had tormented her from the instant she held him. McManamy believed absolutely that the need to resuscitate a newborn should never be a surprise—never. She preached this gospel widely to other nurse midwives in lectures and workshops. Yet she herself hadn't anticipated Tony's condition. She had failed, in the crucible, to meet her own standard of care. Whether it had made any difference in the outcome for the child, she could only guess. But he was severely oxygen-deprived, that much she was sure of, meaning that she might have made some difference. Demanding monitoring strips from Fortuna, doing more to check the twins herself, she'd have known what was happening. She might have rescued some part of Little Tony that instead was lost forever during those terrible hours.

Knowing all this had been excruciating, but unutterable. In medicine, self-doubt was the truth that could never be admitted. Donna's delivery had plunged McManamy into the darkest crisis of her life, and it wasn't over yet. To this day it robbed her of appetite and deprived her of sleep. She knew you could lose your job, your career, your pride, everything. Then there were lawsuits: showing people like the Koskoffs a hint of remorse was plain suicide. So you remained silent, denied everything. And sometimes the unexpressed horror welled up inside you to the bursting point.

She looked tearfully at Humes, how restrained she was. McManamy was desperate to know how Humes had coped with *her* burdens, but she had consciously cut herself adrift from Humes long ago, for her own protection. She saw perfectly that any admission she might make about knowing Little Tony was hypoxic would not hurt her but could devastate Humes. She'd ensured that herself by putting every last bit of accountability on Humes's shoulders. Though she was anguished with guilt—guilt over "the living out of what had happened psychologically, the separation" with Humes; over violating another of her gospels, which is that doctors need not fear being held liable for the nurse-midwives who work under them—she knew now that she could not talk about Humes further without doing additional damage. She was past the point of return.

"Excuse me," she said finally, composing herself.

"Do you want to take a break?" Hunt asked.

"No. I'm fine."

Karen recast the question: "Aside from what she spoke about in terms of Baby B, did she—what did she tell them about Tony?"

McManamy answered evasively. "She told them that Tony was in the intensive care nursery, and as soon as the pediatricians would come and talk to them, they would give a report."

"Did she say that—for any reason that he was having trouble getting oxygen during the time of the delivery?"

"No, she didn't say that."

"Did she indicate that he was deprived of oxygen in any way?"

"Well, I can't say yes to that. I don't remember her specifically saying that, but in the course of an explanation, that would be a logical thing to explain to them."

Karen tried a different angle. "Have you ever talked to Dr. Humes about this case subsequent to the delivery?" she asked.

"Yes."

"On how many occasions?"

"On the days immediately following."

"Can you tell me about those conversations?"

"Yes, we were both feeling very sad for the Sabias about what happened. We talked about helping them through their grief with this. Maybe it would help me if you asked me a specific question."

"Did you ever discuss with Dr. Humes why Baby B died and why Tony was, as you put it, so depressed?"

"I don't think we ever really discussed that."

"Did you ever discuss that with anyone aside from your lawyers?"

"No," McManamy said. "I haven't."

It was true. Bev Hunt was the first one she'd ever told.

~ ~ ~

It was over. Hunt told McManamy she'd done well. She'd placed herself solidly in the role of a supporter, one who'd tried vainly to make the best of a bad situation, but had been powerless and misled herself. She came across as "very capable, very compassionate," Hunt would say, and her breakdown at the end, far from hurting her, would nourish sympathy. "It was so stunning and so genuine," Hunt recalls. "I read it that she felt terrible about what happened. From a callous point of view, it could only have a positive impact."

More worrisome from the hospital's standpoint was Fortuna, scheduled next. Hunt had met with her twice to coach her and had talked with her several times by phone, and each time had found her "terrified" and perplexing. Her story, Hunt recalls, was that she'd admitted Donna, got a fetal heartbeat but couldn't get a second one, then somehow had been able to communicate her findings, but not her concern, to McManamy. "She knew something was very wrong," Hunt recalls, "but she couldn't act on it." McManamy, who'd pressed Fortuna after the delivery about why she hadn't alerted her, says Fortuna told her, "I couldn't. It was like there was a wall of glass between us." Hunt also got this sense of a mysterious and unaccountable lapse. "Something otherworldly was going on here," she says. "I'm not being facetious about this. She was having a bad day."

Fortuna denies this. Years later she would maintain that she told McManamy at around nine forty-five that she couldn't find a second heartbeat, that McManamy gave her orders to arrange to get two units of blood for Donna and start an IV, and that "these orders were done." She was given no further instructions to monitor the fetal hearts, she says, adding "My whole professional life and accomplishment had been destroyed."

Hunt was elated by McManamy's performance, but she dreaded coming back the next day with Fortuna. She wasn't alone. "Pat said we had to avoid a deposition," Hunt says of her discussions with Ryan. "He didn't want to produce her." Both were convinced the Koskoffs knew nothing of Fortuna's firing, since it was inadmissible. But they believed Karen must have been aware of how damaging her testimony would be, especially to McManamy, whose competence had been established, in part, at Fortuna's expense. The Koskoffs were famous for not missing opportunities. Hunt readied herself, preparing for the worst.

The call never came. It was up to Karen to confirm the time of Fortuna's deposition, but after McManamy was through, she didn't mention it. In fact, as a low-level employee with little accountability, Fortuna would have added nothing to the Koskoffs' claims against the hospital and might have seriously weakened their case against Humes. They'd now developed what they considered a "clean" case, with two separate sets of allegations—one against the hospital for Donna's care during pregnancy, the other against Humes for the delivery. Karen didn't want to muddy it by introducing testimony that Humes might not be at fault because of someone else's breach of duty, especially if it was true. Hunt believed the Koskoffs "didn't know how vulnerable Mollie was." But it is just as likely that they dropped her as a witness *because* of that vulnerability. In either case, she was never called. "We were ecstatic," Hunt says.

Karen came away from McManamy's deposition more convinced than ever that Donna had been abandoned throughout her treatment at Norwalk Hospital. "No one was in charge," she'd say. For the next two months, as Little Tony was diagnosed with scoliosis (curvature of the spine) and hospitalized three times at Norwalk Hospital with severe seizures, she pushed hard to finish up the discovery phase. The case had now dragged on for almost three years. Little Tony's health was deteriorating ominously. The Sabias were running out of money and hope, and Donna was pregnant again. Frustrated by how much was being done and how little accomplished, Karen was anxious to begin the next stage, expert testimony.

Then, in February, during a karate workout, she took a blow to the chest after failing to block a punch by her opponent, a ten-year-old boy. Checking the bruise afterward, she felt a lump in her right breast. When it didn't go away, she went to a doctor. A mammogram was negative, but Karen insisted on a more thorough diagnosis. When a biopsy revealed that she had a small, malignant tumor, she didn't hesitate to seek the most radical but assured treatment available. Though the malignancy was at stage one, meaning her chances of full recovery were excellent with limited intervention, she opted to have the breast removed.

Several months later, though the cancer hadn't spread, Karen took the extraordinary step of having a second mastectomy rather than live in fear of a recurrence. Hearing later of her decision, Humes was dismissive of such overkill. But Karen was a malpractice lawyer, an aggressive advocate for women's health, a surgeon's daughter. She'd seen too many mistakes to saddle herself and her son with an unnecessary risk.

But by then Karen and Humes were no longer combatants. Taking almost a year off to recover, Karen relinquished all her files. She was off the case.

TEN

WITH A FIRM-WIDE INVENTORY OF SEVERAL HUNDRED CASES, MIKE KOSKOFF HAD three tests for choosing those to work on personally: sufficient magnitude, sufficient interest, and sufficient social value. Interest alone, he says, would have led him to "be in" *Sabia,* which, because it involved twins, offered more of a challenge than most birth cases. But it was the promise of "huge" damages, he says, that caused him, after Karen left, to take a larger role. The firm committed every resource to its biggest cases, which generally meant retaining the best expert witnesses money could buy. But no asset was more prized than Koskoff himself, who liked doping out cases almost as much as trying them.

The problem with *Sabia,* he realized after reviewing the file, was that after three years of depositions and discovery the firm still hadn't solved the problem of what had happened to Little Tony. They weren't at all sure how Humes and the hospital had combined to cause his injuries, or how those injuries might have been prevented. What they had was a more-or-less routine—and still highly questionable—labor and delivery case against Humes.

It wasn't enough. Personal injury cases are driven above all by the extent of a victim's disabilities, and it now was clear that Little Tony's long-term care needs well exceeded Humes's ability to pay for them: in comparable cases with children far less impaired, lifetime medical costs alone were more than the $2 million available through her malpractice policy. Meantime, claiming that Humes was in total charge of the birth, while crucial to the case against her, had made it more difficult to hold in the hospital, which the Koskoffs were claiming also was at fault during the same period.

"The birth," Koskoff concedes, "was a problem for us because of Humes's inadequate insurance coverage."

It wasn't the only problem. Koskoff knew he would have trouble tying Little Tony's injuries, massive and all but fatal, to the brief period during which Humes was on hand. Huge damage claims were worthless if you couldn't find someone able to pay for them who also appeared culpable. Yet disregarding McManamy's attempts to hold Humes responsible even when she wasn't there, Humes had been at the hospital less than two hours before Little Tony was delivered—hardly enough time to achieve a level of negligence to account for all that had gone wrong, even if all of the damage had occurred during that time. "We weren't dealing with twelve hours of late decelerations," Koskoff says, referring to the sluggish heart pattern that often anticipates fetal brain damage. "I didn't think we were going to get twelve million dollars from a doctor who was with a patient for less than two hours."

Because Humes hadn't been Donna's private physician, there also remained the question of her "agency," the legal doctrine that defines whether an employer is responsible for the actions of an employee. Humes wasn't on Norwalk Hospital's payroll, but she had been on duty for the clinic. If, as St. Paul was asserting, she should be indemnified by the hospital, there would be ample coverage. If not, the firm might be limited to pursuing just Humes's $2 million malpractice policy, which Koskoff considered inadequate. It thus became crucial to develop other grounds for blaming the hospital, besides claiming a mishandled delivery. "We've got to face this case," Koskoff recalls telling himself. "We've got to pull it together."

Frustrated by these concerns, which typically had more to do with identifying who could pay than who was at fault, Koskoff offered the file to another of his cousins, Christopher Bernard, to try to "unify the case"—come up with an explanation that held both Humes and the hospital accountable. Bernard, thirty-eight, now was Koskoff's main associate on birth cases, and Koskoff trusted him to work up medical theories almost as well as he himself did. Despite *Sabia*'s problems, Koskoff knew he wouldn't refuse. "The day he asked me to handle the case," Bernard recalls, "he said it was the biggest case we'd ever had in the office. That was his pitch."

No one who saw Bernard would take him for a personal injury lawyer, much less a Koskoff. He was tall and affable, with a quiet, self-deprecating manner, oblong features, and prematurely thinning hair. He was related by blood—his father was Michael's first cousin—but on Michael's mother's side, the "conservative side of the family," he says. He had begun his career specializing in insurance defense, divorce, and criminal work at the Waterbury firm of Carmody & Torrance, eventually making partner. Earnest to a fault, he had no urgent calling as a negligence lawyer, shared no overt commitment to the firm's progressive political agenda, and had never handled a plaintiff's case before joining the Koskoffs three years earlier, in January 1987.

At the time, the firm's backlog of medical malpractice cases was so great that Bernard found himself at trial three weeks later. During the next twelve months he tried eleven cases, four of which went to verdict while the rest settled. "The first year was a blur," he recalls. Yet when it was over he had proven himself adept enough to join Mike Koskoff and Lichtenstein at the inner circle of the firm's medmal practice. He was more restrained and more ambivalent about pursuing doctors than, especially, Lichtenstein, to whom he seemed constitutionally opposite—a mild, lugubrious Jeff to Lichtenstein's excitable Mutt. Commuting from Litchfield, a picture-book Republican hill town an hour from Bridgeport, he worried about his neighbors' disdain for his new work. Nevertheless, he was appalled by the suffering he witnessed among the firm's clients and in his desire to see them justly compensated he soon became as hawkish as any other member of the firm.

An inveterate list-maker, Bernard reviewed Little Tony's file, then sat down with Koskoff to draw up a to-do list. Like Koskoff, he believed that the focus of the case still was—had to be—a mishandled labor and delivery, with Humes the main offender. The fact depositions, interrogatories, and medical records all pointed, he felt, to such a conclusion. Little Tony's injuries were consistent with an oxygen shutoff at or near the time of birth. There was evidence that Humes had known that there was only one heartbeat, indicating a problem, yet she hadn't delivered him sooner. The damage, reasoned Bernard, therefore must have occurred while she delayed.

But Koskoff had cautioned about depending too heavily on this scenario, and Bernard also began noting other areas to explore, areas that specifically implicated Norwalk Hospital. This was basic hornbook practice for obstetrical cases: if the doctor can't be blamed entirely, screen for liability on the part of the hospital—in its prenatal and postnatal care, whether residents were involved, anything to suggest other areas for blame.

Certain developments suggested that such avenues existed. Before she'd gotten sick, Karen had retained perhaps the world's leading expert on the placentas of twins, Dr. Kurt Benirschke, to review Donna's and Little Tony's medical records. Studying placentas to determine the causes of disease and death had long been a clinical backwater, but due largely to Benirschke's investigations and the strong demand for them by malpractice lawyers, it was now believed that microscopic examination of the placenta could help determine the cause of injury in some birth trauma cases. A disarmingly jolly man in his sixties, jowly, with a thick German accent, Benirschke had emigrated from Germany in 1948, and was thought to be peerless in his understanding of reproductive physiology.

After first reviewing Humes's deposition a year earlier, Benirschke had quickly ruled out twin-to-twin transfusion syndrome as the cause of Michael's death and Little Tony's injuries. In its most common, chronic form, the syndrome invariably killed the anemic twin long before term, literally draining the life out of that fetus bit by bit, with each heartbeat. It was always the engorged, plethoric twin who survived. But Humes had testified that Michael had been dead probably no more than forty-eight hours, and that it was Little Tony, not Michael, who appeared anemic. Benirschke believed that a sudden, acute incident in which Little Tony lost a significant amount of blood was more likely, but he said he couldn't be sure without more data. He'd asked Karen for more complete medical records—pathology reports, fetal weights, autopsy findings, blood tests, a diagnosis for Little Tony. But they had lost touch after she'd gotten sick and he had never received them.

In June, after he'd been working on the case for several weeks, Bernard called Benirschke, who told Bernard about his theory of an acute bleed but said he was puzzled because there had been no mention of bleeding in any of the medical reports. If a sudden loss of blood had caused Little Tony's blood pressure to drop precipitously, depriving his brain of oxygen, the blood would have to have gone somewhere, either into Donna, or the amnion, or, as the Sabias recalled Humes telling them, into his dead twin. Benirschke said he couldn't confirm this theory without looking at the slides of Donna's after-birth. If done properly, he said, they would show where Tony's blood might have gone and the pathways it took to get there. Bernard promised to send the slides immediately.

Bernard understood little of what Benirschke was describing, but he was tentatively encouraged. An acute bleed in a term baby a day or so before de-livery put the burden squarely on the hospital. Bernard would still need to prove that the outcome could have been predicted, and prevented, by routine procedures, but Benirschke's theory was a start. On the other hand, if the damage to Little Tony was clearly initiated before Donna went into labor, where did that leave Humes? A unified theory would need to show that the in-juries to Tony had begun as a result of the hospital's negligence, then had got-ten worse because of Humes's. It would fault them both. But it seemed just as likely, given Benirschke's analysis, that culpability for one might exclude the other, that the reality was like a seesaw. By raising the hospital's exposure, Bernard worried, he might lower Humes's, or vice versa.

The fulcrum of his dilemma was what was known, and not known, about so-called "hypoxic insult"—the temporary, partial shutoff of oxygen that causes brain cells to die and brain tissue to lose function. In nearly all brain-damaged-baby cases, plaintiffs' lawyers seek to show—preferably through the use of fetal-monitoring tapes—decelerations in the heart rate that indicate a drop in the amount of oxygen in the blood. If the slowdown can be linked to the baby's transit through the birth canal and, especially, the mother's uterine contractions, it's considered an excellent case. Bernard and Koskoff were never more indignant, more outraged, than when confronted with an obstetrician who in the face of such "late" decelerations failed to recognize the emergency and take a baby immediately by C-section.

But the mechanism causing Little Tony's injuries was hardly so clear. If Benirschke was right, the boy's problems almost certainly had begun a day or more before Donna went into labor and had been caused by something other than the birth itself. There were no fetal-monitoring tapes, at least none that the Koskoffs were able to obtain through discovery, to show that Little Tony's heart rate fluctuated dangerously during delivery. Then there was the presence of the dead twin, with his torn umbilical cord inserted tenuously in the placenta, a blood clot at its base. Was the clot from before or after his death? Had it contributed to the stillborn's demise by impeding his blood flow? What effect did Michael's death have on Little Tony, and was it immediate and limited or sustained and progressive? Whatever succession of events killed Michael and injured Little Tony could not easily be traced. It was possible they couldn't be traced at all.

Working down his list, Bernard began contacting doctors who specialize in the care and treatment of newborns. He pursued one in particular, Dr. Marcus Hermansen, director of neonatology at Allegheny General Hospital in Pittsburgh. Hermansen, while not widely published like Benirschke, was highly experienced in resuscitating asphyxiated newborns and in teaching the techniques to others. Bernard hoped that Hermansen could tell him whether Little Tony might have suffered additional damage while he was being revived in the delivery room—another period when the hospital might be to blame.

Hermansen didn't think the hospital was at fault, but he was helpful in another area. During their phone conversation, Bernard laid out the scenario suggested to him by Benirschke, and Hermansen replied he wouldn't dispute Benirschke about causation. He then added that in cases of fetal asphyxia, it was believed that the greatest damage occurs toward the end, just prior to death. Bernard seized on the remark. If the effects of oxygen deprivation got worse as time went on, it followed that Little Tony, more dead than alive at birth, must have been suffering brain damage right up to the moment that McManamy took him and handed him off to Danoff, the pediatrician. And if he was, didn't that further implicate Humes, who might have acted to take him sooner?

Here suddenly was the germ of the unified theory that Koskoff and Bernard had been seeking. With Benirschke providing the timing—starting the clock, so to speak, with the sudden drop in Little Tony's blood pressure sometime before Donna went into labor—and Hermansen's opinion that neonatal brain damage was ongoing and progressive, Bernard could now wrap the hospital and Humes into a single scenario of separate, albeit cumulative negligence. They both were to blame, he could say. The hospital had noted two healthy twins when Donna visited the clinic on Friday: two days later one was dead and the other severely depressed and permanently brain-damaged. Norwalk Hospital had failed to anticipate Michael's distress and Little Tony's vulnerability. By the same token, Humes could no longer plead that the damage to Little Tony had been done before she arrived at the hospital, since his brain was being ravaged even as she attended Donna.

Years later Hermansen would qualify his opinion, noting that the mechanism of hypoxia is not nearly so well understood as Bernard came to believe from their discussion. It's true, he would say, that when the oxygen supply to the brain is completely terminated, causing the more profound and destructive condition known as anoxia, the damage is greatest right before death. This had been shown through animal experiments dating back to the fifties. Researchers had taken fetal lambs at term and severed their umbilical cords, inducing 100 percent asphyxia, then watched them die. Within a minute, the animal's pulses shot up as their hearts struggled to continue supplying blood throughout the body. Blood and oxygen were diverted automatically to protect the brain, heart and adrenal glands and directed away from less vital, more resilient tissues, like the kidneys and skin. By three or four minutes, the lambs' blood became more acidic as their hearts slowed. Brain damage began at ten minutes, with the cells at the very end of the blood supply, the so-called "watershed zones," drying up first. Neuronal death began at between ten and twelve minutes, and the lambs died at about fifteen minutes.

As a model, such experiments have been useful in understanding the evolution of asphyxia-induced brain damage in humans, stroke victims as well as babies. But, as Hermansen points out, hypoxia is a subtler phenomenon than anoxia. The loss of oxygen is partial and often more prolonged. Especially in a case like Little Tony's—"one of a kind," he calls it—where an apparent sudden, severe drop in blood pressure ends not in death but spontaneous recovery and survival, where the blood is not dangerously acidic at birth, and where it is impossible to pinpoint when the flow of oxygen was restored, there simply is much less certainty about the course of injury. For obvious reasons, the experiments that would clarify these grey areas can't be done. Doctors cannot bring healthy human infants at term to the brink of death, half-starving their brains of oxygen, then revive them, deliver them naturally, and examine the results. So the grey areas remain grey. "We don't have the data to reproduce these injuries," Hermansen says. "So what you get are opinions. In truth, no one knows how much injury takes place immediately, and how much occurs later on."

Despite such seeming doubts, Hermansen agreed to review the Sabias' files and to consider testifying on their behalf. Bernard was encouraged. Within weeks, toward mid-July, he would send Hermansen copies of Donna's and the twins' medical records, as well as transcripts of Humes's and Mc-Manamy's depositions. "I am most interested," he wrote, "in your impressions regarding the following questions: (1) What was the mechanism of the injury to Baby A (Little Tony); (2) At what point in time was the damage to Baby A reversible?"

But by then the unified theory that Bernard was developing had developed another, potentially more dangerous weakness. On his list had been the need to recruit a third type of medical expert: a senior, practicing obstetrician who could address whether Humes and the hospital had met the prevailing standards of medical care. The Koskoffs maintained contact with numerous such doctors, and Bernard had turned optimistically to Dr. Edwin Gold, a professor emeritus at Brown University Medical School and the main obstetrical expert in another case that Bernard and Koskoff were then preparing for trial.

Bernard had sent Gold the same information he would now send Hermansen, and Gold had reviewed it enthusiastically. Then, on June 22, Bernard called Gold for his appraisal. Gold told him he had looked hard but could find nothing incorrect in any of Donna's treatment. On the contrary, he said, it would have been "absolute malpractice" for Humes to have performed a C-section on Donna when she was in very active labor and about to deliver vaginally. He excused the absence of fetal monitoring because of the intensity of Donna's thrashing and commended the hospital for not giving her painkillers because it could have harmed Little Tony. Gold was almost apologetic about his inability to find wrongdoing. When Bernard suggested that he throw away his records to avoid discovery by the other side, Gold asked if he could keep them in case Bernard discovered something that might cause him to change his opinion.

It was Gold's blanket exoneration of Humes, McManamy, and Fortuna that first drove Bernard to focus more narrowly on Donna's prenatal care—a move that was now yielding promising, if confusing, new data with Benirschke and Hermansen. "It was the first time I started to think, 'There's something else we need to be thinking about,'" he would recall. But it also exposed the hazards of such a strategy. The further back in time the Koskoffs tried to place the advent of Little Tony's injuries, the murkier the mechanism of hypoxia became and the less important—conceivably—Humes's role, which Gold had found under the circumstances to be not only defensible but laudable. The beauty of a unified causation theory was the opportunity to collar two defendants who together could pay the more than $10 million that the Koskoffs now thought the Sabias would need for Little Tony and that they hoped, given their own one-third interest, the case would be worth. It was a bridge. The danger was that in constructing it, Bernard would reach too far, leaving it too weak on either end to stand.

~ ~ ~

April Haskell would have loved to meet Dr. Edwin Gold. Recently named a partner at Montstream & May, she had taken over Humes's defense from Bob Montstream in April and been frustrated by the case ever since. Haskell was a capable, no-nonsense litigator. She'd worked her way through law school, attending night classes, and had cut her teeth defending auto cases and slip-and-falls. At age forty, she had a brisk, competent manner and an appearance to match. She wore trim, dark-colored business suits, had strong features, and hand-swept her shoulder-length brown hair sharply back in a gesture of weary concentration. Scanning files, she licked her fingertips for added purchase, like a bank teller speed-counting fifty-dollar bills. She liked and trusted doctors.

Right after taking over the case from Montstream, she began seeking medical experts of her own, a networking barrage in many ways the mirror image of Bernard's. Where Bernard hoped to find doctors who would say that Humes acted incompetently and that her incompetence had contributed to Little Tony's brain damage, Haskell looked for the opposite. "Our initial defense was based on a dual approach," she says. "One, to establish that Maryellen Humes had met the standard of care. And, two, to show that nothing she did or didn't do had anything to do with Little Tony's problems. All we had to do was show one of them and the case would be defensible."

She took as her starting point the opinion prepared nearly three years earlier by Dr. Alan Pinshaw, Montstream's original obstetrical consultant. Primarily damning of the clinic, Pinshaw also had implicated Humes, saying, "Numerous profound deviations from the standard of care worsened an already probably irretrievable situation." As a baseline, the opinion was troubling but not hopeless. Pinshaw was a diligent ob-gyn with a Harvard pedigree. But "standard of care" ran a broad spectrum—what was routine at Harvard was not routine at a community hospital like Norwalk, a fact the courts recognized. And Pinshaw, no specialist in hypoxic injury, may have been incorrect in stating that Humes's actions "worsened" anything. Haskell thought she could find other obs who would support Humes's performance.

She was wrong. Every ob-gyn she approached was uncomfortable with some part of Humes's story. Some were critical of her reliance on Fortuna and McManamy; they felt she had an independent obligation to order continuous fetal monitoring of the twins. Or else they were troubled by the inconsistencies of Humes's two written accounts of the delivery. None was willing to exonerate her entirely. "We were never able to get anybody who could unequivocally say, 'Yes, she acted within the standard of care,'" Haskell says.

Worse, though she searched diligently, Haskell also couldn't find an expert to say that the damage to Little Tony was over by the time Humes arrived at the hospital. On May 2, for instance, she drove to New Haven to meet with Dr. Solon Cole, a pathologist at Hartford Hospital. Examining the slides that Benirschke would soon request of Bernard, Cole tentatively placed the time of Michael Sabia's death at twelve to thirty-six hours before birth, although he noted that he might be off by as much as twelve hours. Haskell found no comfort in Cole's equivocation: she was hoping the death had occurred at least five days before delivery, far enough back to remove any implication Humes might have altered the final outcome.

Still, the meeting proved useful for another reason. Cole also concluded, significantly, that there were blood vessels in the placenta connecting the twins. Haskell thought the observation salient. The placenta is an "exchange organ," a dense, crenellated, blood-rich sponge. It's packed with blood vessels—separate root systems—which almost but don't quite intertwine and which carry nutrients, sugars, and oxygen from mother to baby and carbon dioxide and waste from baby to mother. In twins there is often additional, direct vascular communication between the fetuses themselves, so-called "anastomoses." Cole urged Haskell to consult a specialist in the placenta, someone like Benirschke, for a more informed opinion about what role, if any, these blood vessels played either in Michael's death or Little Tony's injuries. But to the question of where Little Tony's blood went, Cole saw a distinct possibility that he had bled into his brother, just as Humes had said. Two days later Haskell wrote to St. Paul asking for authorization to pursue the matter.

Haskell felt sympathy for Humes. She didn't think Humes was a bad doctor, that she'd been inept or indifferent to Donna and the twins. But she worried that Humes would look that way in front of a jury, which for the purposes of a lawsuit was all that really mattered. Throughout the spring and summer Haskell struggled to reconcile her sense of Humes as a caring, competent physician with the reluctance she encountered from those who might help defend her. Consulting with doctors, talking repeatedly with Pinshaw, Haskell finally concluded that her best hope was to show that whatever Humes did, it made no difference in the final outcome. Causation was a critical hurdle of any civil action: without it, she knew, the Koskoffs had no case.

Haskell redoubled her efforts. She wrote Bev Hunt in Pat Ryan's office enquiring about Dr. Greenstein's examination of Little Tony and the genetic testing ordered by Travelers. She also, reviving the statute-of-limitations issue, had a paralegal try to track down anyone who worked at the summer camp where Donna met Mary Gay in 1986, to see whether Little Tony had in fact been enrolled. If she couldn't prove Humes wasn't negligent, she also knew she didn't have to. She would try to protect her in whatever way she could.

On July 10, Haskell drove to Boston to consult with two doctors at Harvard Medical School. The first was Dr. Shirley Driscoll, a highly respected neonatal pathologist. After a brief discussion Driscoll agreed to look at the pathology slides and medical records, but offered no opinion. The second physician, Dr. Roy Strand, was a neonatal radiologist specializing in CAT scans. Meeting in Strand's cramped office at Children's Hospital, Haskell watched intently as Strand reviewed in detail the CAT scans taken of Little Tony's brain on April 2, 1984, twenty-three hours after his delivery.

Strand was of little help and, indeed, said much that, had the Koskoffs known it, could have harmed Humes. According to Haskell's report of Strand's consultation, though the images were crude, he believed they showed excessive fluid throughout Little Tony's cerebrum, and that the swelling was consistent with hypoxia. More, he said he thought the brain damage shown in the films was similar to that witnessed with trauma at birth, although it could have been caused as much as three days earlier. The only other possible explanation, Strand said, was a toxic reaction, though as Haskell knew, there was no evidence of that. In Strand's opinion, what happened to Little Tony looked very much like the scenario Haskell most wanted to avoid: severe oxygen deprivation at or near the time Little Tony was born.

It was ironic that each side was now chasing experts whose positions favored the other side's case more than its own, but as Haskell knew, it was also typical. They were seeking opinions about events that were poorly documented and understood, from a class of professionals—doctors—who, unlike themselves, were trained not to tailor their observations to suit their theories. Haskell saw no humor in her predicament. Back at her desk the following day, she wrote to St. Paul, "Unfortunately, we do not seem to be coming up with anything hard to support a good solid defense of this case."

Donna felt Tony's despair rise at the end of May when she gave birth to a girl they named Dayna. She'd hoped to give him another son, but four pregnancies in five years—two aborted—had produced only daughters, and Donna elected to have her tubes tied. She couldn't endure another pregnancy, she told him. Tony said it was okay. "We've got Tony. We've got Rosie and Dayna. We've got Shannon. What else do I need?" he said. More and more, though, Donna sensed a fury gathering in his neck. He bit his tongue as if choking back some inexpressible rage. Though he denied it, Donna thought knowing that Little Tony was the only son he'd ever have was a brutal disappointment, and that he somehow blamed her for it.

It wasn't that he acted defeated, or unloving of Little Tony. Like his father, he was fiercely protective of the boy. Indeed, he was convinced that no one else could do a better job caring for him. When Little Tony had stopped eating and began wasting away, Donna had first thought it was just a phase, but Tony had said, "Bullshit. My son's not going to die in this house because he refuses to eat." He'd insisted that Norwalk Hospital find a permanent way to nourish him, which led to his getting his G-tube at Yale.

Gaining confidence, he'd learned to stand up to Little Tony's doctors. He hated those times when he would bring Little Tony to the emergency room with a seizure and watch as the doctors "blew him out big-time" with high doses of Valium—"They'd pump him up with so much shit, they'd go overboard," he says. Finally, he'd begun handling the episodes himself, at home. At the first sign of a seizure, he'd call the doctor and they'd "play football on the phone," Tony executing the doctor's instructions like a quarterback running plays directed from the sidelines.

Tony imposed a grim normalcy on all of this, as if anything less than obdurate determination was unthinkable. Little Tony was his flesh and blood, which was enough to justify the most extreme disruptions in his own life and those of everyone else in the family. "Guy at work once said, 'Give him up,'" Tony says. "I said, 'You give up your two kids?' He said, 'There's nothing wrong with 'em.' I said. 'What's the difference?'" Adds Donna, "You don't give up your own."

What Tony didn't put into Little Tony and working two jobs he poured into the house. After shoring up the property, he replaced the roof, fixed floors and walls, Sheetrocked an extra bedroom in the basement, painted inside and out, put on a deck, landscaped, and erected fences. He did most of the jobs himself, preferring to puzzle out and do them alone. Much remained to be done—he and Donna wanted a big country kitchen—but the dilapidated bile-green raised ranch that Tony and Donna had moved into five years earlier, a week before Little Tony's first birthday, was now all but obliterated. In its place stood a bright beige slice of suburbia struggling to gleam behind a striving adolescent maple tree and a white picket fence.

≈ ≈ ≈

JULY 4, 1990

Friends of Tony and Donna began arriving at the house by 9 A.M., hauling bags full of food. One of the benefits of homeownership was having the choice not to hassle with beach traffic on busy holiday weekends. Tony liked to borrow a second gas grill, set the two of them up side by side, and barbecue all day long, knowing that he'd probably see everybody he knew and a few people he didn't. He and Donna had a big group of friends who were always dropping by, and Tony used to fill in as a short-order cook at the Silver Star, the diner where Donna had hostessed while she was pregnant with the twins.

Open houses—big, boisterous, and informal—were how they liked to entertain.

With twenty pounds of chicken—thighs and legs—another twenty pounds of ribs, boxes of hamburgers and hot dogs, and mounds of sausage and peppers to grill, Tony knew as soon as he got up that he wouldn't sit down much all day, but he was too wired for that. The forecast was for a steamy summer Saturday. He had worked through the night, slept a little, and awakened bleary-eyed but buzzing. He threw on a psychedelic yellow bathing suit but remained bare-chested and barefoot. Olive-skinned, he was thin and leathery, almost spectral. His hair was freshly permed. The one thing he hoped to do besides cook was play some "hellacious" volleyball.

He came out of the bedroom, downed several cups of coffee, smoked a parade of Kools from a pack on the table, and talked intermittently on the phone. The kitchen was filled with friends, smoke, commotion, laughter. Dayna cried as Donna tried to feed her amid the din. "Normal morning," Tony would say. After a while he went back to the bedroom. As a precaution, he removed the gun and bullets he took to work, carrying them outside and putting them in his truck, a grey 1988 Chevy pickup parked at the foot of the driveway. He stashed them among the springs under the driver's seat. Knowing there would be strangers in the house drinking, and that things might become unpredictable, he didn't want anyone finding them.

The crowd picked up around one. By midafternoon there were cars parked up and down the street. Tony's brother was there, and his sister and her husband. There were Tony's Norwalk buddies, people Donna knew from Sunday morning bowling, families from Little Rascals, the day-care center with the heavy-gauge steel door and tidy lawn on North Taylor Avenue, a few blocks away, where Donna took Rosie. There were friends of friends, people Tony had seen around but hadn't given much thought to. The lawn was set up for badminton, volleyball, horseshoes. There were picnic tables with paper cloths. Tony had rented a keg, and most people were drinking. He abstained. Standing over the grills, pushing burgers and ribs, he seemed happily obsessed, a work demon. Throughout the afternoon he sped between the kitchen and the yard, missing the volleyball games. He never stopped to cool off.

Around dusk, the crowd thinned out. There were maybe fifty people left, and Tony, exhausted but still pumping, had his first beer of the day, then, sometime later, a second. He usually didn't drink, his system being so overstrung by sleeplessness and caffeine that even one or two drinks made him instantly surly. Given his life, he thought drinking "too complicated" and had all but given it up. But now, in the gloaming, with his throat parched and his hands still burning from the grill, the beer felt good. Some friends came over with fireworks and they shot them off. For the first time all afternoon and evening, Tony sat down.

Later, as the light got dimmer, Tony stood around with some friends on the front lawn, talking. Suddenly, he and somebody he vaguely knew exchanged words. As he would recall it, the guy said something and Tony took offense. Tony thought he was messed up on drugs and told him to leave. Refusing, the guy took a swing at him. Before Tony could respond, one of his friends jumped on the guy, telling him, Tony says, "to get the fuck out." Still in his bathing suit, Tony tried to shake it off, but the incident irked him.

Saying he wanted to go for a ride to cool down, Tony started looking for his car keys. Donna thought he shouldn't drive and, sneaking around a hedge, entered the house ahead of him. She snatched his keys and her own and hid both sets. When Tony asked where they were, she wouldn't tell him. Tony blurted something. He was feeling bottled-up, hateful. His eyes were narrowed. Watching him grab a pack of cigarettes and skulk out the front door, Donna could see the frustration poisoning his face. She hoped she'd done the right thing.

Tony went out to his truck, got in and turned on the radio, which he had wired through the dashboard so it could be used without a key. Sitting quietly, he watched Shannon and a friend walking up the driveway. A couple of his friends got in their car, waved, pulled away.

Reaching under the seat, Tony pulled out the gun. He cradled it in his palm, feeling its heft.

≈ ≈ ≈

Donna lurched at the sound of the gunshot, her heart racing. She feared Tony had killed himself. Panicking, she dialed the police, begging them to come. Outside, Tony's sister Donna ducked. Sensing what had happened, she hustled Shannon and her friend up to the house, then took off back down the driveway toward the truck. She could see Tony sitting numbly in the front seat. He was alive, but in what frame of mind she didn't know. A tough woman with a strong face, outweighing Tony by forty pounds, she once described herself as "big as a house, mean as a snake." She'd only been half-kidding. Running, she yanked open the driver's side door and hurled herself into the cab and onto Tony.

Tony still had the gun in his hand and was waving it desultorily when she grabbed his wrist and muscled him down onto the seat. He struggled, but she wedged him into the small compartment so that his arm and shoulder were trapped. He was pinned.

"Get the hell off me, you bitch!" he yelled.

She kept holding him, working his hand. She smelled the burnt powder. Tony had blasted a quarter-sized hole in the floorboard.

Across the street, Jonathan Major's son came racing into the room where Major was lying down. "Daddy, Daddy, get up!" he said. Major jumped up and fled the house in his stocking feet. Janice, his wife, called after him, "If he's got a gun, I don't want you jeopardized," but Major didn't hear her.

A heavyset black man whom Tony respected, Major approached the truck and saw Tony's sister pressing down on Tony's hand with the gun in it. He wasn't surprised. He knew Tony as a mixed-up, hard-bitten young man with a hectic, pitiless life. He often felt sorry for him, believing the Sabias' problems ran deeper than having a disabled son.

"Anthony," Major said sternly. "Cut it out. Just give me the gun right now."

Obediently, Tony relaxed his grip and released the weapon. Major grabbed it. Holding it tentatively, like a newborn, he took it back to his house.

In the distance police sirens gathered and swelled, then burst down the street, a riot of screeching tires and spinning lights. Five cars barreled to a halt and disgorged eight or nine officers, shotguns drawn—"Like they was on the damn SWAT team," Major would recall. Donna watched from the house, horrified. The officers rushed the passenger-side door, yanked it open, and tried to pull Tony's sister off him. With their arrival, the sister's concerns shifted. Afraid of what they would do to him once they got him out of the truck, she clung fast. "I'm not letting him go," she yelled. "Leave him alone." One of her sandals flew off as two officers tried pulling her out by her feet. Another handcuffed Tony's wrist and started yanking him the other way. Tony's brother John jumped on the hood of the truck, but was too late. Ripping Tony from his sister's grasp, several cops pulled him through the driver's side window and hurled him on the ground.

Watching them handcuff him behind his back, she pounded one of the officers. "He just wants to be left alone," she screamed. "He doesn't want nobody around him." Tony said nothing. He was taut, thrashing wildly. The officers tried to subdue him with stun guns, prodding his arms, legs, and back. It took several of them to wrestle him into one of the cruisers while the rest scuffled with his sister and kept back the crowd. As the police car pulled away, Tony's sister Donna shouted, "Don't take him to the police station. Take him to the hospital. He's just upset." Inside the cruiser, Tony tried to kick out the windows with his bare feet.

～～～

Dressed only in his bathing suit, Tony lay on a gurney in a small, windowless examining room in the emergency area of Norwalk Hospital. He was sedated and strapped to the table with leather restraints. He knew where he was, but not why. His arms and legs felt as if they'd been banged with sledgehammers. He had no recollection of firing the gun or how he had got there. A nurse whom he recognized from his visits to the ER with Little Tony came in. Her name was Gail Archer, and Tony had always thought her "good people." She spoke to him soothingly, telling him that they'd tested his blood for alcohol and that he wasn't legally drunk. When she went out again, Tony began unbuckling the straps. He didn't need to be here, he thought. Rising, he peered out the door, in both directions, then walked into the brightly lit corridor. He wanted to go home.

Tony knew the way out—too well. He'd been here maybe twenty times when Little Tony had had seizures. He looked around. There were the familiar bright yellow rolling laundry baskets, metal carts stacked high with bundled blue linen, red occupancy lights above the doors, silver convex mirrors wedged against the ceiling for seeing around corners, security cameras at both ends of the hall. Everything else was white—white walls, white linoleum floor, white fluorescent light.

Halfway down the hall Tony started to run, still half-naked, toward the two sets of automatic sliding doors that led to a covered ambulance bay. Outside, the remaining officers were smoking cigarettes with some ambulance drivers. Seeing him lunge through the doors, they quickly caught up with him and again subdued him. They took him back inside the emergency area, this time handcuffing him to the gurney so he couldn't leave.

All Tony's frustrations now blazed up—his agony over Little Tony, endless exhaustion, money worries, resentment at Donna, fury at the world. All the inescapable wrongs he could never right despite the most heroic acts of will.

"You all killed my fuckin' son!" he screamed. He still didn't know why he was there, but he knew where he was and that he was shackled to the place. "You killed him!" he bellowed at the walls, writhing. "You killed him!" As Archer tried to console him, he raved uncontrollably, his voice a well of anguish and abuse.

It's unclear when he settled down. The officers took him to the police station and booked him on charges of discharging a firearm within city limits, resisting arrest, and assault and battery on a police officer. He spent the night alone in a jail cell, still clad only in his bathing suit. Later the charges were dropped, and Tony was required to see a probation officer. He was allowed to keep his gun permit, though not his gun.

Returning home the next day, his head hurt and his body ached. He said he didn't remember much. All he wanted to know was who had called the cops on him. Donna told him she had no idea.

∾ ∾ ∾

Getting nowhere with Humes's medical defense, April Haskell turned to other issues. The Koskoffs were obliged to show that Humes had been negligent and that her negligence had more than likely caused Little Tony's injuries. Haskell preferred to be able to meet the claims squarely, with rebuttals from medical experts, but lawsuits were seldom fought head-on. There were other ways to divert liability away from a defendant, to point to another cause and show it to be just as likely.

Throughout the summer Haskell flirted with the most obvious—and delicate—of these prospects—blaming Norwalk Hospital. The more it appeared that the hospital was responsible, the less likely a jury would be to find fault against Humes. Certainly, Ryan's office had already begun laying groundwork for the opposite case—that Humes was in charge, thus excusing the hospital—in its coaching of McManamy. But the relationship between codefendants, and between their lawyers, was nuanced and complex. If Haskell sought to exonerate Humes at the hospital's expense, it would invite an inevitable counterattack that might be disastrous for all of them. As she wrote to St. Paul's in mid-July, "It probably doesn't make sense for us to be making totally incompatible claims about the medicine in this case as a jury would be likely to determine that both of us were making it up."

Haskell threaded her way through the conflicting demands of defending Humes while not antagonizing the hospital by courting Bev Hunt, who was working up the hospital's case under Pat Ryan. Like Haskell and Bernard, Hunt had begun shopping for expert witnesses, and was scouring the country's medical schools for qualified doctors who could say what had killed Michael Sabia and devastated Little Tony. And like them, she was having trouble finding anyone to tell her unambiguously what she wanted to hear.

Indeed, as perhaps was unavoidable in a case this specialized, lawyers for all three sides had begun crossing each other's paths, at times almost bumping into each other. Hunt's first choice of pathologist, after scanning the medical literature, had been Kurt Benirschke. Phoning him at his office, she'd reviewed the case for him. She thought Benirschke sounded "supportive" until he called out to his secretary, then came back on the line. "I'm sorry," he said. "I'm only allowed to work for one side at a time." It was then that she learned he'd been retained by the Koskoffs.

In June, Haskell phoned Hunt to clarify the status of another possible witness, Harvard pathologist Shirley Driscoll. After their meeting in Boston, Driscoll had called Haskell to say she thought she'd already been hired by Ryan & Ryan on behalf of Norwalk Hospital. Hunt said they'd considered using Driscoll but had decided not to because they hadn't been able to "establish any rapport." Haskell used the occasion to sound out Hunt on the hospital's defense strategy. Hunt told her that the genetic testing ordered by Dr. Greenstein had been "a bust," although Greenstein suggested redoing the tests with a more sophisticated assay. Hunt also told her that she and Ryan had begun moving the case in a new direction. Like the Koskoffs, they now understood that Little Tony's injuries were due predominantly to a loss of blood. Their most recent thinking was that both twins had bled into Donna and that Little Tony's blood loss, in particular, had been into Donna and not his dead twin. One of the pathologists they'd asked to review the slides was going to place the timing of the blood loss "long before" the birth, Hunt said.

Defendants in birth injury cases commonly try to push the timetable for causation back into the unknown—and unknowable—past. But, as Haskell recognized, this new theory hurt the hospital perhaps more than it helped. Norwalk was accountable for Donna's prenatal care. Thus, Ryan and Hunt would have to defend the fact that its doctors had not known about the lethal exsanguination occurring inside Donna. Maybe it was impossible to know, and that was their defense. Still, Haskell was delighted to hear Hunt's new theory. Nothing would absolve Humes so cleanly as a jury's believing that she'd arrived too long after the damage had occurred to do anything about it. From Haskell's standpoint, Ryan's and Hunt's new thinking was all good news. "I wasn't interested in sinking the hospital," Haskell recalls. "I was just interested in trying to save Maryellen."

Haskell and Hunt each realized the risks posed by the other's case—risks the Koskoffs would no doubt exploit. Before hanging up, they discussed getting together to, as Haskell would report to St. Paul, "determine what might be useful in the way of combined strategy so that we don't torpedo each other." Just as the Koskoffs and Bernard and come to realize the necessity of a unified theory, so had their opponents.

But Haskell had another party to contend with, one less amenable to joining forces with the hospital and its lawyers. St. Paul had distrusted Norwalk Hospital from the start. The company felt strongly that requiring Humes to be on call for the clinic as a condition of having privileges amounted to "blackmail," and its local case managers resented being involved at all with her defense, particularly as it foundered. They didn't like hearing about Haskell's troubles, wanted the case off their books, and pressured Haskell to find a way to get the company out of it. "We always thought," says former claims manager Michael Kaufman, "that the hospital should have defended and indemnified [Humes]."

"The lawyer," the legal scholar Karl Llewellyn used to advise students, "is a man of many conflicts. More than anyone else in our society he must contend with competing claims on his time and loyalty." Haskell's cross-cutting loyalties—to Montstream, to Humes, to Hunt, to St. Paul, to herself—were now sorely tested. She knew that even if Humes was found to be an "agent" of the hospital—serving on its behalf and under its control—it was most likely her responsibility under the terms of her coverage to defend and indemnify the hospital, not the other way around. She told St. Paul that she didn't think it had any choice but to defend Humes as vigorously as possible. Cooperation with the hospital, she said, was essential to that defense.

On August 17, Haskell wrote to St. Paul to outline her progress in the case and to answer its concerns about its obligations to Humes. She said, "I think it is a good idea for the St. Paul to undertake the initial efforts to locate Mrs. Sabia's natural parents, siblings and former husband." Although Donna had always longed to know the identity of her real parents, she had been unable to afford an investigator to find them. Now, in a last-ditch effort to show that Little Tony's problems might be genetic, Haskell and St. Paul set out to do it for her.

～～～

Bernard, Lichtenstein, and Mike Koskoff hunched over stacks of medical books and journals at the black lacquered conference table in Koskoff's corner office. Opulently furnished, the office had once belonged to Ted, and it reflected the old man's Hollywood tastes. There was a sleek, richly veneered, battleship-sized desk flanked by two side chairs and a trio of matching credenzas. Across a sea of salmon-colored carpet, against a bank of windows overlooking the shell of a once-formidable apartment block, sat a low white silk sofa, an oriental coffee table, and a shedding ficus tree nestled on a Persian rug. An obligatory power wall—diplomas, citations, and honors—competed for attention with a framed copy of Richard Nixon's resignation letter to Henry Kissinger and a collage of headlines and photos from Ted's most famous cases.

It was early August, a month after Tony's gun incident. The firm still had no theory of causation to implicate Norwalk Hospital, and Koskoff, in shirtsleeves, failed to disguise his concern. If they couldn't nail the hospital, the value of the case would dwindle to $2 million, Humes's policy limit with St. Paul. Koskoff proudly made a point of not going after doctors' assets except in instances where they weren't "responsible enough" to buy adequate insurance coverage. A certain fellow-feeling toward them as professionals and a distaste for the messy business of inflicting financial ruin on respected individuals, particularly from one's own community, precluded his trying to attach Humes's house and other possessions, much as Koskoff thought she deserved it. "There's not enough there to take care of this kid even if Dr. Humes throws in everything," he said, dissatisfied. "We've got to get a handle on this case."

It was the same exhortation he'd used all spring, but now, having realized just how deficient Humes's coverage was, Koskoff feared they were fast running out of room to pull *Sabia* together, and it showed in his vehemence. Driving his concern was the first, most critical, damage estimate for Little

Tony. Plaintiffs' lawyers rely on outside experts to help them value cases: it was one thing to say a defendant ought to pay millions, but courts and insurers required credible appraisals of losses to justify making big awards. Based on his expert's projections, which the firm had received the previous October but Koskoff had only just seen, he believed that the long-term price of caring for Little Tony might not just be huge, it might be staggering.

Prepared by a Miami-based consultant named Larry Forman, the report itemized every conceivable medical and rehabilitative expense Little Tony would ever have, given his condition and prognosis. For over a year Forman had surveyed all those who'd ever treated him, an army of more than thirty neurologists, pediatricians, surgeons, radiologists, eye doctors, orthopedists, dietitians, physical and occupational therapists, social workers, dermatologists, nurses and dentists, as well as employees of several schools and hospitals. Then, using the American Medical Association's *Guides to the Evaluation of Permanent Impairment* and other predictive tools, he calculated Little Tony's needs over the course of a lifetime and modeled two treatment regimens, basic and preferred. His report, for which Koskoff had paid $4,911.70, ran twenty-four pages.

Forman's projections were nothing if not thorough. There were line-item entries for Attends (Tony's diapers), four cases a month at $48.29 a case for life; Ensure (his high-calorie formula), six cases a month at $54 a case; plastic feeding bags, one case a month at $384.75 a case for as long as he had his G-tube; Dilantin, two bottles a month for life, $31 a bottle. Under "Medical Evaluations" were listed annual visits with eleven specialists (opthalmological, audiological, pulmonary, gastroenterological, orthopedic, neurological) and regular diagnostic tests (X-rays for his recently discovered spinal curvature, $278 a year; CAT scans, $924 a year; EEGs, $275 a year—all as needed). There were expenses for laboratory tests ($227.78 every two weeks for medication-related blood work and liver function tests, for life); one-time surgical procedures ($45,000 to correct Tony's curved spine, $13,400 to release the tendons in his legs—both as needed); therapy (occupational and physical therapy now cost $90 an hour; Forman recommended one hour and two hours a week respectively); education (private school, $47,748 a year for sixteen years); support care ($42,500 a year for a live-in attendant); orthopedic equipment (customized leg braces, $3,000 a pair; knee immobilizers, $2,303.03 a pair; a portable hydraulic lift for getting Little Tony in and out of the bathtub, $1,095); and transportation ($23,000 to $29,000 every five to seven years for a new high-top van with a drop floor and lift for Tony's wheelchair [$2,684]).

More than any other factor, long-term treatment costs set the level of a case. The law allowed for other forms of damages—chiefly loss of income and pain and suffering (punitive damages, with their taint of malice, were rare in medmal cases), but the big money almost always lies in "specials"—care and treatment. Hence Koskoff's urgency. Forman calculated that in present values it would cost $6,833,903 to meet Little Tony's basic medical and rehabilitative needs if he lived to age seventy-three, the average life expectancy for a white American male born in 1984. For the best of everything, and factoring in every possible need, such as further corrective operations for his contractive deformities ($12,000 to $15,000 apiece), the figure jumped to $10,507,273.

Koskoff called Forman's report a "wake-up call." It increased dramatically the firm's incentives to get the case moving and ready for court. Adding $1–$2 million for lost lifetime earnings and perhaps an equal amount for Donna's and Little Tony's pain and suffering, the Sabias could reasonably now claim to be due $15 million for what had happened to them. By that measure *Sabia* wouldn't just be the most valuable case the Koskoffs had ever had; it would be the biggest malpractice case in Connecticut history.

But Forman's report also presented risks. Such towering demands were worthless if the money couldn't be found to pay them. The key was to be able to prove liability on behalf of those with deep pockets. And that, Koskoff knew, they still didn't have.

Koskoff anticipated that Forman's figures would be controversial; they always were. Defense lawyers like Ryan and Montstream derided such forecasts as outrageously inflated, even fraudulent. They correctly pointed out that they neglected other sources of payment and interpreted life expectancy in a staggeringly generous light. Yet if some items seemed excessive—under home modifications Forman had thrown in a therapy pool ($9,000 to $21,000) and a screened-in porch ($2,800 to $5,500)—and others irrelevant (the Norwalk Public Schools were responsible for Little Tony's education and would pay full private school tuition for him until he was twenty-one), Forman's breakout conformed to what those who treated him regarded as essential and appropriate. A good private facility for someone like Little Tony cost about $200,000 a year. Koskoff and Bernard saw nothing in Forman's models that they didn't think Little Tony both needed and deserved.

Nor were they put off by the fact that Tony and Donna had health insurance that covered most vital expenses—a point the defense would surely try to raise, but which was inadmissible in court. Connecticut, like most states, had long held that juries shouldn't be prejudiced by so-called collateral payments in weighing damage awards. Besides, health insurance could easily be lost, as Americans were now learning. In February, Tony's company had eliminated vision and dental coverage, and had reduced his major medical insurance from 80 percent to 75 percent of expenses. Such givebacks normally were justified as tolerable to most families, but the Sabias weren't most families. Little Tony's bills for admission to Norwalk Hospital alone during one six-month period—from December 1988 to June 1989, at the height of his seizures—totaled $39,415.82. A similar siege would now cost Tony and

Donna $10,000 out-of-pocket. Tony had earned in 1988 close to $100,000 working more than eighty hours a week at two jobs; Donna, about $14,000. But Donna was now home with the new baby and resisting getting out of bed. She also was fending off bill collectors. Little Tony's medical bills were a black hole financially, and even health insurance and a good salary no longer guaranteed the family's security.

Huddling with Lichtenstein and Bernard, Koskoff recalls experiencing "a terrible feeling of frustration." He would say he was thinking about the Sabias, their awful futility. He didn't want to let them down. But he, Bernard, and Lichtenstein had their own reasons to be distressed. They had before them what appeared to be the largest malpractice claim in state history, but no theory of malpractice strong enough to implicate Norwalk Hospital, the one pocket deep enough to pay for it.

They had failed so far to answer even the most basic questions of the hospital's liability. If what nearly killed Little Tony and left him disabled was a sudden bleed-out a day before he was born, what, for instance, did that have to do with Donna's treatment? Maybe the event was simply an accident: unforeseeable, undiagnosable, untreatable. The medical texts and journals suggested strongly that "term" women with twins should receive regular nonstress tests to evaluate how the babies are doing. Donna hadn't received any, but if she had, what would they have shown? Koskoff was perplexed. "The main thing that wasn't defined," he recalls, "was the relationship between what was done in the hospital and the medical outcome"—the causal link. In other words, they had no case.

Now, after brainstorming for much of the morning, Koskoff felt he'd hit a dead end. Floundering, he suggested, "Let's call Murray and get his bead on it."

Dr. Thomas Murray was an ob-gyn and perhaps Koskoff's most prized medical contact. An accomplished horseman and former varsity basketball player at Georgetown, he was six feet three and, at age 41, test-pilot trim with drop-dead Irish good looks. He'd graduated from Columbia's College of Physicians and Surgeons, established a thriving practice in semirural Dutchess County, ninety minutes north of Manhattan, had a reputation for skill and integrity, and worked one day a week without pay teaching obstetrics at Harlem Hospital. On the witness stand, Bernard thought he cut a figure as stirring, impressive, and charismatic as John Kennedy.

All this made Murray an ideal expert, but what accounted for Koskoff's great affection was how they had met. In the mid-eighties, at the height of the second malpractice crisis, the broadcaster Fred Friendly had organized a series of seminars for public television that brought together doctors, lawyers, judges, and journalists. Koskoff, by then a leader of Connecticut's personal injury bar, and Murray, an ex-neighbor and old friend of the host, served on a panel together in Hartford. The discussion was predictably contentious. In answer to a question by Harvard Law Professor Charles Nesson, Murray, who'd testified in defense of other doctors but never against them, said he thought plaintiffs' lawyers were corrupt and that the doctors they hired to make their cases for them were "prostitutes."

Koskoff jumped in: "In other words, Dr. Murray, you don't think that we ever use for the plaintiff a legitimate obstetrician-gynecologist." Pausing, he added: "Don't you think an injured baby or mother deserves the best possible defense?"

Murray answered, "Yes, I do."

"Well," Koskoff said, "supposing I had a case in which a woman or baby was egregiously wronged; you've appeared for the defense, would you appear for the plaintiff?"

"Yes," Murray said, "I would."

A month later, Koskoff called Murray and invited him to discuss a case. After hearing the details, Murray agreed to testify. He had reviewed several more plaintiffs' cases since, always for the Koskoffs. Thus Koskoff's delight with their relationship. Doctors willing to condemn other doctors for money were easily branded as jealous incompetents and gold diggers—as Murray himself said, whores. But Murray had been led to do so, it seemed, by honorable intentions, specifically a doctor's mandate to minister to those who suffer, regardless of the cause. That Koskoff had led Murray to such a conclusion, and on national television, made Murray's conversion all the sweeter.

Getting Murray on the phone, Koskoff reviewed the case: the early discordancy in fetal weights, Michael Sabia's velamentous cord insertion, the paucity of fetal monitoring before and during birth, the use of midwives. Donna's delivery at thirty-eight and a half weeks. He outlined Benirschke's suggestion that Little Tony might have bled into his dead brother through the placenta and Hermansen's theory that the boy's condition was exacerbated by the labor and delivery. He questioned Murray specifically on whether the absence of nonstress testing violated the standard of care.

Murray asked several questions, then said emphatically, "They didn't do ultrasounds." He believed that because of the initial disparity in birthweights, Norwalk Hospital should have taken repeated sonograms throughout the final thirteen weeks of Donna's pregnancy, to monitor the relative size of the twins as the dangers to them increased. If it had, he said, Donna's doctors would have seen that Twin B—Michael—wasn't thriving, and would have delivered both babies by C-section at thirty-seven weeks, when the twins reached maturity.

In other words, even if Michael's death and Little Tony's ensuing injuries couldn't have been foreseen, it didn't matter. Michael's low weight—almost 20 percent less than Little Tony's at birth—itself offered sufficient cause for increased surveillance. Donna and the twins had been "abandoned," Murray said. With serial ultrasounds in the last trimester, which any reasonably competent ob-gyn would have performed under the standard of care, her doctors would have known to deliver the twins as much as a week and a half earlier because they were thriving unequally. Certainly, Little Tony, and most likely Michael, would have been born normal and healthy. As Koskoff would later put it, "They'd be running around today."

Here was the unified theory the Koskoffs had long sought: Norwalk Hospital, by failing to do routine monitoring, had callously allowed Michael Sabia to die and Little Tony's life to be ruined; then Humes, also by failing to monitor the twins, finished the job on Little Tony. As Murray would put it, Little Tony's life was ruined by a "cumulative series of mistakes" during pregnancy and childbirth.

The call to Murray sharply reinvigorated the Koskoffs' case. They now had a direction, and a way to proceed. Within days, on August 8, 1990, Lichtenstein sent Bernard a single-spaced three-page memo detailing numerous citations on the necessity of late-stage fetal monitoring in twin pregnancies. He provided capsule biographies of the most prominent authors, anticipating that Bernard would want to contact them and enlist them to testify.

Five days later he sent Bernard another memo, about a recent New Jersey case, *Knoepfler v. Burmin*, which also involved "oxygen deprivation, stillbirth of one twin, brain damage to the other." The case had ended with a $5.08 million judgment against the obstetrician, a structured settlement with an expected life payout to the plaintiff's family of about $26 million. "I thought," Lichtenstein wrote, "this might be of some interest to you."

ELEVEN

OCTOBER 22, 1990

HASKELL HAD ALL OF HER LETTERS TO ST. PAUL COPIED TO HUMES, WHICH WAS how Humes kept up with the case's progress and how she learned of the latest delay. Citing Karen's illness, the Koskoffs had asked for additional time to disclose their medical experts. Lawyers in Connecticut have sixty days from the end of discovery to name experts. After that, a case is assigned to a trial list, where it joins thousands of others trundling toward a court date years in the future. Though the fact-finding period was supposed to have concluded the previous November, the Koskoffs still hadn't given any names. Humes was sure they were stalling.

Haskell was confident their request would be granted and saw it as a reprieve. Since she herself was far from ready to move the case ahead, any extensions, she wrote the company, would "inure to our benefit." Reading the letter, Humes sagged. Sitting at the small French provincial desk in her office, barely the size of an examining room and all but permanently shuttered, she no longer was sure how long she could last. The Sabia matter had consumed her now for six and a half years, the Gay case for most of the five years before that. For almost as long as she'd been in practice, the Koskoffs had been after her, trying, she thought, to destroy her.

Humes abhorred resignation. When she was a girl, her mother had called her Spitfire. She'd always had the ability to get what she wanted either through furious action or by being headstrong, usually both. Nothing deflected her. In 1972, when she was a resident in pathology at Norwalk Hospital, her husband Roland had been in Brazil on a business trip. Refusing to acknowledge that she needed to sleep, she'd dozed off at night in a chair reading a textbook on Rh factors. Some painters' rags under the porch had caught fire. Humes woke up to flames. Racing to get her three daughters, then ages five, seven, and nine, she climbed out a window with each.

Her insistence upon rebuilding the house to perfection precipitated the breakup of her marriage. Living for a year in an apartment owned by the hospital while she finished her residency, she took on every part of the project as determinedly as she later would the house in Westport. To her, remodeling was an imperative. It was her family's home; it should be done right, with a "strong, heavy hand." She recalls saying to Roland, "Pay attention. This matters to us." But it didn't matter to him as much as to her, and the difference eventually drove them apart.

As long as Humes was able to use her confidence as a battering ram, she remained buoyant. But now she felt beset, tired, unable to extricate herself. Her financial problems seemed overwhelming. Connecticut's two other malpractice insurers, Cigna and Connecticut Medical Insurance Company (CMIC), which the state's doctors had set up after the first malpractice crisis to sidestep commercial carriers, refused even to review her application while she still faced an unresolved claim, so she was stuck with St. Paul and its onerous premiums. Meanwhile, her campaign for rate relief had sputtered. In May, 14 months after her first letter, the state's insurance commissioner found no evidence that St. Paul had overcharged on its malpractice coverage and refused to order a further investigation.

The rebuffs drained Humes. She tended to fly from one thing to another, but being sued was like being in irons. She couldn't escape, and the ramifications of the case expanded. In January, for instance, she'd been denied courtesy privileges at Norwalk Hospital, her final break with the boys' club. In a terse letter the hospital's president, David Osborne, had said that the action was based "generally" on the fact that she'd moved her primary office to Stamford and wasn't at Norwalk enough for her performance to be properly evaluated.

Humes was furious. She immediately called Osborne's assistant, Barbara Klein, protesting his use of the word "generally." Klein assured her that there was no other unstated matter implied by Osborne's decision. Still, not long after, word got back to her that a receptionist at the local visiting nurses' association had told a patient that she'd been denied privileges because of a mishandled twin delivery years earlier. Humes dropped everything, drove to the office, and confronted the woman at her desk.

It was a rare public display of anger. Because she was a doctor and a defendant, and because as a woman she felt she had to guard rigorously against being perceived as emotional and weak, Humes felt she wasn't permitted to reveal her pain. But closeting her anguish only added to the injustice she felt.

More than once now, she grew brittle from the strain. "My hurt is as deep or deeper than the Sabias'," she would say. "Their hurt is so out in front, so obvious. It qualifies them for the world's sympathy. But I'm held responsible for something I didn't do. It's horrible. It's like having gangrene in your leg, and having to walk around like everything is okay."

"A sore that doesn't heal," Humes called her ordeal.

Staring down at Haskell's letter, Humes called Madonna Sacco in Bai's office. Bai had always told her, "Maryellen, get on with your life." Now she decided he was right. Impulsively, she asked Sacco to move to settle the case.

Sacco's answer dismayed Humes even more than Haskell's apparent satisfaction at having the case drag on. She told her that she couldn't settle. Nothing could be done, Sacco said, until the Koskoffs disclosed their experts.

Humes scowled. Though the reason was obvious—St. Paul, not Humes, would pay for any settlement, and it would want to see what it was up against before giving in—she was sickened to think that she couldn't back down now even if she wanted to. Her professional life, her livelihood, were at stake, but whether they could be salvaged no longer was in her control. She couldn't even sacrifice herself. She was willing to do the most distasteful thing she could imagine, surrender for the sake of expediency to people she despised— the Koskoffs—on a grave charge she considered baseless. Yet even that excruciating self-betrayal was denied her. Again, she was reminded that it was not her but her insurance policy that the Sabias wanted, and thus it was the owner of that policy who made the decisions.

As she often did, Humes took notes on the conversation, several quick lines in an unflagging hand on the back of Haskell's letter. "Koskoff office delaying and delaying due to Karen K's illness," she wrote. "Sacco will write 'form letter' requesting that we 'get on with it'—the least we can do." She ended the note with a frown—a circle, two dots for eyes, a bitter, downturned line for a mouth—then stuffed the letter in one of several thick folders she now carried around with her, like a petitioner, to keep track of her multiplying grievances.

Humes thought about her lawyers. Montstream she at least saw at depositions, but Haskell remained faceless. She knew her entirely from their phone conversations and from her letters to St. Paul, each inspiring less confidence than the last. She was appalled that Haskell couldn't find any other doctors to support her and was resorting to legalistic smokescreens like trying to find Donna's natural parents. Humes still was fond of Arnold Bai, but Sacco, with whom she had her main contact, wasn't Bai. She'd paid them $10,000 to watch over Montstream and Haskell and now they were saying there was nothing they could do. They were all alike, she concluded. Lawyers started the action against her and only lawyers could stop it. It didn't especially matter whose side they were on; they were all one parasite.

In a way, this was the worst part of Humes's ordeal, this sense of power-lessness. She felt marginalized, a passive spectator to a slow-motion crack-up in which she was the victim. In other endeavors she insisted on asserting her-self, at times too baldly. Now, for instance, she was developing plans to re-model her house, a complete makeover. Eventually, she would go through five architects. She made no apologies. "A lot of people don't want to deal with the extent of my involvement, frankly," she would say. She knew she could be dif-ficult: "I'm a terrible taskmaster; I am. But it's not that I'm any less critical of my own work, too." Yet in this one area, the one that mattered perhaps most to her, the defense of her competence, she felt exiled and excluded. She had failed to find any rapport with her defenders.

Humes redoubled her own efforts. There were doctors, particularly in Stamford and at Yale, who privately had supported her. She knew that they would be hard-pressed to defend her in court; most of them had some rela-tionship to Norwalk Hospital and to the members of the boys' club that they would seek to protect. She thought her best bet might be her old friend Dan Clement. Clement had worked under her when she was chief resident at Stamford Hospital and had emulated her. He'd gone on to a successful career as a perinatologist, managing high-risk pregnancies first as head of maternal-fetal medicine at St. Luke's-Roosevelt Hospital in New York, then more re-cently with a private group in Los Angeles. His longtime partner was perhaps the best-known—and most controversial—perinatologist in the country, Dr. Barry Schifrin, one of the fathers of electronic fetal monitoring who in recent years had turned almost entirely to testifying in obstetrical cases, normally for the plaintiffs. Humes and Clement, a charming, outspoken Canadian, had re-mained close, and he'd once told her that Schifrin, hearing Clement discuss it, had supported her in the Gay case. "She settled?" Schifrin said, according to Clement. "You never settle."

For years Humes had been sending Clement material about the Sabia case: medical records, depositions, review articles. He'd been sympathetic. "She came to help; there was no help to be given," he would say. "It was a dras-tic situation." Even if he himself wouldn't testify, she hoped that he could use his access to Schifrin and Schifrin's California contacts to jump-start a med-ical defense for her in the case, one that she could deliver as a *fait accompli* to Haskell.

As a former pathologist, Humes had always believed that she'd be exoner-ated by pathology. Someone sitting at a double-barreled microscope in a win-dowless room, peering at hair-thin slices of tissue and whorls of granulated cells, would be able to discern the physiological mechanism that accounted for the terrible outcome she'd witnessed in the delivery room. A good pathol-ogist could determine why and when Michael Sabia died. A great one would be able to trace the events, like bloody shoe prints, that led from his death to little Tony's asphyxia. Humes thought perhaps the most capable person in the world for doing such an examination was Kurt Benirschke. She asked Clement to see if Schifrin could help get Benirschke to review the case. Schifrin apparently said he would, then mentioned it to Benirschke on the phone. Clement followed up with a letter, enclosing some of the material that Humes had sent him with the promise of more and asking Benirschke whether he would mind looking at it. Benirschke, for reasons Humes couldn't yet understand, never replied.

A few weeks later, on January 25, 1991, three months after Haskell's letter of mid-October, the Koskoffs again moved to extend the deadline for disclosing experts. Humes, disgusted, wondered if it would ever end.

Mike Koskoff also talked with Schifrin at about this time. Schifrin was an expert in several other cases for him, and Koskoff valued their growing association. He loved going out to dinner with him, getting his "bead" on things. He especially loved having him on the stand. Koskoff had seen Schifrin before breakfast, an hour before court, fail to remember the basic details of a case, then deliver brilliant, flawless testimony on cross-examination. A nineteenth-century editorialist once excoriated the "glorious uncertainty of legal justice and medical testimony." Koskoff thought Schifrin exploited those vagaries better than any physician he'd ever seen. He made cases. Koskoff thought he might be the best medical expert in the business.

Most doctors would consider that a dubious honor. The medical expert industry was rife with incompetent physicians. Some had lost their licenses. There were experts who took out full-page ads in legal journals, or who would say whatever lawyers told them to say—doctors who were fleeing, or had been kicked out of, medicine and saw legal work as a lucrative sinecure. They were doctors who high-end lawyers like Koskoff wouldn't touch.

Schifrin, by contrast, was a ranking academic physician who was—or had been, at least—a leader in his field. Within the malpractice industry, such figures held an almost mythical status. "Many recognized medical experts will not testify under any circumstances," Schifrin himself once wrote; "others are unavailable to the plaintiff." Yet Schifrin's early work with the development of electronic fetal monitoring (EFM) was widely considered pathbreaking even by his enemies. And though his tone was usually more sorrowful than angry, he seemed to relish testifying against doctors who ignored or abused EFM. Obstetricians routinely dismissed him as a publicity seeker, a mercenary, an apostate, an egotist, a whore, but they couldn't deny that he knew perhaps as much as anyone about diagnosing and treating fetal distress during child-birth.

Schifrin's willingness to criticize other doctors where they were most vulnerable, in court, made him highly unpopular with his peers, many of whom despised him even more than they despised the plaintiffs' lawyers who paid him $400 an hour to review cases. "I'm one of the bad guys," he would say. Yet their loathing was more than personal. The advent of fetal medicine—EFM, in particular—was so central to the evolution of modern obstetrics, and even more so to the explosion in malpractice suits against obstetricians, that the emergence of Schifrin or someone like him, a scourge-seer, was probably inevitable. "If Barry wasn't Barry," says Dr. Lawrence Longo, head of the division of perinatal biology at the Loma Linda University School of Medicine, "someone would have had to invent him."

Schifrin would genially concur. A bearish, intimidating man in his early fifties, he exudes a solemnity befitting someone who sees himself as a figure of destiny. He is unambiguously Jewish—Clement calls him "Rabbi"—and his polished Bronx baritone, Ben Franklin glasses, hooded eyes, salt-and-pepper beard, and tendency to pose philosophical questions to which he and perhaps only he has the answers, all attest to a talmudic turn of mind. In a larger sense, he sees himself as having been chosen as God's proxy and stooge in the fight over what makes bad babies bad. "This perverse trick has been played on me," he says, assuming the voice of the deity and intoning, " 'I'm going to show you something that nobody has ever seen—but nobody's going to believe you.' "

What Schifrin had seen was hardly new. It was that obstetricians, by properly monitoring and interpreting fetal heart tones during labor and delivery, can sometimes determine whether a child with an irregular heart rate is at risk of brain damage, and so take action to affect the outcome. What may be unique, though, is his interpretation. Unlike most obstetricians, he believes that doctors should *welcome* the added accountability that comes from being able to discern fetal behavior with EFM, even though, as he acknowledges, it's a notoriously poor predictor of brain injury. For a specialty that feels it has been brought to grief by that same vagary, the position is heretical.

The birth of EFM is generally credited to Dr. Edward Hon, who, while teaching at the Yale School of Medicine in1958, first reported that he had continuously recorded a fetal heart rate by attaching an electrode from a standard heart monitor, an EKG machine, to a woman's abdomen. Up until then, fetal heart monitoring was accomplished intermittently with auscultation—listening, usually with a stethoscope. Hon's device was crude—he would later develop and patent the first commercially available monitors, with their familiar electronic readouts and snaking fetal scalp clips—but with it he was able to probe reliably for the first time what Schifrin would later call "the bewildering array" of fetal heart-rate patterns during the critical hours just before birth. Over the next decade these patterns—fast, slow, variable, accelerated, decelerated—gave obstetricians their first ongoing look at the infant during labor, how it slept, woke, breathed, sucked, burped, moved and, especially, responded to stress.

Suddenly now doctors could *see,* with the heartbeat as their indicator, the minute-by-minute medical status of the babies they were about to deliver. They could determine more easily when something was going wrong and when to intervene. Said Hon, voicing proprietary optimism if not yet the shared opinion of his colleagues, "The fetal electrocardiogram provides a measure of obstetrical care that has never been achieved previously." Certainly, it made that care more complicated. Obstetricians now had to pay as close attention to the health of the fetus as to that of the mother, sharpening the therapeutic knife edge that was the hallmark of their field.

Hon worked for thirteen years researching and developing his new device, yet when he unveiled his first commercial model, in October 1968, reaction was subdued. The *New York Times* reported the announcement in a four-inch story at the bottom of page 78. Like many academic innovators, Hon, a 41-year-old Chinese-born associate professor, was prickly. His specialty—high-risk pregnancy—was new, and most older obstetricians still doubted its worth. His machine was ungainly—six feet tall with a cyclopean display, it was kept in an instrument room outside the delivery area, where doctors couldn't see it—and many patients were squeamish about the silver electrode that he inserted through a woman's cervix, then coiled like a fishhook into an unborn baby's head. The hundred or so obstetricians who came to New Haven to watch Hon demonstrate his new monitor could see that it might be useful, showing in certain difficult labors when a baby's heart rate was perilously fast or slow, although they usually could tell that with their stethoscopes. The rest of the information—the variations, speedups and slowdowns—was provocative. But without some understanding of what they meant over the long term, the data were unintelligible—noise.

A few young doctors were enthralled by EFM's potential and by Hon's confident prediction that it would revolutionize the practice of obstetrics. Schifrin, then thirty, was one of them. After attending Columbia as an undergraduate and Chicago Medical College, and after two residencies in New York, he'd turned down several invitations to go into private practice, opting instead for a surgical fellowship in Miami. In July he'd come to Yale on a second National Institutes of Health fellowship, this time in maternal-fetal medicine—high-risk obstetrics.

Casting around for a specialty, "looking for a father, a mentor," Schifrin quickly found both in Hon and his machine. EFM had generated exorbitant expectations. Its most optimistic boosters predicted that it would all but wipe out cerebral palsy, which for more than a century had been linked to problem births. Schifrin was skeptical, and he and Hon soon had a falling out. But from his first experiences with EFM, Schifrin knew what he would do in his career. He would try to elucidate the connections between fetal heart rate and fetal behavior. He would attempt to discern which heart patterns indicated that a baby's oxygen supply was compromised sufficiently to induce permanent brain damage. He would try to make sense of the noise.

During the next decade and a half, until the mid-eighties, Schifrin plunged into investigating the relationship between hypoxia and fetal brain injury, first at Harvard Medical School and Beth Israel Hospital in Boston, then at the University of Southern California School of Medicine and various Los Angeles teaching hospitals, including Cedars-Sinai, where he was associate director of ob-gyn. Collecting thousands of fetal monitoring strips—he eventually would possess perhaps the world's largest private library—he performed important studies concerning the subtle shifts that indicated whether a baby was at risk of permanent brain damage.

It was frustrating work, and ultimately inconclusive. The new technology, rather than giving a simple answer to a simple question—when does reduced oxygen to the fetus cause brain damage?—generated a mountain of new data, intermittent understanding, and a fog of new imponderables. Schifrin and others discovered that many babies with healthy heart rates were still born with permanent brain injuries. Others with dangerous-looking fluctuations who were born severely depressed survived with no neurological damage. Eventually, even Schifrin would concede: "The correlation between FHR patterns of hypoxia and subsequent neurologic handicap is poor—expectedly so. . . . Unfortunately we have yet to determine reliably how many babies are injured during labor, how many before, and what role if any EFM plays in the detection and prevention of injury."

Nowhere was this inconclusiveness more dismaying than to obstetricians. EFM had indeed revolutionized obstetrics. By 1980 most hospitals had the machines, and they were in constant demand by patients and doctors alike. Electronic monitoring couldn't always predict when a fetus was in danger, but it showed the *absence* of danger more accurately than any other diagnostic technique. Babies with normal heart patterns invariably were born live. With few false positives, EFM was the most reassuring way to know that a preborn infant was, if not entirely okay, at least not being fatally asphyxiated during delivery. The desire for such reassurance by everyone concerned made EFM a cornerstone of modern obstetrical practice, the de facto standard of care for all deliveries.

But EFM's wide acceptance wasn't what most alarmed obstetricians. Far more ominous was its role in stimulating a rash of malpractice suits against them. As long as there had been no way to show how babies reacted to the stress of labor and delivery, a bad obstetrical outcome was a classic black box—the cause of brain damage was anybody's guess. But EFM strips, the pen-scratched printouts pouring out of Hon's machines, represented a paper trail. In the delivery room they might not be reliable predictors of brain damage. But retrospectively, in court, they were the kind of evidence lawyers relished most. They showed quirks and aberrations, enough so that someone interpreting them could claim that the warnings of impending injury were all there, and that doctors and hospitals had violated their obligations to patients by not seeing them.

EFM had become so popular that not having strips could be as damning as having them. Meanwhile, plaintiffs' lawyers found in EFM a near-perfect foundation for bringing negligence suits, one that could be made to bolster their claims either way. By 1987, less than twenty years after EFM's introduction, more than 70 percent of ob-gyns reported they had been sued at least once, most in bad baby cases. One-third had been sued three times. Nationally, obstetrics claims totaled 10 percent of all malpractice claims and almost half of all indemnity payments, thus spurring the malpractice crises of the seventies and eighties. To obstetricians, long the most aggrieved of all physicians, it seemed bitterly ironic. EFM had promised them a tool to avert outcomes like Little Tony's, but it turned out to be far more useful for blaming them when such outcomes occurred. "If you have a baby with a problem," says Dr. Richard Jones III, former president of the American College of Obstetricians and Gynecologists, the obstetricians' trade group, "you know you will be sued."

How Schifrin, a leader in his field, could collaborate with plaintiffs' lawyers to ruin his colleagues was something many of them found unfathomable. Even worse, they thought, were his self-righteousness and the way he justified his behavior. By the late eighties, Schifrin believed more than ever that careful use of EFM and other fetal-monitoring techniques, despite their inherent ambiguities and flaws, were the profession's only salvation. As he pointed out tirelessly in speeches and articles, a doctor can make a mistake and still not be held liable if he or she has met the standard of care. And EFM, despite its flaws, was that standard.

Such public statements favoring a technology that he himself found wanting—yet exploited professionally—struck doctors as offensive enough. But Schifrin, a relentless polemicist, pushed still further, defending lawsuits and the lawyers who bring them. He told obstetricians that their knee-jerk hatred of plaintiffs' lawyers, their unscientific insistence that bad babies are created by God and rarely by themselves, their refusal to condemn incompetent colleagues, and, especially, the "outright perversion" of trying to fault litigious parents by means of their genealogies and habits, as a way of diverting blame, only served to discredit them.

"This sad and pathetic response diminishes not only the available statistics, but our colleagues and ourselves," he wrote in a column in the *Journal of Perinatology*. "Simply stated, if we cannot be responsible for contributing to injury, then there is nothing that we are protecting, and there is little value to our care."

≈ ≈ ≈

FEBRUARY 4, 1991

Ten days after the Koskoffs' latest request to delay announcing their experts, Mike Koskoff received an update on *Sabia*. Years later he would be unable to remember who'd prepared it for him or why, but the news it contained was discouraging and Koskoff wanted someone else to look at it. Within twenty-four hours he would leave for California to consult with medical experts in several cases, including *Sabia*. Scrawling a few notes on top, he dropped the report in his briefcase to show to Schifrin.

It was Koskoff's practice to consult several experts and play their opinions off each other. He claimed never to be concerned when one of them refuted him; he could always find others, just as credible, to agree. Still, there were times when his need to find liability was contradicted so strongly by one of his own consultants that he had to acknowledge the possibility that his case was weaker than he thought. So it was with this memo, which summarized the opinion of one expert. It could hardly have been more exculpatory if it had been written by Humes herself.

"In labor and delivery," the author wrote, "although it is unclear why fetal monitoring was never instituted, it was *not* absolutely required by the standard of care nor *would it have made any difference in the outcome of the labor* [italics added]. . . . Similarly, immediate cesarean section upon admittance to labor and delivery would have made little difference, as twin B was already deceased, and twin A reasonably already damaged."

The consultant's opinion regarding the hospital was more ambiguous. He said that because of the earlier unequal growth of the twins, Donna should have had follow-up ultrasounds and, perhaps, nonstress tests. These were used to assess how a baby was functioning at or near term by means of a monitor strapped to a woman's belly that recorded fetal heart tones for an extended period during normal movement. "With this follow-up," the author wrote, "the impending damage could have been anticipated *although not necessarily prevented.*"

Koskoff knew he had seen worse. Ever since he had read Forman's damage report and talked with Murray the previous August, his sense of the overall liability in *Sabia* had shifted. He now thought their strongest case was against Norwalk Hospital for not treating Donna adequately during her pregnancy; specifically, its failure to perform repeat ultrasounds during her last trimester. He wasn't surprised to see Humes largely exonerated, even though he would maintain that the consultant's position that a C-section would have made "little difference" was actually an endorsement, since "little" difference meant "some" difference, which was all he needed to hold Humes in.

It was the hospital, as the larger prize, that Koskoff wanted Schifrin's bead on. Sometime before they got together, he or someone else crossed out the phrase "although not necessarily prevented." Though the issue of prevention was critical—if there was nothing the hospital could have done to change the outcome, how could it be negligent?—it apparently was this sanitized version that he and Schifrin discussed.

Schifrin told Koskoff what the defense was likely to make of his expert's interpretation. Doubtless, he said, the hospital would say that the acute bleeding that had apparently caused Little Tony's brain damage had nothing to do with his weighing more than his twin three months earlier and that late-stage serial ultrasounds—the centerpiece of Koskoff's negligence theory—were a nonissue. The hospital wasn't required to do them, and even if it had been, the results wouldn't have anticipated a sudden loss of blood from one twin into the other in the wake of the second twin's death due to a cord accident. Although this was a reasonable argument, Schifrin dismissed it. If the hospital had done ultrasounds, he said, it would have seen that Twin B wasn't thriving and would have ordered additional fetal surveillance before Donna went into labor. Doctors would have hooked Donna up to a fetal monitor, seen that Michael Sabia was in trouble, and acted, thereby preventing the disaster that followed.

Here was Schifrin's contribution to Koskoff's unified theory, which so far targeted the hospital for failing to monitor the twins but provided no explanation of how such a failure had caused Little Tony's brain damage. In healthy fetuses the heart rate is an exquisitely sensitive barometer of life in the womb, bouncing up when the baby moves even slightly. Given that Michael Sabia was growth-retarded and about to die, Schifrin said, his heart pattern would *had to have* been sluggish—"nonreactive." A nonstress test on Friday, March 30, the day Donna was last seen by McManamy at the clinic, would have been flat, he predicted. Competent doctors would have read this unresponsiveness as a possible sign of distress and have done more tests to reassure themselves that it was okay to wait for Donna to go into labor before delivering the twins. That, Schifrin said, is what the clinic had done wrong, and why it should be faulted.

Koskoff accepted Schifrin's logic despite knowing he might have difficulty using it in court. Even if a nonstress test had been done, Schifrin's conclusion that it would have been "nonreactive" was speculative at best. Who knew what Michael Sabia's heart rate might have shown during a random twenty minutes of screening a day before he suddenly died? Or how it would have been interpreted? Or whether the hospital would have been able to salvage him and also save Little Tony? Ultrasounds, which Koskoff was prepared to say were required by the standard of care, would no doubt have shown that the twins were of different sizes and perhaps that one twin was less active than the other, but not—this was vital—that either twin was in danger. Koskoff liked to keep cases simple. He may have worried about he tortured logic of arguing that what the hospital should have done wouldn't have made any difference, while what it might have done probably would.

But Schifrin was unequivocal. He prided himself both on his legal sophistication and his ability to educate lawyers, even knowledgeable ones like Koskoff. He especially enjoyed devising legal strategies. In civil actions, he knew, the standard of proof allowed uncertainties that would be untenable in criminal cases. A civil-case jury had only to conclude that there was a hair more likelihood that the plaintiffs were right in order to find in their favor. "More probable than not," was the phrase.

Schifrin's own version of this doctrine was a distinctive brand of retrospective analysis—Schifrin's Law, he called it—which he based on hindsight and what he liked to refer to, philosophically, as "cascading probabilities." It worked like this. Since the one thing that absolutely would have saved Little Tony was not having his twin brother die, and since the only thing that could have prevented that from happening was if Michael Sabia was delivered on the day of Donna's last clinic visit or sooner; and since what would have been necessary for doctors to decide to take the twins early by C-section was some medical justification for doing so, the key question was: "Is it more probable than not that Baby B would have had an abnormal heart rate on March 30?"

Absolutely, Schifrin told Koskoff. Because Michael Sabia was a pound lighter than Little Tony at birth, he said, the child was probably protected by less fetal water than his brother. Since this disparity would have shown up on an ultrasound, the hospital probably would have done a nonstress test, to see if the deprived twin was okay. Since he probably wasn't, his heart rate probably would have been abnormal. Cascading probabilities.

"So what was the hospital's crime?" Schifrin asked inescapably, eyeing Koskoff with a mixture of sagaciousness and glee. "Not providing the information. It was possible to know all this was about to occur, indeed cheap and easy to know, and they still didn't do it." According to Schifrin's Law, *Sabia* was a cold case of original sin, the common sin underlying most malpractice cases—medical hubris. Disaster had been lurking, but the hospital didn't know about it because, trusting its own inadequate procedures, it had failed to look.

After hearing Schifrin, Koskoff knew he had what had evaded the firm for four years: a full-blown theory of medical injury firmly implicating the hospital. A triable case. And though Humes was no longer the central figure, she wasn't excluded either. Within weeks the Koskoffs would end the delaying that had sidetracked the case for more than fifteen months and that had kept Humes from surrendering in a weak moment. On March 11, in a document filed in Bridgeport Superior Court, Bernard disclosed the medical experts the plaintiffs planned to call to trial.

There were four: Marcus Hermansen, the Pittsburgh resuscitation specialist, who would testify about Little Tony's condition at birth and the timing and progression of his injuries; Tom Murray, Koskoff's prized obstetrical expert, who would address Donna's treatment and how it had violated the standard of care for twin pregnancies; Kurt Benirschke, who would lay out the timing of Little Tony's injuries and the mechanism relating it to Michael's death; and, to Humes's dismay, Schifrin, to explain the causal connection between Donna's treatment and the damages suffered by her and Little Tony. The doctor whose opinion formed the basis for the February memo was excluded. Others would later be added to the list. But for now, Koskoff thought, this lineup would more than do.

TWELVE

What is a birth trauma case worth? If the child, as a result of the injury is severely retarded, paralyzed, wholly dependent upon others for survival, blind, seriously deformed, or otherwise so permanently injured as to require constant care and attention throughout a life devoid of most human pleasure, self-reliance and hope, then at trial the attorney for the plaintiffs should be unafraid to ask for seven to ten million dollars, can hope for a verdict of five to seven million dollars, but should reasonably expect a verdict of one and a half to three million dollars.

Lurking in the shadows of each [insurance] adjuster's nightmares is the horrible possibility that a jury might find his insured to be the only culpable party, leaving his company responsible for the full amount of plaintiff's damages. Thus, self-interest spurs multiple defendants, if separately insured, to actively seek an equitable settlement. An interest in self-preservation also causes each of the defendants to point a finger at each other at trial. . . .

Handling Birth Trauma Cases
Stanley Schwartz and Norman Tucker, Esq.

Disclosing his A-list of experts was a watershed for Koskoff. It announced his seriousness, grabbed the other side's attention, and raised the ante. It certified his determination to go to trial and signaled that his clients must be respected. Koskoff could predict the apprehension the lawyers for the other sides would feel upon seeing Schifrin's and, especially, Benirschke's names.

They would realize they had been trumped. It was a rare moment of theater in the otherwise interminable business of bringing a case to court.

He followed with another. During the next two days, March 12 and 13, 1991, Bernard filed two separate "offers of judgment" in Bridgeport Superior Court. Aimed at Norwalk Hospital and Humes, these were largely settlement devices, legal notification of what the Sabias would accept to drop their case. There had been no real talk of settling, either among the parties or between the Koskoffs and Tony and Donna; publicly, all sides remained staunch about wanting a trial. But in the calculus of any malpractice action, settlement had to be considered. Ninety percent of all malpractice cases settled, and doctors won 90 percent of those that went to court. No trial lawyer, even one as sanguine as Koskoff, could disregard these figures.

An offer of judgment started the clock on settlement negotiations whether both sides were interested or not, and it was one of the few tools available to plaintiffs to begin such discussions, in effect by announcing their willingness to settle for, and only for, a stated price, then forcing the other side to respond. Such offers were notoriously unrealistic, but defendants had to treat them seriously. If they refused, and a verdict ultimately matched or exceeded the plaintiffs' offer, they would have to pay for any added losses due to the delay. Explains Koskoff, "What we wanted to say to the defendants and their insurance companies was, 'We think if we go to trial, we're going to get more than this. If you don't accept, you could end up on the hook not only for the verdict, but 12 percent a year for the difference.'" The offers of judgment against the hospital and Humes were $15 million and $2 million, respectively, the top limits of their insurance coverage.

If Koskoff now gloated at the prospect of a big victory, that was typical. Once he'd figured out a case, it often became the best case he'd ever had. He boasted about it and acted as if he couldn't lose. What he didn't know didn't worry him, at least not this long before trial. Not so Bernard. Most birth trauma cases in his experience were "black and white": a protracted labor, a distressed fetus, a negligent doctor, brain damage. But that wasn't the case here. There were still big gaps. Notwithstanding Schifrin's opinion, the causal connection between the hospital's alleged negligence and Little Tony's injuries was doubtful at best. Their case against Humes was weakening. More prone to worry than Koskoff, Bernard believed they'd eventually be able to prove shared liability, but feared that "we were making it up as we went along."

He worried especially about Humes. The more it appeared that the hospital was at fault prior to Donna's labor, the less likely he thought a jury would be to blame her. Unlike Koskoff, he doubted that they could hold the hospital and Humes equally to account. That would mean having to sort out and quantify Little Tony's injuries—day by day, hour by hour—then specify who was to blame for each and to what extent. They would have to offer evidence, for instance, that Little Tony was blind, quadriplegic, and mentally retarded because of the hospital's misconduct, but couldn't speak or eat because of Humes's. Lawyers who argue in front of juries like to keep cases crisp, saying, "Here's what happened. Here's the damages." Bernard worried that by injecting degrees of culpability he and Koskoff were creating a scenario where they might have to let Humes out of the case, leaving an "empty chair" at trial.

Of all possible outcomes, this troubled Bernard the most: a jury knowing that one defendant had been excused while the other blasted away at her in her absence. With the hospital's lawyers heaping responsibility onto a phantom, he and Koskoff would be forced to—what?—defend Humes? Say there was nothing that she could do, that the damage had been done before she arrived? That they'd been wrong in their original complaint? Bernard believed Murray that Humes was somehow complicit. But he fretted that by shifting the case too strongly toward the hospital he and Koskoff inadvertently had eroded the delicate balance that held it together. They were pulling two ends toward the middle, and in between was thin air.

On March 18, less than a week after filing the offers of judgment, he and Koskoff drove together to New Jersey to try to shore up Koskoff's unified theory. Arriving at the New Jersey Medical School in Newark, they first visited the office of Dr. Joseph Apuzzio, a respected perinatologist whom Lichtenstein had identified in his literature search the previous August. A decade earlier Apuzzio had contributed a chapter on twin pregnancies to a medical textbook and more recently had coauthored another book on obstetrical surgery. Though eager to help, he was less than supportive. Having reviewed several hundred pages of documents that Bernard had sent him, he told them there was no question that Donna's pregnancy was high-risk, even by the hospital's own protocols, and that he was angry that it hadn't been treated as such. Like Schifrin, he believed the hospital should have done third-trimester ultrasounds to assess fetal well-being and that there was a "reasonable medical probability"—legal code for "more than likely"—that a nonstress test at Donna's last clinic visit would have had an abnormal result.

Apuzzio hedged, however, on the issue of standard of care. Had late-stage serial ultrasounds been required by the norms of good medical practice? That was the irreducible question the Koskoffs would have to answer affirmatively to show that the hospital had been negligent during Donna's pregnancy. Apuzzio didn't think so. He noted that although Schifrin believed that the earlier discrepancy in the twins' sizes obligated the hospital to follow up, his own chapter in *Principles and Practices of Obstetrics and Perinatology*, published in 1982, two years before Donna's treatment, made no mention of discordant growth. By the late eighties, discordancy had become a recognized risk factor requiring increased fetal surveillance. But what mattered, legally, was whether in early 1984, at a community hospital like Norwalk's, an average obstetrician should have known that a history of discordancy increased both the chance of a bad medical outcome and a doctor's responsibility to try to prevent it. Apuzzio said no.

Apuzzio also had no criticism of Humes. He thought she'd been stuck with an impossible situation and had acted reasonably under the circumstances. Moreover, he told Koskoff and Bernard, she was involved too late; the damage had already been done. If anyone at the birth was at fault, he said, it was Barbara McManamy, the nurse-midwife. Reading McManamy's deposition and comparing it to the hospital's rules and procedures, he concluded that her claim that she had no independent responsibility to care for Donna was, in Bernard's word, "garbage."

Bernard failed to conceal his dismay. Standard of care was the linchpin of any malpractice action. As Schifrin never tired of telling his peers, a doctor could err, kill patients, and be dead wrong time and again, but was not legally at fault if he or she had met the criteria of the profession. To escape blame, doctors and hospitals didn't need to be brilliant, just average and current. Unlike the law, standard of care wasn't fixed and immutable but a rough amalgam of what most doctors were doing at the time, what medical schools were teaching, what textbooks said, and what had been reported in medical journals. In obstetrics, in the eighties, the standard of care for twin pregnancies changed year to year as the ability to monitor fetuses sharpened diagnoses and suggested more aggressive interventions. But because of that rapid progress, the exact date when specific protocols became the norm was an open question. Bernard suddenly had the feeling that he and Koskoff might be working without a net.

Their next appointment, in the same medical center, was with Dr. Leslie Iffy. Iffy was a collaborator of Apuzzio's, a Hungarian immigrant and coauthor both of Apuzzio's recent textbook and of the earlier text to which he had contributed a chapter. A lavish host who likes to provide steaks and drinks at depositions, he suggested that rather than talk at his office they drive out to his house, in nearby Summit. The three climbed into Iffy's gold Mercedes and soon arrived at his rambling "stockbroker Tudor" on Summit's posh north side. With massive stone chimneys and leaded, diamond-pane casement windows, the house had been built in the 1920s, when Wall Street's newest barons strove to appear as if they'd come from Old Money. It was adjoined by a three-car garage that Bernard learned also housed a Jaguar.

According to Bernard, Iffy, who had not reviewed any materials in the case, listened to Koskoff recite the details and was instantly supportive. Bernard found this somewhat disconcerting. Often consultants will ask for time to do independent research before offering an opinion, but Iffy "jumped on board." Recalls Bernard, "He had all the right answers." Bernard didn't

doubt Iffy's conclusions, but was skeptical, given Apuzzio's sobering evaluation earlier in the day. At the same time, Iffy's persona began to worry him. He
was exaggeratedly friendly and polite, but his smile seemed forced. His house
was dark inside, with a large painting of a female nude in the study, and he
kept dogs "the size of horses" that Bernard recalls filled the rooms with a powerful stench. "You could die in there," Bernard would say. "It wasn't the picture
of the witness we wanted." As it turned out, Iffy "spent more time in court and
[on] depositions than I do," Bernard says. "Some enormous percentage of his
income came from medical-legal work." Despite his misgivings, Bernard and
Koskoff decided to disclose Iffy as an expert, but privately Bernard hoped they
wouldn't need him at trial.

On the way back to Connecticut, Bernard was "despondent," he says. If
Apuzzio was right, and serial ultrasounds weren't strictly part of the standard
of care, it didn't matter that if by using them doctors might have diagnosed
Michael Sabia's distress. The case could unravel before they ever got to offer
such a speculative proposition in court. Koskoff, he knew, had become skilled
in cases where the standard of care was in flux or a new standard seemed to
obviate an older one. He encouraged juries to set their own standards of care,
to decide, after hearing all the evidence, what reasonable doctors should have
done under the circumstances. But if Pat Ryan came to trial arguing that as
badly as he felt for the Sabias, no doctor at the time would have been expected
to anticipate their problems, he could trump such a bald appeal. Juries liked
doctors. A doctor who'd followed the rules was almost unassailable. "Who's
the most sympathetic figure in the courtroom?" Schifrin often asked rhetorically. Answer: the sorrowing doctor who'd adhered to the standard of care.

As for Apuzzio's sympathy toward Humes, Bernard agonized: how were
they going to hold her in? Finally, after four years, they'd cobbled together a
workable theory and assembled a core of experts whose testimony almost, but
not quite, corroborated it. They'd just gone hard at the other side, demanding
a total of $17 million. And yet of two leading experts they'd hoped would so-
lidify their case, one exonerated the defendants and the other, in Bernard's
opinion, was unpresentable.

Where was the case? Not knowing made Bernard uneasy. He wasn't a born
advocate like Koskoff; he needed to be convinced a cause was right before he
embraced it. With his friendly face and earnest-college-student demeanor,
Bernard had about him a niceness he couldn't shake even if he wanted to. He
wasn't a shark and took care not to be construed as one, which meant bringing solid, worthy cases and being merciful when fairness dictated. Koskoff, on
the other hand, never seemed conflicted. He was too much a creature of the
trial lawyers' rough-and-tumble—too much of an impresario—to appear to
worry about ignoring unpleasant truths.

Bernard wanted to help the Sabias gain something for their suffering, but in order to do that he had to clear certain hurdles. Grimly, he wondered if he was anywhere close.

≈ ≈ ≈

April Haskell apprised St. Paul of the Koskoffs' latest moves just as Bernard began to worry that he and Koskoff had overreached. On March 18, the day of the meetings with Iffy and Apuzzio, Haskell mailed the company the Koskoffs' offer of judgment and list of experts, along with a two-page letter outlining her progress in *Sabia*. The letter was cautious and self-protective— not the impression Haskell likes to give in person. She had worked her way up in Connecticut's medmal defense bar by being conscientious, a night-school-educated Jewish woman breaching what seemed like a club of shrewd, blustery, mostly Irish-American men. But she was a lawyer telling an unhappy client bad news, and she protected herself by working hard not to offend. Haskell knew nothing, of course, of the Koskoffs' difficulties, only that by asking for the policy limit they had set Humes and St. Paul irrevocably against each other and that she now was in the middle.

The Koskoffs' filings were "fairly significant," Haskell wrote, downplaying their importance. If St. Paul refused the offer of judgment, then went to court and lost, it could wind up paying more than Humes's coverage. Meanwhile, she added, Humes's private counsel also now wanted St. Paul to "settle the matter immediately within the policy limit." As Haskell knew but didn't say, this last was to be expected. Bai and Sacco had one job—to protect Humes's personal assets. Now that the Sabias had offered to settle for Humes's policy, the best way for Bai and Sacco to do their job was to press St. Paul to pay the full amount. Haskell didn't need to point out the irony that Humes and the Sabias were now making the same demand. Or that both were offering to end their dispute but couldn't because St. Paul wouldn't agree to it. For plaintiffs the strategic value of an offer of judgment was that it gave them a common interest with those they were suing, increasing their leverage against insurance companies. It drove a wedge into the other side in hopes of splitting it.

Haskell herself still wanted to go forward with Humes's defense; she thought Humes had been "sandbagged" by the hospital and was too proud to give up without a fight. But she now cautioned St. Paul that it was "somewhat difficult to predict" whether they could win in court. "We do not really know from the disclosure [of experts] what they were going to say with respect to Dr. Humes," she wrote. "Unfortunately, we have not yet been able to find a medical expert who is tremendously supportive of our position.

"My instincts tell me," Haskell cautioned, "that our best defense in this case is the fact that Dr. Humes came on the scene so late, but that it is likely that a jury is going to find in the Plaintiff's favor in this matter, and that the award is going to be significant. I would expect that both Norwalk Hospital and Dr. Humes will end up being held in, although there is some possibility that Dr. Humes will escape liability."

Haskell's ambivalence reflected her role. Deeply involved yet ultimately powerless, she was a conduit. She had no independent authority—even now she had to ask St. Paul for permission to begin deposing the Sabias' experts to find out what they thought Humes had done wrong—yet she was talking regularly, confidentially, with people who didn't talk to each other. Humes and St. Paul's claims people never communicated directly, and neither spoke to the experts Haskell was cultivating on their behalf. Haskell spoke with Sacco, but not, ordinarily, with Humes. Meanwhile, Haskell talked often with Bev Hunt, equivalently situated as a go-between for Ryan's office, the hospital, Travelers, and the hospital's experts. Haskell knew perhaps more about the case than anyone else on the defense, yet she was so restricted in how she could proceed that she seemed to hedge even when she didn't mean to.

Humes, who already distrusted her, reacted peevishly to the letter and what she saw as Haskell's less-than-gallant defense of her. Why, she wondered, couldn't Haskell make clear to St. Paul and the other lawyers what was so patently obvious—that she, Humes, had arrived at the scene of a disaster long after anything could be done about it, that she'd been scapegoated by the boys' club, that the Koskoffs were persecuting her because they thought she was an easy mark? Humes was coming to the conclusion that Haskell's inability to find experts to support her revealed nothing more than incompetence. With each copied letter she received, she grimaced at Haskell's deference to her faceless handlers at St. Paul. "Your insured," those letters now called Humes, as if she were a burden.

Haskell shoved her own feelings about Humes aside, though they, too, were becoming sulfuric. She was deeply worried about putting Humes in front of a jury. Humes was inconsistent, her recollections varied, and her resistance to admitting she'd done anything untoward came off as defensive. One day Humes called and said she wanted to settle; three days later she said she wanted to fight on at all costs. Some days Humes would be buoyant on the phone, telling her about the work she was having done on her house. Other days she would say she didn't care anymore, that the experience of being sued had so poisoned her desire to be a doctor that she was ready to quit. She would go work in the Third World, become a clinic doctor on an Indian reservation, volunteer someplace where she was valued. Haskell worried "which Maryellen would show up in court": the self-pitying victim or the fighter; the Westport home-and-garden doyenne or the long-suffering Che Guevara–style romantic. When Humes mentioned the Indian reservation, Haskell would try to counsel her gently, saying, "Is that really a viable alternative for you?" But more and more, she just rolled her eyes. And will you be taking these lovely things that you have in your home to the Indian reservation, too? she thought.

Haskell believed Humes was "much more psychologically affected" by being sued than most doctors would have been, that *Sabia* had become "a blight on her life," but that "when push came to shove" she wouldn't desert her practice because she couldn't really live on less than she was earning. Her identity couldn't handle it. "This case had a huge significance for her as to how she viewed herself and how she felt viewed by the world," Haskell says. Instinctively a fighter, she was torn. She wanted badly to win for Humes at trial, but weighing everything together, she now resolved, like Bai, to do all she could to settle the case—for Humes's own good, she says. There were still problems: Humes, regarding as patronizing any suggestion that she knuckle under, might dig in, and St. Paul still needed to be convinced to pay out top dollar before the other side's experts even had been deposed. Haskell knew that she was mediating between an aggrieved doctor and a malpractice carrier that didn't think it should be indemnifying her, that while representing both she was trusted by neither. But with the offer of judgment she now saw her first real chance to maneuver them together.

On April 1, Little Tony's seventh birthday, Bai himself intervened, ostensibly at Humes's behest. In what lawyers call a "bad faith" letter to St. Paul's Connecticut claims manager Michael Kaufman, he wrote: "This case should definitely be settled. The plaintiff's demand is reasonable under the circumstances. If necessary, we will not hesitate to pursue action against St. Paul for damages arising out of its continuing unwarranted refusal to deal fairly with Dr. Humes."

Delivered by certified mail, the letter was a naked threat. If St. Paul, by holding out, invited a verdict greater than Humes's policy limit, thereby putting her at risk financially, Bai would sue the company. Besides what it might end up paying in *Sabia*, St. Paul could be on the hook for additional damages to Humes, plus Bai's legal costs. Like the plaintiffs' offer of judgment that preceded it, the letter was meant to apply pressure by raising the specter of a costly future—precisely what insurance companies exist to avoid. Haskell had been faithful about trying to represent two clients with objectively opposing interests, but with Bai's letter, she also now had her own stake to protect. It was possible, given the litigious climate, that if she didn't respond seriously to the Koskoffs' offer, her clients could wind up suing each other or even her and Montstream. But then a glimmer of compromise came from a surprise corner: Bev Hunt. Commiserating by phone on April 5, two weeks after Haskell had notified St. Paul of the offer of judgment, Hunt told her that the hospital wanted to settle.

To a striking degree, Hunt's situation mirrored Haskell's. The hospital and Travelers agreed that, facts aside, they didn't want to go to court, and

Hunt, too, was having difficulty finding experts to support the quality of Donna's care. More, the Koskoffs' settlement offer of $15 million had laid bare certain long-suppressed tensions: Norwalk Hospital was the defendant, but Travelers bore the lion's share of the exposure; Ryan and Hunt were the hospital's lawyers, yet no one in the company knew them; Hunt, like Haskell, a junior attorney unknown by the principals, was handling the brunt of the case. Papering their conversation that afternoon in a letter to St. Paul, Haskell noted Hunt's predicament, though she could have been writing about her own: "Though she is attempting to get experts to support the Hospital's position, she believes that this is simply to posture the case for settlement purposes, and that under no circumstances does she believe that the case ought to be tried. She is going to talk to The Travelers as to what kind of dollars they are willing to pay on the case, and get back to me."

After four years of litigation, the pieces were now in place for Haskell to start feeling out the Koskoffs about their price for releasing Humes from *Sabia*. With multiple defendants, the one willing to negotiate first invariably gains strength: better to move, Haskell thought, than be left out as Ryan, the hospital, and Travelers sought to make their own deal. She would have liked to have an enthusiastic cadre of experts to counter the Koskoffs', but she didn't feel desperate either. A consultant at Harvard and one at Yale had indicated they might testify despite their misgivings about Humes's handling of the delivery, although the Yale expert had ties to Norwalk Hospital that might prevent him from criticizing it. "We felt we had a case to put on," Haskell would say. "We weren't going to be sucking our thumbs."

Haskell had talked with Hunt on Friday, April 5. On Monday, she called Humes and the two spoke for almost an hour. Far from agreeable, as Haskell might have expected, Humes was contentious. She demanded to know why she hadn't gotten a copy of the Koskoffs' witness list or the offer of judgment. When Haskell told her about her difficulty in finding experts to defend her, Humes chafed. What about Dan Clement? she said. Wouldn't he testify? Hadn't Haskell's experts seen her letter to nurse Geri Falcone, two days after Donna's delivery, which described how the dead twin already was decomposing? What else did they need to place her at a safe distance from the events that had harmed Little Tony Sabia?

Now that conditions were becoming ripe for settlement, Humes seemed more adamant than ever about going ahead with the case, and Haskell worried about her unwillingness to stick to her earlier vow. She papered this conversation, too, as many lawyers now did with their phone calls with clients, dictating the next day a three-page confidential letter, copied to Sacco and St.

Paul, in which she tried to answer Humes's concerns. Carefully worded, most of it was an analysis of Humes's letter to Falcone. Humes believed the letter vindicated her, but Haskell, after reviewing it, found it damning, especially when compared with her second written account to Feller's peer review committee two and a half years later.

All Haskell's complaints about Humes now converged. In the letter to Falcone, she noted, Humes's only mention of checking fetal heart rates was her suggestion to one of the nurses, after Little Tony was born, to try to locate the heartbeat of the remaining twin. But in her letter to Feller, Humes had written that Little Tony's heartbeat was found to be normal when the ultrasound was done, prior to his delivery. Similarly, in the first letter she didn't mention Donna's thrashing and combative behavior; in the second, she blamed it squarely for her inability to monitor the twins. "The fact that this is lacking from your first letter might cause the jury to believe that it was 'fabricated' . . . years later," Haskell told Humes. Actually, she wrote, she hadn't shown the first letter to prospective experts at all, since doing so would make it part of the legal record and thus discoverable by the Koskoffs, whom she preferred to know nothing about it.

Humes, because she had written the letters for different purposes—the first to review Fortuna's actions, the second her own—saw no contradiction. But Haskell disagreed. "It is these types of discrepancies," Haskell wrote, "which are probably totally explainable between ourselves, but not entirely understandable to a jury, which cause us to be extremely cautious about releasing these documents." "[Humes's] recollections weren't always crisp and accurate," Haskell would later say, elaborating, "which didn't mean that she was a bad doctor, just that she was going to look bad in front of a jury."

After their phone call Haskell checked to see why Clement hadn't been retained as an expert, and here, too, her finding dismayed Humes. It turned out that Montstream had contacted Clement early on, but that Clement had criticized Humes for not knowing that one twin was dead and the other in distress. "Although Dr. Clement wished to be helpful to your position," Haskell wrote, "he had too many concerns about the care rendered at the hospital to make us feel that we could use him as an adequate witness on your behalf."

If their relationship could get no worse, it was hard now to see how it could get any better. Humes was at a dead end: she felt Haskell had failed her, and even her old friend Dan Clement seemed to think she was damaged goods. Haskell, for her part, felt saddled with a rogue client. Uncomfortable with Humes's veracity and unable to count on her cooperation, she hoped to settle before the case blew up on her. The two had yet to come face-to-face, yet were so estranged that long after they finally met several weeks later, in Sacco's office, with Sacco and Marlene Smethurst, a St. Paul claims representative, Humes would swear she didn't know what Haskell looked like: she'd never seen the woman, she said. "That was typical," Haskell would say, "of the concerns I had about her."

But by then Haskell's desire to settle had turned more urgent. On April 11, the day after she wrote to Humes, she and Bernard went to trial against each other in a case in Waterbury, and during a break in the jury selection they discussed *Sabia*. Bernard told her that the $2 million offer of judgment against Humes was a "take figure"—what they were counting on—while the $15 million offer against the hospital was a "demand."

The next day the two of them talked again by phone, and Bernard, after consulting with Koskoff, elaborated. He said the total demand in the case was $15 million and that he was willing to negotiate separately with the hospital. He also said he would consider discounting something from Humes's policy as part of a package deal if the overall figure remained adequate. Haskell asked him what he meant. He said he thought the $11 million that Larry Forman forecast for Little Tony's medical expenses was realistic, so the total for settling would have to be in the $11 million to $15 million range. In other words, Humes could possibly get away with paying less if the hospital paid more. (Later that day, Bev Hunt, unaware of Haskell's discussions with Bernard, would call Haskell to say that Travelers was interested in settling the case, and had set aside $5 million.)

Haskell no longer had time for Humes's feelings, or her own. Unexpectedly in active negotiations, she now had figures to present to St. Paul—figures which, while miles apart, were nonetheless a start. Each side in a settlement negotiation started with an unrealistic figure, bluffed, then tried to calculate how far up or down the other would go to reach a compromise. That would be straightforward enough if Humes had been the sole defendant, but the hospital was a wild card. Haskell still didn't know how the Koskoffs' experts would try to apportion fault, and how that would affect each side's liability.

As she and Bernard talked, she tried to plum his rationale for a package settlement. Because he and Koskoff were now emphasizing Donna's prenatal treatment, she thought their case against Humes might be weaker than he let on. But she also was concerned about the "agency" issue that had first troubled Pat Ryan years earlier. Humes had been dragged into the Sabias' lives solely at the hospital's behest, because she was on-call at the clinic. If the Koskoffs were going to claim that Norwalk Hospital was responsible for her negligence, making it assume liability for her actions, the hospital could very well turn around and sue her. For Haskell, the key question was, what would the plaintiffs' experts say Humes had done wrong and how had that contributed to Little Tony's injuries?

She asked Bernard outright. As she recalls, he told her that "all" of the Koskoffs' experts were prepared to testify that "there were no problems" with Little Tony until the labor process. According to her notes, he also told her that these experts would say that Humes had breached the standard of care by not monitoring Donna continuously and taking the twins sooner by C-section, and that in so doing she was liable for Little Tony's injuries. Haskell was stunned. "I don't doubt that Chris was mincing his words very finely," she recalls, but she inferred from Bernard's comments that he meant to include the placental pathologist Kurt Benirschke. It was Benirschke who had theorized that Little Tony's bleeding into his dead brother had caused his brain damage. Although Haskell and Hunt continued to try to recruit experts to contradict him, either by saying the cause was genetic or the result of earlier bleeding into Donna, that, Haskell knew, was for posturing purposes. There was no longer any question that Benirschke, whom all three sides had tried to hire, was right, only whether the damage was ongoing and cumulative. If Benirschke was going to testify that Little Tony was harmed right up until the birth, Haskell knew it would be a huge blow to Humes's defense.

In fact, Haskell was misinformed. Benirschke had long felt that all of the damage to Little Tony occurred before Humes arrived on the scene, and he had told Koskoff so. "If the doctor's in," Koskoff recalls Benirschke saying, "I don't want to have anything to do with it." Koskoff had had to choose; either get Humes out of the case before Benirschke was deposed, or risk losing his star witness and main weapon against the hospital. Later Koskoff would dismiss Haskell's belief that Benirschke would implicate Humes as a "misunderstanding"—"spin," he calls it. And Bernard, who has no recollection of the discussion with Haskell, says it would have been "very foolish" to represent in detail how a yet-to-be-deposed expert might testify and that he is "absolutely sure" he didn't do so. But the two sides were now operating under opposing assumptions. Koskoff, if not Bernard, feared that Benirschke would actually exonerate Humes in his testimony; Haskell that Benirschke was "going to tube my doctor."

Haskell put down the phone and concluded that, her personal troubles with Humes aside, she needed to move *Sabia* now, before Benirschke's deposition. If Benirschke was going to testify as Bernard seemed to suggest, there simply was no way left to defend Humes's actions, and Haskell didn't want to wait to learn what else the Koskoffs had in store for her. Scrambling, she searched for a way out that would satisfy both Humes and St. Paul.

Her best hope, she thought, was that Bernard had yet to give the hospital the same preview of Benirschke's opinions he had given her. Benirschke still hadn't been deposed, none of the medical experts had. As soon as he testified—his deposition was scheduled within a few weeks—Haskell knew she would lose any edge she had. The hospital would no doubt turn more aggressively against Humes, claiming that since she was independently at fault for some of Little Tony's damages, she should have to pay. And that in turn would increase the pressure on St. Paul to endorse her policy for the full amount. Time was crucial. If Haskell could settle soon, she thought, she could protect

Humes from a second-front attack by the hospital while saving St. Paul something off her coverage.

The next day she wrote to St. Paul's Smethurst, barely disguising her urgency. "I have some concern about leaving Dr. Humes in the lawsuit for any longer period of time," she wrote, "as I'm concerned that the Hospital may decide to file a cross-claim against her while she is still a party. I would therefore like to get this resolved as quickly as possible so that I can file a withdrawal of action and have the matter concluded." The window would remain open only until Benirschke testified or until Bernard, for reasons of his own, told the hospital's lawyers what he had told her. After that, Haskell believed, all bets were off.

The foyer of Tony and Donna's house was small and carpeted, a narrow platform connecting two sets of half-stairs, one up, one down. Rising on one side to a wrought-iron railing, it adjoined the living room. The ceiling was twelve feet high. On a day in July, Tony stood on top of a ladder, fixing a crack, then fell, breaking his foot in eight places. He grabbed a joint compound bucket, hopped to the kitchen, filled the bucket with ice, and plunged his foot to the bottom. It swelled massively, doubling in size. For the next several weeks he was on crutches and unable to work. During this time he and Donna fought more than usual. Bad as things were when he worked all the time, they were worse when he didn't. During one fight Donna picked up one of his crutches, took it outside, smashed it on the porch railing, and came back to show him the two pieces.

Tony took off after her. He flew down the half-stairs, barely touching them, he says. Chasing her out through the front door, he hurdled a bush and their white picket fence. "If I caught her, I'd have killed her," Tony says. An hour later Donna came back with a new pair of crutches.

Hostility now raged between them. Ever since Tony had shot the hole in his truck and Donna had called the police, they'd been at each other. Everything was so bad, always. In eight years they'd never gotten a break. They never had any time as a couple, or with the kids. They never talked about their feelings about Little Tony, yet because of him they were neglecting the other children, who showed it. Shannon, now a teenager, was acting out, staying out nights, causing trouble at school, socializing with a dangerous crowd. The other two girls had the kind of unfocused, unkempt look that was a red flag for social workers. The family never had enough money, and to keep from going under, Tony recently had borrowed against the house, taking a home improvement loan. Every day the pressure built, and Tony and Donna, beyond burnout, seethed at each other.

Several weeks after Donna broke his crutch, Tony's Uncle Jimmy died in Glens Falls, in upstate New York. Tony planned to drive his mother to the funeral. Donna wanted to go, too, to get out of the house for a couple of days, but they couldn't find a sitter for Little Tony. She erupted. She told Tony he couldn't go, that he couldn't leave her home alone with the four kids. Tony said he was going anyway. When Donna tried to block the door, Tony jerked her out of the way.

Donna called the police. Fearing trouble, Tony went to the bedroom, took his new guns—he now owned a .44 Magnum and a .380—to the Majors' house, and asked them to hold onto them. When the police arrived, he and Donna continued to yell at each other. He was still on probation, but Tony knew law enforcement officers and how to seem reasonable with them. "I sat on the porch and told the cop what transpired," he says. "I said to him, 'If you stood in the doorway and told me I couldn't go to my uncle's funeral, I'd probably move you, too.'" The officer left without arresting him.

More and more now Donna thought of leaving Tony. But how? "Where was I gonna go with four kids?" she would ask. "A shelter? I had nowhere to go." She also had no money. A year earlier, barely a month after Dayna was born, she'd gone back to work one night a week at Standard News, leaving the kids with a sitter. Her first night at work Shannon called to say that Little Tony was sick. A week later the same thing happened, and she quit. "I felt that I was needed at home," she says. Now she had a job a couple of days a week as a cashier in a gift shop on I-95, but it paid less than driving, which was union scale. She was stuck.

Her toughness was deserting her. Never knowing who her real parents were, fleeing her adoptive family as soon as she could, having Shannon at eighteen, running away with Tony—the part of her that ached for a stable home and family had always yielded to the part that kept moving. Her instinct for self-preservation was implacable, yet it was a battle now to get out of bed in the morning, let alone to get through the day. It never stopped. Little Tony. Shannon. The girls. Tony's workaholism and distance, his outbursts. The endless housework. The fighting. The feeling of hopeless desperation and that somehow she was to blame, she'd done all this, she deserved it.

On Sundays, Donna went bowling and left Tony with the kids. It was her one escape. Amid the warm smokiness of the lanes, the smooth rolling balls and crashing pins and echoing laughter, she could forget about home. She didn't have to remember that she'd barely known Tony before she married him, and that ever since then events had conspired to break them apart. Sometimes we would talk enthusiastically about wanting to become a professional bowler, and her friends, perhaps because she was good and because they knew about Little Tony and imagined her stress, encouraged her. Other times she told them that she had money coming from a lawsuit, even though she didn't know about the new negotiations and had been warned by the Koskoffs not to count on anything.

During these brief spells she experienced the exhilaration of being her own person. She could dream, and no one challenged her. Mary Gay had almost lost her marriage by retreating from a similarly desperate home life to a cluttered family room above the garage and staying up all night to talk with strangers on her computer. She had became an on-line addict, a lonely soul who could be anyone or no one in the intimate anonymity of cyberspace. Donna felt a similar sense of possibility at the bowling alley. It was her one sanctuary. But then she went home, and the spell broke. Like air into a vacuum all the old recriminations between her and Tony rushed back. Donna would wake Tony and ask him to carry Little Tony downstairs. Tony would do it, complaining, then instead of going back to sleep would find something to do around the house. He'd blame Donna for waking him, for his chronic exhaustion. She'd tell him to go back to sleep, that it wasn't her fault that Little Tony was getting too big for her to carry. Next thing, Tony would be airing old grievances. The worst, in his mind, was those times Donna "called the fucking cops" on him. Only the familiar hateful, stony silence ended it.

"At times I feel like a villain; at times I feel like I'm being abused," Tony would complain, expressing what both of them were feeling. "I don't know which is worse."

$\approx \approx \approx$

By late summer, 1991, medical malpractice was becoming a hot-button political issue, the leading edge of a new national concern: health care reform. The nation's mood had subsided after the riot of self-congratulation over the Gulf War the previous winter, and was now affected by new anxieties. Chief among them was the staggering price of medical care. The United States had the best doctors and hospitals in the world, but they cost so much they were sapping its prosperity. Americans were afraid to get sick for fear it could wipe them out. Suddenly, America's deepest dread centered not on rogue dictators or nuclear annihilation but on winding up like the Sabias.

The Democrats pounced first, calling for sweeping legislation to overhaul the medical economy. Republicans, reluctant to tangle with an $800 billion growth industry, typically blamed the best enemy they could find. In mid-May, after months of resisting calls for change while enjoying the highest approval ratings of any recent president, George Bush belatedly entered the fray. The solution to the problem of skyrocketing health care costs, Bush said, was to control the fastest-rising part of those costs—malpractice suits. Control lawyers, Bush said, and health care costs will come down. This had been the doctors' *cri de coeur* ever since the malpractice crisis of the mid-seventies, and by adopting it Bush put it in the center of the debate over runaway health care costs. In reality, it was a minor part of the problem.

Malpractice, by the American Medical Association's own estimate, added $21 billion a year to the nation's health bill, or about 2.5 percent. This figure included all verdicts and settlements, insurance premiums, and "defensive" medical tactics. By comparison, doctors earned a total of about $80 billion, or about 10 percent of the total bill. Moreover, the AMA's $15 billion price tag for defensive medicine wasn't what it seemed, since doctors and hospitals were reimbursed for procedures undertaken to avoid lawsuits whether or not they were good medicine. In other words, because they made money on these procedures, they had a material incentive to do them; railing about their high social cost was mostly a smokescreen. If doctors really cared about cost effectiveness, lawyers like Koskoff began to ask, which was better for the country —100,000 unnecessary $40 ultrasounds ($4 million) or the lifetime cost of caring for one severely brain-damaged quadriplegic like Little Tony ($11 million, according to the Koskoffs' experts)?

By parroting the doctors' economic arguments, Bush vastly overstated the role of malpractice suits in the crisis in medicine. But his political instincts were keen. He knew that Americans' anxieties about lawyers were also rising. If working Americans were afraid of doctors and hospitals they no longer knew or understood, or of losing everything because of a catastrophic illness, they also dreaded ending up like Humes—hounded by lawyers and caught in a legal web that required still more lawyers to escape.

Suddenly, doctors and lawyers had become proxies in an all-out war over the future of health care, now the biggest industry in America. Yet their battlefield—medical malpractice suits—chosen by mutual design, wasn't the medical system itself. It was a small, ancillary front where the new economic competition between the two professions was most heated, where each side had a vested stake, and where the outcome mattered more to the belligerents themselves than to those they claimed to represent.

Lost in the squabble were the real questions that underlay it. How much medical malpractice was there actually? And did lawsuits really do what they were supposed to—punish bad doctors while compensating victims? Toward the end of July, as doctors and lawyers began squaring off in Washington, an intriguing answer to both questions emerged. Since the mid-eighties, a team of professors from Harvard's medical and law schools had been studying the relationship between confirmed cases of medical negligence and malpractice claims. The results of their investigation, the Harvard Medical Practice Study, had been published piecemeal throughout the year in various medical journals, with almost no mention in the media. Now, in the last of those articles, in the *New England Journal of Medicine*, the group interpreted its findings.

The researchers reported that doctors and hospitals in fact caused a great deal of medical injury. Nationally, the Harvard group projected more than 300,000 bad outcomes and up to 80,000 deaths each year from malpractice, more than from car accidents and AIDS combined. They also discovered that people without health insurance were far more likely to be harmed by doctors and hospitals than those with coverage. But it was another conclusion that was perhaps most telling. Comparing the records of those who were injured by doctors and hospitals with those who sued, the researchers found almost no correlation. Patients were being hurt and even killed by bad medicine, and doctors and hospitals were being sued with alarming frequency by aggrieved patients. But they weren't the same patients.

Far from being a corrective for identifying bad doctors and getting money to victims, as Koskoff and other trial lawyers claimed, the trend toward malpractice suits revealed a staggering "litigation gap," the authors concluded. "It's similar," said Dr. Troyen Brennan, a professor at both the law and medical schools and the only doctor-lawyer on the Harvard team, "to a situation in which a traffic officer is giving a large number of tickets to motorists who are not speeding, but failing to give tickets to most of those who are."

The Harvard study received wide attention from doctors and lawyers alike, although, typically, each side took away only what suited it. Lawyers cited it as evidence that medical injury was rampant and that the main victims were those, like the Sabias, who could least afford lawyers. The contingency fee system, they pointed out, gave these people access to attorneys they otherwise couldn't afford. Doctors seized on the study as confirmation that malpractice suits were a "lottery," a random exercise in which winning and losing had almost nothing to do with being right: the wrong people were most often compensated, the wrong doctors most often punished, and the only sure beneficiaries were the lawyers themselves.

For once, they both were right. The system of suing over medical injury, Troyen Brennan would say, was "bad on both ends."

THIRTEEN

FOR SEVEN AND A HALF YEARS, HUMES NEVER WAVERED IN HER BELIEF THAT SHE HAD done nothing wrong in regard to the Sabias. On the contrary, she believed that she, too, was a victim, like them. She saw herself and the Sabias as fatefully allied, cosufferers struggling to recover from the same awful event. They'd been dumped together by circumstance, hurt by the same people. The clinic at Norwalk Hospital, the boys' club, Fortuna, McManamy—all had failed, then abandoned them. Not many people sympathized with this interpretation: How, they wondered, could Humes compare her suffering to the Sabias'? Next to them, what had she lost?

And so she'd retreated to where she could go on working without feeling persecuted. She divided the world into friends and enemies. Her patients and staff still loved her, and her daughters, and her sister and brother, and a few treasured friends. But out in the world, she felt wary. She gave off the edgy compulsiveness of someone beset by rumor and conspiracy. And while it was easy to look at her grievances and see why she felt besieged, her persistence only alienated her further. There might be ways to withstand public accusations of incompetence besides nurturing a brittle conviction in your own innocence, but Humes could see only that people were trying to blame her and that she had no choice but to fight or give in.

A battler, she hated to concede. But the case was a war she knew she couldn't win, and there were other things in life she wanted. Since the wedding of her oldest daughter, Martha, in June 1990, she'd been consumed with remodeling her house. The kitchen had always been inadequate, and rather then change it for the wedding, Humes had opted to have it torn out. The room, down to the dirt floor and a slippery whaleback of rock ledge uncovered during the demolition, now sat cold, dank, and empty, closed off from the rest of the house. Humes cooked all her meals in the galley kitchen of the former artist's studio at the bottom of her property. For more than a year she'd had to walk outdoors fifty steps even to make herself tea. At night in winter, under a full moon, the path between the two buildings was a ghostly chute of ice. At various times she'd rented the studio for extra income, but without a kitchen in the main house, the arrangement had become unworkable. She was now carrying the place alone.

Not having a kitchen liberated Humes to think more creatively about the house. What she wanted, characteristically, was extraordinary. She thought the house was a work of art and that it was her "responsibility to keep it beautiful." She also wanted good things. She dreamed of a large master bathroom with an open shower, radiant heat, a marble floor, graceful imported fixtures—a place to luxuriate in and admire. The small back bedroom she planned to use for this bathroom had stone steps leading to what had been a shed. She imagined them leading out to a lap pool.

Her reveries were elegant and grandiose and changed with succeeding impulses. She'd desire something, collect information, then realize that something else, something lovelier, was preferable. She knew that she couldn't do it all herself and began hiring architects. She spent tens of thousands having the place "drawn to death." But as she lugged each new set of rolled-up drawings around with her, unfurling them, studying them, agonizing over each change, her ideas kept expanding. The architects found her difficult to work with.

Living amid the mess and clatter of a work interminably in progress, Humes made frequent stabs at improving the place piecemeal. To finish even small parts of the job indicated progress and a semblance of a settled, more normal life—a sense of completion. But these efforts often proved pointless and expensive, partly because of a lack of a master plan and partly because of Humes's perfectionism and complicated life. A carpenter would install a transom totally plumb and then, because the cathedral ceiling above it was a few degrees off center, Humes would tell him it was all wrong and that the job had to be redone. Having bought a Dutch Colonial antique hutch from Indonesia to hide her TV, she never watched it, forgot to pay her cable bill, and the company kept shutting off her service. When she wanted fabrics for her bedroom, a patient who'd been an art director offered to help, leading her through showrooms in Manhattan. The woman billed her $85 an hour. "I said, 'four thousand dollars for a fabric consultation? When I have no kitchen in my house?'" Humes recalls.

The house had always been a metaphor for Humes's life, an emblem of her self-determination and reach. On the day she'd bought it twelve years earlier, she'd rejoiced in its possibilities. She'd been thirty-nine then, her sense of accomplishment keen. She'd pried herself free of a failed marriage and into two picture-book stone buildings of great charm, secluded in an upland woods close to the sea. She had brought herself to this place of distinction as few women did, by forsaking a husband and working for it on her own. Buying the place was more than acquisition: it was an act of self-invention.

But her attempts to make it over revealed the fullness of her obsession with puzzling out, and taming, two intractable natures: her own, and that of the world. Altering a wood-frame structure like the Sabias' house was one thing, but Humes's house was literally a small mountain of boulders imbedded in tons of case-hardened concrete. It was a bunker, reinforced to defy time and whim. It took a mason a week of hammering and chipping to move a window a few feet, then another week of fitting and cutting and laying stone and cement to hide the emptied space. The ceiling in the old kitchen was too low: to raise it Humes had to reconfigure a major part of the house or try to blast the ledge that lay beneath it. The simplest architect's ideas—moving a doorway here, a step there—became magnificently complicated, an exhausting act of hubris. Everything was ten times harder to do, and ten times more expensive.

Which only made Humes more determined to prevail. Now fifty-one, she was increasingly driven by a desire to do things right. If an architect told her that what she wanted was impossible, she found another to tell her it wasn't. She started to see the project as a life's work in itself, possibly lasting decades and costing hundreds of thousands of dollars. She broke it into phases, hoping that each phase would be easier than the last. The house may have become an albatross, but it was her albatross, and she would carry it through or sacrifice everything trying. She wouldn't give up.

Like all obsessions, Humes's was costly. The house was a sinkhole for money, and she never seemed to earn enough to sustain her vision of it. Karen Brooks, her business manager, hadn't been able to give her a raise in six years. After expenses—Humes still had two offices with two staffs, an associate, and an annual malpractice premium for the two of them, which Humes paid herself, of $146,000—she was earning less in real dollars than she had when she was working alone in Norwalk. With the lost income from the studio, she'd fallen further behind. She couldn't stop the slide. She'd been determined to put her daughters through college on her own, but things had got so bad she'd finally had to turn to Roland for help. He paid the final year of tuition for Anna, their youngest. Humes hated asking him, hated even more that, working tirelessly and living in a half-demolished house, she'd had no choice.

Humes's house and malpractice worries were the warp and woof of her life, and her spirits rose and fell with their vicissitudes. When she lost hope, typically, was in late summer, when her malpractice insurance came up for renewal. When Brooks got the bill around August 15, it always initiated a bitter sag in Humes's morale. Brooks and Humes would meet to discuss how they would manage the coming year. Railing against St. Paul's "extortion," Humes would groan inwardly, "I can't work any harder. I'll cancel, go bare. What can they take from me? The bank owns my house." Brooks would lose sleep for a few nights, then come in and tell Humes she had no choice but to see more patients, bill more hours. There was no other way.

In the spring of 1990, around the time of Martha's wedding, Humes had asked a colleague at Stamford Hospital how he managed his practice. They were standing in scrubs outside an operating room, talking about their financial strains. He told her he'd switched his liability coverage from St. Paul to a company called PRIME, slashing his premium by more than three-quarters. Humes had never heard of PRIME, an acronym for Professional Risk Insurance Management Exclusive. Calling the medical staff officer at Stamford, she asked whether having a certificate of insurance from PRIME satisfied the hospital's requirement that doctors carry their own liability insurance. He warned her against it, saying he knew of the company and that "there'd been some question as to its solvency." She could be putting herself at risk. She pressed him: would a certificate from PRIME be acceptable? He said yes.

Here, Humes thought, was the answer to her problems. Switching her malpractice coverage to PRIME would get her out from under St. Paul, which had the highest premiums in Connecticut. It would satisfy the hospital, allowing her to stay in business and take more money out of her practice, which in turn meant that she could move ahead with renovating her house. Even better, she could use PRIME as leverage to get another insurer to cover her. Every August for the past several years Brooks had applied to CIGNA and CMIC, the state's two other bona fide carriers, and each time they'd turned Humes down. But the state insurance commissioner, so far deaf to Humes's appeals, could force them to issue her a policy if PRIME turned out to be a sham. Doctors in Connecticut deserving of insurance were entitled to coverage. In the interest of public health, carriers were barred from boycotting them. The best thing that could happen, Humes thought, was that PRIME went bad, forcing the state to order another insurer to take her on. It was a risk, but so was paying St. Paul. She'd done that dutifully all these years and look what it had gotten her.

By now Humes was ready to gamble everything to break out of the impasse the Sabia case had forced on her. Although she wasn't eager to sacrifice herself, there was something satisfying about making an end run around a system she felt was destroying her. When she first raised the possibility of going with PRIME in the summer of 1990, however, Brooks, less disposed to making self-defeating gestures to prove a point, objected. So did Dr. Irene Komarynsky, Humes's young associate. "Irene said she couldn't in good conscience do this," Brooks recalls. "It was not a possibility for her." For a year Humes stewed. By August 1991, though, the situation had changed. Despite

Haskell's urging and Humes's willingness, St. Paul had made no move to settle *Sabia*. With no end in sight, Humes thought, she might never be able to transfer to another legitimate insurer. Meanwhile, Komarynsky had announced she was leaving in September to go into solo practice. Heading into what promised to be another distressing fall, Humes again told Brooks she wanted to go with PRIME.

Brooks still was opposed, but without Komarynsky to back her up, she relented, provided Humes also apply to CMIC. Privately, she hoped that CMIC, the company started by the state's doctors to escape the caprices of the big liability carriers, would have sympathy and accept her, thus precluding Humes's desperate gambit. Brooks filed both applications around August 15. She couldn't imagine not being approved by PRIME, but the CMIC application required detailed accounts of any "complaints, incidents, claims and/or suits" against Humes, and Brooks once again, as in previous years, included detailed descriptions of the Gay and Sabia cases. Then they waited.

≈ ≈ ≈

April Haskell knew that St. Paul's local claims people couldn't authorize a settlement of the size being proposed by the Koskoffs and that they were being pressured by their supervisors, which explained why they hadn't responded to her in the two and a half months since she'd talked with Bernard. Settling a multimillion-dollar malpractice claim wasn't like disposing of a $7,500 slip-and-fall. The bigger the case, the farther up the corporate ladder it went and the harder it was to get a carrier to negotiate, especially one that was publicly owned and had hard-driving management and ambitions, as did St. Paul. A $4 billion company, it was the fifteenth-largest property liability underwriter in the country. The executives in its medical services division, which managed its malpractice lines, generated annual profits of more than $100 million—and bonuses and promotions for themselves—not by delicately resolving individual claims but by carving out new markets.

Haskell knew St. Paul's home office had little idea what she was up against and probably wouldn't care even if it did. Its managers wanted results, not excuses. With no trial in sight, they had no immediate fear of losing and therefore no incentive to bargain. And so the challenge for Haskell was to close all the doors. Only by foreclosing every reasonable hope of getting the case thrown out or winning in court could she help St. Paul's local claims managers convince their superiors to grant them settlement authority.

Haskell had to make it appear that Humes could only lose at trial, and that St. Paul would be liable for the full amount of her policy. Not that this was hard to do; even her own experts had offered little positive evidence to absolve Humes. But she was now working at cross-purposes. To protect

Humes personally she had to weaken her in the eyes of St. Paul. She had to render her indefensible, even though, as her lawyer, she'd tried diligently to defend her and wanted to win for her; even though she sympathized with Humes and thought she'd been made a scapegoat.

On August 1, Haskell wrote a seven-and-a-half-page letter to Marlene Smethurst in St. Paul's Hamden office. In it she attempted one by one to answer the objections she understood had been raised by Smethurst's superiors: Why did St. Paul have to indemnify Humes at all? How could Benirschke be sure that Twin B died less than forty-eight hours before the birth and that the whole mess hadn't occurred weeks earlier? What about the outrageously overvalued demands from the plaintiffs? Why wasn't Haskell coming up with her own experts to refute the plaintiffs on the issue of life expectancy, the cost for specials, causation theory, standard of care? Why hadn't they done more genetic testing to try to show that some of the child's problems had to have been hereditary?

Haskell built compelling arguments for each. First she wrote, citing several depositions, that there was no question that the overall responsibility for managing Donna Sabia's labor and delivery was Humes's. She was not a consultant, as St. Paul still wanted to believe, but Donna's attending physician according to her on-call arrangement with Norwalk Hospital. The company, Haskell wrote, was obligated to cover her.

Next she addressed Benirschke's contention that Twin B had died within forty-eight hours prior to delivery. She noted that none of the experts she had contacted found any reason to doubt McManamy's statement that she heard two heartbeats two days before Donna's labor, and that although one of them thought the pathology specimens indicated death somewhere between a day and a week prior to delivery, that wasn't inconsistent with Benirschke's claim. The implication, unstated, was that St. Paul had no grounds to contradict the Koskoffs' theory that the damage to Little Tony began within hours before birth. It wouldn't get itself off the hook by arguing otherwise.

There were those within the company who were appalled by the Koskoffs' damage demands and wanted to know why St. Paul should have to pay to treat injuries suffered on the hospital's watch. Haskell was sensitive to their concerns. It was apparently Benirschke's conclusion that Little Tony had suffered an ongoing, cumulative series of insults, and that those repeated injuries had contributed to massive, if undifferentiated, brain damage. The mere thought of how he or another plaintiff's expert might try to apportion the injuries— how they would explain which of Little Tony's multiple disabilities were attributable to which specific events—had been enough to make Haskell eager to settle before he elaborated under oath at his deposition. Haskell addressed this matter gingerly. It was impossible, she wrote, to know specifically which of the boy's injuries may have been caused during labor and delivery. But that wasn't her main concern. The issue, she said, was what a jury might do if it concluded that the damage had resulted from several factors. It could prorate the blame between Humes and the hospital or, if it so decided, fault Humes for everything, thus leaving St. Paul "on the hook for the overall injury." Even if the Koskoffs' projections about how long Little Tony would live and what it would cost to care for him were wildly inflated, she wrote, "we are probably not going to reduce the value of this case below the policy limits of your insured."

As for the lack of a strong defense strategy, Haskell skillfully laid out the difficulty she was having in building her case. Foremost was the lack of what she called "positive evidence." The Koskoffs' case was based on a theory of cumulative, multicausal brain injury to Little Tony. St. Paul's managers had asked why she couldn't exploit that theory's vagueness; in effect, turn it back on itself by finding experts to say that because the boy was already seriously injured, and because his injury was ongoing, he would have suffered additional damage no matter what Humes did. By this reasoning, even if Humes had done an emergency C-section as soon as she got to the hospital, she'd have been damned. Haskell said she had pressed her experts hopefully on this point, but none felt comfortable supporting it. Without proof that Little Tony's injuries weren't compounded by the stress of labor, they'd told her, there was no way to say for sure that they weren't—even if that were true.

Then there was the issue of genetic testing. From the beginning St. Paul had hoped to reverse the momentum in the case by linking Little Tony's problems to the Sabias themselves. The company had been interested in Tony's three dead siblings, in Shannon, even in Tony's and Donna's pasts. In April, Haskell had written Smethurst identifying a "confidential source" in North Carolina who had access to adoption records and had agreed to try to locate Donna's biological parents. Now, despite the failure of earlier efforts, Smethurst's superiors were urging still more genetic tests. To ensure the accuracy of any new tests, Haskell pointed out, Little Tony would have to stop taking vitamin supplements for several months. She was apprehensive about proposing such a regimen. "I very seriously doubt the likelihood that any Court is going to jeopardize this child's health to allow us to potentially gain an advantage in litigation," she wrote, adding, however, that she would try to get a court order if St. Paul wanted her to.

St. Paul's last hope, Haskell knew, was a straight standard-of-care defense. For more than a year she'd tried to make this the cornerstone of the case and had run into nothing but dead ends. None of the six ob-gyns she'd consulted felt comfortable backing Humes. They thought the lack of continuous fetal monitoring and the timing of the intermittent monitoring that was done betrayed a troubling lack of attention to fetal health. Meanwhile, arguing that others—Fortuna, McManamy—had been responsible for monitoring the twins and had failed to inform Humes that there might be a problem, no matter how true, seemed only to make matters worse. Haskell was sure that trying to blame them would antagonize a jury. Even Humes herself conceded that it was common practice to run an initial EFM strip on all women in labor. "That this was not done in this case," Haskell wrote, "is going to make it very difficult to prevail on [this] issue."

Haskell had said all she could say on Humes's behalf; the case should be settled, now, for all their sakes. What she didn't mention—maybe didn't need to—was what might happen if *Sabia* went to trial. Haskell had never witnessed Mike Koskoff cross-examining a defendant doctor, but it was not hard to imagine how he would bore in on Humes's failure to know that Michael Sabia was dead and Little Tony was distressed despite her own statements that she routinely ordered fetal heart checks for women in labor. None of this constituted proof of malpractice. Who knew whether Little Tony suffered additionally during his short, violent entry into the world? Benirschke seemed prepared to say that he had, but who really could say what happened when the boy was in the birth canal, his brain already darkened, his fluttering heart unmonitored? Not even Schifrin could say for sure what the watery echoes of his galloping heartbeat might have foretold, or swear that the outcome wouldn't have been exactly the same if he'd been taken earlier by C-section. But that didn't matter. In the minds of the lawyers, in Haskell's own mind, the standard-of-care section of the case had already been tried prospectively, and it had been devastating for Humes. Haskell hoped she could save her from the real thing. But time was running out.

Concluding her letter to Smethurst, Haskell recommended that the two of them plan to meet "very soon" with Smethurst's superiors and a lawyer named Phil Chabot, who handled big cases for St. Paul and who was consulting on the case. Perhaps if she could meet with them face-to-face, she could convince them it was in their interest to hear what she had to say.

In mid-September, Humes was turned down for insurance by CMIC. An underwriting committee including several doctors but no obstetricians had concluded that because of her type of practice and claims experience she presented an "unreasonable . . . risk." The company's executive committee agreed, giving Humes fifteen days to appeal. PRIME had no such qualms. It approved Humes's application immediately, without comment. The day after CMIC's rejection arrived, Brooks wrote a check to PRIME for $12,964.05—payment in full for the year starting October 1. Then she called St. Paul to say Humes wouldn't be renewing her policy. She and Humes again argued about the decision. Brooks wanted to pay PRIME another $24,000 for Humes's "tail"—extra coverage that would ensure her against prior claims—but Humes refused. "Buy the tail," Brooks told her. "It's thirty-seven thousand dollars instead of ninety-eight thousand"—the cost of staying with St. Paul now that Komarynsky had left. "What does it matter?" Humes replied. "I know I haven't done anything wrong." Because she had had no bad outcomes in recent years, how, she reasoned, could anyone sue her for care she had already delivered?

Brooks was concerned enough to postdate the check September 20, a Friday; she wanted time to reconsider before the company cashed it. By the afternoon of the twenty-seventh, the check still hadn't cleared Humes's bank, and Brooks was worried. PRIME had an 800-number in Chicago. Whenever she'd called before, there was "always a voice there," she says. Now there was no answer. Alarmed, she hung up, then called the Union Trust Company in Westport to stop payment on the check. The bank was closed. Meanwhile, Humes kept dialing PRIME's number.

Brooks spent Saturday morning investigating. She had the name of a lawyer in the Virgin Islands who'd been listed on one of PRIME's letters as its counsel. She called him and peppered him with questions: Does Dr. Humes have liability insurance come Tuesday? Does the company have a building in Chicago where it can be reached? Does PRIME exist or doesn't it? Embarrassed, the man said he was no longer associated with the company and was trying to stop it from using his name. He was a respectable attorney, he pleaded, a victim himself.

Brooks hung up and called Humes in Rochester, where she was visiting her brother. She said they should try to stop the check first thing Monday morning. If PRIME wasn't real, she said hopefully, maybe that would expedite their getting *bona fide* insurance through the state.

Although Brooks had Monday off, she was at the bank when it opened at nine. She stood in line until a teller told her she could only order a stop payment by phone. She raced back to Humes's Norwalk office and called the bank only to discover it was too late. The check had cleared. A wave of nausea swept through her. In twenty-four hours Humes would be without insurance, and Stamford Hospital would revoke her privileges. She could go on practicing in her office, but she'd be open to ruin if anybody sued her. There was still no answer at PRIME, and Brooks now understood that there wouldn't be, not in time to make a difference. The $13,000 was gone and with it Humes's hope of forcing the state to assign her to another company. When she told her about the check, Humes was disgusted and, Brooks thought, not thinking clearly. "I don't care," Humes said. "I'll go naked."

"The height of insanity," Brooks calls the next twelve hours. She called St. Paul, asked them to reconsider Humes's termination. Then, while Humes saw patients all afternoon, she desperately pulled together piles of paperwork and completed the renewal forms. At 5 P.M. Humes left to plead her case in person at her insurance agent's office. She explained that the claims against her were not her fault. It was her situation, she said, that had put her at risk, and things were different since she'd moved to Stamford Hospital. At Norwalk she'd been vulnerable, required to see staff patients. The hospital had no high-risk specialists and no residents. Stamford, on the other hand, had residents available to see clinic patients around the clock. She supervised these people and they were top-notch, "tested up the gazoo." There was a full-time perinatologist, there were strict protocols, comprehensive case reviews. They went overboard the other way, she said. Something like the Sabia tragedy couldn't happen there.

Talking for an hour, Humes persuaded the agent to give her a policy. Still without a settlement in *Sabia*, she'd managed finally to convince someone connected with St. Paul that she'd been set up. It was cold comfort. What she won was the opposite of what she wanted: she was still with St. Paul. Yielding to what she thought was extortion, she'd debased herself further by pleading for more. "Being falsely accused doesn't make you a better anything," she would say, scoffing at the suggestion that malpractice suits produced more virtuous doctors. "It just makes you cynical."

In September, Koskoff and Bernard started picking a jury in another birth injury case, *Goldblatt v. Sherrington*. Gina Marie Goldblatt, a sunny eight and a half years old, had cerebral palsy, was crippled from the waist down, and, with an IQ of 80, was borderline retarded. Her father Michael was a vice-president for McDonald's, a soft-spoken senior executive with a Ph.D. in nutritional science and a degree in patent law. He and his Mexican-born wife, Marta, now lived in Chicago, but they had lived in Stamford when Gina Marie, their first child, was born. In 1985 they sued Dr. Harold Sherrington, a local ob-gyn. Sherrington had been Marta Goldblatt's obstetrician and had delivered Gina Marie after a long, difficult labor at Stamford Hospital. The Koskoffs had also named the hospital as a defendant.

Neither of the principals had wanted a trial, and there had been more than the usual overtures to resolve the case. Sherrington, whose office was next door to Humes's in Stamford, had a $3 million insurance policy with St. Paul, yet was so fearful of a verdict in excess of that that he had put his house in his wife's name and hired as his private counsel Pat Ryan, who'd threatened to sue St. Paul for bad faith if it didn't settle. Though the Koskoffs' lifetime care expert Larry Forman had projected economic damages alone of about $5 million, they, too, were willing to settle for the policy limit. At a pretrial conference Stamford Superior Court Judge Nicholas Cioffi had admonished St.

Paul's lawyer, Phil Chabot, whom Haskell was now trying to enlist in her campaign with St. Paul's claims managers in *Sabia*, to settle the case. According to both Ryan and Mike Koskoff, Cioffi was outraged when on the eve of the trial St. Paul offered the Goldblatts $50,000 to end their suit.

St. Paul's stonewalling was characteristic: it didn't see why it should pay the full cost when there was another carrier also on the hook. Stamford Hospital's liability insurer was Aetna Life & Casualty, and it, too, had refused to settle, but for other reasons. Aetna considered the case a classic birth trauma action: that is, Sherrington, the attending doctor, was in charge; any fault for not taking Gina Marie sooner by C-section was his. Its lawyer, Edward Sheehy, a partner in the firm representing Travelers in *Sabia*, thought the Koskoffs had named the hospital solely as another pocket and hadn't any real case against it. The Koskoffs' claim against the hospital was indeed thin: because a resident had been assigned to Marta Goldblatt during her labor and, like Sherrington, had reviewed fetal-monitoring strips showing that Gina Marie was in distress, the hospital had an independent obligation to overrule Sherrington's management of the delivery and intervene.

This was precisely the claim of institutional quality control that Humes was now making to St. Paul's salesman, but Sheehy doubted a jury would go for it. St. Paul, on the other hand, appeared to be banking on a joint verdict. Either there was no liability and both defendants got off without paying, or they split the damages. Unless a verdict came in at $6 million or more—an extraordinary amount given Gina Marie's disabilities—St. Paul seemed convinced that it stood to gain by holding fast.

Goldblatt v. Sherrington lasted three months and, as trials do, took its toll on everyone. Bernard, rather than face a two-hour commute each way from his home in Litchfield, moved into the Stamford Marriott during the week. He could remember spending Thanksgiving in the basement of his aunt and uncle's house, reviewing deposition transcripts of a key defense witness. Michael Goldblatt stayed behind to take care of the couples' three girls and to go to work, but Marta boarded a plane in Chicago every Tuesday at 6 A.M. and was in court by 10, often sobbing alone in the back row as the Koskoffs' experts told the jury how Gina Marie had been normal and healthy until just hours before she was born. She stayed in Stamford all week, returning home, tormented afresh, on weekends. Suffering perhaps equally was Sherrington, who, with Ryan beside him, was forced to endure several weeks of public discredit culminating in almost three days of cross-examination by Koskoff, who would proudly remember the grilling as among his most devastating.

The Koskoffs' case rested largely on Barry Schifrin, who testified about fetal monitoring. Meeting at seven on the morning Schifrin was to testify, Bernard worried that his expert seemed unfamiliar with the most basic details of the case. He couldn't even remember the Goldblatts' name. In court, however, under Koskoff's prodding, Schifrin sparkled. Marta Goldblatt's EFM strips were not subtle. They showed a pattern of steadily worsening late decelerations; with each contraction Gina Marie's heart rate slowed more and more ominously and remained sluggish longer, indicated a deepening asphyxia. Schifrin's testimony was so lucid and damning that by the end Bernard felt the jury "knew how to read fetal monitoring strips"—a sign of their interest and attentiveness.

The jury deliberated only four hours. It exonerated the hospital, blamed Sherrington entirely, and voted to award the Goldblatts $5.3 million—$4.5 million for Gina Marie for future medical care and lost income, $500,000 for prior medical expenses, and $300,000 for Marta Goldblatt's emotional distress. Michael Goldblatt, who'd flown in for the verdict and had suffered the strain of the trial more privately than his wife, broke down sobbing at the back of the courtroom. Sherrington soon quit obstetrics.

St. Paul's misstep reverberated at once among the lawyers in the case. The company was obligated for the full $3 million of Sherrington's policy, unless it could get the award rolled back or reversed by a higher court. But that left another $2.3 million. The Koskoffs were determined to recoup the full award, as well as their fees, which totaled more than $1.7 million. Ryan, meanwhile, moved immediately to protect Sherrington's personal assets. A scramble ensued, and an odd alliance. Even as Mike Koskoff started amassing deeds to bring a fraudulent conveyance claim against Sherrington, whose transfer of his property to his wife occurred *after* he was sued, Koskoff teamed up with Ryan, nominally his rival, to sue St. Paul, saying that the company had broken its contractual duty to Sherrington. St. Paul eventually brought an appeal, but after two status conferences with Ryan and Koskoff before a retired state supreme court judge in New Haven, the company dropped it and agreed to pay the Goldblatts $4.5 million. St. Paul's determination to ignore Sherrington's desire to settle and Ryan's threat to sue if it didn't, and to opt instead to face Koskoff and his star perinatal expert Barry Schifrin in front of a jury, had cost the company $1.5 million out of profits.

But even before that, within a week of the verdict, a more immediate consequence of the Goldblatt case emerged. Marlene Smethurst of St. Paul called Bernard, wanting to know if he would consider coming down on his take figure in *Sabia*.

≈ ≈ ≈

With insurance claims, size is destiny. Humes had ceased to be the Koskoffs' main target as soon as they realized she couldn't afford to take care of Little Tony for the rest of his life. They reset their sights on Norwalk Hospital, which could afford it. If she had carried more insurance, Humes would have been more attractive as a defendant and the Koskoffs would have had more incentive to keep her in the case. She'd also have had more clout as an insured: St. Paul, with more to lose, might have been compelled to defend her more vigorously. Now it was the inadequacy of her coverage that decided her fate.

Smethurst might have expected Bernard to posture mightily in the wake of the Sherrington fiasco, but at the time, that case was still in play and Bernard was careful not to jeopardize an ongoing negotiation. His approach to defendants was unfailingly civil. He also knew that his strongest weapon in affecting a settlement was that a doctor was exposed beyond the policy limit, and that the lesson of the Sherrington case was that St. Paul now recognized the full extent of its liability with Humes. He didn't have to start asking Smethurst how much Humes's house was worth to make the point.

Bernard presumed Smethurst had negotiating authority, otherwise she wouldn't have called, and he wasted no time signaling his intentions. He offered a substantial discount, $500,000, if St. Paul would settle immediately. In fact, he had his own reasons for accommodation. With the depositions of Benirschke and Schifrin now scheduled for January, he and Koskoff wanted Humes out of the way, fast. Still named as a defendant, she could only cause serious problems for them. Either she would dilute the case against the hospital, by siphoning a portion of the blame, or by providing it with a foil. "We were willing," he would say, "to take essentially what we could get from Humes to get her out of the case."

According to Haskell, Smethurst countered by offering $1 million or slightly more. But the company had other issues Smethurst was anxious to raise. She feared that even if Humes settled, the hospital might try to bring her back into the case. If St. Paul settled, Smethurst asked, would that end it? Would Bernard be willing to sign a general release denying any further claims against Dr. Humes?

Bernard hesitated. They were still taking depositions; anything could happen. Some yet-to-be-disclosed hospital expert could claim that more of the damage to Little Tony occurred during labor and delivery than anyone had previously thought. The hospital's lawyers could claim successfully that it shouldn't be held liable for Humes's actions, and he and Koskoff could be forced to scramble. He didn't want to foreclose coming back to Humes if the situation warranted—if the Sabias needed more than they could get from the hospital, or if Humes appeared, on the basis of new testimony, to be more than incidentally at fault.

After four and a half years of positioning, only two issues—price and a covenant not to sue—now separated the Sabias and Humes, or at least their proxies. Perhaps it wasn't surprising that the catalyst was another trial in which those proxies had a hand, since the purpose of protracted litigation is not so much to advance to trial as to get to the point at which all sides can reasonably envision one.

∽∽∽

Humes heard about the negotiations from Arnold Bai. She was hardly cheered by them. She knew now that unless St. Paul withdrew its offer and elected to stand by her as staunchly as it had Sherrington, there would be no trial. The realization pained her. It destroyed any chance of public vindication, although in truth few people outside Norwalk's medical community knew about the cloud she was under. Still, seeing how the experience of the trial had almost ruined Sherrington may have caused her to reconsider. As Haskell often pointed out, once a case settled, it sank forever from public view. Humes had to agree that there was release in burying the past. Doctors settled claims all the time simply to avoid being stigmatized. Even without publicity, Humes had been tarnished enough.

Besides, in a sense, she already had had her trial, and the verdict had been favorable. In September, just as the lawyers were picking a jury in the Sherrington case and a few weeks before the PRIME debacle, she had appealed CMIC's rejection to the Fairfield County Medical Association's committee on insurability. Ever since the malpractice crisis of the eighties, this organization, like many local AMA affiliates, had maintained a panel of ten to fifteen doctors to review claims and advise carriers on whether physicians should qualify for insurance. More than a physician's support group, the committee brokered between doctors and carriers, offering something both valued: a second opinion. Humes hoped the committee, as an independent reference panel and an arm of the county medical society, would intercede with CMIC on her behalf. It was her court of last resort.

It also was a model of what many doctors believed to be the only just way to evaluate malpractice claims—putting them before an impartial group of physicians for review—and what plaintiffs' lawyers like the Koskoffs distrusted most about doctors, namely their claim to be the sole legitimate arbiters of professional fitness. Koskoff didn't know about the hearing but would surely have denounced it if he did. He preferred to air questions of medical competence before ordinary citizens drawn—democratically, he would say, and without bias—from jury pools, and to have the issues framed by lawyers.

The committee, drawn from a cross section of specialties and including two ob-gyns, had heard Humes's case on September 11. Meeting after dinner in a private dining room at the Norwalk Inn, a rambling white brick hotel and conference center a few blocks from her office, they were joined by two consultants, also ob-gyns, from outside the Norwalk-Stamford area. Their purpose was to decide whether Humes had violated the standard of care in the two cases against her, Mary Gay's and Donna Sabia's, not whether she was a fair underwriting risk. For three hours the doctors reviewed the charts from the two births. They heard St. Paul justify why it had rejected Humes for insurance, and Humes's defense. Then they deliberated in private.

Humes wanted the insurability committee's finding as part of her CMIC appeal, but the end of the month was a blur and she forgot about it. Finally, on October 1 she phoned the association's office in Fairfield and was told that the panel had exonerated her. It had found no problem with her management of Mary Gay's delivery. As for the Sabias, the committee felt she'd walked into a hopeless situation. Mark Thomson, the association's executive director, told Humes the group had recommended unanimously that CMIC accept her application.

Vindicated, Humes relaunched her defense. She asked Dr. Morton Schiffer, Stamford's chairman of ob-gyn, to support her appeals, and a week later he wrote CMIC that Humes's work was "exemplary . . . beyond criticism." Thomson sent her, unsolicited, an AMA press release about a new study showing that past malpractice claims were inaccurate in predicting future negligence; in other words, doctors who'd been sued before might be bad risks but they weren't bad doctors. Humes bundled the press release with a recent practice profile from Stamford that showed her receiving high performance ratings and sent it to CMIC's underwriting manager. Less than two weeks later she wrote the company again, this time detailing how she'd managed the deliveries of both Michael Gay and Tony Sabia and describing the various protocols she now used to help preempt, if not bad outcomes, lawsuits. "I now insist," she wrote, "on electronic fetal monitoring of all my patients in labor."

Humes's faith in the insurability committee's ruling encouraged her belief that CMIC would now take her. These were doctors speaking, and CMIC was a doctor-run company. For weeks she heard nothing. Then, in mid-November, she called the company's headquarters in Glastonbury and was told that the appeal committee had refused to override her rejection. There would be one final review of her application, she was told, by the company's president, Dr. Kevin Dowling, before Thanksgiving. Running out of time, Humes appealed personally to Dowling in a letter dated November 22. "At the risk of appearing to be precipitous and even abrasive," she began, "I feel I must register with you [my] deep and unmitigated frustration." She was a victim of a "maloccurrence," she said. She had the enthusiastic support of her department head and the county medical society, both of whom had carefully reviewed the claims against her yet had been ignored by the company. CMIC's underwriters had evidently so botched her evaluation that it made her wonder if there weren't many other ob-gyns enjoying CMIC's coverage who had "much more culpability" than she had. Finally, she attacked the appeals process itself. "I feel," she wrote, "I have been judged and condemned without benefit of a thorough hearing. . . . All of the efforts to justify my insurability have been an exercise in futility."

Dowling replied on December 3, ten days before the jury announced its verdict in the Sherrington case and Smethurst called Bernard. Dowling had personally reviewed Humes's file, he said, but had found no basis for overcoming CMIC's concerns regarding her claims history. "Despite this adverse action on your application," he wrote, "please accept our best wishes for continued success." Apparently, it didn't matter whether Humes had done anything wrong, she thought. It only mattered that someone had claimed that she had, and had found a lawyer to make it official by suing her.

It was with this sense of resignation that Humes received the news from Haskell that the Sabia case might finally be at an end. She felt neither joy nor sorrow, not even relief. She'd been exonerated by the only forum she respected and it hadn't helped. Settling, she knew, wouldn't help either. What mattered was having been named in the first place.

Haskell drafted the terms of Humes's future protection while Smethurst and Bernard haggled over price. Haskell hadn't won, but she knew she also hadn't lost. She had rescued Humes from a situation that could only have gotten worse, at a cost to St. Paul that, in light of events, was sure to be a bargain. This is what lawyers did. They compromised, split the difference between people who were at each other's throats. They saved their clients from abuse, hostility, even themselves. Pat Ryan would say later that he thought Haskell had represented Humes as well as anyone could have, under the circumstances.

Haskell herself was less sure, but she knew that if Humes stayed in the case, she'd most likely be "tagged" at trial. In Haskell's experience, juries disliked doctors who were intemperate and, worse, inconsistent. She worried that Humes was both of these. Certainly, she was among the most personally involved of the hundred or so doctors Haskell had represented, and among the most difficult. Haskell couldn't deny a sense of relief at not having to hold her hand at trial. Helping her settle was the best she could do, for both of them.

Yet she'd hoped for more. She had failed in the one thing that would have offset all Humes's problems as a defendant: she hadn't produced compelling evidence to show that Little Tony's injuries had started and stopped before Humes ever got to the hospital—in essence, an alibi. With one or two strong, unequivocal experts to place the boy's injuries entirely in the prenatal period, she might have gotten Humes off completely on lack of causation. But Haskell had never been able to put together a case, and when Bernard seemed to trump her with Benirschke, it was over. All she could do after that was protect Humes's property. Six months later it still nettled her. "It was very frustrating for me," Haskell says. "I would have liked to have found a way to defend her. In my heart of hearts I was sympathetic."

~ ~ ~

Donna worked full-time now at the gift shop on I-95, in Darien. It was a union job, so she took home a decent paycheck. But there were mandatory shifts on weekends and holidays, and some weeks she had to work six days. She worked Thanksgiving and New Year's. She and Tony barely saw each other. When they did, they fought. Donna would ask Tony to do something; he would think she was nagging and walk away in a sulk. "We'd blow out yelling and screaming," Donna says. "It was getting to the point where the kids were hearing it. I'd had it. It was very, very stressful."

When Bernard called in December to say they might settle separately with Humes for more than $1 million, Donna was excited but cautious. She was having trouble at work. She would come in mornings, after the night shift had left the area a mess, and her bosses would blame her. Even with a big settlement, she didn't think she could quit. They might be able to pay off Little Tony's medical bills and their home equity loan, she thought, but what was going to change the constant hemorrhaging in their lives?

She and Tony had long since lost hope of making things whole, and when they talked about the money now, when they talked at all, it was in terms only of making life easier. Tony looked forward to "not living under the fuckin' gun all the time," not having "every day be a fuckin' battle," not, as he always said, "having to rob Peter to pay Paul." They didn't talk about their relationship, but each harbored the hope that money would give them time, they would worry less, and that that would help.

They made no association between the money and Humes as an individual. In eight years they'd seen her only three times—during the birth; the day after, when she'd come to console Donna; and in Ryan's office at their depositions—and their feelings about her were abstract, as if Humes were a well-off stranger with whose Mercedes they'd collided.

Donna had felt, largely because of Mary Gay, that Humes had done something wrong: that it was her job to monitor the twins, and she hadn't done it. It had bothered her especially that Humes was at her deposition—since she hadn't even known that was allowed—and under the glare of her wounded presence she'd felt threatened. But now she bore her no malice, nor did she blame her for what had happened to Little Tony. Though she'd wanted to know the truth, she was happy to get the money without it. "I didn't feel like we had answers," she says. "I felt, okay, now we can pay our bills."

Tony, though they seldom talked about it, felt the same. He thought Humes was an unfortunate bystander, which made her, regrettably for her, a convenient target. He considered the suit, and the settlement, in no way personal. "I'm not resentful of Humes," he would say. "She stepped in the middle of it. But what do you do?"

During the nearly three months of bargaining preceding the settlement, only the Koskoffs viewed the impending deal as in any way just. For four and a half years they'd cobbled together a reasonable, albeit circumstantial, case against Humes. They had the timing of Little Tony's injuries from Benirschke, which set the start of his asphyxia as that Saturday before Donna went into labor. They knew from Hermansen that the nearer to death an oxygen-deprived person is, the more accelerated the brain damage. From the hospital records and from Humes herself, they knew that Little Tony was on the brink of death when he was born. And from Humes and their other experts they had evidence of negligence: no ongoing fetal monitoring despite indications that the twins were distressed, in direct violation of the standard of care. It all added up. If Humes had discovered Little Tony's distress and taken him earlier by C-section, Koskoff and Bernard believed, there would have been more left of him: a higher IQ, more physical control, the ability to eat or go to the bathroom or understand language. Something.

Humes's negligence, Bernard says, was thus a "substantial factor" in Little Tony's injuries. She played a role, so she should be held to account. Koskoff himself was blunter: twice now, in separate cases, he believed he'd seen her so distracted during a labor and delivery that she hadn't done continuous fetal monitoring; both times there had been a tragic result. His attitude toward two-time offenders was, where there's smoke there's fire. He thought Humes was lucky still to be in practice. And yet they were willing to let her go, in order to get money to the Sabias, make their fee, and start concentrating on the larger prize—Norwalk Hospital.

Bernard kept Tony and Donna up to date on the negotiations, calling finally at the end of February to say they had an agreement. The Sabias were both relieved, encouraged finally to be getting a break, but their separate ideas of how the money would improve things seemed only to foment more tension. Driving to Bridgeport on February 28, 1992, to sign papers, they fought all the way up in the car.

The settlement price reached by Bernard and Smethurst was $1.35 million. In return, Tony and Donna agreed "to look solely to Norwalk Hospital for the remainder of the compensation due to them," according to the covenant worked out by Haskell and Bernard. After the Koskoffs took their fee of $450,000 and reimbursed themselves $47,000 for expenses, the Sabias would receive $853,000, about one-fourth cash with the rest in trust for Little Tony. Bernard warned them that payment might take a couple of months.

Various authorizations were needed by St. Paul to issue a check that size and the Koskoffs took their cut off the top. Donna sagged at the news. By then Little Tony would have had his eighth birthday. Donna planned to buy him a clown doll for the collection she'd started and maybe some clothes, which he needed. She felt sad that it wouldn't be a CD player or Rollerblades, things boys that age liked.

For most plaintiffs' lawyers the agreement would have been a bonanza. The Koskoffs regularly ordered champagne and platters of shrimp after closing big cases, and everyone in the office stopped work. But by now deals of this size had become routine. Within a couple of years the firm would have fifty separate million-dollar-plus cases in litigation at one time, most of them malpractice complaints.

Bernard thought it was a good settlement. His purpose had never been to punish Humes personally but to obtain relief for Tony and Donna. "We don't ignore the fact that we're suing human beings, on behalf of human beings," he says. "I don't doubt for a minute that Dr. Humes is a good person. But on that morning she didn't do what she was supposed to do. She can say, 'I didn't do it.' But St. Paul didn't pay $1.35 million because Maryellen Humes wanted out of the case." But Bernard was neither a hardened negotiator nor a malpractice true believer. Joel Lichtenstein, who was both, lamented that they hadn't gotten the full $2 million of Humes's policy. He would soon become the firm's settlement coordinator, handling all cases over $1 million.

Mike Koskoff was pleased to have Humes finally out of the case. At first, when it had looked like a mishandled delivery, he'd been eager to have her as a defendant. But ever since the emphasis shifted to the hospital's prenatal care, she'd just been in the way. Even he had to concede that she'd been "confronted with a terrible situation," and while not enough to spare her, her last-minute arrival troubled him, if only because it might create sympathy among jurors. In terms of value Humes had long been a sideshow, not the main event, and now that they'd disposed of her Koskoff felt revitalized, ready to take on more of the case against the real defendant of interest, Norwalk Hospital. In two weeks he would fly out to California to take depositions from Benirschke and Schifrin. He'd be in the thick of preparations for a major trial, one with a possibly staggering payout. It would be him against Ryan, a formidable match.

He suspected Humes felt she'd been sacrificed, but he disagreed. She should be thankful, he thought. She could have really gotten hurt. Instead, he had let her out at a price her insurance company could accept and had gone out of his way not to sully that which she held most dear—her comfortable life, her livelihood, her reputation, and her home. Another lawyer might think he'd let her off easy.

FOURTEEN

MARCH 13, 1992

FOR MONTHS TONY HAD HAD DIFFICULTY BREATHING. HE HAD POUNDING headaches from frequent sinus infections. His eyes burned. He was inhaling a lot of diesel exhaust and paper dust near the loading dock and thought that was the problem. Finally, it got so bad he opted for surgery instead of waiting to file a disability claim. He drove himself to Norwalk Hospital for the operation. He and Donna were fighting more than ever, and asking for a ride, or accepting one, meant more trouble than it was worth. Their resentments hadn't abated now that they had money coming from the settlement with Humes; if anything, they'd become more reflexive. "I'm supposed to jump, I'm supposed to do this, I'm supposed to do that," Tony would say. "Fuck it." The surgeon had told him he was going to straighten his septum, the wall of bone and cartilage that separated his nostrils. It was outpatient surgery. How bad could it be?

After the operation Tony's nostrils were packed with gauze—he had to breathe through his mouth—and his glasses caused him so much pain he couldn't wear them. Unable to drive, he called his sister for a ride home. That night he and Donna fought again. What caused their arguments no longer mattered; it was all one cycle of abuse. It was as if there was nothing they could say to each other that wasn't a provocation. They exercised that dual accounting, common in troubled marriages, whereby no partner can let the other win, and there are no allowances or time-outs.

They both knew that caring for Little Tony was the overarching cause of their problems, but refused to blame him. Nor did they reconsider putting him in an institution. Tony had long ago said you don't give up your own and

Donna agreed. Nothing, including the settlement, had happened to change that. They would keep him home even though they now could afford a decent place for him; even though, it appeared increasingly, that the cost of taking care of him was their own happiness and that of their other children.

That night Tony didn't sleep. He was doubled-up in pain and had trouble breathing through his mouth. At 4 A.M., sitting at the kitchen table, he sneezed. The surgeon had told him to try to sneeze through his mouth, but he couldn't do it, and the packing from one nostril flew into the living room, like a torpedo, he said. Unable to stop the bleeding, he dialed Norwalk Hospital.

∾ ∾ ∾

Kurt Benirschke's office in the basement of the University of California San Diego Medical Center lies down an echoing corridor of scrubbed tile and linoleum. Across the hall is the battered meat-locker door of the morgue, unmarked but painted, oddly, pink. The area is deserted and smells of disinfectant and bleach. The medical center, a sleek white tower, rises atop a hill overlooking the Pacific; upstairs in the main lobby, a gleaming three-story atrium, twenty-foot palm trees shade plush couches in muted tones. Benirschke, however, is head of the autopsy service. There are no signs leading from the elevator to his office, a warren of small, windowless rooms. The hospital, says a secretary, half-joking, "doesn't like people to know we're down here."

Mike Koskoff arrived around 10 A.M., just hours after Tony, on the East Coast, was wheeled out of surgery. Benirschke's deposition was scheduled for eleven, and Koskoff, uncharacteristically, was worried. He was clean-shaven now, loose-limbed in khakis, a white shirt, silk tie, and sport jacket. His close-set eyes blazed with their usual intensity, but his normal bonhomie was gone, squelched by a studied deference broken now and then by an ingratiating laugh. Benirschke was his star witness, perhaps the one true giant in his field, whom Bernard had led Haskell to believe supported them unequivocally, but Koskoff dreaded what he was about to say. Twice in the past fourteen months he had flown to California to discuss the case with him, and both times Benirschke had been unwilling to blame Humes and the hospital for Little Tony's injuries. His opinions about the mechanism of those injuries served Koskoff's theory, but he refused to be coached.

At sixty-seven, Benirschke was large, tanned, impressively fit. His after-work tastes ran to rugged activity and fine things—he owned a red 1961 Mercedes 300SL roadster that he loved to work on himself—and living in Southern California agreed with him. He had a long, lugubrious face with dark swirling eyebrows that shadowed eyes so deep-set that they seemed gouged, and thin grey hair he kept faithfully combed. His lips tightened when he concentrated, though he wasn't austere: he smiled easily, an infectious grin that overspread his cheeks. His office, so cramped that four people couldn't sit in it comfortably, reflected a grandfatherly, if macabre, sense of humor. Near a dime-store sign that said WARNING: OCCUPANT IS AN INCURABLE CHOCOHOLIC; PLEASE DO NOT FEED hung a print of Salvador Dalí's *Inventions of the Monsters*.

The joke was a droll one. Monsters are a specialty of Benirschke's. A metal cabinet on one wall held his slides, the accumulated grotesqueries of forty years of novel research into the causes of fetal death, injury, and disease. It contained a gallery of freakish images—three-headed babies spontaneously aborted long before term; shrunken, desiccated corpses—which while repellent were, in another light, the laboratory failures of a quirky and experimental Creator. Benirschke seemed endlessly fascinated by their variety. Unsolicited, he liked to pop out slides for visitors, marveling, "Look at this one!" then giggling at the grisliest. An ingenious scientist, he delighted in the ingenuity of nature even when it went hideously awry. Their too-close association with death often marks pathologists as, if not morbid, dull and unsociable, but Benirschke was vigorous and worldly—internationally celebrated in several disciplines—and Koskoff prized him as a rare catch.

He also feared him. It was Benirschke who had determined that the cause of Little Tony's brain damage was the sudden massive bleed into his dead twin through the arteries of the placenta. Koskoff hoped to have him depict those events in such a way as to make clear that both outcomes could easily have been prevented. It was likely that no expert in the world was more capable of doing so—"Benirschke's a god," Bernard recalls a neonatologist once telling him. "If that's what he says, I wouldn't question it." But, Koskoff worried, no expert was more headstrong either. As a witness, Benirschke was famously independent. He had enlightened opinions covering just about all of reproductive medicine and was generally regarded as prodefense. He disliked lawyers and didn't hide it. "As a lawyer," Koskoff says, "you take a certain risk when you hire someone like that. He could kill you."

His career had surely been remarkable. Born in Glückstadt, Germany, a small town on the Elbe, in 1924, he finished medical school at the University of Hamburg in 1948, then emigrated to New York a year later, after a two-month stopover in London to learn English. Unable to find a job, he delivered German-language newspapers until he eventually was hired as an intern at a Catholic hospital in New Jersey. He thought briefly of becoming a surgeon, until a colleague persuaded him to apply for a pathology residency at Harvard. It was at Harvard, throughout the fifties, that Benirschke pioneered the study of the placenta. A more unfashionable specialty would have been hard to find. The organ itself had long been neglected. Obstetricians discarded it; anyone interested in examining placental tissue literally had to retrieve it from the waste. Malpractice claims in bad baby cases were unheard of then, so there was little outside interest in how cellular events could explain what happened in the womb prior to labor. Yet Benirschke, as chief resident at Boston Lying-In Hospital, where young Harvard ob-gyns trained, was intrigued. He started work at 5 A.M. in order to examine surgical and autopsy material before it was thrown away. He collected data on 150 consecutive twin autopsies. Eventually, he began to discern how the structures of the placenta, particularly those involved in the exchange of blood and nutrients, correlated with the grisly outcomes observed in the delivery room.

His interests multiplied. Fascinated with twins, he was drawn to cytogenetics, the study of how chromosomes influence the life and death of cells, making several major discoveries about the causes of fetal abnormalities and becoming a leader in the field. After leaving Harvard to become chairman of the pathology department at Dartmouth Medical School, he took up the study of freemartins, cows that have male twins and are born sterile, which led him to trace the chromosomal basis for infertility in mules, which led to numerous other studies of animal reproduction, which ultimately put him in touch with leading wildlife conservationists and figures at the world's major zoos. By the time he moved to San Diego in the early seventies as a professor of reproductive medicine and pathology, Benirschke had developed a third specialty—animal reproduction—which in 1976 resulted in his being named medical director of the San Diego Zoo, a world leader in saving endangered species. Benirschke drove himself at a murderous pace. He had written more than two dozen books, contributed some seventy chapters to textbooks, authored more than four hundred scientific papers, and served on the editorial boards of journals dealing with topics ranging from genetics to pediatrics. He regularly consulted with doctors, hospitals, and health organizations around the world. He was president of the American Association of Pathologists and the Perinatal Research Society.

And yet the more far-flung his interests got, the more they doubled back to where he'd begun, with the placenta and the causes of illness and death in term infants. It was here that Benirschke made perhaps his chief contribution to medicine, and that he entered his last, most nettlesome, arena: the law. By the early eighties, the explosion of birth injury cases had caught up with him, raising the same questions that he had begun asking thirty years earlier as a resident in pathology. As a medical investigator, Benirschke welcomed the new interest in his work. He started testifying in cases where he thought he could do some good, but he quickly discovered that law wasn't medicine. Law was based on impression, not data; was prosecutorial, not collegial; conferred more value on questions than on answers. It was debating, he realized, not science. No matter how certain he was of the pathology in a given case, he was regularly dismayed by how the lawyers drew their own conclusions, as if they hadn't heard him. He also learned that despite his qualifications, his credibility and intentions were themselves fair game. Once during a deposition an opposing lawyer accused him, "because I grew up in Germany," he says, of dissecting Jews as part of experiments he conducted there as a medical student. When he looked for support from the lawyer who'd hired him, the man remained silent. "It's basically a brotherhood of lawyers," he would say. "The plaintiffs and the defense, neither can do without the other."

Benirschke's frustration had ripened into bitterness, then disgust. He didn't think lawyers wanted the truth, they only wanted to win, and by now he responded to their machinations with thinly veiled contempt. He says he continued to testify to advance the cause of placental pathology and to inject some rigor into the process of litigation. But with each case he felt more and more compromised. At times he joked about it. He had a ranch in the Chaco region of Paraguay where in conjunction with the zoo he was attempting to prevent the extinction of a rare species of wild pig. So hostile was the environment—brutally hot, it was infested with mosquitoes and venomous snakes, covered with an impenetrable thorny bush, and had no potable surface water—it was nicknamed "the green hell." "It's way out in the bush," Benirschke would tell people. "I love it there. It's far from all the lawyers."

Benirschke wasn't hostile to Koskoff, merely disdainful and remote. He'd never been comfortable implicating Humes, convinced that the damage to Little Tony was over before she'd arrived. Now Koskoff reassured him that Humes was out of the case. He didn't reveal that he and Bernard had pressed to force her out before Benirschke's deposition, or that his refusal to testify against her was their primary reason for doing so. The issue now, he explained, was solely whether Norwalk Hospital was culpable. Benirschke voiced no objection, and Koskoff assumed from his silence that he agreed.

It was a slender assumption. Benirschke's opinions had been crucial to the Sabias' case up to this point, but Koskoff worried that they might backfire in court if he seemed to a jury even tacitly prodefense. "I'm thinking," Koskoff says, "'I don't know if he's going to go with us to trial. I don't know if he's going to go with the defendants.' I'm crossing my fingers." Koskoff may have been consoled by the knowledge that if he lost Benirschke as a witness, so would the hospital. Bound by confidentiality, experts weren't allowed to switch sides. At worst it would be a draw, with both sides scrambling for another placental expert.

Bev Hunt arrived shortly after eleven. If Koskoff was surprised that Ryan had left such a critical deposition to an associate, he didn't show it. Mainly, he wanted Hunt to believe that his and Benirschke's collaboration was relaxed and secure. And so he focused on his expert, who rocked slightly, impatiently in his chair, barricaded on three sides by his desk, a computer table, and a table with a microscope with two eyepieces, as he and Hunt said little. The geometry of the tiny office precluded avoidance, but Benirschke, amused, watched the lawyers do their best even as the court reporter arrived, forcing them to shuffle their chairs still closer to one another to make space.

Hunt began her examination first. She and Ryan still were unsure how the settlement with Humes would affect the case against the hospital. Were the Koskoffs still claiming that Little Tony suffered brain damage right up through labor and delivery, and that Norwalk was liable because McManamy and Fortuna were hospital employees? Would Benirschke rule out a sudden cord accident as the cause of Twin B's death or could Hunt make him concede it as a possibility? For weeks Hunt had prepared, poring over Benirschke's writings about twins and discordant growth and the type of veil-like cord insertion Humes had found on the placenta for Baby B. Nothing Hunt found in her preparation ruled out the possibility that what had happened had been a sudden, unforeseeable event—an accident. That was what she had come to believe, but she couldn't prove it. All she knew was that Benirschke, as the Koskoffs' causation expert, stood to implicate her client.

She began, predictably, by asking what killed Michael Sabia. Benirschke steepled his hands against his chin, spreading and unspreading his fingers like a spider on a mirror, as he considered the question. "I don't know the cause of the stillborn's death," he said. His accent was unmistakably German, but his speech precise and clear. "The probabilities are that the smaller baby, in such placentas, had a velamentous of the umbilical cord."

Hunt asked him to elucidate, and Benirschke responded as if giving a short paper. What he believed, he said, is that the arteries anchoring Twin B's umbilical cord to the placenta had become highly vulnerable. The bigger the twins grew—the more crowded Donna's uterus—the greater the chance of the arteries being compressed by the baby itself, perhaps by its head. There was evidence of this in the fact that there had been a thrombus—a blood clot—in one of the arteries that predated the baby's death. Since thrombi don't form where blood is moving freely, Benirschke said, it was most likely that pressure on the vessel had constricted the blood flow through it, a condition called stasis.

"That's the probabilities," he said, concluding, "but I don't think anyone knows with certainty what eventually killed the smaller baby."

Hunt tried to narrow it down. "Was the death of the stillborn sudden," she asked, "or [did it] take place over hours?"

"Death is always sudden," Benirschke said, "I don't—"

Koskoff interrupted. "It's a philosophical question rather than a legal one you're asking," he said. He was trying to head Hunt off—"sudden" implied unpredictable, which implied that there was nothing to be done.

Hunt changed the question. "At what point did the death occur of the stillborn?"

"I beg your pardon?" Benirschke said.

"At what point did the death of the stillborn occur?"

"I would assume about a day, within a day or so prior to delivery."

"And do you have an opinion regarding the functioning of that stillborn up to the time of its death?"

"Well," Benirschke said, "it urinated, because there is amniotic fluid present. And since there is meconium present, it must have been able to defecate, so it was functioning there. It continued to grow. It was smaller, but it functioned to some extent."

"All right. So would you say that the functioning in all probability up to the time of death—the functioning was normal?"

"Oh, I don't know that," Benirschke corrected. "The baby may have been abnormal and functioned in some aspects abnormally. I couldn't say that in the absence of doing an autopsy."

"But there's no indicator here that the child was functioning other than normally prior to its death?" Hunt asked.

"That's correct."

Hunt was fishing. She didn't know yet how long Koskoff would claim Twin B's stasis had gone on, or if it was something that could have been detected through monitoring, but she hoped to establish that there was no positive evidence that the stillborn's demise had been gradual. Satisfied, she moved on.

"Okay," she said. "Now can you tell me the cause of Anthony's damage."

Koskoff cautioned Benirschke. "Based on a reasonable probability."

"In my opinion," Benirschke said, "the probabilities are that Anthony suffered acute hemorrhage leading to hypotension after the first baby had died, through placental anastomoses"—his blood pressure had dropped when he bled precipitously into his dead twin through the placenta.

"Was there a sudden kind of event in terms of Anthony's blood depletion?" Hunt asked.

"Yes," he said.

"And Anthony's damage, in all probability, was solely related to this acute hemorrhage event?"

"Yes."

"Now is it your opinion then," Hunt continued, "that this sudden blood depletion in Anthony occurred at the time of the death of 'B,' which was within a day prior to birth?"

"Within a very short time after the death, yes."

"So the blood depletion in relation to Anthony took place in all probability within minutes of the stillborn's death, is that what you're saying?"

"Yes, a half hour maybe, but within a very short time."

Hunt was encouraged: "So it was within a half hour of that that Anthony's brain damage was incurred in its entirety?"

"Oh," Benirschke hesitated. "I don't know in its entirety, but certainly that is when the major damage is likely to have occurred."

"Okay," Hunt said. "Now what did you just mean by you don't know about its entirety?"

"He may have had many postnatal events or infections that I am not privy to. But I'm saying only that the problems with which Anthony was born were related to this event."

"Okay. And so when you use that qualifier, 'In its entirety,' you have no evidence that there was any other contributing factor . . . to Anthony's brain damage?"

"I don't have any evidence, no," Benirschke said. "I don't know Anthony and I do not know all of the subsequent events that happened in his life."

Hunt could scarcely believe her ears. Benirschke, the plaintiffs' causation expert, had eliminated labor and delivery as a contributing cause of injury. That part of the case was now gone. Hunt felt a fleeting pang of sympathy for Humes but was too exhilarated to dwell on it.

Needing time to think, she asked for a recess. She and Ryan had always figured the Koskoffs would play up the birth. Even after they failed to depose Fortuna, she thought they'd tar the hospital with what had always been the most disturbing part of the case, even for her: the fact that Michael Sabia was dead and Tony Sabia was at the brink of death and no one at the hospital knew it. Koskoff would call that "dead in the water" liability, and though Hunt would strain to deny it, there really was no way to defend such a lapse—except for this, for having the plaintiff's own causation expert assert that it was irrelevant. Where, Hunt asked herself, was Koskoff's case? All he had left was the still unproven claim that somehow the hospital should have known that Michael Sabia was in imminent danger of dying. But Benirschke didn't seem to support that either.

Returning to the deposition, Hunt zeroed in again on the stillborn, Twin B. Was the 20 percent discordancy in the twins' weights significant, she asked? Benirschke said he thought it was. Well then, Hunt asked, would knowing that disparity in itself have been cause for the hospital to take the babies sooner? Koskoff objected; Benirschke was a pathology expert, not an obstetrical expert.

"If you're asking whether an intervention was needed," Benirschke answered finally, "that's not my area of expertise."

Content that she'd got more than she came for, Hunt moved on to some housekeeping. She asked how much Benirschke was being paid for his testimony, how many hours he had spent preparing, whether he charged more for depositions and court time. She then asked, as a matter of routine, whether he'd ever seen any similar cases.

Benirschke perked up, apparently pleased at the opportunity to add some perspective to his testimony. "Yes," he brightened. "It's a common problem."

Could he name some of the other cases? Hunt asked.

"Sure, I can do that now," he said, swiveling in his chair. "That's not a big deal. I can ask my computer to do that for me. Take me a minute, but it's easily possible. I have to find Mr. Norton." Benirschke inserted a disk, typed for a minute, then stared at the screen. "Okay, Barrigan is one," he said.

"Is that B-A-R-R-I-G-I-N?"

"A-N. Brown is another."

"Where was Barrigan?"

"I'll have to tell you that later. I can't tell you that now," Benirschke paused. "Acooley. Fitch could be another one. Horneung. H-O-R-N-E-U-N-G. Evans. Johnson. It's a common problem. Aultman. Sandwell. McKerche, M-C-K-E-R-C-H-E. Oregon, Here, Savarra, and that's it."

~ ~ ~

At trial Koskoff would want to answer one overarching question: should Norwalk Hospital have foreseen—could it have prevented—the death of Michael Sabia? Negligent homicide, in his view, is what the case now came down to. The lifetimes of pain and suffering endured by his clients, Little Tony and Donna, could be traced to a single catastrophic event, an event to which they were both bystanders; an event, Koskoff would argue, that should never have been allowed to occur. His cardinal assumption, the thing that he says drove him as a lawyer and that fueled his outrage, was that if something could go wrong it would, and therefore it was the responsibility of those with the power to do so to ensure it didn't.

With Humes out of the way, the question of when the damage to Little Tony ended was irrelevant. What mattered was simply when—and how—it had begun. Koskoff knew Benirschke's value as a witness rose incrementally the clearer it became that the key events in the case had occurred before, not after, Michael Sabia's death. He was not disappointed with Hunt's examination; on the contrary, she had done him a favor. She had reduced the scope of the questions Benirschke would be asked at trial and set the stage for the real subject of interest—Michael Sabia's condition up to the time he died. On Monday he and Hunt would meet again to depose Barry Schifrin in Los Angeles. Looking ahead to Schifrin's deposition and beyond, Koskoff hoped to erase any doubt that the boy's death had resulted, more probably than not, from factors that could and should have been known by hospital employees through routine medical assessment.

It was rare for lawyers to examine their own experts at depositions, but Koskoff now had several reasons for wanting to question Benirschke directly. The purpose—and value—of deposing someone of Benirschke's caliber was to frighten the other side while planting a flag for trial. But Koskoff felt that

Hunt, in her cross-examination, had "left a lot of misimpressions." She hadn't come close to eliciting how bad Benirschke's testimony might be for Norwalk Hospital. Also, if the deposition ended now and Benirschke eventually testified in court, he would be limited to discussing only those opinions he'd given in answer to Hunt's question. Koskoff wanted to leave a stronger transcript, one that would record more fully where Benirschke stood and, by Connecticut law, could be introduced at trial if Benirschke failed to testify in person. He started off by questioning Benirschke again about the anomalies of Michael Sabia's short, unrealized life.

"Now Dr. Benirschke," Koskoff said, "in this case, you mentioned that there was a difference in the percentage of placenta used by Twin A, Anthony Sabia, and Twin B. Is that right?"

"Yes." Benirschke nodded.

"Twin B had only approximately a third of the use of the placenta. Is that correct?"

"Yes. That's correct."

"And having less of the placenta meant that he was less able to share in the nutrients and blood flow that was present in the placenta; is that fair to say?"

"Yes."

"And having less of the placenta, did that result in Baby B's becoming a smaller baby than Baby A?"

"That's the principal reason for it."

"Okay," Koskoff said. "And Twin B grew at a lesser rate. Is that correct?"

"Yes."

"And that is because, as you indicated, he had less access to the placenta and had a velamentous cord insertion?"

"That's correct."

"Now, Doctor," Koskoff prodded. "Can you tell me: does the velamentous cord insertion lead to the development of thrombi?" The question was critical. If Koskoff could show that Michael Sabia's blood flow had been impeded before he died, it would support his claim that the hospital would have known, by doing a nonstress test, that he was in trouble.

"Yes," Benirschke said.

"And can you tell me whether or not, aside from the thrombosis which ultimately killed Baby B, would it be likely that thrombi would develop in a velamentous cord insertion over the course of time?"

"Object." Hunt shot up. "That wasn't his testimony."

"I don't think the thrombosis killed the baby," Benirschke agreed, explaining that the cause of death was the compression of the blood vessels impeding Twin B's oxygen supply. "But," he clarified, "the thrombosis betrays the compression of the blood vessels."

"So that that played a part?" Koskoff said.

"Object to the form," Hunt said.

"Did it play a part?" Koskoff repeated.

Benirschke paused carefully. He took a breath. "I think," he said measuredly, "the thrombosis signifies that there has been reduced blood flow through those blood vessels and that compression was the most likely cause of that and possibly twisting of the cord, and that this reduced venous return led to the death of that baby."

"Now Dr. Benirschke," Koskoff said. "You were asked whether or not the death was a sudden event, and I think you indicated death is always sudden, in a sense. But did this event—was it a culmination of a number of—of a period of time over which this child was receiving less nourishment and feeling the effects of velamentous cord insertion?"

"Objection."

"The effect of velamentous insertion," Benirschke explained again, "is growth retardation, primarily, and from velamentous insertion, per se, the baby does not die. The baby can die, however, because the blood vessels are torn and it exsanguinates, or there's reduced venous return because the velamentous vessels are compromised by the pressure of fetal parts. Since there were thrombi, compression or reduced venous return can be assumed."

"And the compression you're talking about, is that the compression in utero because of the growing size of the two babies?"

"Yes."

"And that compression takes place over a period of time?"

"That takes place over a period of time."

"And also, the malnutrition of Baby B took place also over a period of time, I take it—"

"That," Benirschke said, "takes place over a much longer period of time."

Koskoff now had all that he wanted. He finished with a coda.

"And that's the sudden event that caused, ultimately, all the damage to— question withdrawn. That's the event that ultimately caused the damage to Twin A."

Benirschke smiled. "That's the overwhelming probability."

Hunt tried to conceal her elation. Koskoff's slip—his accidental use of "all the damage"—confirmed she'd been right about the labor and delivery being moot. She left Benirschke's office as soon as she could politely pull herself away, then raced to a pay phone to call Ryan. But it was after 5 P.M. in Connecticut, and he was gone for the weekend. "I was in a state of shock," dying to share the news, she recalls. Finally, she reached Ryan the next morning at home. "Benirschke couldn't have done better had he been our own expert," she told him. The labor and delivery issue they'd dreaded defending for five years, she announced triumphantly, was "totally gone."

~ ~ ~

A black-and-white 1960s TV commercial about cerebral palsy. An exuberant marionette—a boy—dances gaily, obliviously, as a voice-over states that every hour a child is stricken with the crippling disease. One by one the doll's strings are cut by an unseen hand. First a leg goes lame. Then another. Then an arm. With each loss, the rest of the boy's body twitches out of sync until all the strings are severed and the marionette collapses forlornly in a heap. The image approximates what happened to Little Tony in the scenario laid out by Benirschke, a scenario begun and ended, it now seemed certain, in the last, silently tumultuous twenty-four to thirty-six hours before Donna went into labor.

She was enormous then, the twins stirring yin-yang–like in her belly. It felt as if she were carrying a bowling ball with legs, often two bowling balls. Little Tony's head was wedged so firmly in the pit of her pelvis, she felt she couldn't hold her urine. Michael, in breech position on top, battered her rib cage. With much less water surrounding the babies, she felt every twisting elbow, knee, and shoulder as a sharp, insistent jab. Exhausted and irritable, Donna couldn't wait for it to be over.

Nothing suggests that Little Tony was anything but healthy and normal when Donna arrived at the Norwalk Hospital clinic on Friday afternoon, March 30, and was reassured by McManamy that there were two heartbeats and that all was fine. Michael may well have been healthy, too, although that is less certain. Some part of him may have lodged against the exposed vessels at the base of his umbilical cord long enough to begin starving him of oxygen. Quite possibly, he was already brain-damaged. More probably than not, judging from Benirschke's interpretation, neither boy's condition was affected later that night when Tony and Donna fought and Tony pushed her.

Then, Saturday, something happened, and the shutoff of Michael's oxygen proceeded inexorably. Apparently, sometime around noon he died, his heart stopping. A crucial equilibrium was suddenly shattered. The twins' circulatory systems were joined at their farthest reaches, in the placenta, through the connecting blood vessels called anastomoses. This vascular estuary had served as a buffer between them: as long as both had been alive, each twin's blood was repulsed there by the counterpressure of the other's blood pumping in the opposite direction. But when Michael's heart ceased, each heartbeat pushed Tony's blood farther, as if it were leaking out through a slashed vein. It quickly suffused Michael's portion of the placenta, backwashed through his cord, and spilled into the flaccid vessels of his lifeless body. Thus did Little Tony, as the Sabias recalled Humes telling them, "give his blood" to his brother.

The shock of the bleed caused Little Tony's heart to race, pumping harder a it compensated for the sudden drop in pressure. But because he was losing fluid, fewer and fewer red cells returned with each beat. A major "power failure" now threatened. Not enough blood was getting to his organs and what blood did reach them carried insufficient oxygen. In order to conserve his slender stores of energy, his brain automatically cut blood flow to those areas that could survive temporarily without oxygen and shunted it to those that couldn't.

Brain damage began after about fifteen minutes. By then only Little Tony's brain, heart, and a few other vital areas were getting blood, and most likely he had sunk into a deep stupor. He was severely anemic and his blood pressure was perhaps near zero, which resulted, as he kept hemorrhaging, in a cascade of injuries. It was now that the strings—the bundles of neurons— tying various regions of Little Tony's brain to a normally functioning body and mind were clipped. The brain is perfused with blood saturating outward from a skein of central arteries through an elaborate irrigation system. As Little Tony's blood pressure kept dropping, less blood and oxygen reached the outermost fields of his upper brain. Cells died wholesale as these "last fields" literally dried up. As the blood loss contracted inward, the descending nerve fibers controlling physical movement were also destroyed. In probably less than fifteen minutes and no more than half an hour, Little Tony lost first the use of his legs, then his trunk, then, finally, his arms. His vision and speech, though apparently not his hearing, quickly followed.

More neurons were dying all around. The loss of blood pressure and catastrophic changes in his metabolism that turned his blood acidic decimated the part of his brain that governed thinking, sensation, cognition, motivation, and the interrelated functions that bind them all into what we call intelligence. With the dead cells tending to dissolve, cavities developed, leaving major sections of his white matter porous and spongy—in the words of one expert, "like Swiss cheese." Also lost were inhibitory neurons, which block electrical and chemical reactions and without which the brain fires uncontrollably, inducing seizures.

And then, according to Benirschke—and in the opinion of perhaps the world's leading expert in the neurology of the newborn, Dr. Joseph J. Volpe, who played no role in *Sabia*—the injuries stopped. After an hour or so, Little Tony ceased hemorrhaging, probably because Michael was so engorged that his body acted like a tourniquet, building enough back-pressure to stanch the bleeding. Little Tony stabilized, and his heartbeat modulated. He remained profoundly anemic, even though his bone marrow churned out new, incomplete red cells in a futile effort to get more oxygen to his brain and elsewhere. All that was left of him for sure were the most basic functions needed for survival, the ones the brain guards to the end—the ability to breathe, suck, swallow, digest, and yield waste, and the autonomic regulation of glands and organs. Just over five pounds, he languished this way—cocooned, torpid, tiny heart pounding—until some twenty-four hours later when, after an explosive four-hour labor, he was expelled into the world.

Koskoff had always insisted that because Little Tony was so near death at birth—"incompatible with life," was his phrase—he must have been in a state of continuing decline throughout labor. This, of course, was the crux of the suit against Humes: she had "futzed around" for two hours, he said, while more and more of Little Tony's brain was destroyed. But Benirschke's testimony left little doubt that Koskoff had been wrong. Says Volpe, chief of neurology at Children's Hospital in Boston and Bronson Crothers Professor of Neurology at Harvard Medical School, "By that time the game was over." Imagine someone twenty-four hours after being resuscitated sixty minutes after a major heart attack, Volpe says. Little Tony's devastated condition at birth needn't have resulted from—nor did it indicate—ongoing injuries up to the last minute.

Koskoff prefers another analogy, one that takes into account the added trauma of a vaginal delivery. "It's more like somebody having an insult," he says, "and suffering terrible damage. Then a couple of days later, somebody puts a plastic bag over his head and suffocates him." Still, in 1994, in a phone conversation with Mary Gay, he would concede that even had Humes mishandled the delivery, it was too late to make any difference. "She wasn't responsible for the injury," he said, "through no fault of her own."

Koskoff had no regrets about settling with Humes two weeks before Benirschke absolved her in his deposition. Even if he agreed with Benirschke, which he didn't—even if he'd known exactly what Benirschke planned to say, which he denies, and suspected himself that Humes wasn't at fault—he had far more compelling reasons to keep her in the case until it settled than to release her. One was the empty chair: he didn't want to risk letting Norwalk Hospital blame her at trial. Another, not unironically, was a fear of being sued for malpractice himself. Koskoff had reason to believe that if he let Humes out, then lost to the hospital, the Sabias might find another lawyer to challenge his handling of the case. They would ask to look at his files and learn that he had other experts who'd testified that Humes had violated the standard of care. To drop a case burdened with the promise of so much liability was a liability in itself. Increasingly, in the new dog-eat-dog legal economy, lawyers who lost were at risk of being sued by hungry colleagues. And though doctors applauded this trend as a deserved act of cannibalism, the result often meant that once a suit against a doctor was filed, it was almost never retracted, even if there was reason to do so.

Koskoff's third reason for looking forward, not back, was Benirschke himself. If Benirschke thought Humes was blameless, why was he working for the plaintiffs? Why wasn't he working for her?

~ ~ ~

Hunt stayed an extra day in San Diego. She went to the zoo and took a spectator boat out to watch the America's Cup trials. Then on Sunday morning she rented a car and drove up to Los Angeles to prepare for Schifrin's deposition on Monday. She was still soaring. Hunt was passionate about her work. Now that Ryan, her mentor, had practically given her the case even though it was her first, *Sabia* had come to mean more to her personally than it did to any other of the more than a dozen lawyers who worked on it. She believed staunchly in the hospital's cause and saw it as her mission to win. For lawyers like Ryan and Koskoff, flying to California to depose internationally known experts was part of the drudgery of preparing for trial, but for Hunt, a former nurse, it was powerfully affirming.

Whatever qualms she had concerned Humes. It was, almost to the day, three years since she had coached McManamy through her deposition, encouraging her to testify that Humes bore full responsibility for Little Tony's birth. Knowing what the delivery had done to McManamy and Fortuna, how merely being called as witnesses had haunted them, she could only imagine what Humes had been through. Then, after everything, to have this. It was like a posthumous reprieve, the coldest of comforts. Hunt would later say she wished she could have made it turn out differently, that she might somehow have been more supportive of Humes's position.

Schifrin's deposition took place in his office, on the sixth floor of a modern white office block in Tarzana, and Koskoff was again waiting when Hunt arrived, shortly before ten. He had gotten the flu over the weekend and Hunt thought he looked awful, though she was more aware of Schifrin. He glared at her owlishly, with a mildly annoyed expression that Hunt connected with disdain. Benirschke, with his seniority and independence, didn't go out of his way to bully: he didn't have to. But Schifrin's arrogance seemed palpable, and Hunt, in spite of her bullishness, felt intimidated. She got his name wrong, calling him, perhaps wistfully, "Dr. Benirschke." And she worried about her ability to pin him down during questioning. She recalls, "When you get into giants, it's hard to control them."

Hunt went first. With the birth out of the way, she zeroed in on Donna's prenatal treatment. She thought Benirschke's testimony regarding the cause of Michael Sabia's death had been a wash: though the placenta indicated that he had been compromised for some time, he'd died suddenly, perhaps from a twisted cord. Now she wanted to know how Schifrin thought the hospital had been negligent in not preventing such an outcome. "Oh, sure," he said authoritatively, when Hunt asked how the hospital had violated the standard of care. "The straightforward failure to provide adequate growth testing; failure to provide adequate function testing . . . a seeming failure to understand that twin pregnancy represents a high risk and requires ongoing surveillance." Specifically, Schifrin thought the hospital should have performed an ultrasound every two to three weeks during Donna's last trimester and a nonstress test every week beginning at between thirty-two and thirty-four weeks—a month to a month and a half before her labor. Such tests, he said, were required because of the elevated risks associated with twin pregnancies at term, and would have shown conclusively that Michael wasn't thriving. The implication, unstated, was that both boys would have been saved.

Hunt pursued the issue of the nonstress test. Now, in 1992, the test was standard practice in high-risk pregnancies. With women at or near term, obstetricians recorded fetal heart rates continuously for twenty minutes, looking mainly for accelerations when the fetus moved. A healthy fetus showed accelerations of more than fifteen beats per minute, lasting fifteen seconds—so-called reactivity. An abnormal or nonreactive test showed no such leaps, possibly indicating distress, although, as with other forms of monitoring, the test was much better at predicting when a fetus would be born healthy than when one was in trouble. Typically, Schifrin held that such tests were most reliable when conducted by experienced hands such as his own. But he believed strongly that given Twin B's condition—growth-retarded with a velamentous cord, a week and a half past maturity, hours from death—a nonstress test on the Friday afternoon before Donna's labor would have sent unmistakable signals that he was already compromised.

Hunt pressed him first about Little Tony, who Schifrin agreed should still have been normal. "So does that mean," she asked, "that it's reasonable to believe that 'A' on March thirtieth, four o'clock, would have had a reactive nonstress test?"

"Yes. Absolutely."

"Okay," she continued. "Now in all reasonable probability, would 'B' have had a reactive stress test result on March thirtieth at four o'clock?"

"I believe that's implausible," Schifrin said, "medically implausible."

"Okay. Now what's the basis for that?"

Impatiently, Schifrin repeated himself. He testified by attrition, making the same points over and over, relentlessly. He quickly recounted the 20 percent growth discrepancy between the twins, the abnormal placentation, the fact that Michael's death was imminent, then added one other factor—that Donna never complained of suddenly feeling decreased movement. This last, he implied, meant that Michael hadn't been kicking one minute and dead the next, as expected with a sudden cord accident, but had been sluggish and depressed for some time.

"There is no history of sudden cessation," Schifrin said. "She doesn't suddenly appreciate there is a change in movement." He reiterated. "We have a five-hundred-gram difference in the birth weights. We have obvious growth failure of some duration. We have compromised its circulation. It would be to me implausible, medically implausible, that this baby would be otherwise normal at this stage of gestation."

Hunt felt herself losing ground. Struggling to regain momentum, she asked, "Now, that abnormal placentation, does that always result in chronic deprivation?"

"No," Schifrin said.

"Okay. So you can have a velamentous cord and a child who is delivered healthy?"

"You might, certainly."

"So the combination of the velamentous cord insertion and the one-third placental contact does not translate necessarily into chronic deprivation?"

"A hundred percent of the time, yes, I agree with that."

Scarcely satisfied, Hunt backed into her next question. Assuming Schifrin was right and that Michael was distressed, what, she wanted to know, should Norwalk Hospital have done? "If 'B' was nonreactive March thirtieth at four P.M.," she asked tentatively, "then the course of action would have been to—redo [the nonstress test] within twenty-four to forty-eight hours?"

"Nonsense," Schifrin seethed. "Nonsense. That is too late anyway, if that's the first one. Assuming earlier NSTs were all reactive, nobody would have waited on a nonreactive or abnormal test. One would intervene immediately or almost immediately if one of the twins had gone sour."

The last of Hunt's exhilaration from the weekend now fled as she realized the full impact of Schifrin's testimony. She had believed that eliminating the labor and delivery would simplify the hospital's defense. But Koskoff and Schifrin had surprised her. Suddenly, she had to contend with a much more damaging specter—that Norwalk Hospital might be on the hook for all of the damage to Little Tony because of Donna's prenatal care. By shifting the focus from the birth to the last days of Donna's pregnancy, Koskoff not only had given his case against the hospital a second life, but had come up with a pow-erful new claim. He was a step ahead of her, not a step behind as she had thought. Hunt agonized. "I knew the transcript wouldn't read well," she says.

Her last hope was to discredit Schifrin himself. She had prepared for this, obtaining depositions from other lawyers and asking around about his weak-nesses. She believed he was, if not vulnerable, easily put on the defensive with questions about his legal work and his fees. Schifrin testified so much that he had a separate consulting business—BPM, for Beats Per Minute—to handle it. Unable to discredit his testimony, Hunt still hoped to taint him as a source.

"Okay," she said breezily, changing the subject. "Now, on an hourly basis, what have you been compensated by the plaintiffs' attorney for review and consultation services."

"I think it's four hundred dollars an hour."

"What are you charging for deposition?"

"Five hundred an hour, or, if you book the whole day, you get charged the day rate."

"So you charge us the day rate?" Hunt asked.

"Yeah. But you booked the whole day. So I think it's thirty-five hundred or something like that."

"What are you charging for the deposition today?" Hunt asked.

"Tell me when you're over," Schifrin said, "and I'll give you a premium. The fact is, you booked the whole day. I had to cancel everything else for this deposition. So you get charged thirty-five hundred dollars."

Schifrin and Koskoff consulted for thirty seconds off the record. Returning, Koskoff said hoarsely, "Let the record reflect Dr. Schifrin has agreed to charge the defense counsel for only the hours spent in the deposition despite the fact that he has set aside the whole day."

"And the amount of time that you have expended in terms of review up to the point of deposition is what?" Hunt went on.

"Probably five hours, six hours at least."

"Did you ever provide—have you ever provided testimony concerning facts similar to this?" Hunt asked, repeating the question that had enlivened Benirschke at the end of her examination of him.

"Probably," Schifrin said, then volunteered, "The answer to your next question is no."

"Uh-huh." Hunt nodded.

"That is, I do not remember the case in which I did that."

Hunt's last series of questions concerned whether Schifrin would be testifying about Donna's care during labor and delivery at trial. He said he wouldn't. She then asked a general question about how the standard of care is established.

"It's not the expert who determines the standards," Schifrin said. "The expert is simply there to explain the standards to anyone who will listen."

"And it's a specialty that sets them?" Hunt asked.

"Specialty. And for the most part common sense."

Hunt had no further questions. Neither did Koskoff. He was jubilant, having heard exactly what he had wanted to hear. It was after noon and he was eager to get back home; eager, in a larger sense, to move the case forward. Unlike with Benirschke, he had no worries about what else Schifrin might have to say. In his experience, Schifrin always said just enough. He was a lock.

FIFTEEN

DONNA THOUGHT MORE AND MORE NOW ABOUT LEAVING TONY. SOME OF THE money from the settlement—about $95,000—was to be hers alone. It was the first real money she would ever have, payment for eight years of mental anguish. Maybe she could quit her job and start over. But where? She had four kids, one of them profoundly disabled. She'd walked out on her adoptive parents at age eighteen and never returned. She was now thirty-three. Until the money arrived, she had two choices: stay with Tony or go to a shelter. She stayed.

When they fought, Tony agreed that one of them should leave but swore it wouldn't be him—he would never desert his family. Donna knew he meant it. She predicted to Janice Major that when the settlement came Tony would take off, but in truth she knew the decision was hers. Largely, it was a matter of means. She kept daydreaming now at work about what it would be like to have money that was hers to spend. She could hire a lawyer, get a divorce, maybe have enough left over to put down on a house. She thought about going back to school, learning a skill. Mostly she thought about getting away.

She'd met a trucker at the gift shop. He would pull in from time to time and they'd have coffee together in the cafeteria after her shift. Their friendship was easy and loose and Donna felt strangely normal, the way she had when she and Tony first met and they could talk about anything. When Tony found out about the trucker, he accused her of cheating on him. She denied it. Tony went to Radio Shack, bought a voice-activated recorder, and wired it behind a kitchen counter so he could bug Donna's phone calls. He planned to confront her with the tapes and with phone records. Whatever she was planning, he thought, he wouldn't make it easy.

Then Donna lost her job. In the middle of a fight with a supervisor, she said, "I quit." When she calmed down, she wished she hadn't said it, but it was too late. Her union wouldn't even try to get her reinstated. It was possible to regain jobs for those who were fired, her steward told her, but not for those who quit. When Donna told Tony, he shrugged. For once he took her side.

Without work, Donna grew increasingly restive. Mornings were the worst. She'd always had trouble getting out of bed, but now, dreading what she had to face each day—Rosie's and Dayna's high-energy squealing, Shannon's sullen teen rage, Tony's sleepless, hard-eyed smoldering, Little Tony's uncomprehending stares and endless needs—she couldn't get up. She was exhausted before she started. Work had given her an escape. Suddenly, without it, she felt overburdened.

She kept thinking about the windfall—what to do with it, what it would release her from doing. Her marriage was falling apart, yet she never had time for Tony, or for herself. Donna hadn't had a night away since she and Tony had first run off together and left Shannon with his parents. She imagined what it would be like to get in the car and go. In her reveries she never got far.

Her routine held her fast starting each day with Little Tony. Somnolently, she would disconnect him from his feeding pump and give him his meds by clipping a syringe to his G-tube and slowly releasing the plunger, watching the Tang-colored solution course through the plastic tube. Then she would lift his lifeless head, his eyes locking on hers before fluttering aimlessly away, and remove his T-shirt. Squeezing his mouth open, she would brush his teeth and gums, holding a cup near his chin to catch the drool. Meanwhile, she would talk to him, saying his name a few times and asking him if he would smile for her today.

At more than forty pounds he was becoming too heavy for her to lift, so she would call Tony to take him for his bath. When they came back, Tony would lay him on his rubberized sheet and Little Tony would rasp as Donna toweled him dry, rolling him over this way and that to get his back. He was still—forever would be—helpless, a baby. Lying naked on his mottled back, legs splayed, feet pointed down spastically, twisted hands reaching upward, he was utterly vulnerable. His skin, plump and sallow, was like a frog's underbelly.

Donna would put a new diaper on him, then pull his socks on as his right foot beat a tattoo on his mattress. She would pull on his pants, reaching through the legs to grab his feet, then insert his hands through his shirt-sleeves. Finally came his foot splints and sneakers, a pair of scuffless black hightops. Again with Tony lifting, she would wedge him into the body brace he wore to keep his spine from contorting and tighten the straps. Then Tony would carry him upstairs and put him in his wheelchair, which Donna parked in front of the TV so he could watch Barney with the two younger girls until they went off to Little Rascals and he went to school.

Donna was long past hoping, as Tony still did, that all this would some-day change when Little Tony decided to change it. She knew it would never be any different, that his losses were permanent. And so it took everything she had to perform these rituals, accepting that the best she could provide her son was bodily maintenance. Her own mother, whoever she was, had surrendered her to strangers before Donna had ever had a chance to know her. Little Tony knew her; that much she was sure of. But that was all she was sure of. No won-der she felt confused and accursed. Even when she and Tony finally got away for a few days in March, hurriedly driving down to Florida and back for their first vacation in more than nine years, there was no release from her troubles.

And then, on a night in April, after another fight, Donna quietly packed up and left. With the kids asleep, she loaded her clothes into the van. The money from the settlement still hadn't come. Tony was furious but unable or unwilling to stop her. In the days afterward, he maxed out his Visa card to fi-nance her trip.

≈ ≈ ≈

SEPTEMBER 4, 1951

A warm late-summer night, five years before Tony's birth. His twenty-four-year-old mother, Dorothy, and twenty-six-year-old father, Antonio, a truck driver, quarrel violently in the kitchen of their apartment on Orchard Street in Stam-ford. Dorothy wears a creased yellow housedress. Her hair is disheveled and she chain-smokes. She's been drinking. She accuses Antonio of cheating on her. He denies it. At 7:39 P.M. she calls the police. Two officers respond. Reluctant to get involved in a domestic dispute, they warn them to keep it down.

After the police depart, Antonio—Tony Sr.—gathers up some clothes. Fed up with his wife's suspicions, he announces he's leaving. In the next room Karen, four, Elizabeth Ann, eighteen months, and the baby, four-month-old Anthony Jr., are fast asleep. He avoids waking them.

At the kitchen table, near an open whiskey bottle and a quart bottle of beer, Dorothy sobs, distraught. Sometime after 9:30 she reaches for a piece of paper and a pencil and begins to write.

≈ ≈ ≈

At first Donna moved among motels in Stamford, Darien, and Norwalk. She spent two nights at a Holiday Inn near the bowling alley on the Post Road, but it was expensive, and she started looking for cheaper places. She had no plan other than to get away from it all, clear her head. After a few days, with her money dwindling, she decided to move on. A country music fan, she'd always wanted to go to Nashville. She took off one morning and drove south, sleeping in the back of the van at truck stops to save money. Below the Tennessee border, she got on her CB, and a trucker directed her the rest of the way. She checked into a Hampton Inn. It had no restaurant, so Donna ate most of her meals at a Waffle House next door. She tried one day to board the *General Jackson,* a showboat, but it was booked. She took pictures of it instead. She stayed a week, calling home but refusing to tell Tony where she was. She knew he'd try to find out if she'd checked in alone and would be calling her "nonstop."

On April 28, the Koskoffs finally cut the Sabias a check from the settlement with Humes, and Donna returned to Norwalk, moving in with a girlfriend. Tony told her he wanted her back, but she wouldn't see him. By now she'd lost any hope of saving their marriage: all she wanted was a divorce. That and custody of the kids.

She hired a lawyer who, she says, wanted to "take Tony to the cleaners," yet also urged her to try to patch things up before suing for divorce. He kept asking her, "Are you sure this is what you want?" Donna said it was. Finally, she says, she blew up. "Serve my husband," she told him. "Aren't I paying you? Aren't you working for me?" She later found a second lawyer more willing to do what she asked. When the divorce papers came, Tony wasn't home. The process server, a sheriff's deputy, left them with Shannon.

Tony scrambled to make do while Donna was away. He did all the shopping, cooked all the meals, juggled the bills, got the kids out in the morning, and took care of Little Tony. "You gonna talk to me today?" he'd say to him, racing through his chores. "You gonna smile for me?" He tried to go to work but often didn't make it, and the company threatened to fire him for missing so many shifts. When he did go, he depended on Shannon to watch the other kids, but she resented it and they usually ended up fighting. Eventually, he asked his sister Donna, a home health aide, to quit her job and help him. He paid her $300 a week.

On April 26, before Donna returned to Norwalk, Little Tony had a seizure, his third requiring hospitalization in little more than a month. He arched, his limbs suddenly extending, then he stiffened. His wayward right eye wandered. He started to sweat. At the hospital he was given injections of Ativan, a powerful anticonvulsive, until the seizure stopped. Concerned about his weight—he was eight years old and weighed less than an average five-year-old—doctors consulted the Yale gastroenterologist who'd put in his feeding tube. He was switched to Ensure Plus and given liquid Theragran vitamins. He remained in the hospital more than two weeks.

During his stay the hospital learned of Tony and Donna's separation. Though Donna was listed on Little Tony's intake form as the person to contact in case of emergency, she knew nothing about his seizure. Tony told the nurses not to bother trying to reach her; he'd take care of it. The hospital knew him to be an involved father, but the pediatric staff now grew concerned over Little Tony's welfare. Three days later a hospital social worker called Tony at home, offering to help. Offended, he told her not to call back.

≈ ≈ ≈

By the time Tony Sr. returns to the apartment on Orchard Street at about 11 P.M., Dorothy is on the floor, unconscious. All four jets on the stove are opened, filling the room with what is still called, in 1951, illuminating gas. Tony Sr. stumbles to the windows and throws them open. Gasping, he sucks a few breaths, then sees on the table a grisly tableau: the whiskey and beer bottles, now less than half-full—and a note. He understands immediately what's happened. Shaking, he dials the police.

He finds the children in their beds. Karen is in one bedroom; Elizabeth and Anthony Jr., in their cribs, in another. They aren't breathing. A city ambulance arrives to rush all four to the hospital. After being fed oxygen for almost an hour, Dorothy slowly starts to revive.

She remains in critical condition throughout the next day as page-one headlines in the local paper announce "Three Children Die When Mother Turns on Gas Jets in Apartment." According to the story, police believe that Dorothy, an "embittered young wife," tried to kill herself and her children after she and her husband had fought over his alleged unfaithfulness. Calling the deaths "premeditated," the district attorney says he plans to charge her with first-degree murder—if she lives.

Released from Stamford Hospital the next day, Dorothy appears to remember nothing. She's taken to a municipal courtroom and bound over on murder charges. "Do you know where my kids are?" she asks detectives repeatedly. "Who's taking care of them?" She stands pale, half-stuporous, in her rumpled yellow housedress, chain-smoking absently during the hearing. When police tell her that she killed her children in a futile suicide attempt, she responds uncomprehendingly. "I want to go home and see my children. I can't understand why I can't remember what happened that night." The state's main witness, Tony Sr., tells detectives she tried once before to do the same thing, which is why he returned home after their quarrel.

Only on Wednesday, two days later, does Dorothy realize what she's done. Taken by the county sheriff and a matron from her jail cell in Bridgeport to a Stamford funeral home, she bursts into sobs upon seeing the still faces of her children in their small white coffins. With Tony Sr. standing wordlessly by her side, she cries out, "It can't be true! Oh, it can't be true!" Ten minutes later, crying uncontrollably, she is escorted back to the sheriff's car and returned to Bridgeport.

A huge throng, drawn from Stamford's close-knit Italian community, attends the funeral service, a Mass of the Angels, at Sacred Heart Church. The coffins, resting on stands one before the other, fill the center aisle before the altar. Each bears a small heart-shaped bouquet of roses, the only flowers in the packed, hot church. After the mass, crowds line the sidewalks on both sides as the three caskets, seeming even smaller as they're borne on the shoulders of four pallbearers each, are carried out and placed in a single black hearse. Behind them walk Tony Sr., bent with grief, and his mother. Tony Sr.'s father, holding tightly to his wife and staring ahead, escorts them to the waiting limousine.

Following an open car banked with red and white blossoms, the procession snakes its way from Stamford to Darien, coming finally to a stop in the children's section of St. John's Cemetery, the same narrow riverbank where thirty-three years later Tony and Donna will bury their stillborn son, Michael.

≈ ≈ ≈

Once Tony resolved never to give up his children, there was a chilling finality about it, and Donna knew better than to challenge him. "He kept saying he would fight me to the end," she recalls. "If we had to go to court, the kids just would have to be dragged through the mud. That was his position." What accounted for his ferocity was unclear. He had always been a determined, protective father, but except with Little Tony, seldom warm or affectionate. His demeanor at home was stony, prepossessed. Years of exhaustion and fighting with Donna had cauterized his sense of humor and his parental teasing often seemed ungentle. He was patient with the girls, but his patience always seemed to be wearing thin, and he was too wired emotionally to enjoy them. His playfulness, what little there was, tended to be rough.

His feelings about all his children, including Shannon, seemed to be rooted in something more basic than love, some combination of blood and honor and survival, something he neither understood nor could explain. All he knew was that he would never leave them. He would kill, or die, for them, but he wouldn't abandon them. His "I don't give a fuck" attitude toward the rest of the world was the public reversal of his feelings toward his family, which dictated that you stayed together no matter what. The kids were his; he would stick by them. That was all anyone needed to know.

He did all he could now to take care of them but, with Donna away, it was never enough. Even with help, he barely was able to manage. Rosie, now five and long ago toilet-trained, began to regress. Dayna, almost two, cried inconsolably for her mommy. Together they were shuttled between Little Rascals and the homes of friends and relatives, dropped off without knowing when they'd be picked up or by whom. At times they practically lived at the Majors' house across the street, wandering over on their own. Says Janice Major: "I told Tony, 'I want their Social Security numbers. I'm going to claim them.'" Little Tony spent more and more time in his room, neglected—"pushed to the side," Majors says. Often in the morning Tony couldn't get him ready for the school van. Some mornings there was too much else going on for him even to try. Increasingly, Little Tony languished out of sight, in bed, with the local rock station as his baby-sitter.

It was Shannon who seemed to suffer most. Tony needed her to fill in for Donna, but she was fifteen and long-neglected herself. Pretty and rebellious, she had other ideas. She helped out, but she hated Donna for leaving and perhaps Tony for not stopping her. Shannon also resented Tony for bossing her around. Supervised, she might have suffered in resentful acquiescence, but now she was more or less on her own, parentless and powerfully aggrieved. Tony suspects that at night, when he was at work and she was in charge, she opened the house to boys she knew—"dirtbags," Tony called them. As he would later say regretfully, blaming Donna and himself, "Shannon grew up too fast."

With all his hardships Tony only grew more determined to get by on his own. He was like his father, stubborn. His rage toward Donna frequently consumed him. When she first left, he would hang out the living room window every day and scream to the Majors, "Where is the bitch? Have you seen her?" Yet he also believed that children needed both a father and a mother, and so he resolved to give his marriage another chance. "My lawyer kept telling me, 'Serve her. Serve her,'" he says. He resisted. Despite feeling abandoned, and worse, cuckolded—despite his inconsolable rage—he was careful to leave open the door for Donna to return.

In August, four months after Donna left, Shannon went to live for a month with Donna's sister in Maryland. Around the same time, Donna took a sublease on a condo in Norwalk. For the first time in her life she had a nice place of her own and she spent lavishly, using much of her share of the settlement in setting it up. "I went out and went nuts," she says. She bought a living room set, a videocamera, a stereo, a TV. She bought a car phone and signed up for service. For her birthday she bought herself a motorcycle, a red Harley-Davidson Sportster, then, sometime later, a $400 Harley leather jacket. She enrolled in secretarial classes at the Katherine Gibbs Institute, a couple of blocks from Humes's office. At night she partied with friends, then got up early, dressed herself in new secretarial clothes, and went to classes. She never felt more free.

Shortly after she moved in, Tony started visiting. The thought of getting Donna back, Janice Major recalls, now was "eating him up inside." Major, who was like an older sister to Tony and whom he confided in, disapproved. "This doesn't happen to you unless you allow it to happen to you," she lectured him. "She's made a fool out of you. And who suffers behind this is the children." But Tony refused to listen. He asked Majors where he could buy Donna flowers. By fall he had agreed to go with Donna for counseling.

≈ ≈ ≈

Tony knew nothing about his parents' past. He thought they'd lost three children in a fire. This was the story he'd pieced together on the day of Michael's funeral, when he'd stumbled upon the half-buried headstone bearing the names of three Sabia children and related it to his aunt's blurted suggestion that he bury Michael alongside his sisters and brother. It never occurred to him that it might have been otherwise. Tony didn't ask, and no one volunteered to tell him.

Until high school he'd grown up in Stamford, in the same tight community where his parents had always lived, a hard-bitten world where everyone was related and everybody knew everyone's business. Yet the collective memory of his parents' tragedy had been so thoroughly cleansed by some common agreement, that in thirty-six years, first in Stamford and then in nearby Norwalk, where much of that community later moved, no word of it had gotten back to him. No other kid hearing about it at home had thrown it up to him. No gossip, of which there must have been much, disturbed his innocence.

Thus he didn't know that his mother had spent more than three years in prison, at the women's correctional facility in Niantic, or that his father had tried to escape Stamford and his past by enlisting in the Army. He knew Tony Sr. had fought in Korea, but nothing of the circumstances that propelled him there. His parents were not the sort to regale their children with stories, especially of bad times, and Tony never thought to question them. He'd always assumed that what had happened before he was born had been hard, worth forgetting. He left it at that.

All he knew was that in 1956 he was born, premature, a little over two pounds, and that his parents had named him Anthony Jr., presumably after his father. He knew that his parents went on to have two other children, and that they remained married—not happily, he thought, but with a kind of endurance, like most people—until the day seven years earlier when his dad had keeled over in his chair. He knew that he was like Tony Sr.—everyone said so—and he was proud of the comparison. He knew it must have been hard being married to his mother, a surly, emotional woman with an unpredictable temper.

And yet how much more like his father he was he had no idea. Tony Sr., after all, had taken Dorothy back. He'd been by her side the day she pleaded guilty to manslaughter charges in order to escape being tried for murder. And he met her at prison the day she was released and brought her home. What fears he may have had about her were somehow overcome by his devotion, and he was willing, despite his sorrow, to give her a second chance. Indeed, Tony himself was the legacy of that forgiveness, his conception a kind of ex-culpatory act, an antidote to grief, guilt, shame, death.

Yet what sadness must Tony Sr. have suffered? What must he have thought, leaving Dorothy alone with their new son, named Anthony Jr., like the one who had died? How anxiously must he have behaved around her, knowing what she had done? Had he always blamed himself for provoking her into turning on the gas, and is that why he returned and why he stayed with her? How did either one of them find the strength to go on? Only once did Tony get a glimpse of the answers to these questions—when his father, overcome with grief, refused to attend Michael's funeral. Tony could never know his father's pain, but he experienced something like it as he struggled to keep the wreckage of his own family from going under.

If at the core of Tony's life there was a mystery, one which he wouldn't learn for another two years, his actions now repeated a pattern. He believed Donna had cheated on him and abandoned her children. Both were unpardonable acts in his personal code, but he would not allow his family to be destroyed. And so he would do whatever it took to get her back. He would start over. Like his father, whose faith that Little Tony would someday walk and talk was undying, he would not surrender hope that things would improve.

They couldn't, he was sure, get any worse.

Donna moved back in October. She was spending her money too fast for it to last much longer, and that was now an issue. The Majors and Tony's mother and brother suspected it was the main reason for her return, but there seemed to be other, more pressing factors involved. Living alone, threatened with losing her children, Donna faced the prospect of a terrible isolation. Orphaned once before, she was not about to exile herself again. Family ties had always been the most fragile part of Donna's world, yet when Tony told her the kids needed her, she knew she couldn't bear not to be with them. Insisting on custody, he'd forced her to choose: leave and forsake her kids, drag them through an ugly divorce, or return home to them and, in the bargain, him.

He'd made the choice easier by being genuinely sweet and solicitous on his visits. He'd taken her out, proffered flowers, treated her as if they were dating. They'd had long talks, and though they soon quit going to counseling, they no longer blamed each other exclusively for their problems. Donna knew she was unlikely to meet a Prince Charming on Norwalk's working-class singles circuit; anyone who'd be interested in a jobless, divorced mother of four, among them Little Tony, would surely have some heavy baggage of his own. Tony might be raw and moody, she reasoned, but he was hard-working, a good father, and he didn't drink or abuse her. He had a certain rough integrity that she admired. Eventually, he won her back with the same virtues that had attracted her in the beginning—those, plus his newfound considerateness.

Donna was eager to make their lives better. Leaving her children, she says, had been hard for her, and she felt especially guilty about Shannon. The tenth-grader was begging to come back from Maryland, but Donna told her there had to be some ground rules first. Donna insisted on knowing who she was with, and where; she had to call in to let her parents know what she was up to. Shannon agreed. Within weeks of returning, however, she was back in trouble, flunking out of school, and threatened with expulsion. She transferred to a half-day vocational program where she did well for a couple of months, but there, too, her grades started to slide as she began hanging out with her old friends. Finally, she ran away, spending a week in the Greenwich Youth Shelter. Donna was torn between anger and frustration. She worried that she had driven Shannon away, and that Shannon was now punishing her for it. She didn't know how to help her.

With the two younger girls unwilling to let her out of their sight, Donna quickly felt as encumbered as she had before she left. There was less strife now over unpaid bills, but having money created new tensions. Tony's mother, now in her sixties and diabetic, hoped Tony would help her more financially, even though he explained that the money from the settlement was for Little Tony's future. He also worried about Donna's spending, and arranged with the trust lawyer Bernard had recommended to deny her access to Little Tony's trust.

Inevitably, sulfurous emotions arose. Donna resented Tony's distrust and his mother's claims: Dorothy blamed Donna for driving a wedge between her and her son. "I gave Tony fifty bucks one day and said, 'Here. Take her back to Virginia and leave her there,'" Dorothy would recall. When Tony wanted to give his mother some money, he'd ask Janice Major to take it to her house. Leave it in a drawer next to her night table, he'd instruct her, then call and tell her where it is.

Donna's hold over Tony now seemed stronger than ever, and his frustration about it didn't abate once she returned. He bit his tongue a lot; at times, when Donna expected him to fight her, he was strangely passive. But he had fought to get her back for the kids' sake, not his own, and now that they had some breathing room financially, he was less interested in reliving the battles of the past than in plodding ahead. If having Little Tony had taught him one thing, it was that you do what you have to do. You push yourself every day, then do it again. You don't stop. For the sake of his family Tony had been willing to swallow his pride. But that didn't mean he'd given up. He was conserving himself.

Increasingly, Donna wished they could get out of Sunken Homes and escape Tony's mother's presence. As Little Tony got older and became harder to lift, it would also help if they could live on one level. In November 1992 she showed Tony a classified ad for a three-bedroom Cape on two wooded acres along the Merritt Parkway.

"Call 'em," he said.

"Are you serious?" she asked.

Donna doubted they could afford the house, but she made an appointment with a broker. The house was weather-beaten, with peeling yellow paint, but it came with two small barns and a long dirt driveway. It needed a lot of work, but it sat on some of the highest, rockiest ground in Norwalk: it wouldn't sink. Donna loved it right away. Tony was less enthralled but could see its possibilities. He told Donna they could keep the old house and rent it, building up equity while using the income to help finance the new one.

They borrowed against Little Tony's trust to make the down payment, then moved in on an icy day in February, the girls taking the two rooms upstairs while Tony and Donna had the small bedroom on the ground floor. They gave Little Tony the dining room, off the kitchen. Donna unpacked his clown dolls and arrayed them on top of the breakfront. Tony immediately made plans to build a two-room addition. He would double the size of their bedroom, and build a connecting room for Little Tony. He'd put sliders in both rooms, and a deck off the back, with a ramp for Little Tony's wheelchair. They would have the house they needed, he announced, one that suited their family. Having come this far, they would no longer settle.

SIXTEEN

LIKE SUNKEN HOMES, DOWNTOWN NORWALK SITS IN A BASIN, RINGED BY LOW HILLS.
It feels forgotten. Its slumbering skyline of brick mills, smokestacks, cupolas,
and steeples dates back to the 1920s, when small New England industrial
cities entered the long, low scrape that for some of them has never stopped. Its
business district is spent, a sullen grid of bars, discount houses, minimalls and
free on-street parking. The blackened gash of the Norwalk River, once famous
for oysters, is choked by asphalt plants and oil-stained piers. It washes down
from the hills, cleaves the downtown, then empties out under the spans of
I-95 and the Metro-North train tracks, through a half-gentrified harbor, and
into the Sound. In Norwalk, as elsewhere, high ground is choice ground.

Norwalk Hospital juts like a citadel over the city. Built on a steep hill and
surrounded by low- and moderate-income housing—garden apartments,
double-deckers—it consists of several connected buildings, wings upon
wings, but its main structure, the one that impresses from below, is a gleaming nine-story red brick monolith rising steeply to two top floors sheathed in
metal. The effect is jarring. Like most charity hospitals, Norwalk's was built
originally on high ground for the sunshine and clean air, which as late as the
1930s still dominated its therapeutic arsenal. Since then, it expanded when
money allowed. The result, typically, is an architectural congeries, a sprawling
labyrinth of corridors and building styles grafted from different eras.

The idea of a city hospital was born a century ago among Norwalk's hat
workers. At the time, the 1880s, affluent Norwalk residents were taken by
train or carriage to hospitals in New York or New Haven while most victims

of horsecar wrecks, mill accidents, pneumonia, and childbed fever died at home for want of an amputation or a clean bed. A young hat trimmer named Margaret Cavanaugh, indignant over the sight of a man dying in the street after being struck by a train, launched the hospital's first fund drive, rallying her coworkers until Norwalk's civic leaders were forced to take note. After opening in 1893 with six beds, the facility grew quickly, moving to its present hilltop site on Stevens Street during the 1918 flu epidemic. Inevitably, Cavanaugh's charitable impulse clashed with other forces. As medicine advanced and doctors claimed hospitals as their domain, the nineteenth-century ideal of caring for the indigent sick gave way to the need to compete with other medical centers—for physicians, patients, treatments, technology, and income. Meanwhile, southern Connecticut's postwar suburban boom was tripling the demand for beds. Norwalk, an aging city hospital struggling to draw patients from surrounding towns that were among the wealthiest in America, necessarily became, like other medical centers, more hard-nosed and pragmatic—in other words, a business.

Mike Koskoff liked to see to it that these new exigencies didn't overwhelm the historical mandate of the area's hospitals to do good: at one time or another he'd brought suit against them all. But as a resident of neighboring Westport, he seemed to feel a special urgency about Norwalk's hospital. When CBS newsman Harry Reasoner, for instance, fell down a stairway in his Westport home, a thirteen-room mansion opposite the Fairfield County Hunt Club, he was rushed to Norwalk Hospital, where he later died. Weeks later Reasoner's widow was taken there, too. Apparently distraught over his death, she had fallen thirty feet from a third-floor attic window onto her asphalt driveway, breaking numerous bones and suffering internal injuries. Whatever the gulf between the two communities, Westport had a proprietary interest in Norwalk's medical facilities and doctors, and Koskoff considered it his civic duty to hold the city's hospital strictly to account.

Thus he was especially intrigued when Pat Ryan phoned in mid-September and invited him to talk informally with Norwalk Hospital's executives about *Sabia,* a request as unexpected as it was unusual. Within the context of a lawsuit, lawyers generally talk only with each other. Defense lawyers like to insulate their clients from their legal problems, seldom involving them personally before trial. By doing so, they reinforce their clients' dependence on them, which makes them seem indispensable, which tends to increase their fees. Koskoff didn't know what Ryan was up to but anticipated some kind of settlement discussion.

Ryan had reasons of his own for wanting the meeting, most involving his relationship with the hospital. Now that Humes was out of the case and the Koskoffs were concentrating solely on Donna's prenatal care, both the hospital's liability and Ryan's sense of it had shifted. There was no possibility now that the hospital might still blame Humes for what happened. Nor would it escape the brunt of Koskoff's attacks. Norwalk would be on the hook for the entire value of the case, which really meant that Travelers would be on the hook as its insurer.

All this complicated Ryan's position. He had the confidence of the hospital, but not of Travelers, which hadn't hired him and had counsel of its own. Meantime, only he and Hunt fully understood where the case was heading. They now knew that it would require a straight medical defense—a defense they did not yet have. By engineering a meeting—a trial preview, so to speak—Ryan hoped to show both the hospital and Travelers what they were up against, while defusing any possible complaints about his handling of the case.

Koskoff knew nothing about Ryan's reasoning, but he also wanted to give the hospital and Travelers a foretaste of a trial. As Koskoff knew, Tony and Donna were still separated. He believed juries frowned on awarding large verdicts to—thus reducing insurers' incentives to settle with—broken families, especially those that looked like they might squander their proceeds in an ugly, protracted divorce. Best, Koskoff thought, to present a full-dress rehearsal of his case now, before Tony and Donna's marriage collapsed irreparably and tainted their story as plaintiffs. Koskoff intuited that he should put on a strong show—"divine inspiration," he called it. Although he anticipated an informal session, he prepared for the meeting as if for an opening argument.

He began by cloistering himself in his office. Working from one of his trademark black looseleaf case notebooks—a legacy from Ted, who insisted on them—he broke the case into its essential elements. He scribbled dozens of pages of notes longhand, organized them, then singled out his chief talking points and had them transposed onto Styrofoam display boards to use as visual aids while he spoke. With the boards propped on a chair, he stood up and rehearsed his presentation over and over, slowing his pacing here, spiking his inflection there. Since this was to be a kind of live settlement brochure presented to a hostile group of executives on their own turf rather than an impassioned plea to a lay jury in a court of law, he decided to tone it down. Yet he also wanted the hospital and Travelers to appreciate the full horror of Little Tony's life, and to experience some of the sympathy that a jury might feel. In the end, he opted for a tone of spare simplicity, devoid of histrionics but seething, he felt, just below the surface with portent and outrage.

Arriving at the hospital with Bernard, Koskoff still didn't know what to expect; Ryan had remained vague about the purpose of the meeting and even about who would be there. They enquired in the main lobby, then took an elevator to the executive offices on the fifth floor of the imposing new patient tower. Juggling their briefcases, boards, and a collapsible metal easel, they passed a portrait gallery of dour-faced former presidents of the hospital and trudged down a long, carpeted hallway toward the boardroom.

As he entered the hushed room, Koskoff felt unexpectedly as if he were at a sales meeting. About a dozen people in dark suits sat in matching orange and gold chairs around a twenty-foot oak conference table. Koskoff recognized Ryan and Hunt, but no one else. More empty chairs lined one wall, and at the far end of the narrow room sat an architect's model of the hospital and a table with a speakerphone. He heard the low, incessant hum of air-conditioning and could see out the window the traffic on Route 7 and, beyond that, Norwalk's downtown and port.

Ryan brokered the introductions. David Osborne, the hospital's forty-six-year-old president and CEO, sat at one end of the table. It was Osborne, a coppery, tight-smiling man with a master's degree in public health from Yale, who as vice president for operations had barred Tony from attending the autopsy of the stillborn Michael eight and a half years earlier. More recently, as president, he'd terminated Humes's courtesy privileges. Elegantly coiffed, with upswept hair blow-dried to perfection, he wore a well-cut suit offset by a gold stickpin, tasseled loafers, and a pinky ring. He was surrounded by a number of the hospital's senior staff, including Barbara Klein, now vice president for corporate affairs, who was Osborne's liaison with Ryan, and Linda Nemeth, the former nursing supervisor who had fired Mollie Fortuna and had watched over the Sabias during Little Tony's hospital stays. Nemeth now had a law degree and was the hospital's in-house "risk manager"—point person on all bad outcomes. Travelers was represented by Cathy Gonzales, who managed the Sabias' file. Koskoff took his place at the far end of the table as Bernard fiddled wordlessly with the easel and boards—"playing Vanna White," he called it. When no one spoke, Koskoff cleared his throat and began.

"Mr. Ryan asked me to come here today to talk a little bit about the Sabia case," Koskoff said. His voice was deep and bell-like and he articulated his words with precision, as if there were a slight, censoring feed delay from his thoughts. Like his father, he strove for a kind of vehement simplicity.

"By way of background, Tony Sabia today is eight years old. He lives with his parents here in Norwalk. Tony is spastic quadriplegic and suffers from cerebral palsy. He is, according to the doctors, legally—cortically—blind. He is totally incontinent of urine and feces. He is fed by gastronomy tubing. He cannot walk. He has leg braces which are mainly for preventing contractures, and he also has hand splints, which are used for the same purpose. He is unable to communicate and never will be able to communicate with the outside world. He suffers from grand mal seizures, which are debilitating and life-threatening. And he is severely mentally retarded.

"And the question arises," Koskoff said, pausing, "what happened to cause all of this devastation to Tony Sabia? How could it have been prevented? Could it have been prevented? That," he said, "is what this lawsuit is about."

Koskoff pointed to the first board and continued: "There are, as Mr. Ryan will tell you, three main things that we have to prove in order to prevail in a lawsuit like this. First, we have to prove that there were departures from a standard of medical care. Second, we have to prove causation; that is, that they caused something. And third, that there were damages, or injuries, from these departures from the standard of care. Before going into those departures with you, I'd like to give you a little bit of background on the treatment that Donna Sabia received from the Norwalk Hospital clinic.

"Donna Sabia," he said, "first became a patient at Norwalk Hospital early in her pregnancy. On December 5, 1983, an ultrasound was performed at about twenty-one and a half weeks in which they found that she had a twin pregnancy and that one of the twins, Twin A, was larger than Twin B. They also found, I believe at that time, a condition known as polyhydramnios, which is increased amniotic fluid, and is a risk factor in pregnancy. There was a second ultrasound January 5, 1984, and again it was found that Twin A was larger than Twin B. That was at twenty-six to twenty-seven weeks in her pregnancy. Then a third ultrasound was performed on January 27, 1984, at about twenty-nine weeks, and again it was found that Twin A was larger than Twin B. Of some significance in this case is the fact that even though on each of these three ultrasounds it was found that one twin was larger than the other, there were no further ultrasounds performed during this pregnancy.

"Donna was seen regularly at Norwalk's clinic. Yet even though it was a twin pregnancy, which would have made one believe that she might be at some risk, or that the twins might be at some risk, her treatment was alternated between a physician who happened to be there at the moment one week, and the following week by a nurse-midwife. During the entire course of her pregnancy there were no fetal well-being studies performed. There were no nonstress tests performed to assess the fetal well-being of the twins as they reached maturity.

"On March 23, 1984," Koskoff said, "Donna reached term for a twin pregnancy, which is thirty-seven weeks. On that day she was seen by a physician. But a week later, on March 30, when she had passed term by a week, she was seen by a nurse-midwife. And the nurse-midwife found two fetal hearts, and had no reason at that time, she felt, to suspect anything wrong.

"On April 1, 1984, when Donna was now past thirty-eight weeks, she went into labor. She came into the hospital, one fetal heart was found, and a physician saw her who'd never seen her before, Dr. Humes, who came in in the middle of the delivery. The birth occurred. And when it did occur, one twin, Twin A, was born near death, as close to death as an infant can be and still be alive, suffering from anemia, and suffering from hypoxia. And his name was Tony. And Twin B was born dead, and his name was Michael James. And when they were weighed, there was a twenty percent discordancy in birth weights between the two twins, and Twin B, Michael James, was found to be growth retarded."

Koskoff paused for effect. So far, his recitation had been dry, as if he'd been reading from a medical chart. But he now was heading into the meat of his case. He deliberately started to simmer. "Now as I indicated earlier," he said, "in order to prove a case under circumstances like these, we would have to show that there were departures from the standard of care. In this case there *were* departures from the standard of care. And these are what the departures were." Bernard flipped to the next board, and Koskoff began to read. "First," he said, verbally italicizing the words on the chart, "they failed to treat this as a *high-risk pregnancy*. It was well known in 1983 that a twin pregnancy was considered, just by virtue of the fact that it was twins, to be high-risk.

"Twin pregnancies," he continued, again flattening his voice around key words for emphasis, "suffered from increased *morbidity and mortality*. Yet Donna Sabia was seen by a physician only on every other visit. There was no physician in charge of her pregnancy, as would have been expected. There was no *plan* for this pregnancy, as to what procedures would be performed and when they would be performed. There was no *consult* with *high-risk* specialists, in order to determine how to handle this *high-risk* pregnancy. And," he said, now raising his voice and tapping the chart, "it was a violation of *Norwalk Hospital's own protocols* to allow this pregnancy to be managed in such a haphazard fashion, predominantly by nurse-midwives."

"The protocol here," he continued, pointing to the next chart, "states under section D—that's the protocol for nurse-midwifery management—that 'Women who present the following in the antenatal course will be returned to the doctor for medical management.' And what's the indication? 'Multiple pregnancy.' So," he said, "in a multiple pregnancy the management of the prelabor should have been under the care of a physician, and not nurse-midwives. But if you look at the record here, she was seen by a physician only every other visit, and was handled by nurse-midwives, and *most particularly was handled by a nurse-midwife after she had reached term,* when all the authorities agree there is an *increased risk* of *morbidity and mortality* in a twin pregnancy. So the first-named departure," Koskoff concluded, "was that they failed to treat this as a high-risk pregnancy.

"The second," he said, pausing to compose himself slightly, "is that there was *no fetal growth assessment in the third trimester.* As I said earlier, there had been an indication that there was discordancy and polyhydramnios—increased amniotic fluid. But there was no follow-up. There were no *serial ultrasounds,* as should have been performed. As the discordant growth chart shows," he said, as Bernard again flipped ahead, "on the first ultrasound, on January fifth, Twin A was 990 grams, Twin B was 810 grams. That's a seventeen to eighteen percent discordancy."

Koskoff's voice rose plaintively. "That's *significant*," he said. "That's a risk of increased morbidity and mortality. *That cries out* for somebody to look at this pregnancy to see if this small twin is suffering from intrauterine growth retardation—is in trouble. And yet on the twenty-seventh, at twenty-nine weeks, two weeks later, there was still a significant discordancy of nine percent. And still the ultrasonographer suggested a follow-up ultrasound at thirty-four weeks. But none was performed.

"And at birth, what did they find?" he asked, his voice a well of sorrow and regret. "Discordancy. Twin A, 2,519 grams; Twin B, 2,009 grams. A twenty percent discordancy. That was significant discordancy. And Twin B was growth-retarded, malnourished, and dead at birth. They didn't know about this. They didn't know about it because they didn't do the ultrasounds that would have told them about it. And it had been recommended. The ultrasonographer had recommended a follow-up ultrasound at thirty-four weeks. But they didn't do it."

Koskoff was rolling now. Ever since Benirschke's and Schifrin's depositions he'd thought he had the hospital cold on Donna's prenatal care, yet now, having laid it all out as before a jury, he seemed to have impressed even himself. He was neither the first lawyer nor the last to be carried away by his own story.

"Why are ultrasounds important?" he asked, previewing some of Schifrin's testimony without mentioning him by name. "For these reasons. Twin pregnancies are high-risk, particularly in the third trimester, because that is when a great deal of mortality and morbidity occurs. And that's why, when a pregnancy goes *past term*, at *thirty-seven weeks*, the physicians in charge must be sure of fetal well-being. They don't have very many ways to ensure themselves of fetal growth. The only ways they have are by ultrasound, and by nonstress tests.

"So," he said, doubling back to sum up, "the reasons for the requirement of third-trimester ultrasounds were: first, it was well known that *discordancy and intrauterine growth retardation were associated with greatly increased morbidity and mortality;* second, twin pregnancies in and of themselves carry a *high risk* of intrauterine growth retardation and discordancy, upwards of thirty percent, and in order to find that thirty percent, you've got to do an ultrasound; third, discordancy and intrauterine growth retardation were known to occur most often in the third trimester of a twin pregnancy, *so it doesn't make a lot of sense to do ultrasounds in the first two trimesters, and not in the third trimester;* and fourth, the only way to diagnose intrauterine growth retardation and discordancy is by ultrasound.

"And they didn't do it," he said softly, "even though they had every reason to."

Koskoff waited. "The third departure," he announced. "They failed to perform fetal well-being studies in the third trimester. First, there were *no serial nonstress tests*. Again, the only other thing they could have done in the third trimester to find out about the well-being of these fetuses was to perform nonstress tests, to see how the fetal heart was functioning. But they didn't do it. And second, they allowed the pregnancy to go past term with no fetal assessment. There was no reason to allow this pregnancy to go beyond thirty-seven weeks, when those twins were well developed and well formed and *probably* healthy, no reason to allow them to go past thirty-seven weeks without a fetal assessment, without being sure that they're going to be all right if you let the pregnancy go on to a normal vaginal delivery.

"And the fourth departure," Koskoff stated. "They failed to provide *experienced medical personnel*. They allowed a *nurse-midwife* to handle this pregnancy—*this complicated pregnancy*—after term. They had no consult with a high-risk specialist after term, and they failed to provide the physician who arrived at this delivery without ever having seen the patient before, knowing nothing of the patient's history, to arrive at a complicated delivery and deliver these babies without any knowledge whatsoever of the patient."

Whether this sudden sympathy for Humes meant that Koskoff intended to include the birth after all in his arguments was unclear. But it signaled to Ryan that he might, and he and Hunt both took note.

"So that's the liability," Koskoff said. "Those are the departures from the standard of care.

"Now the next thing we have to prove is causation. And what the pathologists tell us—what the causation experts tell us—is that what caused Tony to be the way he is is this." He gestured to Bernard to flip to the next chart, an illustration of the twins and the placenta, prebirth. "Twin B," he said, pointing to the breech twin, "died in utero sometime within eighteen to twenty-four hours prior to the birth of these twins. This resulted in a drop in blood pressure in Twin B—a loss of blood pressure—and bleeding from Twin A into Twin B. That resulted in a loss of blood pressure and hypovolemic shock to Twin A, which caused the hypoxic brain damage. And that led, of course, to cerebral palsy and the multiple severe disabilities. So the death of Twin B," he said, repeating, "caused the loss of blood pressure, bleeding from Twin A to Twin B, hypovolemic shock, hypoxia, and brain damage."

He lowered his voice almost to a whisper. "How could this injury have been prevented?" he asked. "It could have been prevented very easily, by delivering these twins two days before they were delivered. And how should they have known to deliver these twins two days earlier? They would have known if they had performed an ultrasound, because an ultrasound would have

shown them that the twins were discordant, and would have detected that
Twin B was in trouble, was growth-retarded. And had there been an ultrasound, they would have assuredly known to perform a nonstress test, to see
whether these twins were functioning well, or weren't functioning well. And
what would that nonstress have shown? It would have been abnormal, we
know. And we know it would have been abnormal because one of the twins
was small for gestational age and was growth-retarded—that was Twin B. He
had an *inadequate* share of the placenta, the placental surface. He had a *velamentous* cord insertion. And *he was in imminent risk of death.* All of which
present a *high likelihood* that had they done a simple nonstress test, they
would have detected the fact that that twin was in trouble. And they would
have delivered prior to thirty-eight weeks. And there would have been no injuries to Tony, and no injuries probably even to Michael. And both of them
would be running around in school today."

Koskoff gazed somberly around the room. He gathered his papers. He
was nearing his climax.

"Damages," he said finally, without affect, "are the last thing we have to
prove. These are generally divided into two categories under the law: special
damages and general damages. Special damages are future and past medical
expenses—hospital and custodial care, therapeutic costs, etcetera—as well as
the destruction of earning capacity, for life. General damages are for past and
future pain and suffering that Tony is going to experience, for life. And for
past and future destruction of his ability to carry on and enjoy life's activities."

"The general damages in this case I've already mentioned." Koskoff pointed
to a new board listing Little Tony's injuries. "There's spastic quadriplegia,
cerebral palsy, cortical blindness, gastronomy feeding, leg braces. He's unable
to communicate. He suffers from grand mal seizures, he has severe mental retardation. It's not really known the extent of that mental retardation. At best
for Tony, it is quite profound. And at worst for Tony, it is not as profound and
he is locked into this life of spasticity, quadriplegia—locked in and unable to
communicate with the outside world.

"But what is known," Koskoff said, "is that he will never live independently. He will never play with other children. He will never walk or run. He
will never talk or communicate coherently. He will never eat independently.
He will never go to a normal school. He will never date, or get married, or
have children, or earn a living. He will never have a hobby. He will never have
sexual relations. And he will never enjoy most of the basic pleasures of life. Yet
what we know about Tony so far is that Tony does enjoy personal contact,
with parents, siblings, and therapists. He does enjoy music. And he does enjoy
physical comfort. And he does feel pain. And he does suffer from mental anguish."

Bernard flipped to the last chart, the one everyone in the room had been anticipating. Koskoff modulated his tone once again. He now sounded neutral, like an accountant.

"The special damages in this case are shown first on this chart," he said, pointing to the top line. "Number one is the present value of medical, hospital, custodial, and therapeutic costs in a model home-care setting. Tony could be treated either at home or in an institution, but this particular projection is as if he was treated at home, which is less expensive than if he were institutionalized. That amount, in today's dollars, is $10,174,543. And the economists tell us that the destruction of his earning capacity, in today's dollars, should be valued at $2,052,920. So total special damages are $12,227, 463.

"In addition to that, there is, for loss of enjoyment of life's activities, an additional $5 million. And for pain and suffering, another $5 million. Bringing a total of $22,227,463.

"So that is what the case is about. That is our demand for settling this case. And we welcome any questions."

Koskoff remained standing. No one spoke.

Finally, Osborne broke the silence. "I thought the case was for $15 million. That was the offer of judgment. Where did you get $22 million?"

Koskoff thought for a second. He might have said that he was trying to grab their attention. Or that, as they could see, he was well prepared and they had better be ready to talk serious money because Koskoff thought he could try the case and get a verdict of $22 million. Or that although his professed goal was to go to trial, it was an open secret that 90 percent of cases settled, and he was purposely putting up a big number in order to leave room to negotiate. He might even have said that pain and suffering, those damages promoted so successfully by his father and uncle, had lately become the chief inflator of jury awards and thus the main area where price ultimately was negotiated, so he was now asking for $10 million for those damages rather than the $2.5 million he'd estimated earlier. Instead, he simply told them he had revalued the case.

An uncomfortable silence followed. At last Osborne stood up and thanked Koskoff and Bernard for coming. Koskoff was baffled by this brusque dismissal. The hospital had invited him up to hear his case, yet when he finished, no one responded. He didn't expect them to accept his terms, but he expected something, some discussion. He had never seen anything like it. Outside in the hallway, he turned to Bernard and muttered, "What was *that*?"

≈ ≈ ≈

Ryan liked the meeting. Seldom did he get a chance to hear an opponent air his whole case in time to react strategically. For the sake of fairness the law was designed to bar surprises at trial; that was why there was discovery and depositions, and why each side was entitled to the other's findings. But Koskoff, for his own reasons, had tipped his hand more than that, and Ryan had reason to be pleased. It would help him prepare his own experts, who still hadn't been deposed.

He saw two main weaknesses in Koskoff's presentation. The first was standard of care. Despite Koskoff's indignation about the hospital's failure to do serial ultrasounds, Koskoff would have to prove in court that in late 1983 and early 1984, when Donna was pregnant, an ordinary ob-gyn with no special training would have known to do them *in her case*. That wasn't at all clear. Ryan and Hunt had spoken with Norwalk's current chairman of obstetrics, Dr. David Hunter, who believed strongly that ultrasounds weren't required at that time, and several other experts they contacted had agreed. Nor did the leading medical texts recommend such monitoring. "The evidence was pretty clear to us," Ryan says, "that it was not the standard. No place in any of the books was it saying categorically, 'Do this.'"

The other problem was damages. Ryan thought Koskoff had overreached, perhaps fatally. He knew nothing, of course, about Donna and Tony's marital troubles, but he believed that if Koskoff walked into court and asked for $22 million, he risked losing a jury's sympathy, no matter how deserving his clients might seem. In many states, including neighboring Massachusetts, hospitals were shielded from malpractice claims entirely. They had so-called "charitable immunity," reflecting a long-standing public perception that non-profit hospitals were devoted primarily to the good of their communities and thus deserved protection from rapacious lawyers and lawsuits. Although state law allowed such suits, Connecticut juries were generally far less willing to punish community hospitals with big awards than juries in, say, Texas were. By bringing the case in down-at the-heels Bridgeport, Koskoff had seized a certain advantage, but even there jurors tended to turn against lawyers—and plaintiffs—who appeared greedy. Ryan, whose white hair, empathetic eyes, and avuncular manner contrasted starkly with Koskoff's fervent aura, looked forward to fomenting a backlash.

It pleased him that Koskoff seemed to hold nothing back. "Michael pours it on," he says, "but you have to judge a case by what the jury's going to hear." Knowing Koskoff, he was only moderately surprised by the $22 million take figure, though he doubted the case would go for anything near that. Still, Koskoff's outsized demand served its purpose, alerting Norwalk and Travelers to the "real possibility" that the case could "run the coverage"—cost the hospital's $15 million policy limit and more. From the Sherrington case and many others, Ryan had learned that there was no better way to focus a carrier's attention on a long-neglected file.

At the company's headquarters in Hartford, Travelers' vice president for medical liability, Brian Casey, heard about the meeting from Cathy Gonzales, who seemed more offended by Koskoff's demands than Ryan. It was Gonza-les's job to treat most cases as "no pays"—bald extortion attempts best repu-diated by winning in court. Koskoff she seemed to loathe on principle. But Casey, her boss, took a longer view. He was a former litigator who had once worked for one of the state's biggest firms. Unlike Gonzales, he had the au-thority to settle big cases, which meant he also bore responsibility for the way they were handled. Casey cared less about whether the opposing side's de-mands were realistic than he did about what Travelers might ultimately have to pay and whether its lawyers had done everything possible to limit the com-pany's exposure. He wasted no time responding. He reviewed the file, then called the chairman of the litigation department at his old firm and invi-ted him to take over the case. Within days he paid a visit to Norwalk Hospital, driving down from Hartford with Gonzales to announce that Ryan was off the case.

It was Osborne's job to tell Ryan of the decision. Not knowing him as well as Barbara Klein did, he asked her to come with him. Driving to Ryan's office in Stamford, Klein worried that Ryan would be "devastated" by the apparent loss of confidence. She hoped to reassure him that the decision was Travelers', not theirs. Ryan, however, was strangely compliant, disguising whatever hurt feelings he had. If he was subdued, he would later recall, it resulted less from his disappointment at losing the business than from the novelty of being fired. In thirty-five years of doing insurance defense, he had never before had a carrier come in and take back a case.

Privately, Ryan was relieved. He had long felt that *Sabia* had never truly been his to call. From the start, he'd had to file status reports with Travelers' lawyers every three months. They in turn filed their own status reports to a claims representative Ryan never saw—typical corporate case management. Travelers was a behemoth, a sprawling financial empire with countless divi-sions and tiers, and assets now of nearly $100 billion. Yet unlike St. Paul, it was a spot player in Connecticut's malpractice market, coming in only in big cases where it held a policyholder's excess coverage. Ryan had no ongoing relation-ship with its claims people and little chance of developing one. Even if he managed to get to know its case managers, which was unlikely, nothing guar-anteed that they would be around years from now when the case finally went to court or that the file wouldn't just be kicked upstairs. Koskoff at least knew his clients and could speak for them; their interests were closely aligned. But with Travelers, Ryan was on a string. He had worried especially how the rela-tionship would play out at trial. Travelers and its lawyers would be breathing down his neck, second-guessing him. If he decided it was best to settle, to whom would he go? And why should they trust him?

Meeting now with Klein and Osborne, Ryan told them not to worry about him. Indeed, he said, it was to the hospital's advantage to turn the case over to Travelers because "it was their case." There would be no question about how it was being handled. And if it went bad, none of it could be blamed on them. Besides, Ryan intimated, if it came time to advise the company to settle for $5 or $10 million, he'd rather have someone else do it, someone in whom the company had more confidence. "If somebody wants to take over the case," he said brightly, "my God, let them take it over."

SEVENTEEN

BILL DOYLE HATED PICKING UP CASES THAT OTHER LAWYERS HAD BEEN PREPARING for trial. At fifty-six, he had been strutting into courtrooms and winning defense verdicts for more than thirty years. His firm, Wiggin & Dana of New Haven, had long been general outside counsel for Yale University, making Doyle, its chief litigator and son of a traveling salesman, Yale's top defender in court. Famed for fierce argumentation and hard-nosed pragmatism, Doyle knew what it took to win—credibility. He believed trials were about selling simple messages—themes, he called them. Doyle's success as a lawyer was built on making juries believe what he told them, and it worried him to have to sell a jury a theme based on evidence and testimony that he, or someone who worked for him, hadn't gathered.

The Sabia file troubled him for another reason. Since becoming lead outside counsel for Connecticut's premier medical center, Yale–New Haven, a decade earlier, Doyle had defended too many bad baby cases to think them anything but awful. A battler, Doyle liked to go at his opponents hard, with themes he considered above reproach, theories like "She did it to herself," or "They cheated him, then they defamed him, and when he went to court, which is his right as an American citizen, they defamed him again." But what was the winning theme—the incitement to a jury's sympathetic outrage—in a bad baby case?

"This kid was all screwed up," he says, referring to Little Tony. "There was no high moral ground. Am I outraged that they sued Norwalk Hospital? I don't think so. The whole thing, the most compelling thing, was Tony Sabia with a tube in him."

Not that Doyle hesitated when Brian Casey asked him to take on the hospital's defense. All law firms now struggled for new business. Malpractice defense, defying economic cycles, had become one of Wiggin & Dana's most reliable profit centers: notes Doyle, "Doctors fuck up in good times and bad." Doyle knew *Sabia* was a "big-ticket" case, that Casey wanted him for that reason, and that his fees—$290 an hour—would more than justify his misgivings. Rarely were insurance companies willing to pay what Doyle charged, and when they did, he liked to oblige them. He also liked Casey, who used to work for him and whom he'd helped train. Doyle's status was such that he could get several million dollars to settle a case with a phone call. He knew Casey wouldn't balk at his taking complete control over the way *Sabia* was handled.

Doyle sensed from their conversations that Casey had been frustrated with Ryan, especially with his decision to allow Bev Hunt to depose Benirschke and Schifrin. This gave him no pleasure either. He knew Ryan and liked him; his son, also a lawyer, had worked for Ryan as a summer associate. But business was business, and Doyle wasn't sentimental, not professionally. He knew what Casey wanted from him, which was his full attention and the comfort that went with it—namely, the ability to trust Doyle's counsel because Doyle, not an associate, was driving the case. Trust between insurers and defense lawyers most often was a fool's bargain, but Doyle was known to deliver. He worked up cases as if for trial, the sooner the better. He didn't churn bad cases but "moved" them—got rid of them before they got worse. He provided a level of assurance that insurance companies, as risk managers, aspired to but seldom, in their dealings with lawyers, found.

This was Doyle's way: bluff, pointed, practical. Physically unimposing, he resembles a smaller, younger Tip O'Neill, with a straight shock of white hair, ruddy complexion, sloe eyes, nose going bulbous, Barney Rubble neck, and stocky frame. At five feet seven, slouchingly graceful with small feet and small mottled hands, he looks like an aging Irish bantam and jokes about it. "Short, insecure guys go into litigation," he'll say. "Where else can you kick the shit out of other people and get paid well for it?"

But Doyle is more than hired muscle, even for Yale, whose presidents he counsels face-to-face. He has a politician's warmth and social adroitness, a keen mind, a plodding tenacity, and limpid blue eyes that beseech listeners to trust him. Koskoff and many others consider him the best corporate litigator in Connecticut. Though medmal accounted for only about a quarter of his practice, his work for Yale–New Haven made Doyle perhaps the top defender of doctors and hospitals in the state. And yet when Casey called about *Sabia*, he understood he was being tapped for another distinction entirely—his relationship with Mike Koskoff.

Doyle was Koskoff's nemesis. Part of that was their conflicting ties to Yale. Koskoff had been raised worshipfully in Yale's "penumbra"; all of the Koskoffs had—Yale Koskoff, Karen's father, had been named for the college and medical school he would one day attend. Now, however, Michael viewed both the university and Yale–New Haven more often as corporate malefactors, two of Connecticut's ranking defendants in civil cases. Meanwhile, their chief apologist was Doyle, who not only defended them in court but taught litigation at Yale Law School, one of the country's leading bastions of corporate law. Doyle represented, literally, everything Koskoff opposed.

Their animosity was no secret. The top tier of the state's malpractice bar consisted of fewer than a dozen lawyers, and though Koskoff and Doyle professed mutual admiration—if someone he knew had a medical injury, Doyle liked to say, he'd refer him to Mike Koskoff—anyone who knew them had heard their grievances about the other. But Brian Casey understood something else. Several years earlier, when he'd been working for Doyle, he had witnessed up close Doyle and Koskoff's signature confrontation, a grueling seven-month trial that neither of them had been able to forget; a trial that had nothing to do with Yale or malpractice. Doyle believed it was that memory especially that Casey hoped to invoke by bringing him on.

The case had a bizarre history going back more than seventeen years. For decades, until the early seventies, the B. F. Goodrich Company had operated a large sponge rubber products plant in Shelton, a rusting mill town on the Housatonic River, north of Bridgeport. Faced with mounting losses, Goodrich decided to sell the business in 1974 to a flamboyant Ohio industrialist named Charles Moeller, a tobacco-chewing pig farmer and born-again Christian who believed in psychics and claimed he couldn't read. To buy the plant, Moeller borrowed 100 percent of the purchase price at interest rates well above prime and pledged as collateral all of the assets of all of his other companies. Eleven months later, "Sponge Rubber" was firebombed in what the FBI would call the largest case of industrial arson in American history. A federal grand jury indicted ten people in connection with the fire, including Moeller and his chief psychic, who prosecutors said masterminded the blaze. Moeller's lawyer was Ted Koskoff, then in top form. The elder Koskoff won Moeller's acquittal on all federal charges, then, seven years later, on state charges as well.

Twice exonerated, Moeller hired Koskoff to sue his insurer for $62.5 million. It was this claim, ten years after the fire, that irrevocably linked Doyle and Mike Koskoff. The carrier, Protection Mutual, hired Doyle and gave him an unlimited budget and a free hand, while the younger Koskoff took over the case reluctantly, by default. Ted was then ill with bone cancer, debilitated both by the disease and chemotherapy. "It was clear somebody was going to have to try the case," Mike recalls. "I volunteered, but I didn't want to do it." The trial began in Bridgeport in September 1987 and was billed as "a battle of the titans" by the city's afternoon paper, though the younger Koskoff was plainly overmatched. Moeller had agreed to let him argue the case, but he insisted that Ted examine both him and the key witness against him; otherwise they had just one other lawyer assisting them, a prominent New Haven litigator named Tony Fitzgerald. Doyle, meanwhile, led a small army, including a former FBI agent to track down witnesses and an investigative accounting firm to sift through the financial records of all of Moeller's other companies. Koskoff joked about the mismatch—"My father always said if he ever had a heart attack and he wanted to recuperate, we should wheel him into a courtroom"—but going into the trial he feared being swamped by the sheer exhaustiveness of Doyle's preparations.

With a well-prepared case, a weak plaintiff, and the kind of Runyonesque theme he loved—"He burned it down, then he lied about it"—Doyle was relentless. He barraged the younger Koskoff with objections throughout his opening argument, forcing him to sit down at one point and complain, "You're not letting me tell the jury what the case is about." His hostility intensified as they began to take testimony. Doyle, all florid intimidation, postured feverishly, contested every point, scowled, feigned incredulity—anything to gain the upper hand. He browbeat both Mike Koskoff and his witnesses. The low point for the Koskoffs came with Ted's examination of Moeller. During the two criminal trials, the elder Koskoff had skillfully portrayed his client as a public-minded businessman and a good Christian. But now Moeller was a plaintiff, not a defendant, and his "rags to Jesus to riches story," as Doyle called it, was irrelevant. Ted struggled to paint Moeller in a positive light, but he was frail and distracted. With his hips frozen, he took small, painful steps. His voice had lost its resonance. Doyle had little trouble derailing what he called the "Ted and Chuck Show," leaving Mike to feel he wasn't just carrying his father's case, but his father, too.

Then, on a night in late January, at the beginning of the fifth month of trial, Ted collapsed at home. He was taken by ambulance to Bridgeport Hospital, then moved to the critical care unit at Yale–New Haven. His doctors didn't think he would leave the hospital alive. After spending all day in court, his son began to go to the hospital every night, sustained only by his desperation to have it all be over. It was a "horrible experience," he says, one that affected everyone, even Doyle. "I remember," Doyle says, "we were scheduling, and Ted's in the hospital, and [Judge] Harrigan is talking about when we're going to do closing arguments. And he said to Michael, 'When do you want to do it?' Everybody was being very accommodating, we all were. And Michael just choked up and said, 'I guess I better do it now because I don't know if I'll be able to do it later.' It was very moving, to see the turmoil." After six months of testimony, the summations each lasted eleven hours.

The jury deliberated twenty days. With Ted stabilized, Michael was relieved from worrying that his father would die during the trial, but he still endured the rabid introspection and self-loathing that trial lawyers, spent and defenseless, often suffer when a jury goes out. Doyle, too, was bereft. He second-guessed himself bitterly as he considered the unimaginable: a hung jury. Unable to sleep or eat or work, both men sunk into a kind of torpid depression. They proclaimed great respect for each other, not just out of professional courtesy but because twenty days was the longest a Connecticut civil jury had ever deliberated. They had fought, they suspected, as near to a draw as lawyers could. Each had seen too much of each other not to appreciate the menace to himself.

On March 23, 1988, the jury found for the defendants: though Moeller was never convicted of arson, he was barred from collecting on his insurance policy. Neither Koskoff was surprised by the verdict, though Ted was now too ill to be upset by it. Michael remembers him saying about trials, "One day's going to be bad and the next day's going to be good and they're going to even out in the end. So you just get to final arguments. And, if you lose, it was a bad jury from the beginning, the case was a loser, nobody could have won it, the judge took the case away from us." Even in the hospital his equanimity never deserted him.

During the next several months Ted came infrequently to the office, not to work but simply to be there. Typically, he never made Michael feel he had performed anything but admirably in their last trial together, though Michael had reason to feel he might have won without his father. Nor did Ted feel any malice toward Doyle, who some months after the trial ran into Michael and, not having seen Ted since the verdict, inquired if he was mad at him. Within days Ted had his daughter hand-deliver Doyle a box of Havana cigars with a red ribbon as a Christmas gift. Three months later Ted was dead.

Michael mourned him with deep affection but also with a sense that while he may have surpassed his father's skills as a lawyer, he would never fully live up to his legacy. At Ted's memorial service he told a story about what he called "the soup incident." When Michael was nine, his sister was serving Ted soup at dinner. Approaching the table carefully, she stumbled, dumping the teeming bowl in his lap. Without a word, Ted rose, left the room, and came back wearing a raincoat. Michael said he took from this incident two main themes: "There was nothing so horrible or so disturbing that it should interfere with a good meal," and "If you were a member of Ted Koskoff's family, you could do no wrong." Ted's corner office remained dark for months after his death, as the firm's lawyers wandered in and out to think about him and perhaps smell the lingering cigar smoke. Some of them talked about preserving it as a shrine. In the end, Michael moved in quietly, keeping all the furniture as he assumed his anticipated place at the head of the firm.

Brian Casey could not have known the degree to which the younger Koskoff suffered during the final year of his father's life, but he appeared to be betting that the memory of the Sponge Rubber trial was an acid one for him, and that it would act on him as he learned that he would be facing Doyle, not

Ryan, in *Sabia*. It was a reasonable guess. All trial lawyers have their ghosts, and Koskoff had his: the last time he had gone all out against an insurer, Doyle had beaten him amid the darkest months of his life. Koskoff, who would match his skills against anyone's in a courtroom, would say he had no fear of facing Doyle over the long course of a trial. But after how bedeviled he felt last time, how, Casey seemed to be betting, could he not?

~ ~ ~

Scrapping for advantage after the Norwalk Hospital meeting, Koskoff wasted no time pressing for a court date. Ryan never called with a counteroffer, so Koskoff concluded that Travelers had no wish to discuss settlement, at least for the time being. He wasn't surprised, but he feared the case might fall back into limbo. Ryan had disclosed a corps of experts but hadn't yet deposed them, and Koskoff worried it might take a year or more to get to trial. He believed Ryan had done him a favor by prompting him to overprepare for the meeting. In October he resolved to return it by pressuring the court to speed the case along. Business and professional issues added to his urgency. After five and a half years *Sabia* was now among the oldest files in the office. The Humes settlement had guaranteed that it wouldn't be a loss, but Koskoff was eager to obtain just compensation for the Sabias, whom he admired but hardly knew, earn his one-third share, and close the matter.

In truth, he wanted to go on to other cases, particularly that of a former resident at Yale–New Haven who'd contracted the AIDS virus from a needle stick and was suing both the hospital and Yale Medical School. Ever since Ted's death three and a half years earlier, Mike Koskoff had been frustrated by the limitations of his practice. He still loved the courtroom, but fewer and fewer cases went to trial. Bringing individual malpractice claims, he was able to help one family at a time not to become whole, as the idea of civil justice had it, but to dig out financially and gain something for its suffering. He made sure doctors and hospitals were more vigilant, if only to avoid being sued. What he didn't do, he knew, was change the structure of medicine so that medical injuries declined, victims were cared for, negligence was deterred and bad doctors were weeded out. But he believed the Yale case, by attacking the beast in its belly, had that potential. His client, an HIV-positive Manhattan doctor, claimed never to have been adequately instructed on how to do an arterial line insertion on an AIDS patient. Koskoff believed the case could well crown his career. Here were all his complaints against doctors and hospitals writ large—that the very methodology by which the best young doctors were trained, an imitative technique known as "see one, do one, teach one," begat a culture of negligence so ingrained that it even destroyed its own. With Yale the defendant, and Doyle its lawyer, the case had everything Koskoff could want.

Sabia, meanwhile, was at a stage that could only worry him. He still thought he had a strong case, but there was more to winning lawsuits than merit. Luck, stamina, and timing also counted. Tony and Donna were still separated, ominously; if their marriage collapsed before the case went to trial, it could destroy their credibility as plaintiffs. More critically, Little Tony's health loomed now as an issue. His constitution was good and his seizures largely under control, but he was eight and a half, and the older he got, the more tenuous his hold on life became. The boy's lungs were weak from inactivity; he could catch cold and, unable to clear his passages, bow to pneumonia. He could choke on his own vomit. He could fail to get enough calories and slowly starve to death. As Doyle recognized, Little Tony *was* Koskoff's case. Specific damages for his future care, loss of life's enjoyment, lost income, and lifelong pain and suffering comprised the bulk of Koskoff's $22 million demand. Koskoff had once had a case where an insurance company offered a multi-million dollar settlement, then retracted it after the plaintiff died. He feared a similar outcome now.

Koskoff worried that Travelers and the hospital might simply drag their heels long enough for Little Tony to succumb. But getting a court date for a major malpractice case had become increasingly difficult. Connecticut's civil dockets were stuffed, clogging court calendars. With complex malpractice trials like *Sabia* often lasting several months, judges preferred not to tie up their courtrooms with them, ordering their clerks to schedule shorter cases to help reduce their backlogs.

A pretrial conference on *Sabia* was scheduled for January, and Koskoff hoped the judge, Myron Ballen, would set a trial date then, possibly for April or May. Ballen wouldn't hear the case himself—he was an administrative judge; his job was to route cases through the system—but Koskoff and Bernard had both lobbied him, and Ballen had assured them that he would try to "reach" the case by summer. It was one of the oldest cases on the docket, and Ballen seemed eager to clear it off. That was before Koskoff learned, however, that Travelers had brought in Doyle and that all his calculations might change. Koskoff was unintimidated by Doyle's hiring, as Casey may have hoped; in fact, he claimed to be delighted. Doyle was less charming in court than Ryan, and while he may have beaten him in Sponge Rubber, Koskoff had never considered that a fair reckoning. Rivalries demand rematches.

What heartened him even more was Doyle's likely impact on any settlement negotiations. Koskoff knew that Doyle and Casey were friends and that Casey had hired Doyle not just to rankle Koskoff but to tell Casey whether Travelers could win in front of a jury. The nearer both sides got to trial, the greater their incentive to avoid one would become, and the more Doyle and Casey's relationship might be made to work to Koskoff's advantage. He and Doyle had recently settled a $6 million anesthesia case together. Koskoff trusted Doyle to tell

Travelers what it might cost to avoid a trial in *Sabia* and believed that the company would listen to him more intently than it would to Ryan.

He anticipated that Doyle would need time to prepare his case and expected Ballen to grant him a three-month continuance, but at the January pretrial, in chambers, Ballen unexpectedly turned prickly. He was determined, he said, not to grant any further delays, pointing out that the hospital had had the same five and a half years to prepare its case as the Koskoffs, and that aces like Doyle were often brought in at the last minute to try cases they hadn't developed. These, he said, weren't the court's concerns. "I'm going to put this case on trial unless you both decide not to," Ballen warned them. Koskoff smiled ambiguously, realizing he had gotten what he wanted—and might do better not to take it. All he had to do was say no to an extension and he and Doyle would be picking a jury in six weeks. That was exactly what he and Bernard had been trying to engineer for almost two years, since they'd filed the offers of judgment. A trial sooner rather than later would benefit him and hobble Doyle.

And yet he held back. The case was now between him and Doyle, and the two of them had too much other business together, particularly the Yale case, for Koskoff to want Doyle to feel that he had taken unfair advantage. On the other hand, if he accepted a delay, Doyle would owe him. Whatever he decided, Koskoff knew Doyle would have numerous occasions to repay him, and would, aggressively, when it suited him. In the end, Koskoff agreed to an extension, but not before applying his usual spin. As he would later tell it, Doyle "begged" for a continuance, and he, Koskoff, munificently and at risk to his clients and himself, agreed. Largesse was a Koskoff family trait that hadn't been diluted between Ted's and Michael's generations.

Doyle returned to his office in New Haven suspicious as ever of Koskoff's motives but with a reprieve. He now had time to prepare a case, get some decent experts, develop a credible theme. He would have to work fast, but not so insanely as if Koskoff had insisted on going to trial. He thought Koskoff had done the reasonable thing. As Doyle recalls, he hadn't groveled before Ballen, but only because he didn't have to.

One of the first decisions he'd made after accepting the case was to retain Bev Hunt. Having done Ryan's legwork, she knew the file. She also knew the experts, and Doyle, with neither time nor desire to nurture a fresh associate, needed a competent "second chair," someone familiar with both the testimony and those voicing it. Now he and Hunt got together to review the entire file, going back to the first court pleadings and assembling a chronology so that Doyle could analyze the case. He was struck at once by how Koskoff had lurched over the years from one theory to another. At first the Koskoffs had primarily blamed Humes for the damage to Little Tony. Looking back on it, Doyle suspected this was the real reason Koskoff hadn't also sued on behalf of the stillborn Michael. Having no clue as to what actually had happened, yet presented with the fact of one baby not only dead but dead for many hours, Koskoff, he reasoned, had faced an insoluble dilemma: Either Humes was responsible or she wasn't. Yet if she was to blame, what accounted for Michael's death? And if she wasn't, what negligence injured Little Tony? In other words, where was the case?

Doyle didn't believe for a minute that Koskoff had decided not to file a wrongful death claim for Michael because such claims generally brought small verdicts. He was sure the reason was that Koskoff knew the case against Humes would collapse if he did sue over Michael's death. He found Koskoff's second theory—that the injuries to Little Tony first sustained on Saturday were worsened by a prolonged delivery—equally disingenuous. It suited Koskoff's need to hold in both defendants, but on what basis in reality? Benirschke had said that what injured Little Tony was a catastrophic drop in blood pressure following Michael's death, yet he also testified that the damage was over quickly and conceded that Michael may have been killed by a sudden cord accident. The birth, Doyle concluded, was a red herring.

Doyle expected not to have to challenge Benirschke on causation, and in fact saw him as friendlier to Humes and to the hospital than to the Sabias. He thought Humes had been screwed, paying $1.35 million "for nothing." As for the hospital, he concluded that there was no liability. Hunt told him they had experts who believed that the standard of care didn't require serial ultrasounds or nonstress tests and that even if such tests had been done, Michael's death could neither have been predicted nor prevented. Doyle knew this last would be a hard sell in the face of the devastation to Little Tony, but, listening to Hunt, he concluded it was his best hope. He boiled it down: "Even if we had done what they said we should have done, which we dispute," he said, "that would not have prevented what happened."

Here was Doyle's theme—"a case in search of a theory," he called it. First the Sabias went after Humes and, without proving she was at fault, collected from her. Then they went after the hospital. Typically, it was Little Tony's long-term disability, not whether Humes and the hospital had done anything wrong, that drove them as they shifted targets. Doyle knew he couldn't paint the Sabias as villains, but he believed he could face a jury with the claim that there was absolutely no connection between what the hospital did or didn't do and Little Tony's injuries. Moreover, he could argue that Koskoff's attempts to invent such a connection were both cynical and deceptive, a bald attempt to exploit their sympathies. It wasn't the best theme Doyle had ever devised, but he knew he was unlikely to come up with one better. All he and Hunt had to do now was prove it.

EIGHTEEN

IN MARCH, TONY AND DONNA LEFT THE KIDS WITH TONY'S SISTER AND SHANNON and went to Daytona for Bike Week. They'd been planning the trip for a year. The previous winter, just before Donna moved out, they'd run away together for a few days, getting in the car "basically to talk," Donna says, and had driven nonstop to Florida. Bikers from all over the country descend on Daytona's joints and beaches in the weeks before the college kids arrive for spring break. Tony and Donna had felt engulfed by what seemed like one big party, an all-night eruption of flashing chrome and wide-open bars, mud-wrestling and tattoo contests. Inhaling the noise and heat and attitude, having fun for the first time in years, they swore they'd come back.

Even after they split up, they talked about returning. A month after Donna had bought her Harley Sportster with her share of the Humes settlement, Tony purchased a red 1200 cc Honda Aspencade, a big touring bike. They had ridden to the Poconos a couple of times, but from the day they reunited, they talked about Bike Week, about doing it right this time. Borrowing a trailer, they hitched their motorcycles behind Donna's van and headed to a motel on the beach called Perry's, their first real vacation in ten years.

Their friend Janice Major would criticize them for taking the trip without their children. She thought they should have taken everyone, including Little Tony, to Disney World instead, using their newfound time and money to restore themselves as a family. But others, like Chris Bernard, who'd seen the strain on Tony during their separation and had watched other families destroyed trying to raise disabled children, urged them to go. "Taking kids to Disney World is stressful under the best of circumstances," Bernard says. "I tell people who've been through this kind of ordeal, 'It's like when the oxygen mask comes down on a plane and they tell you to put the mask over your mouth before your child's.' If you can't function, how can you save them?"

The ten-day trip rekindled their marriage but soured their relationship with Shannon, who was consumed with adolescent rebellion. Balky and hostile, she talked back constantly. It was not hard for her to feel that all her life she'd been unwanted by her family, that in a kind of unintentional reprise of her own life her mother had orphaned her just as her mother had been orphaned. At sixteen, she didn't have much sympathy. Donna accepted most of the blame for Shannon's hostility. She felt she had done her best under the circumstances, but their lives had been unrelievedly harsh, and Shannon had suffered so that Donna could go her own way. "When Shannon was born, I didn't have any family," she recalls. "My sister had to sneak her over to see my mom when my father was at work. My mom would never hold her. She was afraid she would get too attached and it would cause problems."

Donna had shuffled Shannon among relatives so she could work, left her with Tony's parents when she was five so she could be with Tony, neglected her for years after that so she could concentrate on Little Tony. When Tony had first volunteered to adopt her after their marriage, Donna says, "it was like a dream come true"; Shannon would have a father. Yet it was far from enough. Donna always meant to do more for her, and always failed to. Now she shook her head ruefully, saying, as Tony did, "Shannon grew up too fast." She didn't know what else to do.

Spring in the new house had been a relief from the mud and shifting ground of Sunken Homes, and on Memorial Day she and Tony threw an open house. Expecting a big crowd, Tony rose early and by late morning was in high gear, setting up the grills, marinating the meat, dragging lawn chairs and sports equipment from the garage, clearing the driveway. He and Donna had made it a rule that on weekends Shannon had to be up by ten, but by noon she still wasn't downstairs, and Donna, knowing that Tony needed her help outside, went up with the younger girls to rouse her. By twelve-thirty she still wasn't down and Donna had to go up to her room again. This time Tony followed her. "Your father's going to blow his stack if you don't get out of bed," she warned.

Shannon finally stumbled down at about one o'clock, shortly before most of the guests were to arrive. Tony, Donna says, "went through the ceiling."

"Clean up the dog mess in the yard," Tony told her.

"Fuck off," Shannon said.

Tony grabbed her by the shirt and began marching her into the house. Going limp, Shannon tried to resist, and Tony, persisting, dragged her across the lawn. "Your daughter's calling you," he called to Donna.

Shannon was screaming wildly when Donna finally heard her and tried to intercede. She was covered with grass stains. Coldly, Donna looked her up and down. "Change your clothes," she snapped. "And stay out of your father's way."

The party was uneventful, but in school later that week Shannon reported that Tony had beaten her up. School officials, required to do so by law, notified the state's Department of Youth Services, which sent an investigator to the house. Shannon returned to the Greenwich Youth Shelter.

It had become impossible for them all to live together, and Donna realized, given the state's involvement and Shannon's age, that she and Tony faced a choice: give her up—make her a state ward—or send her back to live with Donna's sister in Maryland. They chose the latter, telling Shannon that this time she couldn't come back until she finished high school.

On July 20, in Norwalk Probate Court, Donna signed papers to grant temporary guardianship to her sister and brother-in-law, Deborah and Russell Bednarik. Thinking there was no other solution, she didn't contest the reason for the decree: "Parent's ability to control child," it read, "has deteriorated to an intolerable level."

~ ~ ~

JULY 27, 1993

Having persuaded Ballen to assign *Sabia* to a trial list for early September, Koskoff intensified his maneuvers. The date wasn't firm—no civil court date was—but the fact that he and Doyle were scheduled to start picking a jury in six weeks put him solidly on the offensive for the first time, and he meant to use his upper hand to tweak Doyle wherever possible. The case, both of them knew, was entering its penultimate stage. Courtesies like granting the other side an extension were no longer practical. Koskoff and Doyle had talked often by phone, mostly to nail down dates for deposing several last-minute experts. Koskoff knew Doyle's "case in search of a theory" theme and thought it desperate. He also knew that Doyle was concerned about the labor and delivery, which though ostensibly no longer an issue, still loomed as perhaps the most troubling example of how the hospital had neglected Donna's care.

Typically, Koskoff thought he couldn't lose. He believed that Doyle—though he would never admit it—knew it too, and he wanted Doyle to reconsider whether going to court was in his client's best interest. As part of the housekeeping of setting the issues for trial, Koskoff now entered two last-minute pleadings. Both were meant to remind Doyle what he would be up against, all too soon, if Travelers still refused to discuss resolving the case.

The first filing amended the Sabias' original complaint to reflect Little

Tony's current medical status. Now almost nine and a half, he'd been hospitalized more than twenty-five times, and orthopedists at Newington Children's Hospital, where he'd had his hips realigned, were recommending two more operations, including a risky, two-part procedure to straighten his spine. Because of his wasted nervous system and paralysis, Little Tony's spinal column had grown more and more crooked the older he got. Doctors feared that if he survived to adolescence, his twisted skeleton would constrict his vital organs, causing him pain and possibly dysfunction. The solution, they'd told Tony and Donna, was to remold his spine, fuse it, then insert steel rods along its length to keep it straight—an eight-to-ten-hour operation requiring entry through both the back and the chest. For the Sabias to claim that Little Tony's scoliosis and other late-blooming problems were caused by the hospital's negligence, the Koskoffs had to present the court with a fuller diagnosis than they had when the case was first filed more than six years earlier.

Doyle accepted the medical amendments without complaint. He knew he wasn't going to win a jury's sympathy by claiming Little Tony was any less disabled than he was. But he objected strenuously to Koskoff's second filing—a list, running more than seven pages, of witnesses the Sabias intended to call to testify regarding Little Tony's medical condition. Indeed, provoking Doyle was one of Koskoff's main purposes in submitting the three-part roster. First, Koskoff added the name of Dr. Bennett Shaywitz, an eminent Yale neurologist, to his list of medical experts. Shaywitz wouldn't be testifying about what caused Little Tony's injuries: Koskoff seldom relied on neurologists to elucidate fetal brain injury, although that was their field. He preferred instead perinatologists like Schifrin, who had more direct experience with brain-damaged newborns and whose speculations better suited his arguments. Shaywitz would address Little Tony's current condition, treatment, and future prognosis only, testifying to the boy's dire state in order to support Koskoff's claim for damages.

It was a small role—noncontroversial given the general agreement over Little Tony's condition—but disclosing Shaywitz had other, subtler meanings for both Koskoff and Doyle. Most Yale–New Haven doctors avoided testifying as experts in in-state malpractice cases because of the hospital's relationship with local medical centers. Norwalk Hospital itself referred its most serious cases there, thus supplying Yale's physicians with patients and income. It promoted its Yale affiliation in ads and brochures. Koskoff considered it a coup for himself and a black eye for the hospital to have a prominent Yale medical professor on his side, and he knew that Doyle, because of his own relationship with Yale, would be hard-pressed to attack Shaywitz head-on.

Second—the majority of the names—was a list of those who had treated Little Tony and whose therapies, prescriptions, recommendations, and insights formed the basis for the $12 million life-care plan in Larry Forman's damage report. There were enough names and specialties to staff a small hospital: twenty-four treating physicians, more than two dozen nurses, social workers, dietitians, physical and occupational therapists, psychologists, rehabilitation counselors, and special-needs teachers, plus the "agents, servants and employees" of Norwalk Hospital, Newington Children's Hospital, and the Easter Seals Rehabilitation Center in Stamford, where Little Tony had first gone for treatment eight years earlier. Koskoff didn't plan to call all these witnesses at trial, but if he wanted to include their testimony, he had to disclose them first. The sheer size of the list suggested what Doyle would face if he tried to challenge Forman's conclusions.

It was Koskoff's third disclosure, however, that rankled Doyle, for reasons Koskoff could anticipate. "The plaintiffs," he wrote, "may further call Maryellen Humes, M.D. and other agents, servants and employees of the defendant Norwalk Hospital." Doyle had no problem with Humes, McManamy, Fortuna, or anyone else from the delivery being asked to address Little Tony's condition at birth. It was Koskoff's suggestion that they might also testify "regarding the applicable standard of care for their care and treatment of (him), departures from the standard of care and the causal relationship between those departures and the injuries and damages suffered by the plaintiffs" that outraged him. Doyle had been assured by Casey that the labor and delivery was a dead issue, wiped away by the settlement with Humes, and that he wouldn't have to defend the hospital's handling of it. Having to justify Donna's prenatal care would be hard enough; the last thing he wanted was to have to defend to a jury what happened in the maternity suite, where clinic employees also were involved. Long distrustful of Koskoff, he suspected him of using the filing to reintroduce the birth through the back door, perhaps as a bargaining chip.

Doyle called Bernard to complain. He said he understood that the labor and delivery were handled poorly and asked Bernard's assurance that no evidence of negligence during the birth would be brought to trial. Noncommittal, Bernard said he would talk to Koskoff and get back to him.

~~~

AUGUST 3, 1993

Westport filmmaker Bill Buckley arrived at Little Tony's school, the Feroleto Child Development Center in Trumbull, and set up his first shot: a one-on-one classroom sequence involving Little Tony and his teacher. Buckley's videocamera was hefted on his right shoulder. With his soulful eyes, boxy glasses, and pointy grey beard, he looked like Robert Altman. A pioneer, with

B A R R Y   W E R T H   269

Koskoff, in producing documentary-style "day-in-the-life" videos for trial, Buckley had been filming brain-damaged children for twenty years. Before that he had made award-winning human rights documentaries.

This was Buckley's second session of taping Little Tony: the first was done on March 1, 1988, but Koskoff deemed it too dated to be of value. Other than perhaps a brief personal appearance, this was all a jury would see of Little Tony, and Koskoff wanted it to be current and unflinching. He'd learned years earlier that juries quickly became inured to the sight of even the most horribly brain-injured children. A twenty-minute day-in-the-life, he liked to say, was much more compelling than having a wheelchair-bound child "just lying there" day after day in court.

Courtroom videos were a Koskoff trademark. Among the first lawyers in the country to use them, he had helped develop their documentary format and had fought several key legal battles in Connecticut, including a precedent-setting case in the state's Supreme Court, to force judges to admit them as evidence. He also promoted their use nationally, advising trial lawyers how to conceive, script, and edit them for maximum effect. "In a static environment, like a courtroom, what moves attracts attention," he once lectured a group of Maryland trial lawyers. "It's a rule of drama." He also told them: "It's difficult for a jury to distinguish between a vegetable and a human being. Instruct the cameraman to focus on the person's eyes. It is impossible to look into someone's eyes and not sense humanity. If you look long enough, you start believing that there is a consciousness there. There is," he concluded, "that illusion of humanity."

At Feroleto, Little Tony's eyes were determinedly shut. He sat quietly, strapped in his wheelchair, head slumped on his chest. Donna had dressed him that morning in a black and grey short-sleeved sports jersey and matching shorts that she'd bought at Kmart. On his feet were white sports socks and black sneakers. Shooting him from slightly above, Buckley focused on his head, which rolled from side to side. A young woman with a cheery voice approached him from off-camera.

"Hi, Tony, how are you today?" she said. The boy showed no response. She took his hand. "This is Dawn. I'm on your left side and I'm touching your left hand."

Still no response. Little Tony's mouth was frozen in a deep frown, as if he didn't like something, maybe the overhead lights.

"I'm going to put your splint on," Dawn said, reaching for a hard molded plastic device with splayed grooves for Little Tony's fingers. "I'm going to put it on so I can separate your fingers, so your fingers will heal. You need to relax your hand."

Buckley zoomed in on the splint as, finger by finger, she unfurled his gnarled fist.

"Okay, Tony," Dawn said. "Now I'm going to put some cornstarch between your fingers to help dry out your sores." She spread the cornstarch as Little Tony, powerless to help or resist, did nothing. "Nice job," she said.

Little Tony still hadn't opened his eyes, although he now lifted his head in the kind of torpid, aimless movement one associates with drug addicts. Buckley cut from his hand to his face, then zoomed in as Dawn moved to prop up the boy's waxy-looking head.

"You need to hold your head up," she said. "You must keep your head on this side of the headrest here and try to hold it up."

With no sign that he heard or understood her, or that he could will himself to do what she asked if he had, Little Tony's head rolled slightly. Then, with his eyes still closed, his chin sank once again into his chest. Buckley faded out.

It went on this way throughout the morning. Tony's teachers prodding him to roll to one side, to push a plate-sized button on his lap in order to turn on a radio, or, outside, to acknowledge the sun; and he, in turn, registering nothing—no puzzlement, no recognition, just a deep inwardness that translated into a kind of stolid, bovine resistance. It was impossible to say what, if any, intelligence he had, and whether these persistent efforts to engage him weren't wholly futile. At lunchtime one of his teachers pulled his feeder tube from inside his shirt, said, "Apple juice for you today, Tony," poured the juice into his syringe, then asked, "That feel good?" as the juice drained into his gut. Tony sat dully, uncomplaining. Only once, when there was a sudden burst from his radio, did he respond, his mouth and eyes opening into a wide grin of pure infantile delight.

Buckley recorded it all dispassionately. He had veered into making films for court twenty years earlier, when his oldest son was arrested for selling a hundred pounds of marijuana to a federal agent and Koskoff, his son's lawyer, suggested a barter to cover legal fees. He knew that because of evidentiary requirements a day-in-the-life needed to appear scrupulously unbiased. As propaganda, these films were the very opposite of so-called settlement brochures, which Buckley also made and Koskoff used and which were heartrending, made with the express purpose of bludgeoning insurance adjusters into settling claims.

Buckley set up after lunch for what would be the video's last scene. In a few weeks he would spend the morning at the Sabias', shooting Little Tony from the time he got up until Tony carried him into the van to leave for school. He would tape him getting his medications, his bath; Donna and Tony dressing him; his sitting with his little sisters in front of the TV listening to Barney. Though shot out of sequence, that footage would precede the school scenes in the day-in-the-life. Now, as Little Tony slouched in his wheelchair in a darkened corner of the classroom and Dawn once again approached him from the side, Buckley zoomed in on his downturned face.

"Tony," sang a voice, "It's Dawn. I'm sitting in front of you and I'm touching your right knee. We're going to do an activity with a flashlight now. I want you to open your eyes and see if you can follow the flashlight with your eyes."

Little Tony's eyes were open, though what he saw was unclear. Even if his eyes worked, and even if he understood Dawn's instructions, doctors had long ago determined that the visual part of his brain was porous and he was effectively blind.

Dawn pointed the beam at his mouth, which was opened slightly. "I see a smile on your face," she said. "I think you like the light."

"Now I'm going to move it up," she said, "and if you can, try to follow it."

Tony's head lurched, as always when he was sitting, with no evidence that he could control it. Mostly, it swung down or jerked to the right. As the beam lit his hair, his head fell forward.

Dawn spoke again. "Now I'm going to move it down towards your stomach. See if you can follow it."

Again the boy's head motions seemed random. Dawn told him she was going to shine the beam now to his right, touching his right arm, and Tony's head continued in the same stilted arc. "That's a nice job looking to the right, Tony," she said. "Very good."

Feroleto had a substantial reputation. The Norwalk school department, concluding it could do little more for Tony than warehouse him in a special-needs class, were paying $42,000 a year in tuition for him to be here. Donna had fought to get him in, and was delighted with the close attention he was receiving.

Yet as Dawn continued to move the flashlight back and forth across his face, vacant of the slightest comprehension, the value of the exercise seemed questionable. By any measure, his movements bore only the vaguest connection to her directions. Only the most hopeful observer could find in them any real encouragement. He would first have to understand her words. Did he know what a face was? An eye? A stomach? Could he possibly distinguish left from right? Was he capable of moving his head intentionally? What, if anything, did he see? To presume that Little Tony was doing what she praised him for was to credit him with a degree of intelligence and control that neurologists familiar with his type of injury considered beyond imagining. There was humanity in Little Tony, to be sure, but how much was anybody's guess.

The lesson lasted just a few minutes, which Buckley would edit to less than two minutes on the final tape. Toward the end, Dawn brought the light back to Tony's nose, then told him, as she stroked his left arm, to try to follow the light to his left.

Tony's gaze was unchanging. Then his head jerked farther left than at any time before—not much, just a few degrees, but enough to suggest that the motion may have been intentional. Dawn patted his arm encouragingly. "That's a nice job moving your head, Tony, very good."

Buckley panned to Dawn, then returned to Little Tony, who was now beaming. Buckley faded out with Little Tony's smiling visage filling the screen.

Koskoff could only be pleased. Whatever the ambiguity of the moment— had Little Tony turned purposefully to follow the light, or was he responding reflexively to Dawn's less-than-subtle physical cues, or was his sudden lurch just another random motion, an accident of timing?—it would surely leave a jury with a final impression that served the Sabias' case either way. Either Little Tony's brain was so wholly destroyed that he couldn't understand the simplest instruction or perform the simplest task, or, worse, as Koskoff had suggested at the meeting at Norwalk Hospital, within his crippled form was a thinking, feeling human being, a creature imprisoned so deeply inside his wasted body that a faintly deliberate shake of the head was all he could do to scream out that he was there and that he understood. With each fate more monstrous than the other, how could Koskoff lose?

≈ ≈ ≈

AUGUST 12, 1993

Dr. Charles Lockwood, Norwalk Hospital's chief standard-of-care expert, reminded Doyle of Doogie Howser. At age thirty-eight, Lockwood was already prominent in the world of high-risk obstetrics. He was director of perinatal research at Mount Sinai School of Medicine in Manhattan, where he ran a busy clinical service with a youthful hyperactivity that left those around him gasping. He also sustained an important academic career, publishing feverishly and garnering high-profile awards and grants. Doyle, who revered credibility, worried that Lockwood seemed too young to have earned his, despite his energy, rank, and reputation.

Five feet seven, with thick black hair and round glasses, Lockwood had precocity written all over him. He had grown up in a "schizo household" near Boston, the product of a polyglot ancestry. His father was a taciturn engineer whose WASP forebears were lanky Connecticut shipbuilders but who himself grew up in Puerto Rico and speaks Spanish, Lockwood says, "like John Wayne." His mother's parents, whom he resembled physically, were devout Catholics who emigrated to Puerto Rico from Corsica and Calabria, in southern Italy. Bursting with drive, Lockwood had a Latin bearing and metabolism hard-wired to a Yankee industry and surname. What struck Doyle most force-fully was his bouncy adolescent verve. Twelve years after being chosen president of his graduating class at the University of Pennsylvania School of Medicine, he looked, Doyle thought, "about eighteen." Doyle was impressed with Lockwood's views and expertise but fretted about how he would play be-fore a jury, especially against the grey-bearded, rabbinic Schifrin, whose testi-mony he was about to rebut in his deposition.

Bev Hunt had retained Lockwood in 1991 and had nothing but confi-dence in his opinions. Not only did he believe that it was not required in 1984 to perform serial ultrasounds in twin pregnancies—Koskoff's main negli-gence claim against the hospital—but he was equally certain that what had happened to Little Tony could not have been predicted or prevented even had such fetal scans been done. To Hunt, Lockwood was a treasure. His credentials were exhaustive; he testified equally for plaintiffs and defendants, so he couldn't be attacked, as Schifrin could be, as a "whore"; and he believed en-thusiastically that the hospital had done nothing wrong. Moreover, he had been willing to do independent research to support his testimony. On the key issue of whether repeat ultrasounds were standard practice, for instance, he had reviewed back editions of several textbooks, scoured the medical litera-ture for publications that addressed the issue, called leading ultrasonogra-phers to get their views, then contacted numerous older colleagues, inviting them to second-guess him. Hunt, who had never before tried a case, thought he would be unassailable under cross-examination.

Sitting in Lockwood's Mount Sinai office at the corner of Ninety-eighth Street and Madison Avenue, waiting for Lockwood to be sworn in, Doyle knew better. Juries were notoriously fickle, trusting one expert because of his posture, distrusting another because of a bad toupee, factors that had nothing to do with right and wrong. As Doyle put it, he'd had his ass handed to him by too many juries to take any expert for granted, especially one who looked like he might not be shaving yet. Even if Lockwood was right, and Doyle believed he was, law wasn't medicine. What was true was what a jury believed, not what the most authoritative expert said. "Doctors live in a world of black and white," Doyle says. "The appendix is where it is, the esophagus is where it is. But what we do is very messy. Litigation is a sea of grey. There are no facts un-til the trier of facts finds something as a fact. And so your job is to have a fact perceived the way you want it perceived."

Koskoff had sent Bernard to depose Lockwood. He preferred not to meet the other side's experts before seeing them in court, nor did he want them to meet him. Cross-examination, in his view, was raw theater, two actors impro-vising off each other's cues. Koskoff liked to depend on his own "visceral and instinctive reality" of what was happening in a courtroom—was a witness nervous? arrogant? appealing? unappealing?—to decide how best to keep the drama fresh. He also liked to keep the other side's experts off balance by not letting them know what to expect from him. If he met them, he might like them, and that would dull his attack.

Bernard began his examination routinely, by ascertaining Lockwood's qualifications, forcing him to admit at the outset that in 1983–1984, while Donna was pregnant, he was still a third-year resident and not "board-certified in anything." But as he walked him through his credentials, it soon became clear that what Lockwood lacked in age he made up in experience. After graduating from Penn, he'd been a fellow in high-risk obstetrics at Yale, the same program attended by Schifrin and for decades the country's leading training ground for perinatologists. From there he'd gone on to teach at Tufts University School of Medicine while maintaining a busy practice at one of Boston's leading referral centers for women with complicated pregnancies.

Indeed, Lockwood could hardly have been more involved with managing difficult births. At Mount Sinai, he had his own full schedule of high-risk patients, saw about a quarter of the patients at the hospital's high-risk maternity clinic, consulted for thousands of patients whose ultrasound scans were referred each year from other hospitals, and every fourth week was "high-risk attending"—supervising complex deliveries around the clock. On the standard of care for twin pregnancies he was impressively up-to-date, and had been at least since 1985, his first year at Yale. But the main issue in *Sabia,* the one on which it now hinged, was what regular ob-gyns were supposed to be doing a year before that, not what academic specialists did today.

Bernard built to the question slowly. He was now treading in an area where, Doyle's dictum aside, medicine was the sea of grey, not law. In law a statute is a statute, a rule a rule, by legislative or judicial decree. Who, though, ordained what doctors did in their daily practice? Standard of care was merely a kind of mean, what a reasonably competent physician would be expected to do under the circumstances. Koskoff loved asking juries to decide what *they* thought the standard of care should be, based on common sense. Cleverly, he would suggest that Norwalk Hospital should have done serial ultrasounds on Donna *as a matter of course* because it was feasible and because, in hindsight, there appeared to be a need. But Bernard's job was to find out how Lockwood would testify. He wanted no surprises. After several run-ups, he posed the question outright: when exactly did Lockwood think it had become the standard of care to do serial ultrasounds in women expecting twins?

"It's not quite like turning on a lightbulb," Lockwood said, then rattled off his findings. The primary textbooks in 1983 and 1984, especially the sixteenth edition of *Williams Obstetrics,* the ob-gyn's bible, didn't discuss serial ultrasounds at all, he said. Also, a computer search of hundreds of journal articles during that time about serial ultrasounds failed to turn up a single mention of twin pregnancy as an indication. He himself didn't remember doing them in twin gestations before 1985, but "just to be sure," he'd contacted the director of ultrasound at Pennsylvania Hospital where he had been a resident, who said it hadn't become the standard there until 1986. To reassure himself further, he'd checked with several senior perinatologists, including the chairman of maternal-fetal medicine at Mount Sinai, all of whom concurred that it was not the standard in 1984.

"So with that myriad of sources of information," Lockwood asserted, "I am very, very confident that this was not the standard of care in 1984, nor probably the standard of care in 1985. My best and most conservative estimate was that it would probably have become the standard of care between '86 and '87, and I base that on the fact that there were a number of descriptions in ultrasound texts and in maternal-fetal medicine texts that began to discuss it about 1984 and 1985. I think the earliest reference I saw was 1983, so that given the normal lag that it takes for these things to become general practice, my most conservative estimate would probably have been 1986."

Bernard moved on to other subjects, asking Lockwood under what circumstances serial ultrasounds might have been called for with twins, what discordancy was, and whether repeat scans might have been indicated in cases where twins were known to be growing unevenly. Without being asked specifically to discuss the Sabias, Lockwood agreed that if one twin was known to be growth-retarded and the fetuses were at term, the obstetrician's burden shifted—from justifying whether to deliver to finding good cause not to.

"What you are looking for is whether it is safer for the babies to be inside the womb or outside?" Bernard asked.

"That is obstetrics," Lockwood said.

"Let me ask you a hypothetical," Bernard went on. "Suppose you by ultrasound determined there is discordant growth and at thirty-eight weeks you do nonstress testing and you can't assure yourself of the well-being of one of the fetuses. Do you deliver at that point?"

"Yes," Lockwood said.

By carefully evading any mention of the Sabias up to this point, Bernard was subtly enlisting Lockwood for his side; nothing brought a witness up shorter than his own on-the-record comments. Unable to shake Lockwood on the question of whether serial ultrasounds were required, Bernard had nonetheless forced him to concede that they might have been helpful, even critically so, in a case like Donna's. Koskoff no doubt would be pleased.

Finally, Bernard said, "I want to ask you some questions specifically about the management and care of the Sabia pregnancy. First, do you have any criticism of the management of the labor and delivery?"

"I have no comments."

"You have no comments because you haven't reviewed that area?" Bernard seemed suddenly intrigued.

"Yes," said Lockwood. "They were very, very specific that I was to address the issue of standard of care being met during the prenatal care of the patient."

Hesitating purposefully, Bernard went on. "You were specifically requested by defense counsel not to address the issue of the care during labor and delivery?"

"No," Lockwood said. Doyle and Hunt had asked him only to review the prenatal care. They hadn't proscribed his examining the management of the labor and delivery, but hadn't given him any specific documentation about it either.

Acting puzzled, Bernard turned to Doyle. "Are we clear that Dr. Lockwood is not going to offer any testimony regarding opinions as to the care rendered during labor and delivery?"

The strangeness of the question nearly launched Doyle from his seat. Bernard knew the hospital wanted nothing less than to raise the issue of the birth again. Doyle himself had protested Koskoff's attempt to reintroduce it just a week ago, with Bernard, on the phone. Why, Doyle wondered, was Bernard bringing this up?

Agitated, Doyle shot back: "I hope we're clear that not only is Dr. Lockwood not going to do it, that nobody on *your* side is going to do it, because we had this conversation the other day and it's been my understanding since I've been with this case, from conversations with Bev Hunt and conversations with you, that whether or not during delivery Norwalk Hospital complied with or breached the standard of care is not an issue in this case any longer. Is that correct?" Doyle concluded.

Bernard was cool, laconic: "I can confirm that for you, I believe, after we complete the depositions of your experts. I can't make that representation to you until that has been done."

Doyle's face reddened. "I don't understand that," he said, "because I'm not sure—and again it raises my level of concern—why you're even asking him about the business of labor and delivery."

"I need to know if he's going to come into court to express an opinion on it."

"Why would he, if it is not an issue?" Doyle snapped. "As far as we're concerned, based on representations I've had from you and my conversations with Bev, it's not an issue. And I can represent to you that I'm not in the business and don't intend to be in the business in this case of putting on expert testimony about a matter that's not an issue. If you're not in this case attacking, and I understand you're not, what Norwalk Hospital did or didn't do in connection with the delivery, I am sure as hell not going to come forward and try to defend it."

Whether Bernard was simply baiting Doyle or instinctively repelling fire with ice, his tone now grew supercilious. "I'm not sure what you mean by 'what is an issue'?" he said. "Certainly the facts involving the labor and delivery and condition of the child at birth, all of that is certainly relevant in this case. As to whether or not the standard of care was met during labor and delivery, that's a different issue."

"Let's be very frank about this," Doyle said, his voice swelling with indignation. "I don't have any problem if what you want to do is—and you listed Dr. Humes as a possible witness—talk about what Anthony appeared to be like when he was born and the whole business. But if you are going to try to get into, without putting a label on it . . . sequences of things that happened or didn't happen during the delivery that have nothing to do with Anthony's condition after he is born, then we are going to have a problem. I don't understand why this is—"

Bernard cut him off: "I [don't understand how] what you are getting at is my problem. We'll continue to do this on the record, if you like, but I'm going to send you a bill for these pages."

Doyle fumed, "Let's go off the record." His face was scarlet. Either Bernard was goading him, by reminding him that the hospital might still be on the hook for how it had handled Donna's labor and delivery, or else Koskoff even at the eleventh hour was still unsure what had injured Little Tony and was refusing to rule out birth trauma as a secondary cause. Maybe both. Doyle told Bernard flatly that he considered the birth absolutely off-limits and that no amount of gamesmanship would change that. Still, Bernard once again refused to drop it. He preferred, it seemed, to let the matter dangle.

Back on the record, Bernard asked Lockwood his opinion as to what had killed Michael Sabia, and Lockwood ringingly endorsed Benirschke's cord compression theory. Privately, he thought Benirschke a "remarkable person," someone with "phenomenal ability." He had no reason to disagree with Kurt, he said.

Bernard continued. "Dr. Lockwood," he said, "if nonstress testing had been performed on March thirtieth, the last prenatal visit, and one of the twins was found to be nonreactive, what would have been required by the standard of care?"

"Well, in 1984 my guess is they would have done a contraction stress test."

"You prefaced that answer by saying you guess, and that is a word that has some specific legal meaning. Is your answer with reasonable medical probability that that's what was required?"

"Correct."

Bernard was getting now to the nub of the case. According to Barry Schifrin's cascading probabilities, because Michael Sabia was substantially smaller than Little Tony and because his umbilical cord was exposed and vulnerable, he more than likely was already in distress on Friday morning when

Donna went to the clinic. Under that scenario, it was more probable than not that his distress would have shown up as a nonreactive, or sluggish, fetal heart pattern, and doctors, recognizing the elevated risk of allowing him to deliver vaginally, would have induced Donna's uterus to contract in order to see how he withstood the increased pressure. If this was Lockwood's understanding, too, Bernard might well neutralize by force of hindsight his earlier statements that the hospital had no compelling reason to monitor the twins.

Bernard pressed him further. What would happen next if that so-called stress test showed that the baby was in trouble?

Lockwood was unequivocal: "We would deliver the patient," he said.

Lockwood so far had no problem allowing Bernard to lead him. But he could see where Bernard was headed and refused to be brought along. Everything he had said thus far was true; a nonstress test on March 30 would most likely have led to the clinic's delivering healthy twins by C-section. But that wasn't the point. The point was whether the hospital could have, or should have, predicted that Michael Sabia was in trouble.

Lockwood believed unshakably that there was no basis for either argument. Not only was it not the standard of care, but even if the hospital had done fetal monitoring, there was nothing to say that the clinic's doctors would have seen Michael's distress. Velamentous cord insertions were themselves undiagnosable through ultrasound, and the boy's growth retardation was borderline at best. True, there was a small blood clot that Benirschke said was evidence of a previous slowdown in Twin B's circulation, but Lockwood thought it absurd to think that they foreshadowed any recognizable effect on his heart rate. "There's not a scintilla of doubt in my mind," he would later say. "Zero. Didn't happen. It's not an opinion."

Like most doctors, Lockwood despised the way lawyers took the art of medicine and reduced it, retrospectively, to checklists. It was easy enough to say that an ultrasound would have shown that Twin B was significantly smaller than Twin A and that the dangers to such children increased the nearer they got to term. But this ignored the vagaries of real medical practice. For instance, the margin of error for fetal ultrasounds was 15 to 20 percent— about the same as the difference in weights between Michael and Little Tony at the time of Michael's death. Yet medical opinion continues to vary widely on how much discordancy is ominous. As Lockwood now told Bernard: "Discordancy is not a very precise way of defining risk. If a baby is at the seventy-fifth percentile and another baby is at the fiftieth percentile, do I really care that there is a twenty-five percent discordancy? No. But if one is at the tenth percentile and the other one is way below the tenth percentile, then I'm concerned, even though the discordancy might only be four or five percent."

Then there were the technological shortcomings. In 1984, ultrasonography techniques remained primitive, useful for identifying major defects such as a missing brain or kidney or a large spina bifida, but a poor predictor of intrauterine growth retardation. Lockwood knew from seeing thousands of such scans that it was far from clear what an ultrasound on Friday would have shown and whether it would have been reliable. Yet to bring suit and win damages it was necessary to exalt a questionable technology while demonizing those who, perhaps knowing better, chose not to use it. He was not unconflicted. There were "a lot of bad docs," he would say, but he didn't see how randomly "castrating" physicians by subjecting them to simplistic, uninformed lay second-guessing helped weed out incompetence. All such inquisitions did, he lamented, was "poison the relationship between doctors and patients."

Lockwood deflected Bernard's next series of questions, which were designed to suggest that discordancy alone provided sufficient cause to think the twins were in trouble. Then, with Bernard importuning, he at last offered his own theory of what had actually occurred.

"Dr. Lockwood," Bernard began, "did you formulate an opinion with reasonable medical probability as to the cause of death of Baby B?"

"Almost certainly due to a 'cord accident,' quote unquote."

"Can you describe for me what you mean?"

"The vast majority of babies with velamentous cord insertions don't suffer significant harmful effects just from the velamentous insertion. But there are two events that can be lethal. One is where the velamentous vessel tears; there is extensive hemorrhage, and the fetus bleeds out in a matter of minutes. The second is prolonged compression, a contraction of the vessel that lasts minute after minute. The fetus becomes progressively hypoxic, acidotic, and eventually the heart stops. Almost certainly the cause of this death was the latter. There was mention in one of the depositions of a tear in the vessel, but I think that is highly unlikely to be the cause of fetal death because there would have been copious amounts of fetal blood in the amniotic fluid and leaking into the vagina."

"So you are postulating a complete compression of the vessels for some period of time?" Bernard said.

"A *critical* compression," Lockwood corrected.

"Over what period of time?"

"Well, I mean, it's an incredibly rapid event. It's three or four minutes and that's it."

"That's under circumstances where the blood flow to the baby is completely disrupted?"

"Critically disrupted," Lockwood said. "Critically occluded."

"When you say 'critically'—"

"Well, there may be some flow. I mean I can't tell you with perfect certainty that there was complete flow stoppage and there probably wasn't, but there was a crucial reduction in venous return to the heart which results in fetal death."

"It is your opinion," Bernard said, "that that occurred at one single time? In other words, there were no partial compressions prior to the event which led to the death of Baby B?"

"Well, it is unlikely," Lockwood insisted. "Hundred percent certainty I can't give you. And apparently they didn't do a postmortem on the fetus to look for chronic evidence of periods of intermittent ischemia or hypoxia. But I would have expected there to be vastly more pathological findings in the placenta than there were."

"And do you have an opinion with reasonable medical certainty as to the cause of the injury to Tony Sabia?"

"I would completely agree with Kurt on this," Lockwood said. "It's actually fairly well established. In identical twins—you don't want to use that term but basically these are—there are almost invariably vascular communications between the two placentas. If one twin dies, the immediate response of its cardiovascular system is to cause massive dilation, so the blood pressure essentially drops. When that happens, there's a communication between the two circulations. It's just like plumbing: if there is much lower pressure here than there is there, the blood flow is going to be from the area of higher pressure. The result is that the live baby becomes severely anemic, but more importantly in the short term, because so much blood volume is switched over, the baby can no longer pump adequate amounts of fluid, never mind red blood cells, to the brain and it becomes progressively more hypoxic and acidotic and there is a tremendous insult. I mean it's tragic, it's terrible, but it is not an uncommon consequence of this scenario where you have a cord accident."

"And do you have an opinion, Doctor," Bernard said, "over what period of time Tony Sabia continued to sustain damage?"

"Well, it is an almost instantaneous process. Literally a matter of minutes."

"So in other words, the process of injury to the brain of Tony Sabia was completed within a couple of minutes of the death of Baby B?"

"Right. Within several hours the baby would have gotten sufficient plasma from its mother via the placenta to restore its blood pressure, restore its total circulatory volume, and reperfuse the brain. Actually, it's the perfusion that continues the insult because then you add oxygen in a free radical form, which causes further damage. But the whole process, the first part a matter of minutes, the second part a matter of a couple of hours—isn't preventable. This baby," Lockwood concluded, "unfortunately suffered the maximum insult without dying."

Bernard had no further questions. Neither did Doyle. For once, it seemed, there was nothing for either side to add.

NINETEEN

"*Doctor* Iffy," Doyle sniffed. "Isn't it true that most of the lawyers you consult with represent plaintiffs as opposed to defendants?"

Leslie Iffy was the too-agreeable Hungarian-born perinatologist whose record as a medical expert and whose huge dogs had dismayed Bernard during his and Koskoff's scouting trip to New Jersey two and a half years earlier. "Yes," he said. "The majority of them are plaintiffs, yes."

"It's around ninety percent plaintiffs' lawyers, isn't it?" Doyle said, stating more than asking.

"Eighty-five to ninety percent, yes," Iffy said.

Doyle's eyebrows rose. "Can you tell me," he asked, "why the percentage is so high for plaintiffs' lawyers as opposed to defendants' lawyers?"

"I can't," Iffy said, leaning forward, smiling beneath an icy stare, "but maybe some lawyers can."

"Okay. You don't have a clue?"

"Frankly, I don't."

They were sitting with Bernard and Hunt in the upstairs study of Iffy's brooding Tudor in Summit, forty-five minutes west of New York City. A veteran testifier, Iffy was being polite to the point of being hostile.

"And about how many cases do you review a year?" Doyle asked.

"Probably at the range of fifty new cases. I mean formal reviews."

"Can you tell me, Doctor," Doyle said, "how much money you earned from reviewing and, in specific, consulting with lawyers last year?"

"Probably at the range of one hundred fifty thousand dollars."

"And do you have a standard range of charges?"

"Four hundred dollars per hour of my work for review."

"That's for the review?"

"Yes," Iffy said.

"And do you charge on a different basis for deposition testimony, trial testimony?"

"Yes."

"Can you tell me what that is?" Doyle asked.

"Six hundred dollars for deposition with a minimum of two and a half hours equivalent."

"But if the deposition goes five hours, you get—"

"Five times six hundred dollars."

"Right," Doyle said. "And if a deposition lasts fifteen minutes, you still get fifteen hundred dollars?"

"I haven't seen that yet. But this would be the case."

Bernard cringed. Exposing the other side's experts as mercenary hirelings was a routine part of taking depositions, like asking their names or if they were board-certified. Bernard himself had done it countless times. But Bernard shuddered at what jurors in Bridgeport might make of a $600-an-hour gynecologist who earned five to ten times a year what they did, part-time, by condemning his peers.

Doyle continued. "Doctor," he asked, "do you know what killed Baby B?"

"Growth retardation, in all probability, hypoxia."

"Growth retardation," Doyle repeated. "It's your view, in all probability, that growth retardation killed Baby B. Is that correct?"

Bernard interrupted. "Objection. That's not what he said."

Doyle ignored him, confronting Iffy directly. "Is that correct?"

Again Bernard objected.

"Yes," Iffy said, "that is my opinion."

"And what do you base that opinion on?"

"Because once there is a substantial degree of growth retardation that brings the fetus outside or at the margin of the range of normal growth, the fetal demise from hypoxia is predictable."

"I'm sorry," Hunt interceded. "Is predictable?"

Doyle hid his astonishment. Koskoff's theme was that Michael Sabia died when he slowly compressed the exposed blood vessels that were his lifeline: growing too large for his environment, he had cut off his own oxygen supply. Yet Iffy was suggesting something else entirely, that the stillborn had died of persistent starvation. Either it was one or the other; claiming it was both supported Doyle's theme that the Koskoffs didn't really know what killed the stillborn and were compensating by asserting multiple theories. Doyle seized the inconsistency as if it were a maul.

"In terms of what killed Baby B," he asked Iffy, trying to narrow him down, "would you defer to the opinion of Dr. Benirschke?"

"No," Iffy said, "I don't need to, because I think it is within my area of expertise what kills a growth-retarded fetus in utero."

"And it's your opinion that what kills a growth-retarded fetus in utero is what?"

"Hypoxia, finally."

"Finally?"

"Yes."

"And it's your opinion that what happened to Baby B was an ongoing as opposed to an acute—"

Iffy cut in. "Growth retardation is an ongoing process."

"And it's your view and your opinion based on reasonable medical probability that Baby B died because of a chronic process that ultimately resulted in what, hypoxia, killing it?"

"Correct."

"Doctor," Doyle averred, "are you familiar with the term 'cord accident'?"

"Yes."

"What does it mean?"

"It can mean a variety of things. Compression of the cord, hemorrhage in the cord, tying up two cords in the case of twins, knotting the cord. Prolapse of the cord even without compression may amount to a cord accident. These are cord accidents."

"And cord accidents can happen quickly without any chronic condition?"

"They are rare, but they can happen quickly."

Curiosity had so far tempered Doyle's brusqueness. He wanted to see what Iffy would say, wanted, as a point of interest, to see how Koskoff and Bernard had prepared him. Doyle was more than skeptical about the production of testimony, telling his Yale law students that there was "a very fine line" between preparing witnesses and suborning perjury. Now, though, he wanted to pin Iffy down as a chink in Koskoff's armor, and his courtliness evaporated.

"Now Doctor," Doyle went on, "you believe that if the physicians had performed nonstress testing or biophysical profiles—ultrasounds—that Baby B's death would have been prevented. Is that correct?"

"Yes, Counsel, but if—"

Doyle cut him off. "Why—"

"But if Baby B—I haven't finished my answer."

"No, you did," Doyle snapped. "I asked you the question. It called for a yes-or-no answer. You said yes. Okay? And I'm going to ask you another question."

Iffy seemed to shrink. "Okay."

"Why did you say that?" Doyle demanded.

Iffy asked the stenographer to read back his answer as Doyle kept after him. "I want to get the answers to the questions I ask," Doyle said. "I don't want you to give me the answers to the questions that you think I asked. Okay? And we'll get along a lot better, and we'll get out of here a lot quicker."

Bernard objected, but without real vehemence.

Again Doyle ignored him, lecturing Iffy instead. "You can listen to that question and answer that question."

"I object," Bernard said.

Finally, Iffy defended himself. "Your comment is irrelevant to my answers, Counsel," he said. "And my answer is very related to your questions, except you don't want to hear all of them."

"I want responsive answers," Doyle said.

"They were."

"The pending question is," Doyle said, "why do you say that?"—why did Iffy think Michael Sabia's death could have been prevented with fetal monitoring?

"Because almost any kind of fetal death, whatever the cause of it or the mechanism of it, is predictable by fetal well-being studies," Iffy said.

"And is it your opinion that, in this case, Baby B's death was predictable by fetal well-being studies if they had been performed?"

"In all probability, yes."

"What do you base that opinion on, in this case?"

"I thought I just answered it earlier."

"No. You said in other cases and in most cases. What is it in this case that those fetal well-being studies would have revealed that would have led the physicians to conclude that Baby B is going to die?"

"In this case, there were the usual risks for fetuses that derive from twin pregnancy. These risks are growth retardation, twin-to-twin transfusion, sometimes detachment of the placenta."

"I understand that," Doyle said. "But did that happen in *this* case? Was there twin-to-twin transfusion in *this* case?"

"There was—in my opinion, there was growth retardation."

"That killed him," Doyle said.

"Probably that, yes."

Doyle questioned Iffy for another hour, prodding him about how growth retardation could kill an unborn baby, how cases were referred to him, whether he'd ever consulted before in a twins case. Ted Koskoff used to say, "How do you trap a rat? By closing all the doors." Doyle was closing all the doors. But the damage had been done. Although Doyle wouldn't get a shot at Koskoff's chief experts, Schifrin and Benirschke, until trial, his first go at a prized backup witness, the editor of several respected texts who could support their opinions, had been a rout. Furthermore, he had exposed the central weakness in Koskoff's case: namely, if Koskoff's own experts couldn't agree what had killed Baby B, how was he going to persuade a jury that Norwalk Hospital could, and should, have prevented it?

As Koskoff saw it, Doyle's attitude was, "I know Mike thinks there's no way he can lose this case. Well he's wrong. He can." With Iffy, Doyle now forced Koskoff to rethink his position.

Bernard had already rethought his. Working on the case full-time, deposing experts every few days in a dash to prepare for a trial date now less than four weeks away, to-do lists metasticizing, he'd begun culling his and Koskoff's witness list. He knew experts could command huge fees because those who hired them deemed them worth it. Plaintiffs' lawyers did the numbers—$10,000 or $15,000 for testimony on a case valued at maybe five hundred times that—and found them compelling. But having seen what Doyle would do to Iffy at trial, Bernard wanted nothing more to do with him. "Iffy," he would later say, "would not have come to court."

≈≈≈

AUGUST 20, 1993

Dr. Susan Farrell had never examined Little Tony, but she had seen many children like him and she considered his prognosis grim. A pediatrician, Farrell had worked exclusively with brain-damaged children for almost twenty years, ever since she'd been a postdoctoral fellow at Johns Hopkins. She was a pioneer in the field of developmental pediatrics, crusading for its recognition as a medical subspecialty. As director of developmental associates at Moses Cone Hospital in Greensboro, North Carolina, an affiliate of the University of North Carolina Medical School, Farrell designed protocols for treating neurologically impaired children and trained other doctors to use them.

Hunt had recruited Farrell as a damage expert, to help the hospital and Travelers value the case. Koskoff liked to describe Little Tony's condition at birth as "incompatible with life." Now that he was almost ten, and Koskoff was demanding $12 million for his care and treatment over a lifetime, just *how* incompatible had become the core economic issue in *Sabia*. It was Farrell's job to counter Koskoff's claim that because no one knew how long Little Tony would live, it was necessary to provide for the maximum care he might require.

Life expectancy was a delicate issue, and even before flying down to Greensboro to take Farrell's deposition, Bernard understood that it might be explosive. The cruel calculus of any personal injury case, especially one involving birth trauma, was that the *duration* of pain and suffering was the key multiplier. Lawyers for both sides knew that time equaled money: the longer a victim lived, the greater the damages, and thus the larger both the value of the case and the lawyers' fees. Conversely, if the victim died, as Michael Sabia had, damages contracted sharply; there was nothing to claim. A big case—the best cases from a financial standpoint, and the reason why lawyers sued obstetricians more than any other doctors—typically hinged on a macabre knife edge. The victim should be injured permanently, but with the unmerciful expectation of a long life.

Bernard harbored neither pride nor guilt about this equation; it was how things were. If he had an obvious self-interest in extending the life expectancy of a client, so did the client, and the client's family. Their interests were neatly aligned. And yet he knew how traumatic that realization could be for parents. Mary Gay said the worst part of settling her case with Humes was allowing a price to be placed on her son's life. Blood money, she called it. Bernard worried that the Sabias would have similar pangs. He knew they loved their son and, aware of Tony's fractiousness, worried how ferociously Tony would resent the boy's commodification.

Bernard questioned Farrell gently at first, his tone easy and familiar. When he asked her whether she'd passed her pediatric boards on her first try and she responded that she hadn't completed them because she'd gone into labor, he quipped, "Any excuse," and smiled until Doyle, unamused, muttered, "Any excuse, right," cutting him off. Soon, however, his conviviality vanished, and he was all business. If Doyle intended to use Farrell at trial to persuade a jury that Little Tony couldn't live long, Bernard was equally determined to subvert any basis she might have for asserting that opinion.

"Now, Doctor," he said, "just so we're clear, you have never seen Tony Sabia?"

"That's correct," she said.

"You've never met his parents?"

"That's correct."

"You've never spoken to any of his treating doctors?"

"That's correct."

"You've never spoken to any of his teachers or therapists?"

"That's correct."

"And you've not seen pictures or videotapes of Tony?"

"Correct again."

"You've not reviewed any radiologic studies, X-rays of Tony?"

"Outside of what was in the records, no."

"Dr. Farrell," Bernard asked, "have you ever been sued for malpractice?"

"No."

Bernard paused. He asked several more questions about what prognosticators Farrell used to predict the destiny of children she'd never examined, then circled back.

"Now," he said, "do you have an opinion with reasonable medical probability as to Tony Sabia's current life expectancy?"

"Yes," Farrell said.

"What is that opinion?"

"I don't think that Tony is going to live longer than mid-teens. I think he'll probably die within the next five to six years."

"And what is the basis for that opinion?"

"I form that opinion," Farrell said, "on the basis of my review of the records of his condition as well as my clinical experience and medical education."

Bernard wasn't surprised. He knew when it came down to money, Doyle would argue that Little Tony should get only what he needed, and that he wouldn't need much because he probably wouldn't survive adolescence. Still, what were the chances? How likely was it that Little Tony would die in his mid-teens? "Is it fifty-one percent?" Bernard asked Farrell. "Is it seventy-five percent? Is it ninety-five percent?"

"I would say it's better than ninety-five percent," she said, "for this particular child."

Bernard tacked. "In your experience," he asked, "have you ever seen a patient with similar medical conditions to Tony Sabia live past age twenty-one?"

"Yes."

"Approximately how many?"

"One," Farrell said.

"And was that person brain-injured from birth?"

"Yes."

"How old was that person the last time—is it a him or a her?"

"It's a her."

"How old was she the last time you saw her?"

"Well, she died at age twenty-two."

"What did she die of?"

"Pneumonia and sepsis."

Bernard wasn't ready to ask what Farrell thought would kill Little Tony. He was more interested in getting her on the record as to his physical and mental well-being. He and Koskoff planned to argue that because Little Tony was generally in good health, gaining weight, his seizures under control, and being cared for at home rather than in an institution, statistics about life expectancy and stories about children with similar disabilities were irrelevant. He knew from experience that once jurors saw Buckley's day-in-the-life, they most likely would be pulling for Little Tony and resisting anyone who appeared to treat him as less than an individual.

Farrell, having reviewed Little Tony's CAT-scans and neurologist's reports, believed Little Tony's brain was "abnormal"—rife, she said, with "multiple holes"—and that his IQ was below 25. The loss of brain tissue itself, she had told Bernard earlier, left him less equipped to survive than other children equally retarded but with brains that were "structurally intact." Still, enlisting Farrell here could help Bernard in two ways: either she acknowledged the boy's robustness, undermining her own gloomy prognosis, or else she painted a picture so bleak that it only compounded the jury's sympathy. In either case, her testimony would at least have to square with what jurors believed about him based on what they saw on videotape, Koskoff's "illusion of humanity."

"All right," Bernard said. "Now, based on your experience as a developmental pediatrician, can you tell me what effect or effects Tony Sabia's brain injury has had on his ability to enjoy life?"

"Well, Tony Sabia is profoundly retarded," Farrell began. "His abilities have been estimated at a two-to-five-month level based on the documents that I have reviewed through June of '92. I have no records past June of '92, so I do not know what has happened in the last year. But that is an extreme rate of profound mental retardation. He is also affected by the fact that he is legally and cortically blind and therefore cannot utilize information from visual input. He does have brain auditory evoked responses"—he can hear and respond—"which means that the auditory pathways are there. But I have no indication that he has any understanding of auditory information past the five-month level."

"Specifically," Bernard asked, "what does he enjoy?"

"Well, in my opinion, he doesn't enjoy anything. I think he feels comfort when he is well cared for physically and not having seizures and not being stuck with needles for a blood test. And at five months, probably some auditory stimulation like music or talking, because children begin to do some lateralization and turning toward some pleasurable sounds, as opposed to harsh, loud, grating noises, at about five to six months."

"What types of things make him comfortable?"

"Maybe I'm not being clear," Farrell said. "I thought we've been over this. If he is fed, if he is cared for and kept dry and clean, if he is in a temperature environment that is appropriate, those things make him comfortable. Those things make us comfortable."

"In your opinion, Doctor, is there any possibility that Tony will be able to communicate?"

"No. Communicate in the sense of—I should clarify that—sign language or oral speaking of any kind to communicate choice."

"How about communicating his needs?" Bernard asked.

"No."

"Would Tony ever be able to operate some kind of switch, for instance, that would—"

"No."

"—turn on music that he enjoys?"

"No."

"Okay. There's no possibility of that?"

"Not in my opinion, no."

"Okay," Bernard concluded. His groundwork laid, he was now ready to take Farrell head-on. "Do you have an opinion with reasonable medical probability as to what will be the cause of Tony's death?"

"Yes," Farrell said. "It's been my experience that respiratory illnesses are usually the cause of death." She explained that, unable to absorb enough calories through their G-tubes to sustain them through adolescence, children like Little Tony became depleted, making them too weak to fight off infections in spite of aggressive medical care.

"Okay," Bernard said. "You've mentioned two factors. During adolescence there is an increase in growth, and there's an increase in calorie requirements?"

"In normal children, yes."

"And in children like Tony?"

"In children like Tony the data are not fully understood. When they reach adolescence and should be hitting a growth spurt, one of two things happens. Their—they start to lose weight in spite of increasing gastronomy calories. You increase the calories because they're losing weight, and they get diarrhea or the bolus of food is too large and they start refluxing"—vomiting. "So you put them on continuous twenty-four-hour feeds and they are still not getting enough calories and they are losing weight. Or you'll see the reverse," Farrell added, "—that they begin demanding more calories. And though they are very short, they get rapidly obese and develop what we call precocious puberty hirsutism—hairiness. You get excessive testosterone responses."

"Does that also lead to respiratory problems?" Bernard asked.

"No," Farrell said. "That usually—it leads to some exacerbation of seizures."

"And do those seizures then in those infants who become overweight and have this hirsutism . . . do those infants—children—die of seizures?"

"Quite commonly they do, but they may also have respiratory problems."

"And your opinion with reasonable medical probability is that Tony will follow the first path, and that is that he will not grow, and he will become globally weaker and unable to fight off infections and—and respiratory problems and he'll die from a respiratory problem."

"In general, that is correct."

"And can you tell me specifically what respiratory problems will kill Tony?"

"My experience has been that the children and then the adolescents develop pneumonia."

Bernard corrected her: "My question, though, was, do you have an opinion with reasonable medical probability as to what specific medical problem will kill Tony?"

"No."

Here was Bernard's edge, however slim. As long as he could prevent Farrell from opining directly about Little Tony, he could undermine her credibility by painting her as uninvolved. He kept on. "Okay," he said. "And does the fact that Tony has already reached nine years at all impact on your prediction of life expectancy?"

"Yes," said Farrell. "Because children who are this profoundly retarded and handicapped usually die within the first several years of life." She added that the 5 to 10 percent who don't die at that time usually live until their mid-teens.

"So if you were to analyze Tony Sabia's condition at two to three months of age, it would be your opinion that his life expectancy would be another two to three years?"

"Right. Four years. Something like that."

"And once he survives that three or four years, then your opinion becomes that his life expectancy is to mid-teens?"

"That's been my clinical experience. Some of the literature has said that they will estimate an additional four or five years past each critical milestone."

It wasn't difficult to see where Bernard was headed: If Farrell had seen Little Tony as a baby, she'd have predicted he would die in a few years. Now he was almost ten, and she was making the same prediction. Since she'd have been wrong the first time, why was she right now? Bernard would have little trouble making the case that, as doctors themselves often say in offering prognoses, statistics indicate trends but don't predict what will happen to individual patients. The rest was merely mopping up.

"Dr. Farrell," Bernard asked. "Do children like Tony Sabia have increased medical needs in the year or years prior to their death?"

"Quite often they do. It's a gradual thing. Weight and metabolism problems first, then difficulty getting enough calories in by GT tube, and then more frequent bouts of seizure or more frequent bouts of infection, and then one big infection. In the child that lived to be twenty-two, her parents decided to take some rather heroic efforts, surgical efforts, to maintain her life. She had GT tube feedings, a lot of reflux, not enough calories. They did a pharyngotomy—that is, they diverted the back of the throat and all those fluids she was not handling well and choking on out the side into a pouch."

"And do I understand your opinion to be that those increased medical problems that arise during adolescence will continue through the remainder of Tony's life, however long that happens to be?" Bernard asked.

"Well, my opinion is that he is at greater risk for medical problems, no matter how long he lives. If you look at the incidence of hospitalization, for example, with these children, normal children get hospitalized once or twice in their lifetimes: normal adults, leave out automobile accidents, for illnesses once or twice, maybe three times in their life. These children get hospitalized four to five times a year, whether they are ten or twelve or fifteen or twenty-one."

"Okay. And if, to use your words, by some miracle he lives to be thirty or forty, would you expect that to continue?"

"Yes."

"Okay, and if he were to live to fifty or sixty, you would expect that to continue?"

Farrell seemed irritated, but she answered the question. "Again, you're talking about something that I don't think is possible. But if it happened, yes."

～～～

SEPTEMBER 2, 1993

Bill Doyle liked Dr. John Goldkrand in spite of himself. Goldkrand was another of Koskoff's backup obstetrical experts—a perinatologist who, like Iffy, had a sizable medical-legal practice. Since 1981 he'd consulted in more than 275 cases. Goldkrand charged $120 an hour for review, didn't advertise for clients, drew only about 5 percent of his income from consulting, and did 90 percent of his work for defendants. Koskoff had used him only a few times before, most notably along with Murray and Schifrin on the "old Goldblatt team," whose collective testimony drove St. Paul to settle on behalf of Humes. He'd contacted him again in January in the hope that he would buttress Koskoff's claim that Norwalk Hospital had violated the standard of care in its treatment of Donna. After Iffy's deposition, the move seemed prescient.

Doyle admired Koskoff's preparedness. Sitting in Goldkrand's office in Savannah, Georgia, he could see instantly that Goldkrand would help Koskoff's case; indeed, that he might be Koskoff's strongest witness. Credibility was Doyle's gold standard, and Goldkrand, with his solid expertise, pro-defense record, and altruistic fees, was nothing if not credible. None of which meant Doyle would coddle him. Like Koskoff, he worried about holding back with opposing experts that he liked, but with the trial set to begin within two weeks, this would be his last chance to make Koskoff doubt himself. He and Hunt had experts whose depositions they would have to take during jury selection or even during the trial, but Goldkrand was Koskoff's last major witness to be deposed. And so Doyle waltzed him through the usual recitation of his credentials, then hit him—hard.

"Is it your opinion, Doctor, based upon a reasonable medical probability, that in 1983 and 1984, the standard of care required in every twin pregnancy that there be serial ultrasounds in the third trimester?"

"Yes, sir, I believe so."

"And is it your opinion that in 1983 and 1984 nonstress testing was required by the standard of care in all twin pregnancies?"

"I think by 1983, 1984, monitoring was certainly becoming the standard of care."

"You say becoming," Doyle said. "Was it or wasn't it?"

"Well, I'm saying in the early eighties, by my interpretation of how twin pregnancies should have been managed—"

"I'm not asking about your personal opinion. I'm asking you what the standard of care was in '83 and '84 with respect to nonstress testing in twin pregnancies in the third trimester."

"Well. What I was trying to say a moment ago is in my interpretation of the standard of care, the answer is yes."

"Now what do you base that on?" Doyle asked.

"The standard of care isn't cast in stone. It's essentially a consensus of opinion of people doing like work."

"It's an evolutionary process in a sense, isn't it, Doctor?"

"It's an evolutionary process."

Doyle paused meaningfully. "You're not saying, are you, that no reasonable expert with similar qualifications to yours couldn't have a different opinion?"

"If someone chooses to disagree with me, I can't say that's not their right—"

"I'm not talking about right," Doyle snapped. "I'm talking about whether there would be any reasonable basis."

"I've given you what I consider the standard of care. If someone else has another opinion, I would want to know why they based their opinion as they do."

"Are you saying that if you took into account what they had to say you might not reconsider?"

"No, I wouldn't. I feel my opinion is correct and so I—"

Doyle cut him off. "And so it doesn't necessarily follow, then, that anybody else who differs with you is incorrect?"

Goldkrand's admission that standard of care was an amorphous concept over which reasonable doctors might disagree lent scant weight to his opinion that fetal monitoring was required during the last weeks of Donna's pregnancy. As he told Doyle, a single, articulable standard of care was more a legal construct than a medical one. Like Lockwood, he had researched the matter and found several citations in the medical literature to support his opinion. An article in *Current Therapy in Obstetrics and Gynecology*, published in 1983, instructed: "With a patient without evidence of intrauterine growth retardation during twin gestation, routine nonstress tests on each fetus should be performed on a weekly basis beginning at 36 weeks of gestation. . . . For the woman with suspected or diagnosed intrauterine growth retardation, the nonstress test is begun . . . as early as 26 weeks depending on maternal-fetal conditions, and repeated twice weekly until delivery." Another, a 1980 article in *Clinical Obstetrics and Gynecology*, advised, "In multiple gestation, antepartum electronic fetal monitoring of fetal heart rate and uterine contractions should be performed."

Doyle knew it would take more references than these to establish that electronic surveillance was required, but the point was who a jury would believe—Goldkrand, who seemed so reasonable, or Lockwood, who seemed so young. Doyle knew better than to bet on the outcome. He moved on, trying to force Goldkrand to concede that even if such monitoring had been done, the outcome would have been the same.

"Doctor," he said. "Do you have an opinion as to what caused the death of Twin B?"

"I think Twin B withered on the vine, so to speak."

"What do you mean, 'withered on the vine'?"

"Well, it's not growing well, it's growing less well than the other twin. According to the pathologist, the reports, it was receiving about a third of the circulation from this placenta, versus Twin A, which was receiving two-thirds. Then we've also got abnormal vasculature."

"Velamentous insertion?"

"Yes."

Doyle pressed. "But what killed Baby B?" It was the same question he'd used to impeach Iffy.

"I don't know exactly the terminal event," Goldkrand conceded, "but I think it's a combination of vascular impingement from the velamentous insertion and placental insufficiency—insufficient placental mass to keep this kid going."

"Well," Doyle said, "if there was a cord accident, okay, an acute event that led to—"

"You're saying 'if,' or there was?" Goldkrand asked.

"If," Doyle clarified.

"Okay."

"Well," Doyle stopped. "You don't know whether there was or wasn't. Do you?"

"An acute event?"

"Yeah."

"There may have been a final, terminal event, but I think this is a chronic event."

"Well, then," Doyle said, "let me ask you this: If there was an acute event, a cord accident in there, what difference goes growth retardation have? I mean, what bearing does that have on it?"

Goldkrand thought before answering. "Probably because I would have had the baby in the nursery before the acute event. If your postulate is correct, my baby would have already been in the nursery."

"And if there had been an acute event such as a cord accident that resulted in the death of Twin B, there's no way to predict that by ultrasound and non-stress testing, is there?"

"Well, sometimes with nonstress testing, if there is a cord impingement, you sometimes can get fortunate in seeing cord compression patterns during the testing, which—"

"If the compression is going on—"

"Correct."

"—at the time you're doing the testing. But otherwise it doesn't tell you anything."

"Assuming that the baby is otherwise normal."

"Doctor," Doyle asked finally, "what did Norwalk Hospital do wrong?"

Goldkrand thought for a moment. "The medical record," he said, "doesn't present any apparent care plan for a multiple gestation which would have treated this as a high-risk pregnancy. Such a plan should have included serial ultrasounds and serial electronic fetal monitoring of the heart rates during the third trimester of pregnancy. Norwalk Hospital also erred in allowing this pregnancy to continue with discordant twins to the point of demise of Twin B and injury of Twin A.

"Had they been delivered earlier," Goldkrand said, "this outcome would not have occurred."

$\approx \approx \approx$

SEPTEMBER 3, 1993

During the long Labor Day weekend, Koskoff reflected that there had never been a better moment for taking a high-end obstetrical case like *Sabia* to court. The value of such cases, according to several journals covering the malpractice industry, was now at an all-time high and rising fast. The largest verdict in Connecticut for a birth injury case, for instance, had been $9.7 million, yet the September issue of *National Jury Verdict Review and Analysis* reported two awards, one in Boston, one in Philadelphia, for $20 million each. There simply was no more powerful engine for generating large verdicts in individual negligence cases than a child whose brain had been deprived of oxygen at or near birth.

Koskoff noted happily that Schifrin was the plaintiffs' main standard-of-care expert in the Boston case. Even more encouraging was a twin case reported in the latest issue of *Medical Liability Week*. The case had two defendants, a woman ob-gyn and a hospital, and facts nearly identical to those in *Sabia*. A Kansas housewife named Faye Aves had been hospitalized during pregnancy with preeclampsia, a disease known to increase the risks to newborns. One of the babies was breech. Yet when Aves arrived at the hospital with an apparently ruptured membrane in December 1984, her doctor, Nasreen Shah, hadn't taken the twins by C-section; she'd only administered Pitocin to speed up Aves's labor. Although there was an electronic heart monitor available, the printer was broken, so no fetal-monitoring strip had been produced.

Shah delivered both twins naturally. The breech, healthy, came first, but the second twin, a girl named Darcy, wasn't breathing. Multiply disabled, Darcy Aves, now almost nine, had suffered from birth the same afflictions as Little Tony: epilepsy, cerebral palsy, mental retardation, cortical blindness, microcephaly. The medical parallels alone were enough to invite comparison, but it was the legal outcome that buoyed Koskoff. The hospital had settled before trial, but a jury, assessing Shah for 90 percent of the damages, awarded the Aveses more than $21 million. Though Shah appealed, the Tenth U.S. Circuit Court of Appeals had upheld the verdict. "Darcy Aves will need extensive medical treatment throughout her life," the appellate judge wrote. "To be sure, the award is large; however given the court record before us, the award does not shock the conscience of the court."

The conscience of the court. It was one of those incantatory phrases that Koskoff loved, a benediction. For juries in Boston and Philadelphia to come in with back-to-back $20 million verdicts was one thing—big-city awards were generally high, and these two were still fresh; the courts could still knock them down. But three appellate judges in conservative Kansas supporting a verdict this size was like the *Good Housekeeping* seal. It would have repercussions even in Connecticut, where verdicts still lagged behind those in other states.

Koskoff knew less about settlements in comparable cases because settlements, unlike verdicts, were seldom reported. Claims managers for liability carriers loathed above all else the "shark effect"—schools of ravenous lawyers made more voracious by knowing what companies were willing to pay—and usually demanded strict confidentiality when they resolved cases. A few trade journals, such as *Medical Malpractice Verdicts, Settlements and Experts,* managed to pierce the industry blackout, but they tended toward the low end of the market, with such headlines as "Mentally Retarded Woman Chokes to Death on Peanut Butter Sandwich Despite Orders Not to Give Her Peanut Butter—$52,976.37 Wisconsin Settlement" and "Popcorn Hull Stuck in Throat Leads to Death—Plantiff Claims Airway Not Properly Established and Improper Transfer Occurred—$1.2 Million Minnesota Settlement." These journals might report a $2 million cash "structure"—a time-released payout favored by insurers—in a birth injury case, but Koskoff disdained such agreements and didn't pay them much attention. What mattered was that verdicts and settlements moved in lockstep. If verdicts rose, so did settlement prices, because settlements were almost always a last-ditch means of avoiding the uncertainty of putting a case to a jury. Koskoff took comfort in the fact that significant verdicts only gave insurers more incentive to sit down and talk.

This was truly a Golden Age for malpractice lawyers—with one ominous caveat: it might all soon come to an end. In Washington, Hillary Rodham Clinton's Task Force on National Health Care Reform was racing to complete four months of furtive deliberations. Almost every day front-page stories in the *New York Times* forecast an overhaul of American medicine, a shake-up likely to be so profound that the country's $700 billion medical economy was already reeling from the advance shocks. The conventional wisdom was that doctors were going to be the big losers in the Clinton proposal. What worried Koskoff were rumors that the Task Force would recommend steep limits on malpractice awards as "sugar coating" for the doctors—something to soften their opposition to the overall plan. ATLA, the trial lawyers' lobby that Ted had headed as president, already had begun to gear up for an all-out fight.

Koskoff knew the Clintons would soon roll out their plan, and while the effect wouldn't be immediate, if the rumors about curtailing lawsuits were true, there would be a backlash. He thought plaintiffs' lawyers might again be vilified as they had been during the malpractice crises of the seventies and eighties. Other industries that decried large negligence awards would be massing for attack, hoping that an ATLA defeat on medical malpractice—its first ever—would open a wedge for wholesale liability reform. Not only cases like *Sabia* but Koskoff's very livelihood might be imperiled.

Koskoff felt restless. Even if *Sabia* started the week after next, as Judge Ballen had promised, talk of "malpractice reform" could be rife by the time the jury started deliberating, most likely in December. By then, Koskoff knew, he could well be thinking about much more than the disposition of one case; he might be worrying about the future of his firm, which did predominantly personal injury work. Nothing in the recent depositions had made him doubt his case or himself. He still thought he would win. But the key was getting to court, and after six and a half years they still weren't there. The time for trial was ripe, and running out.

≈ ≈ ≈

SEPTEMBER 13, 1993

For months, every time Bernard saw Ballen he'd lobbied him about *Sabia*. It was Ballen who, in April, had scheduled a trial date for early September, but Bernard had kept after him, letting him know that the plaintiffs' experts were deposed and available, and that the case was ready to go. Ballen had listened, but he took it with a grain of salt. Every day lawyers pleaded with him to reach their cases, yet while his job was to expedite lawsuits, Ballen had other factors to consider. Sometimes he had two judges available for trial, sometimes five. Why should he commit himself to tying up a courtroom for three months with a large insurance case that nine times out of ten would settle before opening arguments? Whose interest was he serving, lawyers playing dare or the public's?

A cantankerous former Bridgeport attorney, Ballen knew that plaintiffs' lawyers used the threat of a trial to force insurance companies to negotiate and that they blamed everyone else for judicial delays. But how many times had he listened to them grovel as they explained why they couldn't go forward? *My witnesses are from all over the country,* they would plead; *I can't get them in to testify.* Or, *I've discovered new information.* "I have a saying," Ballen remarks. "Every case is ready until it's reached."

On the day before *Sabia* was to begin, Ballen told Bernard there were no judges available to hear the case and promised to try to get it on the October calendar. Bernard struggled to contain his frustration. Every setback in obtaining a trial date meant a gear-grinding downshift in emotion. He had been going full speed, flying around the country tangling with Doyle, working to the limit, and now he had been dumped into limbo. He returned to his office. He and Koskoff had enough cases in process that a delay meant some juggling, but no real loss of income. He'd have a paralegal contact their experts, tell them the trial was delayed, and get their schedules for November and December, when they were likely to testify. Feeling let down, he turned to other matters.

What bothered him, he says, was the effect on the Sabias. What other case did they have? And what else was there for them to turn their attention to?

Bernard was enraged when he considered what they'd been through because of Little Tony. He admired them, Tony especially, and knew their hardships wouldn't lift until the case was at an end. He and Tony had talked frequently since Donna moved out, and Bernard knew that Tony wanted more than anything else the *vindication* of a trial. He had done all he could to keep his family from coming apart. What he craved now was recognition, not for his efforts but for his injury. Tony wanted the world to acknowledge his family's suffering and concede that they had been wronged. As the one to have to tell him about the latest delay, Bernard worried about how much more he could take. He needed for Tony to be calm and rational when the trial finally began; his and Donna's behavior in front of a jury would be crucial. Knowing Tony better than anyone in the office, Bernard's job was to manage his raw attitude, which, while perhaps justified, could prove perilous if allowed to flash over into rage.

To that end, Bernard wrote Tony's boss, and not for the first time. The company had tried to fire Tony for absenteeism after he'd missed several shifts when Donna had moved out, and Bernard had made irate phone calls and sent strong letters to get him reinstated. Now, however, he appealed to a common purpose. Explaining that it was "absolutely essential" that Tony be "awake and alert" during the trial and that he might be needed on some evenings to prepare his upcoming testimony, Bernard implied it might be good for the company to give him some time off. "I am sure that Anthony will try to keep the amount of time to be missed from work at a minimum," he wrote, "but I cannot overly stress the importance of his participation at this trial. This is the one opportunity that we have to provide for his son's enormous health-care needs for the rest of his life and we must make every reasonable effort to avoid jeopardizing this goal."

Publicly, Bernard and Koskoff remained set on going to trial, their posture stalwart. But with Ballen's latest decision they also recognized that the case might not be reached in October either. It could be continued into January or beyond. What if Little Tony died by then? Koskoff kept asking. Farrell was right: the boy should have died at birth, or when he'd stopped eating. He was frail, undernourished, and living on borrowed time. Koskoff had begun to regret letting Doyle off the mat at their first pre-trial conference in January. Posturing aside, he knew he had to make an effort to try to settle, if only to find out what Travelers was willing to offer. Whether Ballen had said so or not, overworked judges expected lawyers to attempt to have their cases mediated first by outsiders, a proof of reasonableness and good intentions that judges valued heavily in deciding which cases to reach.

Proposing a mediator was tricky, however: you didn't want the other side to interpret it as a sign of weakness. Koskoff finessed the problem by suggesting to Doyle in a phone call that they seek mediation and then offering to let

Doyle pick the mediator himself. The move suited Koskoff's purposes neatly. Although he himself had settled several major obstetrical cases through mediation, he knew that Doyle hadn't. At the same time, he "wanted somebody who was going to carry weight with Travelers," which had led the insurance industry in pushing mediation as an alternative to going to court. By appearing generous, Koskoff engineered the situation so that whatever movement—and possible loss of face—came from the other side.

As it happened, Travelers responded by proposing a mediator from Chicago, David Ferguson, whom Koskoff knew. Ferguson, thirty-seven, was little known in Connecticut, but in ten years as a full-time mediator he had successfully resolved nearly one thousand disputes. His success rate was 85 percent. Using what he liked to call a "facilitative" style—he tried to get opposing parties to negotiate their own settlement rather than impose his own views—he had worked his way up from doing slip-and-falls to big-ticket, multiparty conflicts. His was a delicate art, requiring smoothness and empathy. Ferguson had once settled a $50 million legal malpractice claim arising from a car dealership that had gone bad. He'd resolved a wrongful death claim involving a roofer who'd fallen headfirst onto cement while on the job. A year earlier he'd been brought in by the other side in a major birth injury case of Koskoff's and had managed to broker an agreement.

On a routine sales call to Travelers' headquarters in Hartford a few months before, Ferguson had met with several adjusters, including Cathy Gonzales, the claims representative on *Sabia,* and had made a good impression. Gonzales, after determining that he also was acceptable to Koskoff, called him now. Ferguson was between jobs. He had just signed on with Endispute, one of a burgeoning number of companies in the world of assisted negotiation—also known as alternative dispute resolution—now being touted by insurers as a way out of the costly and uncertain business of going to court. Ferguson agreed to take the case. After a round of phone calls, a mediation session was scheduled in Koskoff's office for September 30, enough time for all sides to finish their last-minute trial preparations and resume their march to court if the talks went sour.

TWENTY

KURT BENIRSCHKE GLARED AT THE VIDEO CAMERA IN FRONT OF HIM AND FIDGETED with his clip-on microphone wire. He wore a blue oxford shirt and no jacket, and his burgundy tie hung limply askew. He was sitting behind the desk in his windowless office across from the morgue at the UCSD Medical Center, waiting for Koskoff and Doyle to start questioning him about what had happened to the twins. Releasing the wire, he grabbed a pen, looked away, then leaned forward to scribble something. Next, he scooped up a pair of wire-rim reading glasses and began twisting the stems in his large, liver-spotted hands. When still nothing happened, he sank back in his chair, returned his gaze to the camera, steepled his index fingers, and assumed a look of murderous impatience, his dark eyes burning beneath the great cirrus of his brows. Finally, he reached for a coffee mug that said I LOVE YOU, GRANDPA and took a gulp.

Space was severely limited. Shoehorned in front of him, Koskoff and Bernard craned to stay out of the camera's view. Doyle and Hunt squeezed together off to the side. Beside them crouched a young court reporter and, just inside the closed door, a camera operator with a tripod. There was no way out for any of them without climbing over each other. Behind Benirschke's left shoulder, filling the only floor space left in the room, stood an easel supporting several schematics with overlays depicting the critical events that had led to Michael Sabia's death and Little Tony's brain damage.

The lawyers had flown to San Diego because Benirschke had said he was too busy to appear in court. Videotaping witnesses for trial was common, yet examining him here raised the stakes for both sides. Benirschke was the most important witness slated to testify. What he said regarding proximate cause—whether Norwalk Hospital's alleged negligence resulted directly in Little Tony's devastation—could well decide the trial's outcome. His storied independence, which Koskoff and Hunt had encountered at his first deposition, made him unpredictable. The lawyers had agreed to examine him prior to jury selection because afterward there would be no time. As a result, what the jurors saw of him, six weeks or so into the trial when both sides were laboring to establish their own themes while slashing away at the other's, would consist of a small-screen TV performance taped three thousand miles away and out of sequence.

The jury would see Benirschke, an austere-looking but surprisingly jolly German-accented doctor, but not the lawyers, who could be identified only by their disembodied voices, questions, and objections. These last a judge could rule on in the interim, which could lead to Benirschke's testimony being edited. The tape would be a static piece of crucial evidence in a dynamic proceeding, and how it played would depend in part on how well the lawyers could anticipate the courtroom events preceding its airing. For the lawyers, it was like shooting a movie climax on a soundstage before the cast and crew flew off on location.

It was also the first time, because of Koskoff's policy of avoiding the other side's witnesses before trial, that he and Doyle were facing off over an expert in *Sabia*. Koskoff still didn't know how much Benirschke would support him, but Benirschke was too central to the case not to testify and for Koskoff himself not to conduct his direct examination. What Koskoff knew was Doyle's defense strategy, as articulated by Lockwood, that what killed Michael Sabia was a sudden cord accident. Bernard had written him a long memo after returning from Lockwood's deposition five and a half weeks earlier. In it he'd urged Koskoff to find out whether Benirschke thought there was any "pathologic basis" for claiming that the cord compression that killed Michael Sabia occurred "over an extended period of time (at least several days; hopefully weeks)"—an opinion that would fortify their obstetrical experts' claim that his death had been preventable. Ever since, Koskoff had thought carefully about what—and, more decisively, what not—to ask Benirschke.

Whatever apprehensions Koskoff harbored about his expert's opinions he now concealed behind a studied casualness. Benirschke was his witness, and he would let the jury know it by the obvious rapport between them. Unlike the procedure at depositions, experts at trial were questioned first by the lawyers who hired them, so Koskoff led off with a flattering walk-through of Benirschke's credentials. Benirschke answered dutifully at first, but soon seemed annoyed. Koskoff picked up the cue. After asking Benirschke whether he was listed in *Who's Who in Science and Engineering*, *Who's Who in the*

World, Who's Who in the East, Who's Who in the West, Who's Who in America, and *Who's Who in Technology,* he apologized. "I'm sorry to embarrass you, doctor," he said with a laugh, "I have to do this." Benirschke tried to speed up the pace, interrupting Koskoff's listing of the chapters he'd contributed to textbooks with a bored, "and on and on and on." After twenty minutes the recitation ended with Benirschke chortling, then shaking his head in amazement at what lawyers will do to make a point.

Formalities done, Koskoff moved on to the first major part of Benirschke's testimony—that Little Tony had been injured when his blood pressure dropped as he bled into his dead twin. In order to answer, Benirschke swiveled his chair to refer to the charts at his back, and pointed out the twins in utero, the sac, the placenta, the velamentous cord insertion. Using the overlays, he showed how the boys' circulatory systems communicated through the blood vessels in the placenta and speculated that they were connected artery to artery, the commonest form of anastomoses, he said. He also specified where the pathologist's report indicated there had been thrombi—blood clots. There were two—a small one in Michael's cord vessels indicating an earlier slowdown in his circulation, and a much larger one between the placenta and the uterine wall that had been caused by a partial separation called an abruption. This second clot, drawn by a medical illustrator Koskoff had hired to consult with Benirschke, was depicted as an angry red blot, much larger and more pronounced than the first.

Doyle objected to introducing the illustration as evidence. He knew from the pathologist's report that there had been such a placental abruption, but no one had previously suggested that it was major, or that it had anything to do with the ultimate outcome. He suspected Koskoff of deliberately trying to make it seem more ominous than it was.

As Benirschke lectured, Koskoff questioned him gently. There had never been any doubt about how Little Tony was injured; Humes herself had seen it in the delivery room nine and a half years earlier, when Tony and Donna recall her saying that Little Tony was lifeless and anemic because he "gave his blood" to his brother. The mystery—the center of the case—was what had killed Michael. That was the question upon which both sides' claims hinged, and to which Koskoff and Doyle most feared Benirschke's answer. Koskoff edged delicately toward it, then broached the point directly.

"Can you tell us, Doctor," he asked, "based on reasonable medical probability, whether Twin B died of a sudden cord accident?"

Benirschke answered slowly, "No. It's a progressively . . . increasing . . . embarrassment, as it were, because of reduced flow through the circulation."

"How do you know it wasn't a sudden cord accident?"

Doyle interrupted. "I'm gonna object to that. He didn't say that."

"Well, I'll withdraw. I thought he had said that."

Benirschke smiled ambiguously. Lawyerly gamesmanship both amused and dismayed him.

"Can you tell us," Koskoff began again, "based on reasonable probability, whether Baby B died of a sudden cord accident?"

"I see no evidence for that, so I don't think it's a sudden *cord* accident, a knot of the cord or something to that effect."

"Is there evidence that you see to the contrary?"

Benirschke paused. He'd been pinching a pencil and twirling it across his lips. Now he used it as an enumerator, tapping his unfurling fingers with each new point. "Well, in the first place," he said, "it's a common feature in the velamentous insertion of the umbilical cord to see that that baby is growth-retarded, and when one dies, it is that one rather than the other. Second, we find that there's a thrombus, which we see in other such babies is a common consequence of slowing of the circulation. To me, death is sudden anyway. I mean, you know, you're either living or you're dead. But it is a progressive injury that is exemplified by the thrombus. I don't conceive of this as a sudden twist in the umbilical cord"—he wrung his hands as if strangling a snake—"or knot"—he pantomimed tying a bow—"in the umbilical cord."

Here, it seemed, was the far edge of Benirschke's cooperation and of Koskoff's comfort level. There were other vital follow-up questions Koskoff could have been asked: Could a velamentous cord insertion be detected by fetal monitoring? (The answer was no.) What about the reduced blood flow betrayed by the thrombus? (Possibly, but only if it occurred at the exact moment of the test.) But these would have muddied Koskoff's theory. He chose not to ask them. Instead, apparently satisfied, he said he had nothing further and yielded his seat to Doyle, whose deliberateness as he approached the same uncertainties was palpable.

"Doctor," Doyle began funereally, "with respect to that retroplacental bleed"—the second, embellished blood clot that Doyle suspected Koskoff of throwing in as a ringer—"isn't it true that it's impossible for you to say that that was implicated in B's death?"

"Yes," Benirschke said.

"Okay. So when we're talking, in your opinion, about the *causes* of the death of Baby B, you're not saying that that was a cause?"

"That is correct."

Doyle spoke as if he was worrying every word. His voice was flat, less sonorous than Koskoff's, but deeper and slower. Each of his sentences seemed to have, like each of his cases, a simple theme, which Doyle reduced to a key word or words, then seemed to italicize.

"Now you also mentioned discordancy," he said slowly. "In that context, also, isn't it true that you're *not* saying that the growth retardation or the discordancy caused Baby B's death? Isn't that correct?"

"Correct, yes."

"In your opinion, based upon your training and experience, and your reading of the material that was supplied to you, the cause of Baby B's death was the *pressure* on the blood vessels of the velamentous cord?"

"Correct."

"All right." He paused meaningfully. "And it's also true, isn't it Doctor, that you *cannot* say with reasonable medical probability how long that process of compression was present?"

Benirschke shook his head. "No, I cannot tell you exactly."

"And isn't it true that you cannot say with reasonable medical probability when that compression began?"

"No, I do not know exactly, no."

"Let's talk a little bit about cord compression," Doyle said. "Even in cases of singletons, cord compression does happen."

Benirschke fiddled with his glasses, put them to his mouth. "Yes, *cord* compression occurs in prolapses of cords."

"And in any pregnancy—I don't mean every pregnancy—but it's not unusual for there to be intermittent pressure on the cord. It comes and it goes."

"Ah, I don't think that's correct," Benirschke said. "I think that in labor perhaps it is, but not during the intrauterine state of affairs."

"Okay. Now in twin pregnancies, as opposed to singletons, is there an increased risk of cord pressure, from whatever source?"

"In monoamniotic twins there is, not in other twins." Little Tony and Michael, each held in their own sac, were diamniotic.

"And, in cases where there's velamentous cord insertion, which is what we have here, isn't it true that the risk associated with that condition increases dramatically the mortality and morbidity rate?"

Benirschke's steepled forefingers played against his lips. "Yes," he said. "Twinning does. Monochorionic twinning does. And velamentous insertion does. All of them are incremental."

"All right," Doyle said. "And the reason there's more risk of undue pressure is that the cord of the twin is *not protected* with what's known, as you describe, as Wharton's jelly."

"No. The cord is. The blood vessels, from the point of insertion of the cord onto the membrane, are no longer protected."

"And that increases the risk of problems related to pressure on those vessels?"

"Yes."

Doyle sweated each new answer. He didn't know what Benirschke would say, only that he would "call it as he sees it." Like Koskoff, he wanted to take him as far as he could, then stop, but he was groping in the dark. He didn't know where the edge was. Measuring every word, he tiptoed on.

"Now, you've told us that it is your opinion, based on reasonable medical probability, that Baby B died on Saturday, March thirty-first. That's the day before delivery. Is that correct?"

"Yes."

"And isn't it true that, in your medical opinion, the sole cause of the injuries to Twin A—Tony—is related to the death of Twin B on Saturday, March thirty-first?"

"That's correct."

"Because of the process that you described to Mr. Koskoff."

"Yes," Benirschke said. He was suddenly grim.

"And isn't it true that prior to March thirty-first there is nothing in the medical records that you reviewed to indicate that there was a problem with this twin pregnancy?"

"I did not see any such evidence."

"Now something happened on Saturday that killed Baby B. Is that correct?"

Benirschke smiled at the obviousness of the question. "Sure."

"Because that's when he died. Right? Correct?"

"That's *apparently* when he died. Because two days before, somebody heard two heartbeats."

"You know from the records that the nurse-midwife heard two healthy heartbeats on March thirtieth."

"I know she heard two heartbeats," Benirschke said, quickly adding, "I don't know about the health."

"And then something happened between that time and the time of Baby B's death on Saturday, March thirty-first."

"Yes."

Doyle so far had been "dancing on eggs," he says, but he now grew bolder. He still didn't know what Benirschke would say about the cause of Michael's death—the next obvious question—but he knew what he *had* said, at his deposition. Doyle seized on it. He handed Benirschke a copy of the transcript and asked him to follow along as he read aloud.

"Mr. Koskoff asked you a question," Doyle said. He was pleased to discover that it was Koskoff, not Hunt, who'd asked it. "*'Can you tell me whether or not, aside from the thrombosis which ultimately killed Baby B, would it be likely that thrombi would develop in a velamentous cord insertion over a period of time?' Ms. Hunt: 'Object to the form. That wasn't his testimony. The Witness'*—this is you, Doctor—"

"I'm going to object to that question," Koskoff said.

Doyle, ignoring him, kept on. "*—Yeah, I don't think that the thrombosis killed the baby. I think it is the compression more likely of venous return that eventually led to so significant a hypoxia that the baby died, but the thrombus* betrays the compression of the blood vessels.' Question: 'So that plays a part.' Answer: 'I believe the thrombosis signifies that there has been reduced blood flow through those blood vessels and that compression was the most likely cause and possibly . . . twisting . . . of . . . the . . . cord, but that this reduced venous return led to the death of that baby.' Did I read that correctly?"

"Yes," Benirschke said.

Doyle lit up. "Isn't it true, Doctor, that you're not ruling out that what happened on Saturday, March thirty-first, was a cord accident, such as you described in your deposition, as a possible twisting of the cord? That could have happened, isn't that true?"

"It *could* have happened, but—"

"Right. And isn't it true that because you cannot tell us when the compression began that you can't rule that out?"

Koskoff interrupted: "I'll object to the point of that question. I don't think that—"

"I don't care what you think," Doyle snapped. "You can object to the form and it'll be ruled on at the time of trial."

Benirschke clarified: "If a sudden twisting of the umbilical cord is what killed the baby, then there would have been no thrombi. The thrombi are clearly from some prior event."

"I understand that there were some thrombi," Doyle said, his voice ascending contemptuously. "But that thrombi didn't kill Baby B, did it?"

"It betrayed the slowing of the circulation."

"It betrayed that there was some pressure, earlier on; you can't exactly say when, but you described it as at a different time, two, three days. But we know this," Doyle asserted. "Whatever caused that thrombi two or three days before delivery did not kill Baby B?"

"The thrombi didn't."

"What killed Baby B was what happened on March thirty-first. Isn't that correct?"

"Sure. It died—"

"Right," Doyle snapped. "And something happened. And so, now, isn't it true that you can't sit here and tell us that based on reasonable medical certainty that there wasn't a sudden cord accident, a twisting of the cord, that led to Baby B's death? Isn't that correct?"

"I can only tell you what the medical probabilities are," Benirschke said, clearly frustrated. "Those probabilities are, because it happens in many other babies, that there is an *incremental* decrease in venous return because of compression of the velamentous vessels. That's all I can tell you. I was not there, I did not know the position of the baby; I have no evidence that there was a sudden twisting of the umbilical cord."

"And you don't have any evidence that there wasn't."

Benirschke shrugged and shook his head, his palms lifted. "I don't know," he said.

"You don't know," Doyle repeated.

"The obstetrician could tell you at the time of the delivery," Benirschke suggested.

For fifteen seconds the camera's eye lingered on Benirschke as Doyle pondered his next move. The doctor nibbled on his half-folded plastic eyeglass temples, staring in anticipation. Then, when Doyle said nothing, Benirschke's expression changed. He didn't admire Doyle's gamesmanship, but he had to admit that it had worked. It was true, he didn't know what had killed the baby, and he couldn't exclude a sudden accident, though science and probability suggested a gradual demise. A faint smile flickered across his lips. Then, seeming to think better of it, he closed his mouth, shot a glance at the ceiling, and resumed his vigil.

"Doctor," Doyle began, slowly again, "in this case, the only evidence you found of cord compression prior to Saturday, March thirty-first, when Baby B died, was the thrombosis that you indicated was produced two or three days before birth. Is that correct?"

"Right." Benirschke looked glum. He picked up his mug and drained it.

"And there wasn't evidence, from what you saw, of thrombosis prior to that time?"

"No. There was none."

"Thank you," Doyle said. "I have nothing further."

Koskoff jumped in immediately. "Doctor," he said, "did you see if any *tests* were run by anyone in order to *detect* the presence of any such compression?"

"Objection," Doyle interrupted. "Beyond the scope of my cross-examination."

Benirschke acknowledged that he hadn't.

Koskoff went on. "And you mentioned that the thrombus formed two to three days before delivery. Can you tell us whether or not the slowing of the circulation preceded that?"

"That's the commonest antecedent to thrombus formation."

"And you expressed the opinion to Mr. Doyle that that's what occurred in this case. Is that correct?"

"That's correct."

"And the cause of the slowing of the circulation was what?" Koskoff asked.

"My opinion is the compression of the branch vessels in the membrane."

"And the compression was caused by what?"

"By an expanding fetal mass," Benirschke said. "Commonly, it is the head, but it could be other portions of the body."

"The baby's getting bigger," Koskoff said.

"That's right."

"And is that a sudden process or an incremental process?"

"I'm going to object," Doyle said, "on the grounds that it's leading."

"I'll withdraw the question. Earlier," Koskoff said to Benirschke, "you said that it was an incremental process. What does the word 'incremental' mean?"

"I stated earlier, as the baby grows, the pressure increases on those vessels."

"And you also mentioned that there was no evidence to support a sudden cord accident?"

"I'm gonna object," Doyle blurted, "on the grounds that the question is leading."

"Is there any evidence of a sudden cord accident?"

Doyle repeated: "I object to the question on the grounds that the question is leading."

"I know of no such evidence." Benirschke generally regarded lawyers' objections as attempts to stanch the flow of truth. He suppressed a sneer.

"I have no further questions," Koskoff said.

"Nothing further," Doyle said.

Benirschke snickered, then plucked the microphone wire from his tie as if it were a leech. He was disgusted. All he'd wanted to do—all he ever wanted to do—was to say what, medically speaking, probably had occurred. But lawyers, he believed, "don't really want the truth, they just want to bend the truth to their party's interest." They were conspirators *against* the truth, he thought, asking narrow, partial, indirect questions from which they hoped certain assumptions would be inferred, then objected when the other side made the least effort to enquire further. "They never hear what you want to say," he says bitterly. "That's what hurts so much."

Doyle left Benirschke's office worried that Koskoff had won. "Michael didn't get all he wanted," he would say, but he thought Koskoff had gotten most of it. Benirschke had clearly depicted a pregnancy gone sour, a progressively worsening situation in which Michael Sabia's death and Little Tony's injuries had been amply foreshadowed. With so much going wrong, how could a jury not conclude that the end was inevitable?

True, Doyle had kept Benirschke from ruling out a sudden cord accident, but the doctor had done so grudgingly, only conceding that in a case without a precise diagnosis anything was possible. His concession wasn't much to stand on, and Doyle feared Koskoff had more than made up for it with his drumbeat of dangerous anomalies—velamentous cord insertion, thrombi, unequal placentation, growth retardation, discordancy. He was miffed that Koskoff had even slipped in the placental abruption, which was a nonissue. "Michael's very clever," he says.

And yet both of them had stopped short of asking the real question—was

Twin B's death preventable? Koskoff most likely avoided it because he knew what Benirschke's answer would be; Doyle, because he didn't. Did the presence of the thrombi indicate an event that could have been diagnosed with fetal monitoring? And if so, could the outcome have been foreseen? These issues were the heart of the case.

Benirschke himself strongly believed that the answer to both questions was no, that what had happened, while gradual, was beyond anyone's ability to diagnose or arrest. He had no faith that the twins could have been saved. As competent perhaps as any expert in the world to say whether or not the hospital was at fault by not anticipating Michael Sabia's death, he was convinced that it wasn't. He says today that he regretted not being allowed to say so.

But the jury would never hear Benirschke's opinions. In a courtroom, unlike a morgue or a lab, truth emerges not from an accretion of carefully collected information but from a paradox: the only questions answered are those that are asked, yet the only ones asked are those to which the answers are already known, or at least suspected. Benirschke had hoped to tell the jurors what he thought about the issue of the hospital's blame. No one's views were more authoritative or crucial to their ability to reach a proper reckoning. But Doyle and Koskoff, joining preemptively to edit him, combined to bar him from addressing the subject.

TWENTY-ONE

SEPTEMBER 29, 1993

KOSKOFF AVOIDED DRIBBLING OUT INFORMATION TO CLIENTS DURING THE LONG
years of a lawsuit. They suffered enough, he thought, without having to endure the "twists and turns and deviations and highs and lows" as their cases
staggered through pretrial procedures. "Live your life as if you don't have a
suit," he counseled, both to try to spare them and to dampen their expectations. Now the time had come. The day before the mediation, he met for more
than an hour with Tony and Donna to brief them on their case's progress. Six
and a half years after filing suit, they still knew little about what had happened
to their sons and how the hospital might be at fault. They knew less about the
recent developments affecting Koskoff's thinking—Ryan's departure and re-
placement with Doyle, Judge Ballen's reversals and the trial delays, Little
Tony's worrisome life expectancy, the soaring value of comparable cases, the
prospect of health-care reform, the decision to seek mediation. Ushering
Tony and Donna to the white satin sofa in his sitting area, he worried about
their capacity to absorb these militating issues.

He also feared, he recalls, how they would "present" at mediation. Koskoff
wanted Doyle to see them as he thought a jury would, as a good family, long-
suffering and terribly wronged. They should appear not only deserving but
likable. Donna, he knew, had impressed Ryan at her deposition almost five
years earlier. And Tony, soothed by Ryan's supportiveness, had withstood the
harassment of Humes's first lawyer, Bob Montstream. But that was before
Tony "flipped out," as Tony himself put it, before Humes settled and Travelers
took over, before a trial was imminent—before, Koskoff noted, the arrival of

Bill Doyle, who was expert at vilifying plaintiffs to gain the upper hand. "They're going to be sizing you up," he told them. "Doyle believes that cases are won and lost by who the bad guys are and who the good guys are. He tries to prove that people are liars."

Tony and Donna struggled to take it all in as Koskoff walked them through the case. It was a year to the day since the Norwalk Hospital meeting, and his presentation, though simplified, was the same. He used the same display boards with their boldfaced headings—VIOLATIONS OF STANDARD OF CARE, CAUSE OF INJURY, GENERAL AND SPECIAL DAMAGES—to make, essentially, the same points. Norwalk Hospital, he told them, failed to treat Donna's pregnancy as high-risk despite compelling reasons to do so. It had caused Little Tony's injuries and Michael's death by neglecting to do a series of follow-up sonograms after Donna's second trimester and by not delivering both boys on Friday, March 30. The difference between their having two healthy sons, he said, and one son who was dead and another profoundly brain-damaged, was "a forty-dollar ultrasound."

Then, before all this sank in, he flipped to the last board and told them what he considered the cost of the hospital's "indifference"—$22 million. Koskoff qualified the figure as a demand, but he also wanted them to know he wouldn't sell them short. "We have a trial date," he said. "We want top dollar. If we don't get it, we'll go to court."

Tony and Donna remained silent at first. They were thinking about what to do. For years after the birth they had not known what to believe. Later they accepted that what had happened was the result of a concatenation of negligence by the hospital and Humes. Then, despite settling with her, they came to absolve Humes, who Tony concluded had been "bluffed" into settling and had arrived at the hospital too late to give help. Now they welcomed Koskoff's answers, yet declined, it seemed, to consider themselves victims. In truth, they had always been too consumed with just getting by to dwell on who was at fault. When they thought of blame at all, it was to ask, as Tony put it, "Why me? What'd I do?" It was hard for them even now to see far enough beyond their own bewilderment to accept Koskoff's view that they and their sons had been devastated by appalling medical care.

Koskoff had feared that Tony was a "loaded cannon" and had expected him to seethe, rail, explode—do something. He was relieved when he didn't. Yet this was how Tony absorbed life's shocks: he was slow to take them in, slower to react. Years later, when he learned that his mother had killed his sisters and brother, he would sit impassively for several minutes before muttering, "I'm okay," then lapse back into a brooding trance, his knee pumping like a piston. He built grudges painstakingly, brick by brick, and dismantled them the same way. It was too soon for him to express his outrage, if that was what he was feeling. Knowing his capacity for violence, Koskoff continued talking but tried to say nothing further to inflame him. "I wanted him calm," he recalls.

He returned to the issue of price. During the past few years he'd settled three other brain-damaged-baby cases for $9 million, $7.75 million, and $7.5 million. This, he said, was the range he'd be seeking to establish during the mediation, minus the $1.35 million they'd already gotten from Humes. "I told them," he recalls, "if the offer was less than $5 million, I'd recommend that they reject it; that between $5 million and $7 million was a judgment call; and that anything over $7.5 million they ought to take."

Hearing the breakout, Donna felt excited. Like Tony, she wanted the vindication of a trial, but she wanted other things more—a feeling of independence, of not being so strapped and desperate. If Travelers and Norwalk Hospital were willing to pay that much money at mediation, she thought, how could she refuse? But how would they know how much was enough? Should they hold out for more? She and Tony had been through "hell"— Michael's death, Little Tony's problems, the years of hardship, the separation, giving up Shannon. If she'd learned anything, it was that financial security was the best first step toward easing their suffering.

"No amount of money is going to justify what's happened to this family," she recalls telling Koskoff indignantly, but money could buy respite, time, comfort. Enough money could mend a broken family. For all their sakes, she said, they had to be realistic.

Warily, Koskoff agreed. Now that they were verging on negotiations, his interests and the Sabias' were about to diverge. It was easy to conceive of a situation, say with $3-to-$5 million on the table, where he might want to take the money, but the Sabias should not. Likewise, if Tony and Donna insisted on going to court, for pride or vengeance or some imagined duty to Little Tony, he could lose millions of dollars in fees. Lawyers could steer clients toward making deals, but it had to be handled without a trace of coercion. As it was, Koskoff knew he had to elicit a competitive offer, lest the Sabias become disgruntled.

Donna's remarks led Koskoff to suspect that she would be no problem. Strong and sensible, she came across as knowing what she wanted. Like Bernard, he admired her for returning to face her life when she could have run away. It was Tony who worried him. Koskoff liked to say provocatively that plaintiffs' lawyers actually saved doctors' lives; he'd had clients far less volatile than Tony tell him it was good they'd won, because if they hadn't, they'd planned to gun down those responsible. At least when Tony had exploded before, he hadn't shot Donna, or Humes, or Ryan, or his foreman, or a night clerk at a 7-Eleven. He'd shot his truck, his one means of escape. Still, mediations could be rough. They were like trials, he explained, exposing plaintiffs as targets and causing them other torments. Defense lawyers, Doyle especially, fought back with everything they had, including character assassination.

Koskoff didn't want Tony so near the action during the mediation that he might lose it, giving Doyle an excuse to wait until trial, when a similar outburst could be far more damaging. Explaining the risks, he offered him the option of staying away for the day, but Tony insisted: "I want to see what's going on," he said. At Bernard's urging, he considered staying home from work that night to sleep, but, driving back to Norwalk, he decided to go in. The best way to handle the mediation and someone like Doyle, he reasoned, was to be tired. "That way," he says, "I wouldn't have an attitude."

$\approx \approx \approx$

SEPTEMBER 30, 1993

David Ferguson preferred to know next to nothing about the cases he was hired to settle. Unlike most top mediators, he wasn't a litigator or a retired judge: his strengths were in conflict management and communications, not business and law, and when he joined a dispute, it was with the strict intention of getting the parties to talk to each other, not telling them what to do. "A mediator enters a trust vacuum," Ferguson liked to say. Knowing *Sabia* was a brain-damaged-baby case, he expected emotions and distrust to run "sky high," but he was conciliatory by nature and training. He believed he could somehow broker a deal.

After flying in from Chicago the day before, he arrived at Koskoff's office by eight-thirty. A youthful thirty-seven, his squarish face was handsome and earnest, his dark hair thick and well trimmed. Round wire-rimmed glasses made him seem vulnerable and pleasant; "easy on the eyes," Koskoff's secretary Joyce Russ recalls. But choirboy innocence and idealism weren't what Ferguson hoped to project, especially in a roomful of veteran trial lawyers and claims managers. "I have a baby face, I do," he would lament. "I wish I had some grey hairs."

Protocol dictated diplomatic-style seating for the opening session. Ferguson, as moderator, took the leather armchair at the head of the long polished table in Koskoff's conference room, where four years earlier Humes and McManamy had given their depositions. At his right, backs to the window, sat Koskoff, Lichtenstein, and Bernard, in that order. At his left were Doyle, Hunt, Casey, case manager Cathy Gonzales, and another lawyer from Travelers. For the first time in the more than seven years since Donna had first visited Lichtenstein's office, all those with the authority to settle the case were gathered in one room. Or almost all. Tony, Donna, and Little Tony waited just down the carpeted hallway in Koskoff's office, which was pressed into service during high-stakes mediations as a combination clients' lounge and green room. It had been agreed that they would be introduced before the morning session, then remain on hand as both sides caucused separately throughout the day.

They were dressed as Koskoff and Bernard had instructed. Tony, who still lived in boot-cut jeans and T-shirts with beer logos, wore a green double-breasted suit, one of two he'd had made in Okinawa as a Marine almost twenty years earlier, and a tie that Donna had picked out for him. His hair cascaded almost to his shoulders, and he had a greying, billy-goat beard. Drinking coffee and pacing, his eyes were hard, magnified behind thick, tinted aviator glasses. Donna wore a blue suit and medium heels and her raven hair was pulled back in a topknot. She looked tanned, although not rested. After three pregnancies she was heavier now than when she and Tony had met, but she had the same high cheekbones and forehead, the same world-weary gaze. With nothing to do while they waited, she fussed nervously over Little Tony, as if preparing him for a school play. Crumpled in his wheelchair, he wore navy blue slacks, a new shirt and sweater, and black wing tips, his dress shoes. His eyes darted. His breathing, shallow and labored, was punctuated now and then by a throaty groan.

In the conference room Ferguson brokered the introductions. He carefully wrote down names and seat positions so as not to forget them later on, then reached into his briefcase, removed a stack of releases, and distributed them for signing. The need for confidentiality was profound here. Simply by agreeing to talk, both sides were conceding that there was something to talk about. It could be ruinous to them if their strategies became known, particularly to each other. Ferguson's releases offered a kind of double-walled secrecy. Not only did they bar the parties from discussing the mediation with anyone else; they prohibited Ferguson from divulging what they told him in private. Even if they couldn't trust each other, they needed to trust him. The releases guaranteed that they could speak openly with Ferguson without subverting their bargaining positions. (Later, as negotiations developed, he would conspicuously stop taking notes to further this sense of security. In case the mediation failed, he wanted both sides to know that he had nothing written down about their proposals, nothing that could be subpoenaed for trial.)

When the Sabias were introduced, they said little. They walked stiffly, Tony wheeling Little Tony ahead of him. As Koskoff had intended, they presented a tableau of a good and worthy family. Tony, eager to know which one was Doyle, zeroed in on his red face and white hair, and tried to stare him down. He wanted Doyle to know that he and his family weren't the only ones being evaluated. Half-turned in his chair, Doyle returned Tony's gaze. He was not unmoved by the sight of Little Tony, now nine and a half, his broken-marionette body twisted and immobile in his seat, his frantic eye movements betraying a lost mentality. Nor was he immune to Big Tony's solicitousness as he bent over, stroked the boy's ear, and cooed his name. He looked at Donna, whom years earlier Ryan had identified as both smart and honest. However Doyle fought this case, he knew it would be a mistake to denigrate these people. He wouldn't accept such tactics himself, and they would score him no points with a jury. "Everyone agreed," he would say, "[Little] Tony was very well cared for."

In fact, Doyle understood their hardships more than anyone could have guessed. Although he seldom discussed it—his own partners, some of whom he'd known for thirty years, didn't know—he had grown up in a remarkably similar household. He had younger twin brothers, one of whom was crippled with cerebral palsy that Doyle had come to believe had resulted from a birth injury. As a child, he had watched his mother fight desperately for special services for her son. He understood firsthand how the boy's living at home "sapped so much" from her and from the rest of the family. "I have an appreciation of that," he says, although he adds that he never thought about this in relation to the Sabias.

Tony and Donna left to drive Little Tony to school as the proceedings got under way. As moderator, Ferguson would first hear both sides present their cases. Koskoff began shortly before ten. With another mediator, he may have made preemptive concessions, acknowledging that he had demanded $22 million to "get noticed," and that his take figure for settling was less than that. But Koskoff knew that Ferguson, who didn't pretend to be able to judge "content," only process, wasn't going to push him to be more realistic, so he had no incentive not to posture. Speaking for almost an hour, delivering almost the same talk he'd given at Norwalk Hospital and to the Sabias, he stuck to his $22 million figure. "My feeling," he recalls, "was that since the mediator didn't start out saying, 'You people are crazy. This is a good case, but it's not going to bring $10 million at a settlement,' it wasn't our responsibility to start coming down until there was real money on the table."

Doyle was scowling by the time Koskoff finished. He had expected him to ask for top dollar; mediations, after all, were bargaining sessions, a chance to cut through the posturing and home in on the one thing that could end a dispute—money. Every case had its price, and that price was determined by what the buyer was willing to pay, not what the seller imagined he was due. Doyle knew that Koskoff, recognizing this, negotiated according to a simple rule: the higher you start out, the higher you end up. Nevertheless, insisting that Travelers pay more than twice the largest malpractice verdict in state history, Doyle thought, wasn't merely provocative, it was "stupid."

"I mean, I looked at him and said, 'Are you out of your fucking mind?'" he recalls. It was one thing to start high in order to grab an insurer's attention; another, Doyle knew, to set—and stick to—a demand so preposterous it could only invite a backlash. Within insurance companies, claims managers like Casey and Gonzales are commonly maligned for giving away profits that higher-status underwriters labor to produce. In negotiations, they had to feel they were getting a break. There was nothing to gain from antagonizing them.

Doyle failed to conceal his annoyance. Snarling, he told Ferguson that Koskoff had no case, then set out to prove it in a typically acerbic rebuttal. What had killed Michael Sabia and injured Little Tony, Doyle told Ferguson, wasn't negligence by Norwalk Hospital but a simple, unpredictable cord accident. Worse, he said, Koskoff had known this all along. First he'd blamed the doctor who'd delivered the twins; then, after she settled, he'd come after the hospital. Doyle vowed to be able to show in court that it was *not* the standard of care in 1984 to conduct serial ultrasounds during the third trimester, as Koskoff had claimed, nor was the discordancy between the twins' weights as clear-cut, or perceived to be as dangerous, as Koskoff had made out. In other words, Doyle said, there was no malpractice. The hospital had done all it was supposed to, and couldn't have detected any danger even if it had done more.

Unable to read Ferguson's reaction, he went on. He explained that several legal challenges were pending that could result in some or all of Koskoff's case being thrown out in court. He and Hunt still intended to argue that the Koskoffs had blown the statute of limitations, the first-line defense initially considered by Ryan years earlier. And, he said, they would soon move to dismiss Donna's and Little Tony's complaints on two other grounds.

The first, he explained, was a lack of "proximate cause." The linchpin of any civil suit is that the alleged negligence contributes directly and substantially to the injury being claimed. Doyle believed Koskoff had failed to demonstrate such a connection. Earlier in the week an associate had sent him an eleven-page memo outlining eighty years of Connecticut and federal case law articulating why. In it, she'd cited a 1913 Connecticut case between two dairy farmers, *Kelsey v. Rebuzzini,* in which the plaintiff, Kelsey, had charged his neighbor with negligence for failing to fix a wire fence that ran between their properties. According to the suit, Doyle explained, Kelsey blamed Rebuzzini for killing several of his heifers, who had wandered through the opening, crossed Rebuzzini's land, reached yet another lot where they grazed on poisoned grass, and died. Rebuzzini won.

"Now it was the poisoned grass the killed the cows, not the broken fence," Doyle told Ferguson, who dutifully copied the statement down. Doyle was making a parallel point—that what had injured Little Tony was solely the death of his twin, not Norwalk Hospital's failure to anticipate that Michael Sabia might die. Indeed, Doyle said, no matter how experienced or wise the hospital's doctors had been, they simply could not have foreseen such an indirect outcome, and so should not be held to blame. "The connection between the two isn't there," he said.

Doyle said he also planned to oppose any damage claims made by Donna.

According to the Sabias' court complaint, Donna "observed the negligence of the [hospital]" while it was occurring. She alleged that those who treated her should have known that their conduct was "likely to cause severe psychological, physiological and emotional distress" to her as "the mother of the infant plaintiff." Yet, as Doyle pointed out, Donna had "flatly contradicted" those claims in her deposition, saying she hadn't suspected anyone had done anything wrong until after she met Mary Gay, two and a half years after the birth. Moreover, the state supreme court had recently ruled that "a bystander to medical malpractice may not recover for emotional distress," Doyle said.

Doyle raised this point only as a threat, for while he wanted Donna's claim stricken at trial, he also preferred to have it on the table for now, as a bargaining chit. "This is Tony's case," he told Ferguson. "This is not his parents' case." Yet in fact he hoped to use Donna's self-interest as bait. "If she's got a separate claim," he would say later, "you have a basis for getting money directly to her, which will help settle the case."

Doyle now built to his last, most critical argument: Little Tony's life expectancy. To Travelers, this was the crux of the case: Why should it pay anywhere near $22 million to support a child who, according to its experts, had almost no chance of surviving beyond a few more years? Making this argument at trial would be a "hard sell," Doyle knew: "'We've screwed up this kid so badly that he's not going to live very long. So let us off, don't hit us too hard.'" But now he was adamant. Travelers, he said, was in the business of calculating risk on the basis of statistical probabilities. In order to justify settling, Casey and Gonzales needed to satisfy themselves that the other side's price had some validity. Yet Doyle had two experts, Dr. Susan Farrell and another yet to be deposed, Dr. Herbert Grossman, prepared to testify that Tony would most likely die within five years. Bluntly, Doyle told Ferguson he had seen nothing in Koskoff's case to contradict such an outcome. And so he was putting Ferguson on notice: if he had any hope of facilitating a settlement, it would have to be at a price far below Koskoff's asking figure.

Ferguson stopped writing. He tensed as the lawyers searched his face as if he were a surrogate juror, but he betrayed nothing. Affirming lawyers' arguments wasn't his role. What's more, he considered the question of blame irrelevant, and so he steered clear of it. It had no bearing on what he wanted to accomplish and could well get in the way, as any sign of partiality could only undermine the trust he hoped to establish. Now that he had let both sides vent publicly, he had only one goal: to meet with them in private to find out what they really wanted—"had to have," he says—to make the case go away.

≈ ≈ ≈

It was lunchtime when Doyle finished. Ferguson suggested he meet with the defense team first in the conference room while the Koskoffs caucused elsewhere. Throughout the years of litigation Travelers had never made a settlement offer, nor had Doyle made one in his rebuttal. Ferguson knew there was nothing to talk about until they did.

Koskoff, Bernard, and Lichtenstein headed to Lichtenstein's office, two doors down from Koskoff's, to meet with Tony and Donna. They ordered sandwiches for everyone, but when the sandwiches that arrived were huge, Tony felt ludicrous trying to squeeze the bread flat enough to take a bite. For years he'd always worn a pager in case Little Tony, somewhere else, had a seizure. Now "a bucket of nerves," he stood up and announced, "You want me, you beep me. I'll be outside smoking a cigarette."

In the conference room, Ferguson gently prodded Doyle and Travelers to make the first move. This was his style, to shuttle between the two sides and cajole them into making ever-better offers to "elicit the maximum movement from the other side." Tony called it "playing hopscotch." Ferguson's skills were as an intermediary, not a negotiator. Eager to listen, all he heard now was outrage and indignation. Hunt and Gonzales expectedly took the hardest line. Both believed the hospital was in the right, that they would win at trial, and that making an offer sent the wrong message. But it wasn't their call. It was up to Doyle and Casey, who despite having little faith in the negotiations or in Ferguson saw the session as the only way to find out what Koskoff was after.

They proposed, as if on cue, a "structured" settlement of $1.7 million—$700,000 up front; the rest invested in a pair of annuities. These were policies that insurers sold to other insurers to help them avoid paying out claims in cash. Travelers proposed to spend $1 million to buy two annuities from a firm called National Home Life and Accident, of which Little Tony would be the beneficiary. The policies would yield $60,000 a year, in current dollars, to pay his medical expenses for as long as he lived. Doyle said the amount was predicated on his also being eligible for public assistance. As a sweetener, Doyle added, Travelers also would pay the cost of putting the Sabias' two other children through college—$12,500 a year each for four years.

Doyle thought the structure was a reasonable offer, in the best interests of the Sabias and Travelers alike. It allowed the hospital and Travelers to settle at a discount, and because the money wouldn't go into trust, Tony and Donna wouldn't have to pay taxes on it. Structures generally, he thought, were a "macabre business," the insurer and the annuity company betting, in effect, that the recipient wouldn't survive. In a case like this, however, where there was irresolvable disagreement over life expectancy, Doyle believed annuities could deliver "a hell of a lot more money" than an upfront cash settlement if Koskoff was right and Little Tony lived to old age. "You wanna talk about life expectancy," he told Ferguson, "forget it. Take life expectancy off the table. I'll take that risk." True, with a structure there would be no estate when Little Tony died, but Doyle thought that was only fair, since the goal was to provide for his well-being, not to enrich his parents.

Moderately encouraged, Ferguson took the offer to Lichtenstein's office, where Donna sat cloistered with Lichtenstein, Bernard, and Koskoff. This office was smaller than Koskoff's by half, with a large catercornered desk and a small round conference table. Ferguson was met by a mood as somber as that in the conference room, though for another reason. "People get excited around here when there's a mediation going on," Koskoff says. "My fear is that someone's going to slap me on the back and say, 'How's it going? What're they up to?'" The antidote was to remain poker-faced at all times, even, apparently, behind closed doors. They paged Tony, then settled in to review Travelers' offer. All three lawyers rejected it at once. Ordinarily, Koskoff would have called a consultant, just in case, to price out the deal, make sure the numbers squared, and find out whether the annuity company was solvent. Now he didn't bother. Dismissing the structure proposal as ludicrous, he sought to refocus the discussion. "Let's talk about the price," he told Ferguson. "Then let's talk about the financing."

Ferguson hoped to elicit a counteroffer, but before Koskoff could make one, Tony, who'd been fuming, erupted. "I hate to tell you, but you were misinformed," he growled at Ferguson. "You've got your facts wrong. First of all, Tony isn't entitled to Medicare, Medicaid, or Social Security because I make too much money. Second of all, I've got four kids, not three. And third of all, it costs a lot more than sixty thousand dollars a year to maintain Tony. His school alone is forty-two thousand dollars a year. A case of diapers is a hundred dollars." Tony didn't explain that Little Tony's tuition was paid by the City of Norwalk, and Ferguson didn't ask.

Tony was trembling. For ten years he'd held his family together, trying to provide for his son. Throughout that time, Norwalk Hospital, on which he continued to rely, had never once acknowledged responsibility. Now, finally forced to address him, its minions were not only lowballing him because they thought Little Tony was going to die soon, they didn't even know how many children he and Donna had. Tony wanted to tell "Doyle and them" that he'd see them in court, but Koskoff and Bernard intervened. "They're still here," Koskoff counseled, implying that since Doyle and Casey hadn't left, it would be useful to see what else they might be willing to offer.

Ferguson beseeched Koskoff to give him something real to take back to the conference room, something to jumpstart negotiations. He also understood now that he would have to appease Tony directly and that Koskoff wasn't making the calls, Tony was. Clearly, Doyle's and Casey's mistakes had hurt his efforts to build trust, and he resolved to "go back and educate them." But he also needed for Koskoff to show some genuine movement. Finally, after discussing the matter with Bernard and Lichtenstein, Koskoff agreed to lower his initial demand. Two and a half years earlier he'd filed a $15 million offer of judgment that said, in effect, pay this amount now or pay it with 12 percent interest when the final bill comes due. Koskoff's new figure reflected that formula: $19.5 million.

"Right off the bat we were in trouble," Ferguson recalls. The sides were so far apart that it would be next to impossible to convince Doyle and Casey that Koskoff was serious. Still, he carried the offer down the hall and delivered it to the defense, along with his report on Tony's reactions to the factual inaccuracies in Travelers' offer. Now it was Doyle's turn to explode. "Will you get out of here," he growled. "Talk about *move!* When I move, we're talking real dough, but he starts with this bullshit twenty-two-million-dollar demand, then goes to nineteen, and I'm supposed to go *up?* His numbers are fantasy numbers. Mine are real. It's stupid." Doyle reddened with disgust. The cash value of his original offer was almost $2 million, which, he says, "when you bet on a short life expectancy for Little Tony could pay out a lot each year," maybe more money than the Sabias had ever had. He suspected Koskoff of jerking him around.

But this was what negotiations were: a grinding game of high-low. You raised your ceiling; the other guy dropped his floor. You both postured, hoping privately that somehow you'd slip within range of each other and, if the mediator knew what he was doing, get close enough to reach a deal. Still preferring the process to a trial, Doyle and Casey hung in. They made no counteroffer, but admonished Ferguson to go back and see if he could talk some sense into Koskoff. Their message, Ferguson recalls, was: Bring back some justification why we should pay a lot more money. Otherwise, we're nearing our top offer.

≈≈≈

Ferguson felt dejected as he left the conference room for the second time. He'd struggled through enough mediations to know that people were easily discouraged and that it was the mediator's job "to keep the process going when it would otherwise stop." This one, though, had a meanness to it that made him think his efforts could well be futile. What, after all, did he have to keep the process going *with,* other than his own enthusiasm? Both sides seemed to want him to tell them what the case was worth, but that was beyond his competence. He had no idea how a jury might value it, whose case was stronger, what comparable cases were settling for. All he knew was that if he prodded and persisted and didn't let them stop talking they might inch toward a realization of what they and their opponents needed in order to settle.

"I kept going," he says, but after more than two hours of only the most desultory movement, he didn't know how much further he could push.

He sensed an unlikely ally in Koskoff. Most lawyers, in his experience, conducted negotiations in the same state of high dudgeon. They felt they had to act intransigent to prove their mettle. Koskoff, however, seemed different. Whether it was the enormous cushion he'd provided himself by starting out with an astronomical demand—he could come down by half and still trump the largest malpractice *verdict* in state history—or his confidence in himself as a trial lawyer or some elemental calm, he seemed eager to keep going even when his clients weren't.

Only Koskoff seemed undismayed when Ferguson trudged into Lichtenstein's office with the news that Doyle had refused to make a counteroffer. Koskoff explained his position to Ferguson: if they went to trial, the range for a jury verdict would be from $7 million to $30 million. (How he'd come to add $10 million to the August record-setting obstetrical verdicts was unclear.) "We don't need to get the thirty," he told Ferguson, "but we need better than the low end of the range." Otherwise, he asked, why settle? "But," Koskoff added, almost as an afterthought, "if they were at five million, we would go to fifteen."

It was more a casual aside than a counteroffer, but Ferguson was encouraged. Sensing that there was hope after all, he decided not to write the figures on his master sheet, committing them instead to memory. He put aside his pad, as if to announce the beginning of more serious discussions. He returned to the conference room buoyed by Koskoff's willingness to move, but Doyle again demanded to know how he and Travelers could justify paying more than they'd already offered when Koskoff kept dallying in the "stratosphere." "What are we doing here?" Doyle asked.

By now Doyle believed Ferguson was in over his head; worse, he suspected him of being used by Koskoff. Scrambling, Ferguson pleaded with him to keep trying. "What you need to know is what they have to have," he told Doyle. The implication was, if you stop talking, you won't find out where Koskoff's bottom line is. It was a thin reed, but Doyle grasped it. He said he would consider raising his counteroffer if Koskoff came down to $7.5 million.

Following the "usual mediation script," Ferguson shuttled between the conference room and Lichtenstein's office for the next hour, trying to overcome both sides' frustrations by sticking to the same speech: "I hear what you're saying. I know you're disheartened. But the process always makes sense." He was going on faith. *Sabia* was a big case. Both sides had set aside the whole day and no one had left. As long as he could keep them involved, he had momentum, and momentum was Ferguson's wedge. "One of my greatest strengths and greatest weaknesses," he says, "is I don't know when to quit."

What he hadn't anticipated was Koskoff's cynical view of insurers and his determination not to be bullied by Doyle. Soon after presenting Koskoff with Doyle's proposal that the Sabias drop their floor to $7.5 million, he got an earful regarding both. "They're telling us what to demand," Koskoff admonished. "We can leave the room and they can negotiate with themselves." Koskoff was losing patience. Angrily, he told Ferguson he believed that Travelers was negotiating in bad faith. The company had sold Norwalk Hospital a liability policy with a $15 million limit. He and Bernard thought there were additional layers of coverage that could bring that up to $20-to-$30 million. "You wouldn't sell a policy that size if you didn't think there was some injury that was worth it, would you?" he asked Ferguson rhetorically. The implication was that no injury could be more costly than Little Tony's; if Travelers was offering less than $2 million in his case, it was defrauding the hospital. Koskoff knew he had no legal basis for a bad-faith claim against Travelers, but as the offers of judgment and the Goldblatt verdict had showed, it was never too soon to raise the threat of one.

Koskoff's saber-rattling had its effect. Doyle increased his offer to $2.5 million, either a structure or all cash. That induced Koskoff, during Ferguson's next pass, to drop his demand to $14.5 million. Officially, the two sides were still $12 million apart, though unofficially Ferguson sensed that each was willing to move further—Doyle perhaps to $5 million, Koskoff to $10 million—provided the other moved first. But it was nearing three-thirty; at this rate, Ferguson thought, they'd be here all night.

Glumly returning to the conference room yet another time, Ferguson thought he'd pushed both sides almost to their limit. The process, he says, was "grinding to a halt," and he was running out of reasons why anyone should remain hopeful. "People were so discouraged," he says. "They were so far apart. I felt like I was hitting a wall and that I had to do something different." He received no help from Doyle, who refused to raise his counteroffer. Ferguson pleaded with him not to leave. Then he returned to the gloom in Lichtenstein's office, where he appealed to Koskoff. "You don't have to respond to me," he said, careful not to lock Koskoff into a figure that wasn't his, "but my sense is you're looking at $10 million." Koskoff was silent as Ferguson continued: "I've got a read on the defense's bottom line, and I can tell you, it's not eight figures."

Koskoff was no longer blithe. The day had been a grueling disappointment, and he was irked by Doyle's stonewalling. They'd made scant progress. Only Ferguson's relentless willingness to plod ahead suggested that there was any more room for movement. Still, if by coming down, say, to $10 million, he could tempt Doyle to cross the $5 million threshold, they'd be in real negotiations. Koskoff thought it through. Even if the discussions went no further, at $10 million they'd still be safe. It wouldn't compromise their bargaining position and, heading into court, it still gave them plenty of room to negotiate if

Doyle and Casey had second thoughts. Koskoff hinted that $10 million might be acceptable.

Then he had another idea. Officially, he was still at $14.5 million, and the day was getting late. Knowing that Doyle was fed up, he was reluctant to continue the arduous scrape that had gotten them to this point. Nor did he want to inform Doyle needlessly that he had dropped his floor to $10 million. If Doyle refused to make a counteroffer, Koskoff would be sacrificing $4.5 million of bargaining power for nothing. So he proposed an alternative to Ferguson. Instead of going back to Doyle and Casey with his latest offer, he said, why not float a compromise figure and give each side a chance to evaluate it in private. If both sides agreed, they had a deal. If not, nothing would be lost and they could resume negotiating.

All but out of ideas of his own, Ferguson jumped at the notion. Unless he could draw the Sabias and Travelers closer together, neither side would have to confront their bottom line. Still, he was troubled. How could he handle the proposal so as to assure both sides that their bargaining strategies wouldn't be compromised? And what was a reasonable figure, given that officially they were still $12 million apart while, unofficially, probably much less than that.

At four o'clock, Ferguson called both sides together in the conference room and said he wanted to make one last attempt at a settlement. He would propose, he said, a figure for both sides to think about overnight. "This is not what *I* think the case is worth," he stressed. "I'm not here to say somebody's right or wrong. But I think this is a number, based on what I know about your positions, that you'd both have to think very hard about."

Then, trying to put everyone at ease, he set the terms for disclosure: "If both sides say yes, we have a done deal. If both say no, I'll report no. If one says yes, I'll also report no, so that the side that agrees isn't compromised." Worried that Doyle, especially, distrusted him, Ferguson had struggled to come up with a figure that neither "split the baby" nor in any way seemed to favor Koskoff. They were talking real money now, and he had taken seriously Doyle's admonitions about the difference between his real figures and Koskoff's artificial ones. On the other hand, he didn't want to betray what seemed to be Koskoff's most recent movement.

He reasoned that if Koskoff is hinting at $10 million, he'd "take $8.5." And if Doyle was indicating he might consider $5 million, he could probably be pushed to $6 million, maybe higher. Reaching for a number "that would make each side squirm," Ferguson proposed his own figure: $7 million.

Ferguson felt beat-up. It had been one of the most grueling mediations he'd ever handled, and it wasn't over. More, the "trust vacuum" he'd tried to fill with his earnest goodwill had defied his efforts; people distrusted *him* now. Leaving to find a hotel room, he announced that he would meet separately with both sides in the morning to hear their replies.

~ ~ ~

The next morning Ferguson met with Doyle and Casey first, although he already knew their answer. Doyle had called him the night before to say that Travelers had rejected his figure. "Despite all my disclaimers," he recalls, "they seemed to feel that my number set a higher standard than would otherwise have been set in the case." Ferguson tried to reassure them that the $7 million price tag was arbitrary, based solely on his sense of what it would take to settle, but Doyle and Casey remained unconvinced. There was now an unofficial, albeit sanctioned, value on *Sabia,* and it was considerably more than they were willing to pay.

Ferguson felt they blamed him for torpedoing their position—an unconscionable blunder for any mediator—and that they were, if anything, testier and less cooperative than they'd been the day before. Gonzales, driving down from Hartford that morning, had hit a deer, which may have added to the sour feeling. ("I hope she didn't have Travelers' insurance," Tony said on hearing about the incident.)

Ferguson plodded down the hall to tell the Sabias and Koskoff the news. "Since I already got a no," he said dispiritedly, "don't bother telling me your answer." Tony and Donna buckled. Ferguson's proposal had forced on them a terrible reckoning. After he'd left the day before, they'd stayed at Koskoff's office until eight, agonizing over what to do. Donna had called Tony's sister to ask her to take care of the kids, who were asleep by the time they got home. They'd talked anxiously all through dinner, then until midnight, drinking coffee and smoking at the kitchen table.

They had expected more money and still wanted Norwalk Hospital to concede what it had done to them. They were spent, disappointed. But Koskoff and Bernard had been blunt: no matter how good a case they thought they had, they could lose in court. Hold out, they said, and you could wind up with nothing. In the end, they had reluctantly decided to accept Ferguson's proposal, though they doubted Travelers would agree.

Even after they'd decided, Tony had remained restless, unable to let go. Though he'd been up all the night before, his nerves were jangly, and every time he tried to sleep, his eyes popped open. Should he take the money? Is this what it came down to, a bunch of suits playing God with his kid? As Donna said, "Half these people have never been around a child like Tony. They don't know what it takes. All they know is money." It was this, this unacknowledged suffering, that disturbed Tony more than anything else. It didn't matter to him how much money they got: he'd still keep his job, still have the money from Humes, still be "so tight I fucking squeak." It was the fact that people thought that money could salve his and Donna's and Little Tony's wounds, that it would buy his acquiescence, that filled him with such contempt. Those people had no idea. Now, in Lichtenstein's office, Tony turned to Ferguson, fixed him in his gaze, and said, "You caused me a sleepless night."

The Sabias, Koskoff told Ferguson, were willing to accept his figure, provided that the money was up-front—no structures. Ferguson was staggered. He'd expected Koskoff to accept nothing less than top dollar, yet here he'd dropped his floor by more than two-thirds in less than a day. Koskoff reassured him: "You heard it from the boss," he said, pointing to Tony.

Ferguson scrambled to consider how to exploit this new knowledge. By his own ground rules, he was obligated to report that there was no deal, yet he now knew that the two sides were tantalizingly close; not separated, as Doyle and Casey believed, by a gulf of $12 million, but by a narrow strait of perhaps no more than $2 million. As far as the defense still knew, the plaintiffs' demand was firm at $14.5 million. The difference between the Sabias' official position and what they'd indicated they would now take to settle was $7.5 million—if only Ferguson could find a way to use this information.

He returned to the conference room with a renewed determination to keep going, but Doyle and Casey refused to budge, growing increasingly impatient with his entreaties. Ferguson sputtered for more than an hour before giving up. "I got a pretty clear message," he says, "that that was it." Afterward, Ferguson tried to understand why he felt so demoralized. He remembered a review he'd once read of a book on plaintiffs' lawyers. After reading about their exploits, the reviewer said, he'd been forced to admire their determination to obtain answers and redress their clients' suffering. Nevertheless, the reviewer had felt thoroughly "repulsed by a system that punished everyone who came in contact with it." Ferguson told himself, "Win some, lose some," but he couldn't escape feeling that same revulsion. Lawsuits bred mistrust. Sometimes, he thought, the adversarial rancor damaged everyone around it. Ferguson feared that *Sabia* was one of those cases, and that by failing to end it he had only made it worse.

Koskoff was more sanguine. The mediation, he says, "was a real moment of truth for me. It's easy to say you don't want to settle when no one's offering you any money. For the first time I had to decide what we had to have." Typically, he'd felt diminished by the process, saying, "Mediation is not what I was born to do. It's like an actor doing commercials." And he regretted the "huge disappointment for the Sabias," although he didn't think it all bad that they'd "got a little taste of what a trial was like." Mostly, though, he was happy to have gotten beyond the negotiations unscathed. Doyle still didn't know his floor. They were going to trial. His blood was racing. He now knew Doyle's entire defense and was unimpressed. If he had to roll the dice, this was as promising a case as any. As he would say afterward, "There aren't a lot of cases around that are this good."

TWENTY-TWO

AFTER THE MEDIATION, THE CALCULUS IN SABIA SHIFTED. HAVING SEEN EACH other's cases, both sides knew what to expect at trial. With real money on the table, Doyle and Koskoff could see that the best deal for everyone was one that they, as middlemen, controlled. Only two obstacles remained: finding a satisfactory price that wouldn't embarrass anyone, and getting the Sabias and Travelers to agree to it. None of which altered the lawyers' pretrial preparations. The more desirable a deal became, the more each side wanted the other to believe that it had lost any hope of settling and that a trial was unavoidable. Psychologically and strategically, the case had entered its endgame, a familiar masquerade to the lawyers in which the desired goal—settlement—required them to exert all their energies toward its opposite—courtroom supremacy. It was the legal equivalent of stepping up bombing raids in order to force an enemy to accept a cease-fire. Either Sabia would reach trial, assumably within the month, or it wouldn't. Either way the lawyers had to prepare as if it would.

Each side tackled last-minute details. Bernard's to-do lists again lengthened as he prepared to depose the last few experts. As second seat at trial, his job would be to marshal the flow of witnesses and evidence, handle the legal arguments, act as Koskoff's right hand, plug holes in the case as they occurred, and minister to Tony and Donna. And so he plowed through more than a decade's worth of medical records, consultants' reports, articles, memos, pleadings, and transcripts that filled four file drawers in Joyce Russ's office. He arranged to have Little Tony reexamined at Newington Children's Hospital, to secure another opinion about his life expectancy. He began researching a brief to counter Doyle's promised motion to exclude Donna's damage claim and hired a consultant to develop a settlement structure more favorable to the

Sabias. Aware that all else would go on hold once jury selection began, he scrambled to clear his desk, and life, of other commitments.

As the pressure built during the first two weeks of October, he struggled with conflicting feelings. Approaching trial was one thing; going to court after turning down a multimillion dollar offer was another. Protective of Tony and Donna, Bernard was nagged by doubt. He worried that by encouraging the Sabias to reject Travelers' proposal, however inadequate, he and Koskoff may have doomed them to a far worse fate: "How would you like to be the one to say to Big Tony Sabia, 'I'm sorry, we lost. You're going to have to go back to living the way you've been living.'" Mediations, he knew, are more difficult for trial lawyers than trials are. In court everything is black and white—you argue your case, give it all you've got, and if you lose, as Ted Koskoff used to say, the judge and jury were against you from the start. But failing to reach a settlement once negotiations began left only yourself to blame and carried the legal and moral weight of having rejected a suboptimal deal for possibly none at all.

If Koskoff had such qualms, he didn't show them. The tense weeks before trial were an overture, the prelude to showtime. This was when he became fully engaged in a case and when he earned his money. One of his chief pleasures as a plaintiff's lawyer was that, unlike defense lawyers, he got to design and engineer trials. He not only starred, he produced and directed as well.

His most crucial work routinely occurred before—not after—the curtain went up, as he shaped on paper the impending trial's architecture, pacing, and drama. As much as the trial itself, this was Koskoff's art. He had inherited from his father a feeling of entitlement, a sense that when he walked into a courtroom it was his. Lacking his father's natural ease and charisma, though, he attained his mastery through meticulous preparation. Alone in his office, he spent every day now ordering and reordering his black loose-leaf trial notebook, writing questions in his quick sprawling hand, a hybrid of script and print, then crossing them out, or shuffling them between pages. A trial was a narrative, and the notebook, with its inserts labeled ARGUMENT and CHARGE and DAMAGES and POINTS OF LAW, contained the structure of the story Koskoff proposed to tell.

He knew the trial would be long and confusing and that the jury would forget a lot of what it heard. And so he worked methodically, untangling the pieces, ordering every step, making each detail seem simple and logical. He assembled an exhibit list, including major items such as Donna's prenatal records and minor ones such as Michael Sabia's death certificate. As much as possible, he anticipated the order, tone, and context of every question he planned to ask. Most critical was his witness list, since it was through the careful ordering of testimony that the rhythmic tension of a courtroom drama was established. Koskoff liked to create a favorable impression of the plaintiff's case, then build inexorably to a series of climaxes. Fifteen years earlier he'd written that a malpractice trial consisted of four parts—exposition, factual history, expert witnesses, and damages. Now, looking at *Sabia*, he laid them out.

The first part, setting the stage, consisted solely of Donna and Tony describing what had happened to them in the winter and spring of 1983–1984. Koskoff hoped to cement an impression of hard-working, family-minded virtue so compelling, and of catastrophic loss so devastating, that it would last through perhaps six weeks of dense, often mind-numbing medical testimony. At the same time, he didn't want Tony and Donna overexposed. Best, he thought, to keep their testimony tight—a quarter day and half day, respectively.

Next would come those who treated Donna at the Norwalk Hospital clinic: Dr. George Patterson, the elderly Harvard-trained ob-gyn who agreed to let Donna be seen by nurse-midwives on alternate visits; Barbara Mc-Manamy, the caring but in-over-her-head midwife who saw Donna two days before the delivery and again during labor; and perhaps two other treating physicians, including then-ob-gyn chair Dr. Daniel Adler, who was in charge of the clinic around that time and had supervised the writing of its protocols. The impression Koskoff hoped to make here was wholly different from the one he'd elicit from the Sabias: profound institutional indifference to the risks of twin pregnancies, especially discordancy; medical expedience so cynical that accountability devolved to the least-credentialed person on staff, the nurse-midwife.

Rounding out the historical phase—perhaps the first two weeks of testimony—would be Humes, who, as a result of Doyle's pressure, would address the condition of the twins at birth but not the delivery, then, in probable order, Dr. Avelino Maitem, the radiologist who saw Donna during labor; Dr. William Cronin, who performed the three ultrasounds earlier in her pregnancy; possibly two of the labor nurses, although not Mollie Fortuna, whose lapses Koskoff had still overlooked; and perhaps—Koskoff hadn't decided yet—Tony's sister, Donna, who accompanied Donna Sabia to the hospital and attended the delivery. Koskoff would use this aggregate testimony to lead up to his theory that the hospital had caused Little Tony's brain damage by neglecting to treat Donna properly during pregnancy.

It was the second half of the case, building to his closing argument, that Koskoff considered most assiduously and, paradoxically, left loosest. Among his medical experts, Iffy was still a question mark, but he now put down Murray, Schifrin, and Goldkrand—the old Goldblatt team—for a day each of testimony, followed by Benirschke's climactic videotaped deposition. He then planned to bring in his damage experts, the four doctors and economists he'd hired to assess Little Tony's injuries and their costs, followed by up to eight back-up witnesses—therapists, pediatricians, and neurologists—who'd treated Little Tony and could testify about the extent of his disabilities and hopeless prognosis. It was during this final phase that he would show Buckley's day-in-the-life video. The jury, after hearing Little Tony's helpless state endlessly described, and possibly seeing him once in the courtroom if Koskoff thought it useful, would at last witness what getting through each day was like for him, and for Tony and Donna. After that, Koskoff was considering putting on Shannon, who would testify to the impact of Little Tony's afflictions on her family.

Koskoff could look at this list, some thirty names, and see the trial unfold before him. He could read his notebook as a script. Then again, so could Doyle. For almost fifty years, ever since the U.S. Supreme Court abolished "trial by ambush" in *Hickman v. Taylor,* one side's court preparations mirrored the other's. As the Court had put it, "mutual knowledge of all the relevant facts gathered by both parties is essential to proper litigation," which meant that while Doyle might not know everything about Koskoff's strategy, he knew more than enough to counteract it.

Deep in his own preparations with Hunt, Doyle still thought "the whole thing, the most compelling thing, is Tony Sabia with a tube in him." He was "scared to death," he says, of the emotional impact Little Tony's condition would have on jurors. He also had to smother some of the same pangs Bernard had felt, fearing that he may have made a costly mistake by rejecting Ferguson's float figure at the mediation. Beyond that, however, Koskoff's case failed to impress him. Basically, he thought, it came down to a single, questionable claim: that if Norwalk Hospital had done serial ultrasounds in the last trimester of Donna's pregnancy, it would have seen that Twin B was smaller than Twin A and would have taken them both by C-section sometime before Twin B's death. Yet according to Lockwood and Dr. Richard Jones, another defense expert yet to be deposed, the complaint was wrong on all three counts.

First, Doyle planned to argue, the hospital wasn't required to do such ultrasounds under the standard of care. Second, it wasn't clear, given the wide margin of error, that the discordancy would have set off alarms even if it had. And third, the hospital wouldn't have been required to take the babies even if the discordancy had been recognized. Add to that Benirschke's ambiguity about what had eventually killed Michael Sabia, and Doyle was confident he could mount a persuasive case. "I didn't anticipate being able to convince a jury that it wasn't the standard of care, although I think there's some real question about that," he says. "But in court you need both; you need a breach of the standard of care and you need evidence that the negligence was a substantial producer and cause of what you're complaining about. Our case was that there was no connection between the negligence, if that's what it was, and what actually killed the twin, which resulted in the damage to Tony. You're not taking the twins out to prevent a cord accident."

Among the defense lawyers, Bev Hunt alone had been with the case from the start. She had coached McManamy and sheltered Fortuna when it was mainly a birth trauma complaint against Humes, then helped bury that part of the case with Benirschke's deposition. She'd tangled with Schifrin and survived Ryan's ouster. Having literally grown up on the case as a lawyer, she was eager to reap justice, win for the hospital and Ryan, beat the Koskoffs, and work the second seat with Doyle. On October 6, a week after the mediation and the same day that Little Tony was reexamined at Newington by Koskoff's newest life-expectancy expert, Dr. Lawrence Kaplan, Hunt began sending Doyle a series of trial memos. Since the mediation, she'd become more vehement than ever about exonerating the hospital.

Hunt's first memo briefed Doyle for his cross-examination of Barry Schifrin. Aside from Benirschke, Schifrin was Koskoff's most valuable expert; certainly, he had the highest profile and the most imperious manner. Not only did Schifrin believe that fetal monitoring would have prevented everything, he insisted that the dangers to Twin B would have been glaringly obvious to anyone who had looked. It was a damning analysis—Schifrin's Law, which in hindsight made doctors look inept for not seeing the aggregate risk of individual anomalies that by themselves might appear marginally important at the time. Schifrin was famous for winning cases, and Doyle looked forward to attacking him on the witness stand. Hunt thought this wouldn't be hard. To counter Schifrin they had Lockwood, who was equally convinced that the hospital had done nothing wrong. Lockwood would testify that none of the problems attending Michael Sabia's death—growth retardation, velamentous cord insertion, compression of the cord arteries, placental abruption, thrombi, and hypoxia—would have been detectable in the days and weeks leading up to it, and even if they had been, no doctor would automatically have taken the babies. And they had Schifrin himself, an increasingly controversial figure whom Hunt set out to discredit in her memo.

Citing recent depositions she'd gotten from other defense lawyers, Hunt advised Doyle how to tar Schifrin as a one-man medical-legal boutique catering cynically to plaintiffs' lawyers in bad baby cases. Schifrin, she wrote, made $90,000 to $100,000 a year testifying. He was sole owner of Beats Per Minute, a company he'd set up, in Hunt's words, as a "conduit for legal fees." Demanding an up-front, nonrefundable retainer of $2,500 for reviewing cases, he hired nurses and "contract labor" to review medical records for him and hadn't held an academic appointment in ten years. Hunt also pointed out that at his deposition in *Sabia* he'd said that what had killed the stillborn was, essentially, chronic starvation as a result of reduced access to the placenta, and that, based solely on an ultrasound finding on March 30 showing a 20 percent weight discordancy between the twins, the standard of care would not have called for medical intervention.

The implications, Hunt noted, were striking. Now that Koskoff's chief liability claim was the lack of ultrasounds, Schifrin appeared to be contradicting his own side's case. And because the Sabias' argument on causation hinged entirely on Benirschke's cord-compression theory, he seemed to be opposing Benirschke as well. Either way, Hunt felt assured that Doyle could ruin his credibility before a jury. Doyle could depict Schifrin not just as a mercenary but as an unreliable one at that.

The buildup by both sides crested on Monday, October 18. With Judge Ballen having all but promised to get the trial on in October, Koskoff spent part of the morning at his desk, typing a last-minute memo: an eight-point outline, all in capitals, of Doyle's defense. He and Doyle had now spoken so often by phone, testily pressing their cases while trying to inch each other toward settlement, that the list could well have been written by Doyle himself. For instance, Koskoff wrote, "LOCKWOOD AND JONES ARE TESTIFYING THAT THE STANDARD OF CARE WAS DIFFERENT FROM WHAT WE CLAIM. NO ROUTINE ULTRASOUND AT OTHER HOSPITALS DURING 1984." And "EVEN SCHIFRIN AGREES THERE WAS NO REQUIREMENT FOR A [sic] INTERVENTION BASED ON ULTRASOUND FINDINGS ALONE. NO REQUIREMENT FOR SERIAL NONSTRESS TEST." Koskoff dismissed these weaknesses as manageable but had learned not to underestimate Doyle. He reproduced the memo and placed a copy in the front of his trial book.

Meanwhile, Doyle as promised filed his last-minute motion to strike Donna's claim for emotional stress. With a trial imminent, he wanted the Sabias to know that one of the costs of refusing to settle was that Donna might well end up with no money of her own. Whether or not he knew the intimate details of the Sabias' domestic history, he, like Koskoff, knew exactly which buttons to push to make his opponents squirm.

A few eleventh-hour depositions aside, there was nothing left for Doyle and Koskoff to learn about each other's discoveries, facts, talking points, and strategies, and hardly anything else to know about each other. They could envision the trial with the same clarity: who would say what when, where to push, where to let go, how to respond. With Hunt and Bernard scrambling to finish up, everything was accounted for except the judge's prejudices and the unknowable inclinations of the jurors.

Which is where they stood—and would remain, suspended, indefinitely—when Ballen notified them that afternoon that he'd again been forced, due to an ongoing shortage of judges, to delay the trial until January.

TWENTY-THREE

BERNARD CHOSE TO DISCREDIT DR. HERBERT GROSSMAN JUST ENOUGH TO WORRY Doyle. The hospital's main damage expert, Grossman was slated to testify regarding Little Tony's life expectancy. Although Bernard believed he could weaken him so much at his deposition that Doyle would dump him before trial, he *wanted* Grossman in court.

A pediatric neurologist at the University of Michigan Medical School, Grossman was best known as coauthor of a controversial 1990 article in the *New England Journal of Medicine (NEJM)* entitled "The Life Expectancy of Profoundly Handicapped People with Mental Retardation." The article described the first large-scale study of death rates among people with severe developmental disabilities, including brain damage. Grossman and his colleagues had found a widespread pattern of early death among 100,000 multiply handicapped patients who had received state services in California during the mid-1980s. Those who were mobile but couldn't walk and were fed by others, they calculated, were likely to live an estimated twenty-three additional years from the time of study. The next group, who were fully immobile but could eat, could expect to live an additional eight years. The third, most "medically fragile" group had a "very short life expectancy"—only four to five more years from the time their records were reviewed. These were people, like Little Tony, who were immobile, incontinent, and required tube feeding.

The study was peculiar. Based exclusively on statistics, it relied on the same predictions regardless of age and precise medical status. It had far greater value to malpractice defendants and insurers than to physicians, since its conclusions were largely economic and avoided any mention of treatment. Still, publication in *NEJM,* loosely affiliated with Harvard Medical School, was a strong endorsement of scientific validity, and it had brought Grossman a certain notoriety and a lucrative second career as a medical-legal consultant—as Bernard put it, "traveling around the country predicting death for kids like Tony."

Bernard had spent three days in his office preparing to cross-examine Grossman, twice as long as for any other defense expert in *Sabia,* yet he had been unable to plow through all the transcripts from other cases in which Grossman had testified. He'd flown out to Michigan the day before, worried anew about how long Little Tony would live and whether he would last until trial. The longer the case dragged on, the more pressing this issue became. Life expectancy was the key measure for both sides in valuing the case, and the major stumbling block to settling. With the latest delay, Bernard and Koskoff feared losing everything if *Sabia* was delayed much longer.

Earlier in the week, Bernard had talked with Dr. Lawrence Kaplan, whom he'd recently hired to examine Little Tony and give another opinion as to how long he might live. Kaplan had told him that, "clinically speaking"— based on his medical examination, not statistics—he thought Tony had a normal life expectancy. He'd also agreed to testify, though he said he was reluctant to do so. Bernard had been reassured. Now, sitting across from Doyle and Hunt in a court reporter's office in Ann Arbor, Bernard planned to undermine Grossman and his statistics in order to support Kaplan's strict medical evaluation.

He doubted it would be difficult. Grossman, who'd become interested in the life expectancy of severely retarded and disabled people more than thirty years earlier and was something of a pioneer in the field, appeared to make Doyle uncomfortable. He seemed almost a caricature of the shopworn professional testifier, so at home in the offices of the court reporting firm where he regularly testified that he had his own coffee cup there. "A strange man . . . a lonely man," Doyle would say. Bernard wasn't displeased to see Doyle's discomfort. He interpreted it as a sign of the other side's desperation.

"Doctor," Bernard said after walking Grossman through a brief recital of his credentials, "during the past year, how many depositions have you given on a monthly basis?"

"I have no idea."

"When was the last time you gave a deposition?"

Grossman thought. "I believe earlier this week," he said.

"And how many depositions have you given this month?"

"That I can't remember."

"Today is the twenty-ninth. Think about it for a minute. Any idea how many?"

"Oh," Grossman said, as if recalling, "there may have been one more. I can't remember."

"So it would be two or three this month?"

"Maybe. Two definitely, maybe three."

"How about last month?"

"I have no idea."

"Is it unusual for you to give two or three depositions in a month?" Bernard asked.

"That would be high," Grossman said.

"What is it usually?"

"Maybe one, sometimes two."

"For how long have you been giving depositions in medical negligence cases?"

"Oh, let's see, about ten or twelve years."

Bernard persisted. "And in the past year, how many times have you testified in court?"

"I'm not sure. I don't really know. No more than—I'm trying to think. Maybe two or three. I can't really remember."

"Is that about average for you, two or three times a year?"

"Oh, sometimes it's not at all."

"Sometimes it's not at all?"

"Or maybe two or three. I suppose once in a while it might be more, but I can't remember."

"When was the last time you testified in court?"

"I think that was earlier this year."

"Where was that?"

"In California."

"What month was that?"

"I think it was February."

"Can you tell me," Bernard asked, "on average about how many medical-legal cases you review on a monthly basis?"

"I have no idea."

"How many have you reviewed this month?"

"I don't know that either."

"Can you give me an estimate?"

"No," Grossman said. "I think certainly those that were related to the depositions, but other than that I can't say. Maybe an additional one, two. I really don't know. I don't keep any records."

Bernard arched an eyebrow. "You don't keep any records of cases you've reviewed?"

"I mean," Grossman responded, "they're sitting in piles."

"So you mean in terms of numbers you don't keep any records?" Bernard said.

"That's correct."

"Am I correct, Dr. Grossman, that the vast majority of testimony that you've given in court and at deposition is where you've been retained by the defense to give opinions regarding reduced life expectancy?"

"Yes," Grossman admitted.

"And have you ever testified in court on behalf of a plaintiff in a medical negligence case?"

"Yes."

"On how many occasions?"

"One or two."

"And that was over the course of the last ten or twelve years?"

"Yes."

"Do I understand, Dr. Grossman, that you are a full-time employee of the University of Michigan?"

"Yes," Grossman said.

"And when you testify in medical-legal cases, does the money go to you or to the university?"

"To me."

"Can you tell me what your fees are currently for reviewing medical-legal matters?"

"Three hundred and fifty dollars an hour."

"And for deposition time?"

"Four hundred and fifty dollars an hour."

"And for trial time?"

"Trial, actual testimony would be four hundred fifty dollars. Other time would be three hundred fifty an hour."

"When you say other time, that would be travel time?"

"Travel time, waiting time."

"So you charge door-to-door three hundred fifty dollars an hour, except for the time that you are in court?"

"Not necessarily door-to-door. I don't charge for eating. I don't charge for sleeping."

"I take it you're reimbursed for travel expenses."

"Yes."

"Do you travel first-class?"

"Usually," Grossman said, "but I get a reduced rate. You'll find that out when you get older."

"Dr. Grossman," Bernard continued, "in 1992, how much money did you make from your consulting in medical legal work?"

"I don't know," he said.

"You keep records of *that,* don't you?" Bernard asked.

"Oh, yes."

"And you report that to the IRS."

"Absolutely."

"And you have those records going back three years."

"Yes."

"Can you tell me what percentage of your income comes from this type of work?"

"No."

"You can't tell me or you won't tell me?" Bernard blurted.

"I can't," Grossman said.

"You have no idea?"

"No," Grossman said. "My wife keeps all those records. I don't. I sign them."

"And you have no idea what the total amount is that you earn from this kind of work?"

"No."

Bernard redirected his attack. "Dr. Grossman, with regard to Tony Sabia's medical condition, I would like for you to list for me all the factors which are relevant to your prediction of his life expectancy."

"He's profoundly retarded in all spheres of function, including mental," Grossman began. "He's immobile. He has a paucity and almost no meaningful voluntary movements, including his upper extremities. He is totally dependent. He is incontinent. He is fed primarily by gastrostomy. He also has a seizure disorder which is not a primary correlation, but he has that problem, too. He's totally immobile."

Bernard went on. "Now, I'd like to ask you some questions about Tony Sabia's condition. First, do you know the cause or etiology of his injuries?"

"No."

"Do you know the timing of his injuries."

"Not precisely."

"Can you tell me what his current weight is?"

"No."

"Do you know what his current caloric intake is?"

"No."

"Do you know anything about his ability to take in any nourishment by mouth?"

"Minimal."

"Do you know what percentage of calories he takes in by mouth?"

"No."

"Do you know what his head circumference is?"

"No."

"What his present medications are?"

"No."

"Do you know if he has any respiratory difficulties."

"The last year has been quite good," Grossman said. "He has had a history of difficulties in the past, but not recently."

"Do you know if Tony Sabia has shallow breathing?" Bernard asked.

"I can't say. There's not a lot of reference to respiratory excursions in these records."

"Do you know if he has impaired ability to cough?"

"That's not clear either. It's probably so, but I can't give you an exact answer."

"Do you know how often he gets physical therapy?"

"No."

"Occupational therapy?"

"No."

"Speech therapy?"

"No."

"Do you know what his IQ is?"

"Not by number, but certainly clinically he is profoundly retarded."

"And by definition," Bernard said, "what would the range of numbers be?"

"Below twenty, twenty-five," Grossman said. "That is very obvious, unfortunately."

Bernard paused. He still believed his strongest argument in terms of life expectancy was that Little Tony was a person, not a statistic, and that he had already defied heavy odds. He also knew that Grossman's role in conducting the California study was largely that of a consultant, someone who examined data, not people, and rendered judgments from a comfortable distance. Grossman's publications might confer academic legitimacy, but Bernard thought he could trump it by depicting Grossman as less a physician than a macabre social engineer and statistician.

"Doctor," he began again, "how many of the one hundred thousand people in this study did you examine?"

"Few, if any," Grossman said.

"Is it few or is it any?"

"I said, few, if any."

"Do you know if you examined *any* of them?" Bernard asked.

"I might have," Grossman said. He had worked in California before moving to Michigan. "But not for the purpose of this study."

"You didn't examine any of these people for this study?" Bernard clarified.

"None of those clients were examined by any of the investigators for the purpose of this study," Grossman said.

"Did you fill out the questionnaires for any of these people?"

"No," Grossman said.

"Did you observe any of these questionnaires being completed by any-body?"

"No."

Bernard was not surprised. There was a growing body of scientific litera-ture that had arisen not out of the normal channels of inquiry and investiga-tion but to succor defendants in malpractice cases; studies, for instance, that challenged the correlation between birth injury and brain damage. Bernard put Grossman's *NEJM* article in that category. He expected less-than-rigorous methods, just as he expected skewed conclusions.

"Would I be correct, Dr. Grossman, that adults who did not continue to receive services from the California Department of Developmental Services would not have been included in this population?" he asked.

"People who drop out are dropped," Grossman said, "whether they're adults or children."

"And in terms of the people who died during the time period of this study, the cause of death for over ninety percent of them was not available?"

"That is correct."

"And in fact you didn't use the cause of death in this study in any re-spect?"

"It wasn't discussed," Grossman said.

"Do you know, by the way, Dr. Grossman, how many of the people who died during this study died in car accidents?"

"No."

"Do you know how many died in fires?"

"No."

"Do you know how many died from abuse or neglect?"

"No."

"Am I correct, Dr. Grossman, that Tony Sabia would be categorized in Subgroup One in this study?" Subgroup One were those with the shortest life expectancy.

"Yes," Grossman said.

"And how old was the oldest person in that subgroup?"

"Well, if you look at the census, there are one-point-six percent over fifty, and I think somewhere—oh, somebody reached sixty-one, I think."

"Do you know what the etiology is of the damage to the person who reached sixty-one?" Bernard asked.

"No," Grossman said.

"What is the age of the oldest person who you would categorize in Group One that you've ever seen?" Bernard continued.

"Oh, I may have seen somebody in the sixth decade of life, but they are very, very uncommon. Obviously it's possible. Highly unlikely, but it's possible."

"Dr. Grossman," Bernard said. "Without regard to probabilities, do you have an opinion as to how old Tony Sabia could possibly live to be?"

Doyle interrupted sharply: "I object to the form of the question." He wanted Grossman's testimony held tight to the study. He didn't want him speculating.

"No," Grossman said. "It's an impossible answer. We can only talk in probabilities. Otherwise you're talking about the lottery."

"Now, Doctor," Bernard said. "If I was to categorize—if I were to be able to categorize a person into a particular subgroup, and I knew which table to look at and which line to read it off of, and I were to come up with the number, is that all I would have to do to come up with a life expectancy for that individual?"

Doyle again jumped in: "I'm going to object to the form of the question."

"I don't know," Grossman said. "Maybe, maybe not."

"Under some circumstances it might be accurate and some circumstances it might not?" Bernard asked.

"Well, let's say you know somebody smokes four packs of cigarettes a day," Grossman explained. "Is he going to have a shortened life expectancy? Probably. Inevitably? No."

"So what you're telling me," Bernard said, "is that there may be other factors that are not included within the characteristics of the subgroup that may affect life expectancy one way or the other?"

"No," Grossman complained, "that's not what I said. There may be other characteristics in the reader."

"In the reader?" Bernard asked, curbing his incredulity.

"Whoever is reading the article."

"I don't understand."

"In terms of knowledge, experience, sophistication."

"What difference," Bernard asked, "does my knowledge or experience or sophistication have to do, Dr. Grossman, with reading a number off a table?"

"Object to the form of the question," Doyle snapped. "He's not here, and he's not going to give his testimony just by reading a number off of a table. He's read and studied Tony Sabia's medical records. He's looked at both the videotapes of Tony. He has his own clinical experience, and he's giving an opinion based upon all of that and not simply reading. So I don't understand the point of the question."

"The point of the question," Bernard responded, "for your edification and the doctor's, is whether it is necessary, once we know what subgroup to put Tony in, to have other information in order to come up with an estimate of life expectancy."

Grossman interceded. "Yes and no," he said. "Because those are guide-lines, that's all. Our studies are ongoing. They confirm our original hypothe-sis. That's all I can tell you. It's a yes-and-no answer."

Bernard continued. "Doctor, do you have an opinion with reasonable medical probability as to what Tony Sabia will die of?"

"Most probable is some respiratory compromise or infection," Grossman answered.

"Can you be more specific?"

"No."

"Do you know what the course will be of that respiratory infection?"

"Usually, it's insidious. It's a series of repeated episodes. It's rarely one episode."

"Do you know how many episodes he'll have before he dies?" Bernard asked.

"No."

"Do you know how he'll be treated when he has these episodes?"

"No."

"Do you know how long it will be from the onset of these episodes to the time they are diagnosed and treated?"

"No," Grossman conceded.

"Dr. Grossman," Bernard asked, "in how many of the cases where you have predicted an early death for a plaintiff have you gone back to check to see if you were right?"

"None."

"I don't have any other questions," Bernard concluded.

"No questions," Doyle said, not wanting to hear anything further from Grossman.

$$\sim \sim \sim$$

Much of a lawyer's job is to deny publicly what is known privately. Doyle re-alized it would be dangerous to let Grossman answer questions in front of a jury. Nevertheless, he continued to brandish his testimony, vowing to use it in court. Koskoff had had the same problem with Iffy and, perhaps, Schifrin, al-though Schifrin had powerful credentials and a record of reversing seemingly weak preparations with bravura court performances.

Doyle still thought he had a "decent case" on damages. He had Susan Far-rell, who actually treated children like Little Tony. And he had Grossman's sta-tistics, which despite his record and research methods "are very compelling as to what happens to people who are immobile," Doyle says. What he didn't have was much faith that claiming that Little Tony was likely to die soon would stand up well either to Koskoff's argument that "only God" knew how long he would live or, more to the point, to the onerous cost projections for lifelong medical care posed by Koskoff's chief damage expert, Larry Forman. "If the jury gets to the point that you caused it and you were wrong, are they going to take a chance on life expectancy? I don't think so," Doyle says. "Arguing that there's a lot of water in Forman's stuff is fair. But Jesus, how do you look doing that? Are you going to try a case by saying you can buy that wheelchair for thirty-nine ninety-five instead of eighty-nine ninety-five? Or you can buy a used one. You can't. They'll kill you for that."

Doyle's problem was how to make Koskoff think he could lose against such a defense, while persuading Travelers it most likely would backfire. "I wanted to worry Michael, obviously," he recalls. "And the life expectancy issue did concern him the most, as it should have."

It was Travelers that was harder to persuade. The company had yet to see any compelling reason why it should pay up to $14.5 million to support a child who, its own experts were predicting, wouldn't live more than a few more years. Hence Doyle's bind. The more he promoted Grossman's figures as real, the more Travelers believed them, and the more it resisted settling. Casey had hired him to advise Travelers what to do, but Casey couldn't authorize an eight-figure settlement on the basis of Doyle's fears about unsympathetic jurors. Nor would Doyle, who was being paid to develop a winning defense, ask him to. What they needed was more data, something to justify their paying a higher price to resolve the case.

On November 10, eleven days after Grossman's deposition, Judge Ballen's office sent Doyle and Koskoff identical computerized letters telling them to be in court on December 8 to pick a new trial date. After receiving the notices, the two of them talked, and Doyle proposed a second mediation. This time, he said, they should get "a couple of lawyers" who, unlike Ferguson, might be able to tell them what the case was really worth and how a jury would most likely decide. Koskoff agreed. Despite his usual bravado, he knew his case also had weaknesses that could blow up in court. *Sabia* was rife, even after nearly seven years of investigation, with unanswered and unanswerable questions: What was the standard of care? Had it been violated? What killed Twin B? Could the death have been prevented? How long would Little Tony live?

Koskoff was too smart and too competitive to think he wouldn't win, but he knew juries were fickle. That was why he was willing to discuss settling. Yet the dynamics of settlement were such that it was Doyle's clout with Travelers, not his own abilities, that would be the crucial factor in any deal. Indeed, this was why he'd welcomed Doyle into the case and had yielded to his request for a continuance—an agreement he'd begun to regret more each day. Koskoff liked to counsel other lawyers: "The case always settles for the other side's figure. All kinds of people on the other side have to look good—claims managers, claims adjusters—and the only way for them to look good is by not giving me exactly what I want. The art," he told them, "is to get them to come up with a number I like." If Doyle thought a couple of big hitters backing him up would help his credibility with Travelers, Koskoff was happy to oblige.

They agreed that each side would pick one lawyer, subject to the other's approval. The arrangement guaranteed three things: that the mediators would be people that Koskoff and Doyle both knew and trusted; that they'd be "players," drawn from the small circle of top litigators who handled most of Connecticut's major personal injury and insurance cases; and that, because of this, their personal and professional entanglements with both sides would be complicated. Connecticut is a small state; there are counties in Montana that are larger, and Alabama has more people. Koskoff and Doyle knew they'd be fishing in the same shallow pool.

Doyle's choice was an urbane, conspicuously well-to-do New Haven plaintiff's lawyer named Stanley Jacobs. Jacobs, sixty-seven, was perhaps best known for winning the largest birth injury verdict in state history, $9.7 million. That victory put him one up on Koskoff, to the extent that they trolled for the same kinds of cases and competed for bragging rights. The patriarch of a small, elite firm, like Ted Koskoff he embodied the flamboyant style of an earlier breed—those mostly first- and second-generation Jewish and Irish lawyers who, excluded from establishment firms, had taken personal injury cases and alchemized them into unrepentant high living.

Jacobs was trim and fit, a bald bullet of a man with a corona of close-cropped grey curls and a prominent nose; he looked like Mike Koskoff might look in twenty years. He spoke Italian, peppering his summations with quotes from Dante, owned a substantial sailboat, and liked to boast that he played tennis with David Halberstam on Nantucket, where he summered. His office, on one of the top floors of a gleaming waterfront business tower, treated clients to sweeping views of Long Island Sound. Yet Jacobs professed no pleasure at the source of his prosperity. "There's no sense of triumph with these cases," he says sorrowfully, "just an overwhelming sadness. I never celebrate them. Even after a big verdict, I'm suffering because all I could get my clients, who've been brutalized by the most appalling malpractice, was money."

Doyle wanted Jacobs mainly because he thought he was a more conservative negotiator than Koskoff. He and Jacobs had been on opposite sides in numerous cases, some of which had settled. He knew what Jacobs was willing to accept behind closed doors, and thought he could use it as ballast in *Sabia*. He had even represented Jacobs when he and his brother, his former law partner, fell out and were suing each other over the breakup of the firm. "I've always been able to do business with Stanley," Doyle would say. "He's got this Jewish shtick; he's always telling Abie and Rosie jokes. But dealing with him is entirely different than dealing with Michael. Michael gives up nothing when you're talking with him about a case. He asks for too much, and what's frustrating is you don't know whether he means it or not. With Stanley that's not a problem." Although at the time Doyle had a major birth trauma case against Jacobs and he worried that Jacobs might inflate his assessment on *Sabia* to gain leverage in that other case, he neutralized his fear by telling himself that, as Koskoff's "biggest competitor," Jacobs would also have an interest in valuing *Sabia* on the low side.

Koskoff was pleased with Doyle's choice. He thought Jacobs could listen to both sides in *Sabia* and give an independent appraisal, something Ferguson couldn't do. Moreover, there was another, deeper connection between them. The Koskoffs and Jacobses went back generations. Stanley's father, Izzy, had been a friend of Koskoff's grandfather. The families had summered together in Woodmont, a Jewish enclave on the Sound. Jacobs considered the Koskoffs "the quintessential Russian Jewish family," and though he and Michael were not close, they understood each other. Whatever their rivalry, Koskoff knew he could rely on Jacobs to give his honest judgment.

Koskoff's own choice was Tony Fitzgerald, his cocounsel in the Sponge Rubber case. A widely respected New Haven trial lawyer, Fitzgerald, forty-eight, hadn't handled a medical malpractice case in years and was best known for corporate defense work, but Koskoff considered him a "really smart guy," and Doyle agreed. He had grown up in Waterbury, a rusting milltown north of Bridgeport, where his father, William, a Harvard-trained lawyer, was a former state's attorney and pillar both of the local bar and the city's dominant Catholic laity. In 1938, before the younger Fitzgerald was born, Bill Fitzgerald's twin fealties to the law and the church merged when he prosecuted a local clinic for distributing birth control information—the first such case anywhere in the country.

Tony Fitzgerald inherited from his father a first-rate mind yoked to a sense of high moral purpose. He'd gone to Yale, then to Columbia Law School, graduating cum laude from both before returning to Waterbury in 1969 to enter practice with his father and brother. After quickly becoming one of the best young trial lawyers in the state, he'd engineered a merger with Carmody & Torrance, an old-line Waterbury corporate firm, moved it to New Haven, and built it into a litigation powerhouse with fifty-five lawyers. He was six-five, wore monogrammed shirts and aviator glasses, and had a self-conscious, Bill Bradleyish air of being both smarter and having more expected of him than the people around him. His work on the Sponge Rubber trial alone would have been enough to recommend him to both Koskoff and Doyle. However wrenching, especially for Koskoff, that trial had been "very much an above-the-belt fight" that "in a funny kind of way solidified things between the three of us," Fitzgerald recalls.

He was connected to them in other ways. He and Doyle frequently referred cases to each other when they had conflicts. Doyle's wife, also a lawyer, had worked for Fitzgerald at Carmody & Torrance, and the couples had become social friends. Fitzgerald had also trained Bernard, whose first job out of law school was with Carmody & Torrance and who had worked there until joining the Koskoffs. And Fitzgerald was now opposed to Koskoff in an already famous industrial liability case now slouching through discovery. Families living near an electrical substation in New Haven had sued the local power company, United Illuminating, blaming it for a cluster of brain tumors in their neighborhood. The *New Yorker* had featured the case in a controversial two-part story investigating the link between electromagnetic fields and cancer.

It would have been hard to find another lawyer so enmeshed with, and so respected by, both sides, yet when Koskoff, after clearing it with Doyle, called Fitzgerald to ask him to mediate, Fitzgerald resisted. "I don't think I'm really the right guy," he said. "I'm just not steeped in the issues." Pressing, Koskoff told him not to worry. They were also asking Stanley Jacobs, he said, who knew brain-damaged-baby cases as well as anyone. What they needed was someone they both could trust. Fitzgerald, a federal court-appointed special master and certified mediator, recognized the problem. He believed that mediation was probably the most "socially efficient" way of resolving disputes, both because it had become harder and harder to get to trial and because the "barbaric level of unhappiness on both sides" made having "a major winner and a major loser" less and less palatable to everyone. Finally, he agreed.

After several more phone calls, the issue was decided. Koskoff and Doyle, careful to dampen their clients' expectations, scheduled a second mediation in Koskoff's office for mid-December, after the status conference with Ballen but before the earliest date for a trial. Then they resumed their game faces, girding themselves for court, posturing, hoping not to peak too soon.

TWENTY-FOUR

KOSKOFF GLADLY BROKE HIS OWN RULE—AVOIDING THE OTHER SIDE'S WITNESSES before trial—to depose Doyle's last expert. Dr. Richard Jones III was an eminent-looking, nationally known ob-gyn from Hartford with a Yale pedigree. Unlike Lockwood, he didn't specialize in high-risk births, nor did he seem too young to be an authority. He was a senior nonacademic physician whom Doyle had hired to defend Norwalk Hospital's decision not to do late-stage ultrasounds during Donna's pregnancy. At fifty-nine, Jones was retired from obstetrics, but he was Doyle's last best shot to imbue his liability defense with some maturity; he would play Marcus Welby to Lockwood's Doogie Howser.

Koskoff believed he could "demolish" Jones at deposition: an old-boy and a nonspecialist, he was bound to be out of his depth regarding a rare, complicated case like Donna's. But like Bernard with Grossman, Koskoff wanted Jones in court. Having deposed Jones once before, he had neither the advantage of surprise to preserve, nor any fear that he might like Jones too much to go at him hard at trial. Both knew exactly how they felt about the other. Koskoff thought Jones a richly deserving target; Jones detested Koskoff and all he stood for—a "parasite," he called him.

Their hostility was as much political as personal. Jones was immediate past president of the American College of Obstetricians and Gynecologists (ACOG), with 35,000 members the profession's main lobbying group. ACOG was to ob-gyns what ATLA was to plaintiffs' lawyers—a powerful champion charged with advancing their interests in Washington. In the twenty-year fight over medical malpractice now coming to a head with the Clinton health-care plan, the two groups were avowed enemies, the most militant proxies for the nation's doctors and lawyers in their battle over liability reform. Thus the enmity between Koskoff and Jones. Jones was a respected national spokesman for curbing malpractice suits against doctors, especially obstetricians; Koskoff, a scion of ATLA, was an apostle for the rights of victims of bad med-ical outcomes to sue. Meeting in *Sabia* was a rare chance for each to attack the other's side not in the statehouse or in trade journals but in the trenches. "Who better," Koskoff would ask, "than the man who'd been the chief of all the obstetricians and gynecologists in the country to be the expert on stan-dard of care?"

Who, indeed? In the war between doctors and lawyers, standard of care was the most fiercely contested front, and Jones was identified with what many lawyers deemed its most infamous offensive. In January 1992, at around the time of the Humes settlement and when Jones was ACOG's incoming president, the organization released a long-awaited "technical bulletin" on the relationship between fetal-monitoring and brain injury. Best-known by its publication number, 163, the document was largely an educational advisory, telling ob-gyns of the latest medical findings about the link between birth as-phyxia and cerebral palsy. One-Sixty-Three was also a legal and financial bombshell. Estimating that only about 10 percent of cerebral palsy in term in-fants involved a loss of oxygen, and only then when the asphyxia was "nearly lethal," the authors concluded that there was "no evidence" that neonatal hy-poxia accounted significantly for cerebral palsy. They also cited recent con-troversial studies showing that there had been no drop in cerebral palsy rates despite the near-universal use of electronic fetal monitoring in American hos-pitals. EFM tracings, the authors wrote, "[do] not reduce the risk of cerebral palsy when compared with frequent auscultation [listening, with a device like a stethoscope]" and "are only fair predictors of fetal asphyxia."

Here was an attempt to sweep away what the authors called the "continu-ing misperception," rooted in William Little's observations more than 140 years earlier, that cerebral palsy resulted from a loss of oxygen at or near birth and that doctors should thus be able to prevent it. The brief also undermined the very basis for most brain-damaged-baby suits—the presumption that fe-tal monitoring can foretell future injury. To plaintiffs' lawyers it was a bald at-tempt by obstetricians to shield themselves from liability by establishing their own ex cathedra standard of care.

Trial lawyers attacked 163 as a tissue of lies, an example of organized medicine cynically perpetuating junk science to relieve itself of blame for its mistakes. Schifrin, whose medical career—and status as a pariah—was based on upholding EFM as a way to make ob-gyns more accountable, railed against

163 as "a fiction . . . created out of vapor to defend doctors." Jones, who had not written the report but was closely associated with it as former chairman of the committee that had prepared it, soon found his name on an ATLA most wanted list posted on a bulletin board in a Hartford courthouse.

If Koskoff couldn't wait to get at Jones, Jones wanted equally to have at him. He blamed Koskoff and those like him for all the ills of the malpractice industry and, in a more general sense, for the breakdown in society he believed that industry exemplified. Jones came from hickory-hard Connecticut Yankee stock. He was about six feet tall, with wispy white hair and thin-boned-yet-sturdy patrician good looks. After attending Exeter, Yale, and the University of Virginia Medical School, he served as an army major in Germany before going into obstetrics. He favored hand-tooled cowboy boots and lived in a handsome house atop a bluff overlooking Farmington, a prototypically prosperous New England town that had become a wealthy Hartford suburb. Jones liked to point down from a guesthouse on his property to Farmington's Town Farm Road, named more than two hundred years before for the local poor farm, and admire the ideals of puritan New England, which, he says, "had a system in place to take care of people who couldn't take care of themselves." An heir to those ideals, he was appalled by a civil justice system he considered neither civil nor just. He hated the idea that the only way to sustain people like the Sabias through unexpected losses was to find someone to blame.

Jones compared lawyers to "gorillas, always posturing." This bellicosity, he believed, was a show, but since those who put on the best show won, they were rewarded more for their bullying than for discovering the truth. "Michael Koskoff is a pro at it," he would say. "He makes an insane amount of money. Most people who appear before him are terribly intimidated by him." Jones claimed to feel unthreatened, seeing himself as a kind of avenger who, because of his status and power—and the fact that he could no longer be sued in bad baby cases because he'd stopped doing deliveries—had a responsibility to stand up to Koskoff even if he hadn't a prayer of winning.

Sitting now in a conference room at Wiggin & Dana, nineteen floors above the neo-Gothic spires of the Yale campus, Jones bristled with indignation. He likened depositions to "an exam where the lawyer's got the open book and you're supposed to answer out of your head." He doubted that he would be a match for Schifrin, who "most of us view as a terrible waste, a guy of enormous talent who could put it to better use." He even believed that Koskoff "could make mincemeat out of me in terms of my credibility and factual knowledge" and that he himself was a "minor league parasite" for collaborating for pay in an exercise he despised. Yet he had watched his profession fill up with people like Humes, people who'd been sued and were terrified of being sued again. "You become emotionally unglued, your sex life goes to pot, you can't sleep," he says. And so he resolved not to stand down, to try to "turn the tables."

Contrary to expectations, Koskoff led off breezily, with a series of questions designed less to embarrass Jones for his lack of specialized credentials than to establish just where he got his information. He seemed to go out of his way to bolster Jones's credibility, declining at one point to follow up when Jones mentioned that he himself had once been sued for malpractice, then showing absolutely no interest when Jones volunteered to tell him how the case was decided. Coddling Jones almost as if he were his own witness, Koskoff questioned him for more than an hour without once seriously trying to impeach him. Then, broaching the issue of standard of care, Koskoff turned suddenly more aggressive, pelting Jones with leading questions.

First he asked him to enumerate the increased risks in twin pregnancies as they were known in 1983. Jones answered with the first two to come to mind—maternal diabetes and prematurity. Then Koskoff asked him if there were others, specifically velamentous cord insertion, the splaying of the umbilical arteries that had put Michael Sabia at risk. When Jones conceded that that, too, was a risk, Koskoff pressed him for specifics. What percentage of twins had the problem, Koskoff asked.

Jones was already beyond his area of expertise. This was a question to which a regular ob-gyn wouldn't be expected to know the answer. Benirschke, Schifrin, and Lockwood would know, but probably not someone who wasn't steeped in the physiology of multiple pregnancies. Jones sputtered, "I can't tell you, but I—"

"Would it be fewer than one percent," Koskoff interrupted coolly, "or greater than one percent?"

"I don't know the number," Jones said, "but you're certainly not talking, you know, ten or fifteen or twenty percent. I mean, one to five percent, I would suspect."

"One to five percent?" Koskoff asked.

"If that," Jones said.

"And five percent would be a significant incidence, wouldn't it?" Koskoff said.

"I say, if that," Jones said. "But let's go back. In 1983, in fact even now, there's no way to diagnose it—"

Koskoff lunged to rein Jones in. "I didn't ask you that question," he snapped.

"Just a second," Doyle said. "You may not like his answer—"

"I don't like it when he answers questions that aren't asked, to try to get little things in," Koskoff said. "Now if he's going to answer my question—"

"I don't like it when you interrupt him before he finishes," Doyle fumed.

"I think he finished—"

"Don't interrupt him."

"Doctor," Koskoff continued, "were velamentous cord insertions a threat to a pregnancy and to a fetus?" Again, it was an area Jones was unlikely to have any special knowledge about, other than what he'd read in general texts and experienced in his own practice.

"Obviously, if they had it, they would have been," he replied.

"And they can result in all kinds of problems, intrapartum, can't they?"

"Of course."

"They can result in intrauterine growth retardation, can't they?"

"They can."

"They can result in failure to thrive of a fetus, can't they?"

"They can."

"And they're significantly greater in twin pregnancies than in nontwin pregnancies, aren't they?"

"As I say, I don't know the number, but they are more frequent."

"And that was known in 1983, wasn't it?"

"It was."

"They can result in unequal placentation, can't they?" Koskoff asked.

"No, I don't think velamentous insertion is part of the etiology of unequal placentation," Jones said.

"Are you familiar with Dr. Kurt Benirschke?" Koskoff asked. He wanted Jones to know that his last assertion wouldn't go unchallenged.

"Yes," Jones said.

"Is he an authority when it comes to the placenta?"

"I think so."

"And what about vascular anastomoses?"—the communication of the twins' blood flow through the placenta.

"What about it?" Doyle complained. He didn't like Koskoff lording it over his witness.

Koskoff ignored him. "Are they present in twin pregnancies?" he asked Jones.

"Yes," Jones said.

"And do you know whether vascular anastomoses poses a threat to twin pregnancies?"

"Well, some more than others, but the answer is yes."

"And discordancy. Is that something that also can occur in twin pregnancies?"

"That's correct."

"And you knew about that prior to 1983, about discordancy, didn't you?"

"Yes," Jones answered.

"And what is the incidence of discordancy in twin pregnancies?"

"I don't have an answer for that."

"But it would be infrequent?"

"Infrequent."

"And what is the effect of discordancy, if any, on the risk posed, the risk of morbidity and mortality"—injury and death—"to the babies?"

"It depends on the degree you're talking about," Jones said. "If you're talking about a fifty percent difference in size and weight, that has far more significance than ten percent." Your "index of suspicion" goes up, he added, when you reach a certain degree of disparity.

"And what's the degree?" Koskoff asked.

"Well, it's variously quoted, but around twenty percent difference."

"And that is considered significant discordancy, isn't it?"

"Yes."

"And so there is some degree of discordancy that you as an obstetrician would not have to be concerned about and others that you would have to be concerned about?"

"Yes."

"And that was true in 1983?"

"Yes."

Koskoff was approaching the core of his case. The discordancy between the twins at birth was eighteen percent—a shade less than Jones himself agreed would warrant medical suspicion. The hospital had measured an identical disparity earlier on, at the time of Donna's second ultrasound, on January 5. Both times, the percentage was sufficient, given the margin of error, to arouse concern, yet the hospital neglected to do the one test that would have confirmed that the twins were in trouble.

Proceeding slowly, Koskoff moved to ensnare Jones in his own trap.

"How would you tell," he asked, "if there *was* discordancy?"

"Well," Jones began, "the only way you can tell about how babies are growing obviously is initially by clinical examination. You try to see how big the uterus is as to whether that's a clue that you should be looking for uterine size and total fetal growth, then with ultrasound."

"The only way to tell the degree of discordancy is by ultrasound, isn't it?" Koskoff asked.

"That's correct."

"And where there is discordancy in excess of twenty percent or in that area, what is the increased risk of morbidity and mortality?"

"I can't give you a percentage number. It's significant. I don't—"

"And what is the type of morbidity that is most frequently associated with this type of discordancy?"

"Well, it depends," Jones said. "If the babies are delivered early, one may tend to be more mature than the other."

"What I mean," Koskoff clarified, "is the morbidity. Brain damage is morbidity, isn't it?"

"Surely."

"And cerebral palsy is morbidity, isn't it?"

"Correct."

"And these are very, very serious conditions, aren't they?"

"Yes."

"And as a conscientious obstetrician in 1983, you'd want to do what you could, wouldn't you, to prevent these things from happening?"

"Of course."

"And death can result from discordancy, or be associated with discordancy, can't it?" Koskoff said.

"Yes."

"And you certainly want to prevent a fetal death if you possibly can, don't you?"

"Correct."

"Are you familiar, Doctor, with intrauterine growth retardation?"

"Yes," Jones said.

"And that's something that can occur in twin pregnancies, too, isn't it?" Koskoff continued.

"Correct."

"And where there is discordancy, one twin can be growth-retarded and the other twin not growth-retarded; isn't that right?"

"That's correct."

"And how would—in that situation where one twin is growth-retarded, is there an increase in morbidity and mortality in growth-retarded twins?"

"Yes."

"And do you have an idea of the extent of that increase?"

"I can't give you a percentage," Jones said.

"It's a significant increase, though, isn't it?" Koskoff asked.

"Yes."

"And, again, the morbidity we're talking about can encompass brain damage, cerebral palsy, those types of conditions?"

"Yes."

"And death."

"Yes."

"Mortality," Koskoff echoed. "And there were methods available in 1983 for diagnosing intrauterine growth retardation in twin pregnancies?"

"Yes."

"What was the method?"

"Principally ultrasound," Jones said.

Koskoff was racing now to close all the doors.

"And in order to make the diagnosis one would have to use the ultra-sound; isn't that right?" he asked.

"That's correct."

"Doctor," Koskoff said, "do you know what the cost of an ultrasound was in 1983?"

"No."

"Would forty dollars be considered a reasonable cost for an ultrasound in 1983?"

"Perhaps. Probably less than a hundred dollars, anyway."

"So for less than a hundred dollars a doctor can have a patient undergo an ultrasound?"

"I assume so. I don't know what they charged in Norwalk in 1983, but I suppose."

"Now, in 1983," Koskoff asked, "what would be required to be done in a pregnancy where discordancy was found?"

"Again, depending on the definition. If it's minimal discordancy, I would think nothing would be done. If it's an enormous amount of discordancy, more than twenty, twenty-five percent, then I think that more surveillance should be done."

"What type of surveillance?"

"I think another ultrasound would be done."

"And if the discordancy is going to be in the third trimester, you'd have to do an ultrasound in the third trimester to diagnose it, wouldn't you?"

"Yes," Jones said.

"And one of the things you would have to do if you had diagnosed dis-cordancy in the third trimester is you'd have to do fetal well-being studies, wouldn't you?"

"We would now. I don't—in 1983 that was not the standard."

"Did you know—did you have nonstress tests available in 1983?"

"We did."

"And you would have had to make an ongoing assessment, would you not, as to whether or not the fetus was better off in the womb or delivered?"

Here was Koskoff's main claim: Norwalk Hospital should have known the twins were in distress and taken them earlier. Jones avoided the trap. He said that he had gone back over texts from the period and records from his own group practice to "figure out when it was that that sort of became what we were doing" and that he had concluded that in 1983 and 1984 nonstress test-ing in twin pregnancies was not required "automatically" because it was twins. "We just weren't doing it. We would now," he said. What he failed to say was whether he'd have done such testing if an ultrasound had revealed that the twins were developing unequally.

Koskoff pressed him, but indirectly. "Once you diagnose discordancy, this becomes a high-risk pregnancy?" he asked.

"Okay," Jones said.

"And you have to make an assessment then as to whether or not the fetus is better off in the mother's womb or delivered at some point?"

"Yes. At some—okay."

"And that assessment is going to be made upon all the data that you could have available to you?"

"Okay."

"Now, one of the negative things about getting the baby out, delivering the baby, is that the lungs may not be mature?"

"That's right."

"In fact, it's the primary problem, isn't it?"

"Yes."

"And once the lungs are mature, you would presume that the baby is capable of surviving in the outside world; isn't that right?"

"Yes."

"And so once the lungs are mature, it becomes essentially better to take the baby out than to have them in a high-risk environment; isn't that right?"

"Again, I think you would have to try to figure out the degree of the discordancy, the severity, then ask, what's the risk of delivery versus the risk of leaving the babies in utero? There's the mother to think about as well as the babies, and there's an increased risk of cesarean section if you try to induce labor and fail," Jones explained. "The other thing," he went on, "that always comes up is what peril do you put one baby in for the sake of getting the other out? Let's say, for example, earlier in pregnancy if you diagnosed that a baby had bad IUGR [intrauterine growth retardation], that baby's better off outside than in, but the other baby seems to be okay but would probably be premature, how do you—those sorts of decisions make it more difficult."

"Now, Doctor," Koskoff said, "nonstress testing was available in 1983 at Hartford Hospital, was it not?"

"Yes, it was."

"And what kind of conditions would nonstress tests show?"

"Obviously, a baby that's sick, in quotations, in utero, from a whole host of different things, genetic problems, growth problems—a whole series of things that might affect fetal well-being."

"I think my question was probably pretty inartful, but one of the things you mentioned was growth problems?"

"Right."

"Okay. Is growth retardation something that can have an effect on performance on a nonstress test?"

"Correct."

"And that can make the nonstress test an abnormal one?"

"It could."

"Can the presence of a placental abruption"—separation—"show up on a nonstress test?"

"It could."

"Can interference with placental blood flow in some way show up on a nonstress test?"

"Yes."

"Can the presence of thrombi in the placental vessels show up on a nonstress test?"

"It would clearly depend on the degree, which is true of every one of those questions you just asked me."

"Now, Doctor," Koskoff asked, "does moving blood clot?"

"No."

"So wouldn't you say, Doctor, it's likely that if a pregnancy had—that if a twin pregnancy had the following characteristics, all of which are present—a placental abruption, thrombi in the placenta, intrauterine growth retardation, discordancy—isn't it likely that this is going to show up on a nonstress test as being unresponsive or nonreactive?" In other words, cascading probabilities.

"I object," Doyle said, "to the form of the question on the grounds it's vague and ambiguous."

"I don't see how you can say that," Jones answered. "I mean I think each one of those has the possibility of causing a problem, depending on degree."

"The only way to find out, I suppose, is to do the nonstress test."

"That would certainly prove it one way or the other," Jones acknowledged.

"And isn't it true that each of them individually could result in an abnormal nonstress test?"

"That's correct."

"And altogether, if all of them were present in one pregnancy at the same time, that increases the likelihood of them showing up still further, doesn't it?"

"I'm going to object to the form of the question," Doyle said.

"I think it would increase it, increase the likelihood," Jones said.

"Yes?"

Jones clarified: "Again, I think it's a matter of if the additive factors reach the critical mass where the kid is going to get into trouble, it's obvious."

"And the reason you do a nonstress test is to see if the kid is going to get into trouble; isn't that why you do it?"

"Yes," Jones said.

Koskoff abruptly changed the subject, as if he feared that lingering on this point would call unwanted attention to how damaging Jones had been to the hospital's case. Although Jones had all but conceded that Norwalk Hospital was negligent, Koskoff didn't want to destroy him as a witness; he only wanted to give Travelers "no comfort" in using him. So he veered into safer territory—exhibit identification—and then into a brief discussion of whether the clinic doctors appeared to have had a "plan" for treating Donna's pregnancy. Jones didn't think they had, at least not that anyone had written down. After querying Jones for a few more minutes, Koskoff yielded to Doyle, who had no questions.

Koskoff had achieved all he had hoped to, not only with Jones but with all of the experts on both sides. After almost five years of taking testimony, this would be the last deposition. The status conference with Ballen was scheduled for the next day, and the judge would be hard-pressed to delay the trial a fourth time without the lawyers agreeing to it, meaning they most likely would be on the docket for early January. That was not to say the trial couldn't be postponed again; Ballen had told the lawyers to find out when their experts would be available to testify, and Koskoff, to be safe, had had a paralegal obtain their schedules through May. But it was too late now for Doyle to find, disclose, and prepare another major expert. Without another continuance, their lineups were set.

In other words, they were done. By more or less mutual agreement, there was nothing left for the lawyers to investigate, no more opinions to enlist, no one else to consult, nothing else to learn. With the completion of Jones's deposition both sides knew as much as they ever would about the central mysteries of the case: What happened to Little Tony Sabia? Why? Could it have been prevented? Indeed, they knew nearly all that was knowable within the framework of a lawsuit, given the combined limits of law, which obscured the truth by sanctioning some questions but not others, and medicine, which asked the right questions but in the end liked to answer circumspectly, with probabilities.

In a sense, the case remained, as Doyle would say, a sea of grey, and it was anyone's guess as to how a jury would find. Yet deciding who was right or wrong was largely now beside the point. The point, heading to trial, was, who was likelier to win? That was the pivotal question facing Koskoff and Doyle as they prepared for the second mediation. That, and one other: how to inform their clients.

TWENTY FIVE

DECEMBER 17, 1993

WHEN BERNARD HAD FIRST SUGGESTED A SECOND MEDIATION, TONY SHRUGGED, "Why waste the time?" In the weeks after the first mediation he and Donna had surrendered all hope of settling. "They threw us a bone, and we were supposed to bite, and it didn't go," Tony recalls. Dug in, they braced for trial and told themselves they would win. Tony, especially, clung to the hope that "all the neglects and abuses and realities" of their lives would at last be recompensed.

Donna, as usual, was more cautious, figuring that Bernard and Koskoff wouldn't enter into a second negotiation without good reason. "I felt," she says, "that if they were suggesting this to us they must have felt there had been a change, or something good could come from it." Trusting Bernard in particular to tell them what to do, she persuaded Tony to go along. Now that they were back together, they both knew they needed to show a united face.

They arrived at Koskoff's office by eight-thirty, sinking into their customary places on the couch. Donna was nervous, though less lost than in the past; Tony was typically on edge. Koskoff knew he craved accountability, but that wasn't what mediations were about. Their purpose was to wipe blame off the ledger in order to allow the parties to justify making a deal. As at the first mediation, Koskoff preferred that Tony and Donna stand by but not be present when the lawyers and Travelers spoke face-to-face. This time Tony refused. "If somebody's gonna talk," he said, "he should talk in front of all of us."

"There may be some things you don't want to hear," Koskoff said.

"Tough shit," Tony said.

Koskoff and Bernard knew not to argue. They agreed to let Tony and Donna in on the entire mediation, providing they held their questions until the end. Recalls Tony, "I told them, 'If I'm gonna see it at trial, I wanna see it now. I don't want to blow my stack in court.'"

Donna also wanted to hear everything that was said. She'd known since the first mediation that deciding whether—and for how much—to settle would be the biggest decision she and Tony would ever face. "We had to decide what was going to be best for Little Tony moneywise," she says. "But who was to say what it would cost? He could outlive us all, and wouldn't that be funny?" She wanted Koskoff and Lichtenstein and, especially, Bernard to steer them toward the right decision. "Between us and Chris," she explains, "things got very intimate."

Bernard had first gotten in the middle of Tony and Donna's troubles during the settlement with Humes. He'd helped them split the money, then set them up with a financial counselor. When Donna left, he'd talked with Tony almost daily by phone, "trying to hold him together . . . afraid that he was going to fall apart." A former divorce lawyer, Bernard was used to dealing with anguished people, yet rarely had he seen a family so troubled—or resilient. He'd tried hard not to take sides, resisting Tony's haranguing about Donna and her countercomplaints about him. The problem was, what now? Like Koskoff, he believed they should settle, but the last time they'd gotten the Sabias some money, Donna had left and Tony had nearly been destroyed. Bernard feared they could split up again, though he thought he knew Donna well enough now, and that she knew herself well enough, that they wouldn't. "I honestly think that if the money was sitting in a box in the living room there might be days that Donna would think about it, but she wouldn't pick it up and leave," he says.

Now he tried to dampen their hopes. He knew what Tony and Donna wanted was "to put Little Tony together again," he says, but "what they're out for they can't get, so they'll settle for money. But because there's so much emotion, there can be an enormous letdown."

Fitzgerald and Jacobs arrived after nine. Driving down together from New Haven in Jacobs's Mercedes, they'd agreed on their assignments. Fitzgerald, a head taller than everyone, would run the mediation; he would manage the discussion, then lean on Doyle and Koskoff to come to terms. Meanwhile, Jacobs, more of a schmoozer, would tell him—and them—the market price of the case. It wouldn't be a linear process. Both sides would circle each other apprehensively until one of them, sensing an advantage, would risk some real movement. Fitzgerald would hover, then try to sweep in and close a deal.

The opening session was held in Koskoff's office, which was less formal than the conference room. Doyle, who arrived now with Hunt and Travelers' Brian Casey and Cathy Gonzales, took his place in one of the side chairs in front of Koskoff's desk. He noted that the Sabias weren't leaving—Donna, who was now all but deaf in one ear, had moved over to sit behind him in the big executive chair at Koskoff's desk, while Tony leafed through Koskoff's trial notebook on the couch—and began estimating the effect of their presence. He knew that Casey, himself a single father, admired Tony, and that the two of them, along with Donna, would decide whether or not the case went to court. Privately, Doyle was hopeful. For the first time in nearly seven years, since the suit was brought, those with the authority to resolve it were now in one room. That it had taken the wiles of a dozen lawyers and an impending trial to bring them here only proved how inefficient a lawsuit could be. Doyle thought face-to-face negotiations would relieve some of the pressure on him and Koskoff as go-betweens by shifting the onus to their clients, where it belonged.

Fitzgerald invited Koskoff to lead off, and he obliged with the same quasi-opening he had presented to Tony and Donna ten weeks earlier, on the eve of the first mediation. Then they had needed time for it to sink in; now, Donna recalls, they were both infuriated. "It was very, very hard to hear what Michael was saying," she recalls. "If somebody had done something a week earlier, we'd have two babies. We might have had trouble with Michael, but Tony would have been fine." Adds Tony, "Basically the kid ran out of room and he popped his own cord. Everybody's life was ruined all because of a fucking forty-dollar ultrasound."

Doyle spoke next. Fitzgerald and Tony would later remember that he all but conceded Koskoff's claims on liability, but he gave a short, vigorous rebuttal. "The Sabias' case is a case in search of a theory," he announced as Donna's gaze bored into the back of his neck. "I bolster that by saying—and I'll be able to put this into evidence—that they first sued us and Dr. Humes with the emphasis clearly on alleged malpractice during the birthing process. And indeed Dr. Humes paid $1.35 million to settle the claim. It wasn't until they got Dr. Benirschke that the theme was changed and that they decided to come after Norwalk Hospital."

Doyle continued. "Even if the standard of care required serial ultrasounds and nonstress testing, which we dispute, what killed the twin and resulted in the damage to Tony was most likely a sudden and unexpected cord accident. Such an accident was not predictable by ultrasound, and was not preventable by ultrasound or nonstress testing. In other words, even if we had done what they say we should have done, that would not have prevented what happened.

"They've also claimed that if we'd done the ultrasound, we'd have seen that these twins were large enough so that we should have taken them out. You can say that now in hindsight, that if you'd done that Friday this never would have happened. But the fact is there are risks associated with cesarean sections. And there's not unanimity of opinion when you go in"—he paused, then said emphatically—"*if there are no indications that these kids are anything but healthy.*"

"And there wouldn't have been any such indication," Doyle said, "even if you *had* done the ultrasounds. The size would have been seen," he acknowledged. "But that size, absent something else, would not require that you go in and remove the kids."

Tony glared at Doyle. Even before Doyle had begun to speak, Tony had pegged him as a legal eagle, hired by Travelers to muscle him and Donna into settling cheap. But after hearing him disavow all responsibility—"legal bullshit," Tony called it—his bile was rising. He felt as Humes had, years earlier; that he could stand his own pain, but not the world's denial of it. Doyle embodied that denial. All he seemed to care about was whether Norwalk Hospital could be held in for Little Tony's injuries, but that was just the beginning of Tony and Donna's grief, and of their grievances. The real damage had come later, as Humes said, like gangrene from a wound. Tony thought people like Doyle had no clue about what it was like to care for a child like Little Tony. Now, he wanted to make him pay.

He stood up shakily. "I had to work two full-time jobs," he said to Doyle, not knowing that Doyle had grown up in a household like his, with a crippled, birth-injured child, neglected siblings, and a hard-bitten father and suffering mother struggling against defeat. "For what?" Tony asked. "For what? I had to work at night, catch an hour of sleep and go back to work, and worry about killing somebody behind the wheel of a truck. I used to make eighty thousand dollars a year and we never had anything in the bank. Never."

He switched subjects. "Doctor says Tony's got a couple of years to live," he said, referring to Grossman, "but he doesn't know what the hell he's talking about. By his statistics, Tony should be dead already. But you have to go on the basis of the kind of care an individual receives. So in Tony's case statistics are trash."

He turned to Gonzales: "Lady," he said, "how many vacations have you taken in the last ten years?" He paused. "You couldn't put anybody in my shoes. Ain't nobody gonna fill my shoes."

Here was Tony's final, consuming plaint: The world had no idea how he and Donna and Little Tony had suffered, and that ignorance itself was the larger crime, even more than whatever had been done to them in the first place. He wanted Doyle to acknowledge that the hospital was at fault for killing Michael and devastating Little Tony and making him and Donna wrecks. He wanted Travelers to pay, dearly. But what he seemed to want even more was a formal recognition of what his family had been put through, how violated and alone they were, and what it had taken for them to survive. He wanted Doyle and Casey to concede that he, Tony, had withstood all the mental abuse the world could throw at him and was still standing.

He wanted respect.

"Come stay at my house for a week," he challenged them, almost brightly. "See what life is." He wasn't surprised to see there were no takers.

Fitzgerald, wanting to talk with Jacobs alone, let Tony finish, then "threw everybody out" of Koskoff's office, he recalls. The key issue, he thought, on which the case was likeliest to hinge in court, was causation. "What's to say," he asked Jacobs privately, "things would have been very different if they had intervened when they should have?" Essentially, it was the same question Doyle and Koskoff had avoided asking Benirschke. Jacobs considered it a nonstarter. Even if Koskoff offered no proof that the outcome could have been changed, he said, a jury no doubt would believe him. Jacobs himself had never had a malpractice case where a causation expert's report had been rejected by a jury, and until recently most insurance companies failed even to rebut claims of cause. Intervention was the capstone of modern medicine; it was simply self-defeating to argue that it was better to do nothing than something.

"So what do you think?" Fitzgerald asked, agreeing that Koskoff's case on liability "looked very strong." "What are these things worth?"

Jacobs listed the key measures—Little Tony's short life expectancy and lack of voluntary ambulation; strong liability; Koskoff's record with juries. Later he would summarize, "Mike was very impressive. And juries are very sympathetic. Normally, they'll give you something in excess of a figure, provided you have a nice client and a nice family. They also have to like the lawyers; you can't be a putz." He told Fitzgerald he thought the case might net about $7.5 million at trial.

And a settlement price? Fitzgerald asked.

About $5 million, Jacobs said.

Fitzgerald called Doyle, Hunt, Casey, and Gonzales back into Koskoff's office around midmorning. He wanted to meet with them first, since it was Travelers' money they would be discussing. With Tony, Donna, Koskoff, Bernard, and Lichtenstein holing up once again in Lichtenstein's office down the hall, he proposed Jacobs's settlement value of $5 million—$2.5 million more than Doyle and Casey had previously offered. Doyle, he recalls, "wasn't interested." He and Casey weren't about to move without a sign that Koskoff, who officially was still demanding $13 million—a discount of $1.5 million from the first mediation—had become more realistic.

But eliciting a formal offer was only the first of Fitzgerald's goals. Because Doyle and Koskoff trusted him, he also intended to get them to tell him in confidence what they needed, bottom-line, to end the case. Ferguson had had to work for seven hours until he could even propose such double-blind bidding, and then only after Koskoff had prodded him. Fitzgerald, however, meant to have both sides discuss real numbers from the start, with him if not with each other. Reminding Doyle and Casey that they were about to go to trial with a weak liability defense, he again suggested $5 million as a possible settlement figure. "I just need to know if we can get to yes here," he demanded. "I think this is where the case is going to end up. Tell me if I'm wasting my time."

Fitzgerald was depending on Jacobs, who knew what it cost to care for children like Little Tony, to back him up on price, and on Doyle, who "knew Stanley's values because he'd paid them" at settlement, to sell Casey on a compromise. But again Doyle and Casey said no, and Fitzgerald sensed that his faith might be misplaced. The more they talked, the more Jacobs, inveterately chummy, appeared to sanction Doyle's hard line, and the more Doyle, fed by Jacobs's approval, seemed locked into a defiant posture. It was that posture—on both sides—that Fitzgerald realized he had to break to get a deal, yet every time he confronted Doyle and Casey, rattling their confidence, trying to beat them up on price, Jacobs tacitly encouraged them to stand firm. "Yes," he said hopefully whenever one of them pointed out that the other side's case had liabilities as well, "you've got them there." Fitzgerald was dismayed. Perhaps too late, he had to admit that he and Jacobs had different approaches to mediation, and that they were working at cross purposes.

For the next hour the mediators shuttled between the two caucuses, scrambling to keep the process afloat. Fitzgerald was blunt, telling the Sabias and their lawyers that Little Tony could die before they ever got to trial; Jacobs, undermining their efforts, praised them for the life-care plan they'd devised for the boy in case he lived to advanced age. Despite the mixed messages, the mediators did manage to stimulate some movement. Officially, Doyle, who started the day at $2.5 million, went to $3.5 million; Koskoff dropped from $13 million to $8.5 million. "Everybody moved quicker," Koskoff recalls, adding, "we also reached an impasse quicker." Unofficially, Koskoff indicated to Fitzgerald that he would go down to $7.5 million and Doyle that he would come up to $5 million, but Fitzgerald wasn't free to report these figures, only to use them to gauge whether to keep going. By eleven-thirty he concluded there was no more room on either side to move. He talked on, but with a steadily weakening conviction that it would do any good.

In both offices the mood sank into desperation. They had come this far, and now they had to choose. Tony and Donna agonized, hoping it would be for the last time. Should they take $3.5 million, a small fortune even after the Koskoffs took their cut? Even though they still might be able to go to trial and get much more? Even though it would mean surrendering their crusade to avenge Little Tony and punish the hospital? Even though, in the end, it might not be enough to support him? They depended on their lawyers to advise them what to do, but Koskoff and Bernard wouldn't have to live with the result, they would.

Koskoff and Bernard had their own reckoning to face. Should they counsel Tony and Donna to take the money or hold out? Koskoff, especially, was offended by Doyle's offer. He thought his side was making all the effort and that Doyle and Casey were lowballing them. He worried about the consequences for Tony and Donna of taking what they felt was too little. Nor could he be expected to neglect the issue of his and Bernard's one-third fee, which would almost triple to nearly $3 million if they could push Travelers to pay what he still believed the case was worth. On the other hand, Koskoff wanted to get the Sabias some money, and $3.5 million, plus the $1.35 million from Humes, was a considerable sum. Reject it now, and they could all wind up with nothing.

For Doyle and Casey there were risks, too. Casey would have to answer to Travelers if he turned down an opportunity to settle and then lost big at trial. Doyle, meanwhile, would make a lot more off the case if they went to court, but if he then lost a $20 million verdict, how could he face himself or his client? He gauged his performance in negotiations by a simple measure: Should I have paid? For his relationship with Travelers, his business, his pride, he dreaded a wrong answer.

As Fitzgerald and Jacobs gathered their things and prepared to leave, Koskoff and Doyle wanted to convey to each other what they had to have, but they were hostages to their own recalcitrance, and to the fear that no matter how well they might have done, they could still do better. The only route out seemed to be to go to court. Doyle didn't disguise his frustration. Railing in a voice that boomed through Koskoff's closed door and into the next office, he blamed Koskoff for the deadlock. He, Doyle, was ready to pay, but Koskoff was making it impossible by demanding too much. He was leaving him no choice. It was stupid, Doyle bellowed. Doyle needed some justification to pay more than market value, but Koskoff wasn't giving it to him.

What Koskoff had always refused to concede was that in the end the value of the case came down to life expectancy. Even if Koskoff had Doyle on liability, which Doyle doubted, price was another matter. The main issue there was what it would cost to care for Little Tony as long as he lived—that, and what a jury might do. Until Koskoff accepted that Travelers wasn't going to pay $8.5 million to support a child who might not survive beyond a few years, there was nothing left to talk about. To his own question—should I pay?—Doyle now answered a resounding no. He told Fitzgerald stormily the mediation was over. He and Hunt and Casey and Gonzales gathered their things and walked grimly toward the elevator.

Tony and Donna sagged at the swiftness of their departure. "They didn't even stay till lunch," Tony recalls. "We didn't see 'em leave. Michael and Chris just came back and said, 'It didn't work out.'" They sat in Lichtenstein's office, bathed by the low December sun, and wondered what to do. After Jacobs left for an appointment in Manhattan, Fitzgerald stayed on to talk with Koskoff, Lichtenstein, and Bernard to see if there was yet some way to make them move. He detailed Doyle's last unreported offer: a structured settlement of $2.75 million, which would pay the Sabias $167,472 a year increasing by 4 percent annually as long as Little Tony lived; $600,000 in cash, $1.8 million in attorneys' fees, for a total of $5.15 million.

Koskoff told him it was too little too late.

The workaday din of the law office swelled around Tony and Donna, still sitting alone. After realizing there was nothing left for them to do but leave, they decided to catch up on some last-minute Christmas shopping. "It was a total waste of time," Tony recalls. "They throw this figure at you. Psychologically, it hammers you. Physically, it hammers you. You go home, you don't wanna eat."

When Koskoff came back to say goodbye and urge them not to lose hope, Tony snapped at him. "Fuck this," he said. "We're going to trial."

Koskoff nodded glumly. "Yeah, I know."

≈≈≈

DECEMBER 23, 1993

For the lawyers a trial carried a certain welcome clarity. You knew exactly where the handles were and what to do. You argued your case, did your all, and let someone else decide if it was enough. There was none of the painful moral ambiguity, the free-floating guilt, of trying to work out a deal and having it collapse. You could lose and still sleep at night. After the mediation Koskoff was fretful. He still didn't have a trial date, there was real money on the table, Little Tony could die any minute, and the Sabias had every reason to doubt him because after seven years he still hadn't delivered. It was two days before Christmas and all anyone was thinking about was clearing out for the holidays and closing out the year. "The genius of mediation," he says, "is you get in negotiating mode." Despite his confidence in himself, Koskoff was anxious to find a way to settle before it became too late.

He phoned Fitzgerald. The previous week, talking as friends after the mediation, they had expressed similar frustrations. The case should settle—everyone knew that. But a mixture of pride and spite and greed prevented their coming to terms. Now, Koskoff cast around for some way to revive the negotiations that wouldn't compromise his hard line yet would leave room to maneuver if they didn't work out. "You know, we're really not that far apart," he said tentatively. "We're not really even five million dollars apart. So what I think an effective mediator might do is figure out a way to bridge that gap."

Koskoff was careful not to indicate any change in his position, but Fitzgerald understood that he was in fact willing to drop his demand—providing he could deny it if it didn't work out. "Mike's call was sort of Delphic," he recalls, "which I interpreted to mean that if I could come up with a settlement number that was midway between where we'd left off, he could do it." But where had they left off? Only Fitzgerald knew the "real figures" he had elicited the week before, when Koskoff indicated privately that he would take $7.5 million and Doyle that he could deliver $5 million. Those numbers were 50 percent closer than their formal bargaining positions. On the other hand, Doyle and Koskoff each had to know that because they'd moved in confidence, the other must have moved as well.

Fitzgerald temporized. The midway point between their official positions was $6 million; unofficially, $6.25 million. Deciding to leave Koskoff some negotiating room in case Doyle still needed to haggle, he asked Koskoff if $6.325 million would do. Koskoff seemed noncommittal. Now that he'd got Fitzgerald to utter a target, the last thing he wanted was to associate himself with it. He hadn't spoken with the Sabias yet, he said. Nor did he want to be on record as shaving more than $2 million from his take figure without the least assurance from Doyle that he would reciprocate. "I didn't get any numbers from Mike," Fitzgerald recalls. "But I began to think maybe we weren't as far apart as everybody said."

Fitzgerald phoned Doyle, who, relieved of the need to posture, listened intently. "There's no way I can do that," he said, but Fitzgerald didn't take Doyle's refusal as a no. He believed Doyle was shopping for a better deal. Doyle told him he needed to talk to Casey and would get back to him. Fitzgerald urged him to take his time. Several minutes later Doyle called back with a counteroffer.

Bound by the same need for his client's approval as Koskoff, Doyle, too, had to be vague. He said he might be able to do something at just over $5.57 million, which, in the hair-splitting calculus of the discussion, meant Travelers was willing to move—as long as Koskoff and the Sabias moved further. The counteroffer, like Fitzgerald's float figure, was confidential. But it was a real number—the first in what both sides now seemed willing to agree was the ballpark—and Fitzgerald seized on it, determining to use it to move the sides together. Calling Koskoff back, he became uncharacteristically insistent. "We really have to talk turkey now," he said. "No more Delphic statements."

Koskoff sensed from Fitzgerald's urgency that he was close to a deal. "You said you could commit the Sabias to the midpoint," Fitzgerald said. "Can I report that?" Koskoff told him he could. Fitzgerald promptly called Doyle to relay the news. "I've got a commitment," he said. Koskoff was willing to settle for $6.25 million and thought he could deliver the Sabias for that price.

Doyle didn't answer. The figure was still more than he thought the case was worth. On the other hand, he'd forced Koskoff down from $22 million, which meant a theoretical savings to Travelers of more than $15 million—real money. More to the point, he knew *Sabia* could still cost three times as much at trial, which was, in the end, all that mattered.

Fitzgerald prodded him. "The case is settled, right?" he asked, knowing Doyle's mind as if it were his own.

Doyle, not bothering to call Casey, answered, "Right." He knew he'd neither won nor lost, but had simply done what he had to do.

Fitzgerald arranged for a conference call. The discussion was brief, with Doyle and Koskoff confirming for each other what they had previously told Fitzgerald. "Okay," Fitzgerald said less than triumphantly. "The case is settled. You guys work out the details."

Within minutes Koskoff was on the phone to Tony and Donna, asking them to come to his office first thing the next day. He didn't explain why, and Tony didn't ask.

"I told him," Tony says, "'I'm not going to any more goddamn mediations, and I'm not wasting any more goddamn time.' The only reason I went up is because I thought it was about the trial."

≈ ≈ ≈

DECEMBER 24, 1993

Sitting once again with Tony, Donna, Bernard, and Lichtenstein in his office, Koskoff laid out the terms of Doyle's offer. It included an upfront payment of $4.25 million, plus a $2 million structure. Koskoff elaborated. Travelers would buy an annuity that would yield $164,000 a year, tax-free, and would rise by 4 percent annually. It would be guaranteed for ten years. If Little Tony dies after that, he told Tony and Donna, "you lose it all." They listened carefully. Structures had exceptional tax advantages, delivering plaintiffs more money than deals for cash. But Tony didn't like the idea of Travelers throwing him "another bone."

"To hell with the annuity," he snapped. "It's not even Triple-A. Let *me* invest it."

Donna was bewildered. It was all happening too fast. After the terrible anticipation and bitter disappointments, they suddenly were talking about what kind of deal to take before she and Tony could even consider whether they wanted to settle. She felt strangely distant, like they were talking about someone else's life. Too embarrassed to say anything, she scowled at Tony, who seemed not to notice.

He was wheeling, gruff as always, but focused. By force of experience, Tony was now so expert at managing their money that Donna tended to defer to him on finances even when she thought he was wrong. She wanted to be alone with him. Alone, she could cut through his attitude. But Koskoff seemed to expect an answer, and Tony seemed to want to give one.

Not that he would decide himself. He was paying Koskoff, Bernard, and Lichtenstein for that. "What would you do if you were me?" he asked them.

Koskoff spoke frankly. He believed he had pushed Doyle and Travelers as far as possible and wanted Tony and Donna to understand the gravity of the offer: there would be no other opportunity to weigh this. If they hesitated, Doyle could withdraw. Now was the time. "Think about Tony," he said solemnly. "It's a great deal of money." He and Bernard had calculated that the settlement would yield six hundred dollars a day in interest. "If it works out right," he said, "it'll probably take care of him his whole life." "If it works out," Bernard echoed, "you can live like normal human beings."

Tony stared at them and grumbled, "What do normal human beings live like?"

It was Bernard whom Tony most trusted. He more than anyone else knew their turmoil and had always steered them right. He cared. Tony asked him the same question he'd asked Koskoff, but beseechingly. Bernard agreed it was a good offer but seemed less comfortable than Koskoff in advising them to settle for money alone. Recalls Tony: "Chris gets red in the face when he's upset. He basically said, 'You could get less, you could get more. You got almost eight million dollars, including the money from Humes. Take it. Take the money and run.'"

Only Lichtenstein advised them to reconsider, recounting the story of another family at a similar moment. The carrier had offered them $300,000. Troubled that they might accept too little and regret it for the rest of their lives, Lichtenstein had asked them, "Is your life worth more?" The family said yes. "Well, let them pay more," Lichtenstein had said. He told Tony and Donna they had to ask themselves the same thing. "Go from the gut. Go from the heart," Tony recalls Lichtenstein telling them. "*You* decide what Tony's life is worth."

That was the unacceptable question Tony and Donna had to answer. A decade of dealing with Little Tony's deficits, and seven years of anticipating some kind of payback, made it no easier. Their desire for justice conflicted with their desire for a better life, and when Tony tried to reconcile the two, he couldn't. "Show me an admission of guilt," he said bravely at one point, "and I don't want a thing."

But it was a dying protest. As Koskoff said, they were talking about a lot of money, enough money to obliterate at last the wreckage of Tony's and Donna's past lives. Besides the money for Little Tony's lifetime care, which would be put in trust, they would net nearly $1 million compensation for past medical bills and for Donna's mental anguish. Tony knew he wouldn't quit his job, and the notion of material comfort held little allure for him. "What's gonna change? Nothing," he said. He planned to arrange it so that if Donna wanted to withdraw any of the settlement money for herself, he or a trustee would have to cosign. Still, the prospect of financial security held out the hope that they could now complete the makeover of their lives that had begun so unpromisingly with Little Tony's birth.

Tony had already raised his family's station in life through his unflinching will. He'd transformed himself, taught himself several trades, salvaged one house and improved another, and with the help of the Humes settlement, moved his family into a better neighborhood. He'd become a landlord while Donna had mastered the complex network of services required to keep Little Tony at home. Against all odds, they were still together. Shannon, meanwhile, was doing so well in high school in Maryland that they had begun talking hopefully about bringing her home in six months, after she graduated. She wanted to go to college.

All this hustling for upward mobility had given them new strength and determination. Which is why the decision to take the money was now largely inevitable. Much as Tony wanted to punish Norwalk Hospital, he wanted to keep improving his family's prospects even more. Donna had grown up abandoned and adopted; he with a legacy of family tragedy. His children had all grown up wounded by what Tony called "extreme mental abuse." Now, he thought, they had a chance to reverse the cycle. How could he—how could anyone—not grab it?

"Let's do it," Tony announced.

Donna recoiled. She had expected the lawyers to leave the room to let Tony and her talk alone for a while. But there was no discussion. Now that Tony had spoken, it seemed as if whatever she thought didn't matter, and so she said nothing, only nodded uncomfortably. Later she would admit: "I wish I'd spoke up. It was a very strange feeling. It happened as fast as whatever happened with Michael and Tony. One minute we're going to court, the next minute we're not."

Koskoff went to the phone to call Doyle and finalize terms. Doyle still wanted a partial structure—it would save Travelers money—but after hearing Tony's position he agreed to an all-cash settlement. Koskoff took notes as they ironed out how and when the money would be disbursed. Then Doyle introduced what he knew would be the last significant issue for Travelers: confidentiality. Doyle demanded that the Koskoffs not discuss the price publicly, and Koskoff agreed. Though it was a healthy settlement and he would like, for advertising purposes, to have announced it, he wasn't about to scotch the deal.

Tony and Donna, however, balked at signing what Tony considered a "gag order. We told Michael, 'Forget it. No way. Under no circumstances are we going to sign anything that covers this up.'" Having sold out their claims, they were unwilling to pay also with their silence. Doyle finally relented: their lawyers would have to adhere to the agreement, but not the Sabias.

The issue of disclosure was a sticky one. Now that the deal was done, how it was perceived would have significant implications, most notably for the hospital. Most people construed the act of settling as a tacit admission of guilt; if you'd done nothing wrong, why pay? Yet Norwalk Hospital remained unequivocal. What had happened was an accident. Donna had received competent treatment. The decision to pay was purely a business expedient for Travelers. The hospital regretted that it wouldn't have the chance to be vindicated in court. True or not, this was the party line.

Long exiled from its own defense, the hospital had no say over Doyle's decision, although its stake in it was huge. Keeping the settlement quiet meant not having to placate alarmed consumers at a time when Norwalk, like many hospitals, had begun promoting high-risk obstetrics as a major selling point and income producer. In April, 1,200 people had turned out for the opening of its new Maternity Center. Described in brochures as "unsurpassed in Connecticut as a childbirth environment," the facility boasted a high-risk diagnostic unit, state-of-the-art, high-resolution ultrasound, staff perinatologists, a neonatal intensive care unit—all services that, had they been available when Donna was a patient, almost certainly would have saved both Little Tony and Michael. Such facilities were now compulsory for community hospitals drawn into stiff new competition with their neighbors.

Norwalk's administrators knew the hospital would suffer if pregnant women learned that it had paid more than $6 million because of a bad outcome it was now set up to prevent, and so they welcomed the settlement. They had little to gain and much to lose by a trial. Only Hunt, on the defense side, still protested. To her the settlement was a lie, invalidating everything she believed in. Unlike Doyle, she'd been unable to put her identification with her client aside, and the mediations had proved insupportable—"the most castrating experience of my life," she calls them.

Despite its savage oddness, it was an apt description. Now that the case was over so abruptly, any unresolved feelings were likely to remain that way. They would linger like the phantom pain of an amputee. Pat Ryan liked to say that settling a legal claim was "buying out of an uncertain future." What was impossible to buy out of, of course, were the uncertainties of the past, and it was those that a trial was meant to resolve. A settlement was a paradox: you surrendered your hope of winning so as not to lose, then lost something vital anyway because the thing that sustained you all along was the desire to win. Feelings of debilitation were not uncommon.

The Koskoffs' customary shrimp-and-champagne victory celebration did not take place. Because it was Christmas Eve, no party marked *Sabia*'s end. The office's secretaries and paralegals waited impatiently for Tony and Donna to leave so they could beat the holiday rush and get home to their families, while the lawyers and the Sabias remained cloistered in Koskoff's office until noon, talking quietly. Bernard tried to cheer up Tony and Donna, calling Little Tony "the six-million dollar kid." Koskoff said something about their "having a different kind of Christmas this year." Tony and Donna thanked them, but were too conflicted to be consoled.

"You mean I'm going to walk out of here with a check and that's going to be it? Is that all it means?" Tony asked, his voice steeped in remorse. Already he was "kicking myself in the ass, because I watched that guy [Doyle] agree with everything Michael said." They had gotten it over with, Donna would say, but for what purpose, and at what price, she and Tony still didn't know.

After they left, Koskoff chatted with Bernard and Lichtenstein, and then sat alone at his desk, decompressing from the past week. He understood the Sabias' regrets but thought he had saved them from something much worse: yet another crushing disappointment followed by the wait for a trial that still might not happen. "That," he says, "would have really destroyed them." By ending their case now, he had done probably as well for them as any lawyer could have. A trial might have satisfied their craving for justice and revenge, but not their need to get on with their lives, which Koskoff considered ultimately more important. Tony had once asked: "Who the hell could ever dream that a fucking nightmare like this would ever happen? Not us." Yet Koskoff saw nightmares like theirs every day; most not as bad, a few worse. As a trial lawyer and public performer, he preferred to go to court, but he had learned that it was far better for everyone not to, provided the defendant's insurer could be forced to pay.

That was the whole exercise now—compelling carriers to pay—and Koskoff was proudly ambivalent about doing it as well as anyone in the state. As his fees proved, he had become a kind of legal bounty hunter. Today's phone calls alone would net him and his firm a little more than $2 million. Doctors and insurers, neglecting how they came about, considered such fees unconscionable, but Koskoff defended them, saying that they enabled the poorest people to afford the best lawyers. He defied doctors to make the same claim about their own incomes.

What troubled him was the exercise itself. It was all calculation now, and the law, the part of it he loved, was mainly an elaborate charade. Because insurers only settled when they were facing trials they thought they could lose, it was necessary to make them fear losing. And so for years you geared up for trial, knowing that what you were really doing was designed not to try the case but to settle it. It was another paradox: prepare your case well enough to win in court, and the other side is likely to give in before you ever get there; do less and you end up, naked and underprepared, before a jury. No wonder defendants won 90 percent of malpractice trials. The good cases almost always settled; it was usually only the bad ones that made it to a jury.

Sabia had been a good case; Koskoff knew that. He had levered Travelers up from nothing to more than $6 million in less than three months. Yet it had taken six and a half years of work, and torment for the Sabias, to reach that point. All of it—Lichtenstein's initial appraisal of the case; Karen Koskoff's frustrating attempts at discovery; his and Bernard's search for a unified theory; the offers of judgment; cutting out Humes; his dog-and-pony show at Norwalk Hospital and outsized $22 million demand; all the flying around and taking depositions and massaging the testimony of $500-an-hour experts until much of it became meaningless; the endless legal maneuvering and the weeks of meticulous trial preparation culminating in the ordering of witnesses; even, and perhaps chiefly, his decision to let Doyle off the ropes when he had every edge—all of it had been necessary to move Travelers to the point at which it was finally willing to pay what the case was worth.

The question of exactly what Travelers had paid for remained unresolved. Koskoff believed absolutely that it was for Norwalk Hospital's negligence in causing Little Tony's brain damage in 1984. Travelers and Doyle, just as vehemently, thought the insurer had paid in order to avoid paying much more if a jury agreed with Koskoff.

But that, Koskoff knew, wasn't the point. The point was, civil justice was virtual now. Almost all malpractice cases were decided not on the basis of fact but on the perception of what a jury was likely to think was fact. You didn't need a trial anymore. You just needed to make the other side imagine one.

EPILOGUE

OCTOBER 23, 1996

SWADDLED IN THE POSTOPERATIVE AREA OF CONNECTICUT CHILDREN'S MEDICAL Center in Hartford, a heat-circulating thermal blanket pulled tight to his chin and a white towel wrapped turbanlike around his head, Little Tony sputtered awake. Surgeons had just finished releasing his hamstring muscles, severing them at the upper rear of his thigh and behind his knee, only seven days after an eight-hour operation to straighten his spine. He was shivering, still chilled from the operating room. A zephyr of oxygen streamed past his nose and mouth from a clear plastic tube draped across his chest.

The hamstring operation was undertaken less for his comfort than to make him easier to care for. Unused muscles contract and contort, and as he grew, his paralyzed legs had become so splayed and taut that it had become difficult to pull on his pants. Snoring gently, he looked like a healthy seventh-grader after, say, an appendectomy. He had Donna's upturned nose, Big Tony's long eyelashes, a strong chin like Tony's brother John, and incipient sideburns. A hint of a mustache shadowed his full upper lip. At twelve and a half years old and eighty-four pounds, and with his newly straightened spine and legs extending his height to almost five feet, he was nearly a young adult. His eyes fluttered open. He looked as if he were about to open his mouth.

Big Tony talked to him. "Toe-knee," he sang familiarly, then higher. "Toe-knee." He and Donna hovered at opposite sides of the bed, leaning in so close that their heads almost touched. They'd been living on coffee and cigarettes and looked tense and worn. Almost simultaneously, they began brushing Little Tony's cheeks with the backs of their hands, as if he were a sleeping infant.

"Can you say 'Hi, Dada'?" Tony said. "Can you say 'Hi, Dad'? Can you say 'Hi'?"

Little Tony silently closed his eyes.

In the thirty-four months since the settlement with Norwalk Hospital, his condition had remained remarkably stable: no better, but no worse either. His seizures continued to abate, he suffered no major respiratory problems, and he was generally robust, putting on weight. Most days he attended the Feroleto School, where staff members tried to teach him to communicate, identify numbers and shapes, stand with support, express his wants and feelings, and answer yes or no to questions such as whether he was wet and needed to be changed. Though neurologists familiar with his type of injuries considered these goals ludicrous, the school reported he was making good progress, and Donna was encouraged by the attention he received there.

He still lived at home, as Tony and Donna had taken steps to ensure that he would for the rest of his life. With the income from the settlement, they hired a live-in home-health aide to care for him, paying her $300 a week. Tony, meanwhile, completed a spacious new bedroom for him adjacent to his and Donna's, then began building him a private, handicapped-accessible bathroom.

Tony's life, too, remained much the same. He tore a rotator cuff at work, which required surgery and resulted in nerve damage. He was in pain for over a year, pain from which he still suffers. He was unable to raise his arm above his shoulder, he says, without severe headaches and neck pain. He went on disability but never stopped working on the house, which became, like Maryellen Humes's, a perpetual work in progress. He finished the basement, creating three new rooms, including one with a hot tub, and installing a pool table, a bar, and a home entertainment center. Despite his crippled arm, he did most of the framing and Sheetrocking himself. He also put in an in-ground swimming pool with a stone patio a few feet from the ramp leading from Little Tony's bedroom. He tore down a breezeway and built a new family room.

Out of work, Tony became a developer, using some of the settlement money to finance, then rescue, a failed housing subdivision—five lots on a deep parcel in South Norwalk that bordered an area of miniestates near the Westport line. After taking the development over, he fixed up the half-finished houses to sell.

Donna, managing their ever-chaotic household, still complained about his workaholism, but their relationship improved. On Valentine's Day, 1996, Tony gave her a dozen long-stemmed roses. She sent him a card with a picture of a toy poodle with the inscription "From your little bitch." With most of their financial worries relieved, and the settlement providing them an inducement—and a way—to work things out, they seemed hopeful together for the first time since before Little Tony had been born. Shannon started community college in Norwalk, but soon dropped out and took a job at a convenience store.

The family lived well but not extravagantly. Tony disliked the idea of dipping into Little Tony's trust and agreed to do so only when the boy might benefit, as with the additions to the house and the pool. The Sabias bought a used twenty-six-foot motor home and a black sports utility van for Donna. Donna got several tattoos, including one on her upper arm that read FREEDOM. And they went to Daytona every year for bike week. But most of the time they worked to improve their lives. The money, they agreed, helped enormously, but perhaps no more than their years of hardship.

Maryellen Humes put the Sabia case behind her. Although many of those involved in *Sabia* would concede that she hadn't harmed Little Tony, no one apologized for the way she was treated. She loved medicine and, despite her frustrations, still enjoyed being a doctor. She continued to work alone, doing fewer deliveries and more surgery. Few patients knew about the two settled malpractice claims against her, and she continued to add new business and receive excellent ratings from Stamford Hospital and from HMOs with which she did business. Unable to switch insurance carriers, she remained with St. Paul.

Her house project advanced slowly but inexorably. She had a two-story addition built, with a kitchen and family room on the first floor and two bedrooms and a bath on the second. Humes served as her own general contractor, importing framing specialists and roofers from out of state when she couldn't find capable subcontractors in Connecticut. To preserve the house's architectural integrity, she matched the original stone facade with stone quarried from her property. She expected that when she was done the place would be worth more than $1 million. She felt strongly that she had created something enduring and beautiful.

In late 1994, after a prolonged labor, one of Humes's patients delivered a brain-damaged baby. The couple contacted the Koskoffs, who investigated and sued Humes a third time for malpractice. The child eventually died, but Stamford Hospital, after reviewing the birth, brought no disciplinary action against Humes. The Koskoffs, however, continued to pursue the family's claim, with Mike Koskoff personally taking Humes's deposition. The case is still pending.

Mike Koskoff stopped trying medical malpractice cases, not because his office wasn't handling them but because virtually all of the large cases in which he was personally involved now settled through negotiation. Part of this was due to Koskoff himself. Insurance companies doing business in Connecticut recognized that his careful screening of cases, his ability to hire and prepare top medical experts, and his courtroom skills made it risky to go to trial against the firm in cases with high exposure. Other factors also militated against claimants holding out for trial: plaintiffs' frustrations with ever-lengthening delays, the availability of alternative methods of dispute resolution, the rising cost of litigation, and the fact that there was no longer much guesswork about what big-ticket medical malpractice cases were worth. Jury verdicts in excess of $20 million were routinely knocked down on appeal to between $7 and $8 million. Even without malpractice reform or health-care reform, both of which collapsed with the failed Clinton health-care proposal, the medical liability system had become more rational because it had become more market-driven, at least at the top. Lawyers still needed to prepare as if trials were inevitable, but trials were no longer necessary to determine what cases were worth. Disputes like the one over Little Tony's life expectancy started to disappear from the bargaining table.

Koskoff, who loved to try cases, claimed to be bored by the new system. Still, his firm prospered, his reputation grew, and he found other interests. He served as a commentator on Court TV during a medical malpractice trial. Like his father, he lectured other lawyers, becoming one of the trial bar's best-known experts on birth asphyxia, and leading workshops around the country. He was invited to participate in several high-profile lawsuits, including two arising from the Ron Brown plane crash and the Oklahoma City bombing. He looked forward to meeting Bill Doyle in court on the Yale-HIV case, scheduled for trial in late 1997.

Kurt Benirschke announced his retirement soon after the *Sabia* settlement. Although he continued to do research, he stopped consulting in malpractice cases. After learning about Norwalk Hospital's decision to settle, he wrote in his file, "This is the second case of gross misjustice in a twin case that I have seen."

Back in his room at Children's Medical Center, Little Tony lay dreamily in bed, his head propped on a pillow, an arterial line sewn into his chest and attached to an IV pump on a portable stand. Donna tucked a plush dog toy under the top of his blanket. "I've got Chester," she told him. "I told you he'd be waiting for ya." Tony, standing across from her, lifted Little Tony's arms to exercise them. One by one, he unfurled the boy's gnarled fingers.

It had been raining for a week and, in the dark, invisible drops pelted the window. Donna observed how much Little Tony was starting to look like a young man. He was using mouthwash and deodorant now. Soon, she said, they'd have to learn to give him a shave.

"I wonder if he got his afternoon meds," she mused, remembering that he had been in surgery when he should have been given his anticonvulsives. Afraid he might have a seizure, she left to find a nurse.

Tony lowered Little Tony's arms. "Toe-knee," he said. "Tony boy. Are you gonna talk to me? You gonna smile for me?" But Little Tony's eyes skittered away. As Donna returned, Tony tried again. "Hey, buddy," he said, less brightly this time, "ya hear us talking?"

Little Tony's head lolled sideways. He flashed a happy-face, jack-o'-lantern grin toward Tony, and a deep, unearthly sound erupted from his throat. His voice had recently begun to drop.

"He knows you're here," Donna said encouragingly.

Tony didn't answer. Rubbing his chin, oblivious, he gazed at his son. He knew this was all the recognition Little Tony would ever give them—a gaping smile; a sweet, inchoate groan. But somehow it had become enough.

Acknowledgments

THIS BOOK WOULD NOT HAVE BEEN POSSIBLE WITHOUT THE COOPERATION OF MANY of the people who appear in it. I especially want to thank Tony, Donna, and Little Tony Sabia and their family, Maryellen Humes, and Michael Koskoff. My gratitude also to Kurt Benirschke, Chris Bernard, Troyen Brennan, Karen Brooks, Mike Buckmir, Joe Calve, Dan Clement, Bill Doyle, David Ferguson, Tony Fitzgerald, Mary Gay, April Haskell, Marcus Hermansen, Beverly Hunt, Stanley Jacobs, Richard Jones III, Barbara Klein, Karen Koskoff, Joel Lichtenstein, Charles Lockwood, Barbara McManamy, Thomas Murray, Linda Nemeth, David Osborne, Alan Pinshaw, Pat Ryan, and Barry Schifrin. I owe a special debt to Larry Longo and Joseph Volpe, who were not involved in *Sabia* but helped clarify important matters, and to Joyce Russ, Mike Koskoff's remarkable secretary, who good-naturedly kept up with my requests.

Dan Okrent first suggested the idea for a book about a malpractice case; Art Cooper and Marty Beiser at *GQ* supported my initial efforts; Joseph Nocera, Anthony Giardina, Jonathan Harr, Ellen Kaufman, David Sigelman, David Hoose, Eileen Bonder, Kathy Goos, and Bill Newman read drafts of the manuscript and offered valuable advice; Alan Sosne and Fred Eisenstein were there whenever I needed them; Chris Jerome was indispensable in the final stages. I owe them all a great deal.

I want to thank my agent Amanda Urban, my editor Bob Bender, and, also at Simon & Schuster, Johanna Li, Jennifer Weidman, and Gypsy da Silva.

My greatest debt, as always, is to my family: Kathy Goos, Emily Werth, and Alex Werth. Their love and patience sustained me.

A Note on Sources

I FIRST LEARNED ABOUT THE SABIAS AND THEIR LAWSUIT IN DECEMBER 1993 FROM Michael Koskoff. I was looking for one medical malpractice case through which to explore the conflict between doctors and lawyers—specifically, one that was about to go to trial—and had been directed to Koskoff by George Gombossy, an editor at the *Hartford Courant*. After the case settled later that month, Koskoff told me that he was bound by a confidentiality agreement not to discuss the settlement, and I resumed my search. At the same time, I was gathering information for a magazine piece about malpractice reform for *GQ* ("Doctors vs. Lawyers vs. Patients," August 1994). Intrigued by what I knew about the Sabias' story, I asked Koskoff if he would introduce us, and he agreed. It was when I met the Sabias, with the intention of writing an abbreviated version of what had happened to them for *GQ*, that the idea for a book-length project about them and their case arose.

The obstacles, I realized, were considerable. Because there had been no trial, there would be no final public resolution to draw on, meaning no courtroom drama or access, two mainstays of nonfiction legal thrillers that I would have to find a way to do without. Also, there were the various confidentiality strictures, of which the settlement agreement with Norwalk Hospital was only the last. Most medical malpractice claims are settled in part because of the defendants' wish for anonymity, and attorney-client and doctor-patient relationships are privileged, as are medical records. Cases resolved through negotiation remain buried under several protective layers. Still, the more we spoke, the more impressed I became with Tony and Donna, whose determination to keep Little Tony at home and to keep their family together I admired. And because 90 percent of malpractice cases settle, I considered it a worthy challenge to write about one such illustrative case—the submerged part of the medical liability iceberg, so to speak.

Much of the reporter's craft is leveraging access. After meeting several times with the Sabias, I wrote to Maryellen Humes and Norwalk Hospital requesting interviews. The hospital rejected my request, but Humes responded immediately. Not being a party to the December 1993 agreement, she was free and—for reasons I soon understood—eager to tell her side of the story. Humes availed me of her files, then authorized her lawyers to speak with me. That, in turn, led Norwalk Hospital to reconsider, and it, too, eventually agreed to discuss the case and to release its lawyers to be interviewed. With the Sabias granting me similar permission to meet with the Koskoffs, who also opened their files for me, and authorizing Humes and the hospital to release Little Tony's and their medical records, that completed my access to the main parties and most vital materials in the case. I then was able to obtain releases to discuss the case with each side's experts and, ultimately, the three mediators. In the end, only the insurance companies, St. Paul and Travelers, refused to discuss the case, although they, too, didn't bar their lawyers from speaking with me and were occasionally helpful with general information.

All of the characters and events depicted in this book are real. Scenes were reconstructed primarily on the basis of in-depth interviews, letters, memoranda, medical records, court documents, and deposition transcripts. In those scenes where there is lengthy dialogue but for which there exists no written record, such as the meeting between Donna Sabia and Mary Gay or the two mediations, I relied on the recollections of those who were there, as corroborated by the other participants. In one scene—Michael Koskoff's presentation at Norwalk Hospital—I took the liberty of allowing Koskoff to re-create his speech several years after the fact. Koskoff, who has an actor's talent for remembering opening and closing arguments, spoke from the same notes he'd used previously—not his trial notes, which would have changed some of what he said—and tailored his delivery, as he had earlier, for an audience of hospital executives rather than a jury. I believe the scene in the book accurately reflects what took place.

For background, I relied on a variety of published sources. The most useful, listed by category, are cited below:

Reproductive Medicine

Benirschke, K. 1990. The Placenta in the Litigation Process. *American Journal of Obstetrics and Gynecology* 162, 1445–1450.

———. 1991. The Placenta in the Context of History and Modern Medical Practice. *Archives of Pathology and Laboratory Medicine* 115, 663–667.

————. 1993. Intrauterine Death of a Twin: Mechanisms, Implications for Surviving Twin and Placental Pathology. *Seminars in Diagnostic Pathology* 10, 222–231.

Berkowitz, R. L. 1993. Should Every Pregnant Woman Undergo Ultrasonography? *New England Journal of Medicine* 329, 874–875.

Blickstein, I., and M. Lancet. 1988. The Growth Discordant Twin. *Obstetrical and Gynecological Survey* 43, 509–515.

Cetrulo, C., C. Ingardia, and A. Sbarra. 1980. Management of Multiple Gestation. *Clinical Obstetrics and Gynecology* 23, 533–548. New York: Harper and Row.

Chervenak, F. 1986. The Controversy of Mode of Delivery in Twins: The Intrapartum Management of Twin Gestation (Part II). *Seminars in Perinatology* 10, 44–49.

Chervenak, F., et al. 1984. Twin Gestation: Antenatal Diagnosis and Perinatal Outcome in 385 Consecutive Pregnancies. *Journal of Reproductive Medicine* 29, 727–730.

————. 1985. Intrapartum Management of Twin Gestation. *Obstetrics and Gynecology* 65, 119–124.

DeVoe, L., and H. Azor. 1981. Simultaneous Nonstress Fetal Heart Rate Testing in Twin Pregnancy. *Obstetrics and Gynecology* 58, 450–455.

Eddleman, K., et al. 1992. Clinical Significance and Sonographic Diagnosis of Velamentous Umbilical Cord Insertion. *American Journal of Perinatology* 9, 123–126.

Findley, P. 1939. *Priests of Lucina: The Story of Obstetrics.* Boston: Little, Brown.

Freeman, R., T. Garite, and M. Nageotte. 1991. *Fetal Heart Rate Monitoring.* Baltimore: Williams & Wilkins.

Hagay, Z., et al. 1986. Management and Outcome of Multiple Pregnancies Complicated by the Antenatal Death of One Fetus. *Journal of Reproductive Medicine* 31, 717–720.

Hamilton-Rubenstein, T., B. Schifrin, and J. Shields. 1991. Conversion of Fetal Tracing from Equivocal to Chronic in a Patient with Subsequent Cerebral Palsy. *Journal of Perinatology* 11, 279–282.

Hays, P., and J. Smeltzer. 1986. Multiple Gestation. *Clinical Obstetrics and Gynecology* 29, 264–285.

Hill, L. M., and R. Breckle. 1983. Current Uses of Ultrasound in Obstetrics. *Primary Care* 10, 205–223.

Hobbins, J. C., ed. 1979. *Diagnostic Ultrasound in Obstetrics.* New York: Churchill Livingstone.

Hobbins, J., and R. Berkowitz. 1977. Ultrasonography in the Diagnosis of Intrauterine Growth Retardation.

Hobbins, J., R. Berkowitz, and P. Grannum. 1978. Diagnosis and Antepartum Management of Intrauterine Growth Retardation. *Journal of Reproductive Medicine* 21, 319–325.

Kassberg, M. 1995. Deciding When to Save the Placenta. *OBG Management,* January, 43–45.

Miller, P., R. Coen, and K. Benirschke. 1985. Dating the Time Interval from Meconium Passage to Birth. *Obstetrics and Gynecology* 66, 459–462.

Mitford, J. 1993. *The American Way of Birth.* New York: Plume.

Montagu, M. F. A. 1962. *Prenatal Influences.* Springfield, Ill.: Charles C. Thomas.

National Institute of Child Health and Human Development. 1984. Diagnostic Ultrasound Imaging in Pregnancy. Public Health Service, NIH Publication No. 84-667.

Newton, E. 1986. Antepartum Care in Multiple Gestation. *Seminars in Perinatology* 10, 19–29.

Pritchard, J., and P. MacDonald. 1980. *Williams Obstetrics,* 16th ed. New York: Appleton-Century-Crofts.

Sabbagha, R. 1987. *Diagnostic Ultrasound Applied to Obstetrics and Gynecology.* New York: Lippincott-Raven.

Schifrin, B. 1994. The ABC's of Electronic Fetal Monitoring. *Journal of Perinatology* 14, 396–402.

Schifrin, B., T. Hamilton-Rubinstein, and J. Shields. 1994. Fetal Heart Rate Patterns and the Timing of Fetal Injury. *Journal of Perinatology* 14, 174–181.

Shields, J., and B. Schifrin. 1988. Perinatal Antecedents of Cerebral Palsy. *Obstetrics and Gynecology* 71, 899–905.

Storlazzi, E., et al. 1987. Ultrasonic Diagnosis of Discordant Fetal Growth in Twin Gestations. *Obstetrics and Gynecology* 69, 363–367.

Warenski, J., and N. Kochenour. 1989. Intrapartum Management of Twin Gestation. *Clinics in Perinatology* 16, 889–896.

Wertz, R., and D. Wertz. 1989. *Lying-In: A History of Childbirth in America.* New York: Free Press.

Birth Injury and Neurologic Impairment

American Academy for Cerebral Palsy and Developmental Medicine. 1988. *Perinatal Asphyxia: Its Role in Developmental Deficits in Children.*

American College of Obstetricians and Gynecologists. 1992. *Fetal and Neonatal Neurologic Injury.* ACOG Technical Bulletin 163.

Bennett, D. D. 1985. Mysteries Surround Infant Brain Damage. *Science News* 127, 231.

Cardwell, V. E. 1956. *Cerebral Palsy: Advances in Understanding and Care.* New York: Association for the Aid of Crippled Children.

Collis, E. *A Way of Life for the Handicapped Child.* London: Faber & Faber.

Dinnage, R. 1986. *The Child with Cerebral Palsy.* Philadelphia: NFER-Nelson.

Eyman, R., et al. 1990. The Life Expectancy of Profoundly Handicapped People with Mental Retardation. *New England Journal of Medicine* 323, 584–589.

———. 1993. Survival of Profoundly Disabled People with Severe Mental Retardation. *American Journal of Diseases in Children* 147, 329–336.

Fink, L. 1986. Pregnancy and Birth-Related Brain Disorders. *Children Today,* May-June, 26–27.

Freeman, J. 1992. Cerebral Palsy and the "Bad Baby" Malpractice Crisis. *American Journal of Diseases in Children* 146, 725–727.

Freeman, J., and A. Freeman. 1993. Perinatal Hypoxia and CP: Just the Facts. *OBG Management,* April, 22–26.

Hurley, R. 1969. *Poverty and Mental Retardation.* New York: Vintage.

Kumar, R., and I. Brockington, eds. 1982. *Motherhood and Mental Illness.* London: Wright.

Little, W. J. 1861–62. On the Influence of Abnormal Parturition, Difficult Labours, Premature Birth, and Asphyxia Neonatorum, on the Mental and Physical Condition of the Child, Especially in Relation to Deformities. *Transactions of the Obstetrical Society of London* 3, 293–344.

Longo, L. D., and S. Ashwal. 1993. William Osler, Sigmund Freud, and the Evolution of Ideas Concerning Cerebral Palsy. *Journal of the History of Neuroscience* 2, 255–282.

Lord, E. 1937. *Children Handicapped by Cerebral Palsy.* New York: Commonwealth Fund.

Nelson, K. B. 1988. What Proportion of Cerebral Palsy Is Related to Birth Asphyxia? *Journal of Pediatrics* 112, 572–575.

Nelson, K. B., and J. H. Ellenberg. 1986. Antecedents of Cerebral Palsy: Multivariate Analysis of Risk. *New England Journal of Medicine* 315, 81–86.

Oe, K. 1969. *A Personal Matter.* New York: Grove Weidenfeld.

Osler, W. 1888. The Cerebral Palsies of Children. *The Medical News* 53, 29–35.

Richmond, S., et al. 1994. The Obstetric Management of Fetal Distress and Its Association with Cerebral Palsy. *Obstetrics and Gynecology* 83, 643–646.

Volpe, J. 1987. *Neurology of the Newborn.* Philadelphia: W. B. Saunders.

Perlman, J. M., and F. G. Cunningham. 1993. *Fetal and Neonatal Hypoxic Ischemic Cerebral Injury.* Supplement No. 21 to *Williams Obstetrics,* 18th ed.

Medical Malpractice

Barr, R. 1989. "I'm One of the Bad Guys." *OBG Management,* November-December, 38–44.

Bovbjerg, R. 1992. Medical Malpractice: Folklore, Facts, and the Future. *Annals of Internal Medicine* 117, 788–791.

————. 1993. Medical Malpractice: Research and Reform. *Virginia Law Review* 79, 2155–2207.

Brennan, T., et al. 1991. Incidents of Adverse Events and Negligence in Hospitalized Patients: Results of the Harvard Medical Practice Study I. *New England Journal of Medicine* 324, 370–376.

Charles, S. C., and E. Kennedy. 1985. *Defendant.* New York: Free Press.

Danzon, P. 1985. *Medical Malpractice: Theory, Evidence, and Public Policy.* Cambridge: Harvard University Press.

De Ville, K. A. 1990. *Medical Malpractice in Nineteenth Century America.* New York: New York University Press.

Fineberg, K., et al. 1984. *Obstetrics/Gynecology and the Law.* Ann Arbor, Mich.: Health Administration Press.

Gibson, J., and R. Schwartz. 1980. Physicians and Lawyers: Science, Art, and Conflict. *American Journal of Law and Medicine* 6, 173–182.

Hamacher, E. 1968. Toward an Effective Attorney-Physician Relationship. *Georgia Law Review* 4, 45–64.

Hay, I. 1992. *Money, Medicine, and Malpractice in American Society.* New York: Praeger.

Hiatt, H., et al. 1989. A Study of Medical Injury and Medical Malpractice. *New England Journal of Medicine* 321, 480–484.

Horan, M. 1993. The Real Medical Malpractice Crisis. *Public Citizen.*

Huycke, L., and M. Huycke. 1994. Characteristics of Potential Plaintiffs in Malpractice Litigation. *Annals of Internal Medicine* 120, 792–798.

Institute of Medicine. 1989. *Medical Professional Liability and the Delivery of Obstetrical Care.* Vols. 1 and 2. Washington, D.C.: National Academy Press.

Kassberg, M. 1995. Placental Pathology: The Neglected Defense. *OBG Management,* January, 36–41.

Lander, L. 1978. *Defective Medicine.* New York: Farrar, Straus & Giroux.

Law, S. A. 1978. *Pain and Profit: The Politics of Malpractice.* New York: HarperCollins.

Lewin-VHI. 1993. *Estimating the Costs of Defensive Medicine.*

Lewis, H. R. and M. E. Lewis. 1970. *The Medical Offenders.* New York: Simon & Schuster.

Localio, R., et al. 1991. Relationship Between Malpractice Claims and Adverse Events Due to Negligence—Results of the Harvard Medical Practice Study III. *New England Journal of Medicine* 324, 245–251.

Miller, F. 1985. Medical Malpractice Litigation: Do the British Have a Better Remedy? *American Journal of Law and Medicine* 11, 435–463.

Minnesota Department of Commerce. 1989. *Medical Malpractice Claim Study, 1982–1987.*

Rolph, E., ed. 1991. *Health Care Delivery and Tort: Systems on a Collision Course?* Rand: Institute for Civil Justice.

Rubsamen, D. 1976. Medical Malpractice. *Scientific American* 235, 18–23.

Sandor, A. 1957. The History of Professional Liability Suits in the United States. *Journal of the American Medical Association* 163, 456–459.

Schifrin, B. 1987. Polemics in Perinatology: The Tango of the Sharks. *Journal of Perinatology* 7, 133–134.

Schifrin, B., H. Weissman, and J. Wiley. 1985. Electronic Fetal Monitoring and Obstetrical Malpractice. *Law, Medicine, and Health Care,* 100–105.

Schwartz, R., and J. Gibson. 1981. Defining the Role of the Physician: Medical Education, Tradition, and the Legal Process. *Houston Law Review* 18, 779–799.

Schwartz, S., and N. Tucker. 1985. *Handling Birth Trauma Cases.* New York: Wiley.

Stryker, L. P. 1932. *Courts and Doctors.* New York: Macmillan.

Wagner, J., and J. Corrigan. 1993. *Impact of Legal Reforms on Medical Malpractice Costs.* U.S. Congress, Office of Technology Assessment.

Walter, E. J. 1993. New Hope for OB: Pure No-Fault. *OBG Management,* April, 29–34.

Weiler, P. C. 1991. *Medical Malpractice on Trial.* Cambridge: Harvard University Press.

Weinstein, L. 1988. Malpractice—The Syndrome of the 80s. *Obstetrics and Gynecology* 72, 130–135.

Zobel, H. B., and S. Rous. 1993. *Doctors and the Law.* New York: Norton.

History of Law and Medicine

Baker, L. 1991. *The Justice from Beacon Hill.* New York: HarperCollins.

Friedman, L. M. 1985. *A History of American Law.* New York: Simon & Schuster.

Gawalt, G. W., ed. *The New High Priests: Lawyers in Post-Civil War America.* Westport, Conn.: Greenwood Press.

Glennon, M. A. 1994. *A Nation Under Lawyers.* New York: Farrar, Straus & Giroux.

Koskoff, Y. D. 1962. Rules and Responsibility. *Connecticut Medicine* 26, 7–10.

———. 1977. The Nature of Pain and Suffering. *Trial,* July, 21–26.

———. 1978. Proving Suffering: A New Challenge. *Trial,* July, 46–49.

Koskoff, Y. D. and R. Goldhurst. 1968. *The Dark Side of the House.* London: Leslie Frewin.

Koskoff, Y. D., and S. Hagg. 1981. The Syndrome of Suffering: A Pragmatic Approach. *American Journal of Clinical Biofeedback* 4, 111–116.

Lieberman, J. K. 1981. *The Litigious Society.* New York: Basic Books.

Nuland, S. B. 1988. *Doctors.* New York: Vintage.

Starr, P. 1982. *The Social Transformation of American Medicine.* New York: Basic Books.

Stevens, R. 1989. *In Sickness and In Wealth.* New York: Basic Books.

White, E. G. 1980. *Tort Law in America.* New York: Oxford University Press.

Index